Nature and Nation

AF668298

HEDGEHOG AND FOX

ashoka UNIVERSITY
HISTORY SERIES

the fox knows many things,
but the hedgehog knows one big thing

SERIES EDITOR

RUDRANGSHU MUKHERJEE

Nature and Nation

Essays on Environmental History

MAHESH RANGARAJAN

permanent black

in association with

ASHOKA UNIVERSITY

Published by

PERMANENT BLACK

'Himalayana', Mall Road, Ranikhet Cantt,
Ranikhet 263645
perblack@gmail.com

in association with

ASHOKA UNIVERSITY

Distributed by

ORIENT BLACKSWAN PRIVATE LTD

Bangalore Bhopal Bhubaneshwar Chandigarh Chennai
Ernakulam Guwahati Hyderabad Jaipur Kolkata
Lucknow Mumbai New Delhi Patna
www.orientblackswan.com

Copyright © 2015 MAHESH RANGARAJAN

ISBN 978-81-7824-500-3

First paperback printing 2017

Typeset in Adobe Garamond
by Guru Typograph Technology, Crossings Republic,
Ghaziabad 201009
Printed and bound by Sapra Brothers, New Delhi 110092

for

GEETHA

Contents

III. Nature's Future

Preface and Acknowledgements

Nature and Nation brings together a selection of my essays written over the past several years as part of a larger engagement with issues in ecology and history, focussing mainly on animals, politics, and history. I have not revised the papers, except occasionally to additionally cite some of the relevant literature that has appeared since the original publication; I have instead written a long Introduction which tries to tie together the larger argument as it looks to me now. The effort is not so much to give a rounded view as to assess the state of the field, and do so in a manner that gives a more coherent shape to the issues discussed, the sources used, and the approach adopted.

In the mid and late 1990s there was a small gaggle of scholars—a noisy one, sometimes resembling cackling geese but more often clamorously provocative—raising issues about the environment that needed to be heard. Two decades on there are many more such small groups thinking about and investigating the questions raised here. What remains striking to me is the salience of some older concerns—such as turning points and departures from past patterns; the fascination with extinction and collapse—as much as the rise of newer, equally fascinating tropes, such as the resilience of ecosystems and the longer-term patterns that show continuity. So, these essays are part of a continuing enquiry which tries to locate present-day concerns in a long-term perspective. Historians, when asked 'why' about any specific social phenomenon, usually say the time periods they need to look at need to be longer, and the answers they come up with need to show greater complexity and depth. In these two respects I hope this book is no different.

One source of pleasure in this long and complicated process of discovery and retelling of stories is the existence of other storytellers, listeners, and fellow travellers. The *Panchatantra*, the great Sanskrit epic, is a set of five tales told to a king's errant son. The 'five' in the title is a misnomer, for one story leads into another, and every character tells a story. If written in that vein, my account of how these essays came into being could grow into a nested edifice revealing the many friends and scholars with whom I have exchanged thoughts and learnt from. For the moment, refraining from the nostalgia that would make for a very long expression of gratitude, I can only mention a special few to whom I owe a deep and everlasting intellectual debt. The usual disclaimers apply, but I acknowledge the generosity and candour with which these scholars and practitioners shared their insights with me and frequently rescued me from error.

The ideas presented in this volume first took shape during my tenure as Junior Fellow at the Nehru Memorial Museum and Library (NMML), where many were tried out in early, more hesitant, versions. For the fellowship, and even more for his stimulating and encouraging and warm presence, I remain deeply indebted to a former NMML director, the late Professor Ravinder Kumar. His departure cannot dim memories of his institutional stature and intellectual influence. It was at his urging that I tried initially to widen the broader setting of what began as a somewhat narrow study of hunting and conservation in imperial and independent India. NMML's fellows of that period, mainly older eminent scholars, were forthcoming and helpful.

The ideas worked out over the past many years also gained from my stints at other enriching places. The Mario Einaudi Center, Cornell University, where I was 'visiting faculty' for three years, was very congenial. Valmik Thapar and the Ranthambhore Foundation were unstinting in their support during a period in 1999, for which I remain grateful.

Visiting positions at the Jadavpur University, Kolkata, the Centre for Ecological Sciences, Indian Institute of Science, and at the National Centre for Biological Sciences, Bengaluru, helped widen my horizons. The Nature Conservation Foundation, Mysore, as well as the Centre for Herpetology near Chennai, were sounding boards and incubators for many ideas. Visits to Uppsala University, Sweden, and to the Rachel Carson Center, Munich, and on more than one occasion to Yale University, gave me the chance to interact with a range of scholars. The four batches of the MSc Wildlife Biology I taught at the National Centre for Biological Sciences, Bangalore, contained among the finest young minds I have had the privilege of working with. Special thanks to Umesh, Meghna, Nandini, and Nachiket.

Inevitably, as one's horizons broaden, the ground surveyed grows less familiar, the trails all seem strange, and to whom can one turn but those who know the way—and know it far better than I ever can? For help with early and medieval contexts I am indebted to Nayanjot Lahiri, Upinder Singh, Kathleen Morrison, R.C. Thakran, Farhat Hasan, S.Z.H. Jafri, Sunil Kumar, Najaf Haider, Heeraman Tiwari, T.R. Shankar Raman, Mudit Trivedi, and Shibani Bose. Environmental history, in its broadest sense, continues to widen, and the scholars in it are very numerous. So, though I cannot thank them all I acknowledge with gratitude and affection Amita Baviskar, William Beinart, Ritu Birla, Jane Carruthers, G.S.L. Devra, Gunnel Cederlof, Rohan D'Souza, Heather Goodall, Radhika Govind Rajan, Ramachandra Guha, Richard Grove, Sumit Guha, Annu Jalais, Shashank Kela, Mayank Kumar, Joan Martinez Alier, Michael Mann, Christoph Mauch, Vasudha Pande, Jose Augusto Padua, Meena Radhakrishna, Usha Ramanathan, Aarthi Sridhar, Kartik Shanker, Ajantha Subramanian, Arupjyoti Saikia, Vasant Saberwal, Richard Tucker, Michael Lewis, Peter Perdue, William Pinch, and Nandini Sundar. I am also grateful to those with distinct interests who have put up with me for trying out arguments and ideas: Pranay Sharma, Srinath Raghavan, Charu Gupta, Dinesh C. Sharma, Leela Gandhi, Heidi Tinsman, Anshu Malhotra, and the energetic trio at *Seminar*—Mala, Harsh, and Tejbir.

Over the years there has also gathered a wider ecumene of scholars which straddles the all-too-familiar divide between biological or life sciences and the humanities. Related to but distinct from this is work by people who cross the human–animal boundary. Among these are many who will see traces of past conversations in these pages: Vidya Athreya, Rohan Arthur, Yashveer Bhatnagar, Pallava Bagla, Seema Bhatt, Bahar Dutt, Madhav Gadgil, Ajay Desai, Suparna Ganguly, Aparajita Datta, A.J.T. Johnsingh, Ullas Karanth, Jagdish Krishnaswamy, Ajith Kumar, Asmita Kabra, Divyabhanusinh, Janaki Lenin, Vivek Menon, Charu Dutt Misra, Divya Mudappa, Sunita Narain, Rishad Naoroji, Y.V. Jhala, Deepak Pental, Aaron Lobo, Nitin Rai, M.K. Ranjitsinh, Sindhu Radhakrishna, Ravi Chellam, Vasant Saberwal, Anindya Rana Sinha, Nishath S., Raman Sukumar, Nitin Sethi, Gopi Sundar, Romulus Whitaker, K. Vijayraghavan, and Arun Venkataraman,

The papers here have been discussed and reworked after interactions in fora too numerous to mention individually. An extra word of thanks to those I worked closely with on edited volumes that sometimes emerged from those conversations: Vasant, Madhu, Shivi, and Ghazala for ideas and debates that will linger long in my mind.

Each of us gains in immeasurable ways from the wider moral and material support of our institutions, as also from colleagues, students, and staff. In particular I thank the head of department and all members and students of the Department of History, University of Delhi, and the chairman, fellows, and staff of the NMML, New Delhi.

Anuradha Roy and Rukun Advani have long been a bedrock of support and my appreciation for their patience, especially with unreadable and tangled prose, is deep and abiding. A word also for their dog Biscoot, who passed away in January 2015 after thirteen and a half years during which, my editors tell me, she supervised the creation of Permanent Black with an iron paw.

A special word of thanks to my family and friends, especially to Geetha, Uttara, my mother Shantha, and Wing Commander and Mrs Venkataraman.

This book is dedicated to Geetha. Since words in her praise cannot suffice, I will attempt none.

Sources of first publication are given below.

'The Raj and the Natural World: The Campaign Against "Dangerous Beasts" in Colonial India', *Studies in History*, vol. 14 (1998).

'From Princely Symbol to Conservation Icon: A Political History of the Lion in India', in Nariaki Nakazato and Mushirul Hasan, ed., *The Unfinished Agenda: Nation-building in South Asia*, Delhi: Manohar, 2001.

'Gandhi's Notion of Ahimsa and the Human–Nature Relationship', *Seminar*, no. 466 (1998).

'Nature and Nationalism: Rethinking India's Nehru', in William McNeill, Jose Padua, and Mahesh Rangarajan, ed., *Environmental History: As if Nature Existed*, Delhi: Oxford University Press, 2010.

'Striving for a Balance: Nature, Power, Science, and India's Indira Gandhi, 1917–1984', *Conservation and Society*, vol. 79, no. 4 (2009).

'Five Nature Writers: Jim Corbett, Kenneth Anderson, Sálim Ali, Kailash Sankhala, and M. Krishnan', in Arvind Krishna Mehrotra, ed., *An Illustrated History of Indian Writing in English*, Ranikhet: Permanent Black, 2001.

'The Politics of Ecology: The Debate on People and Wildlife in India, 1970–95', *Economic and Political Weekly*, vol. 31 (1996).

'Parks, Politics, and History: Conservation Dilemmas in Africa', *Conservation and Society*, vol. 1, no. 1 (2003).

'Contesting Conservation: Nature, Politics, and History in Contemporary India', in Sujata Patel and Tina Uys, ed., *Contemporary India and South Africa: Legacies, Identities and Dilemmas*, Delhi: Routledge, 2012.

1

Introduction

Issues in the Writing of Environmental History

Writing India's environmental history entails comparing and contrasting the subcontinent not only with Europe and North America but also, and most specially, with societies and territories in Asia and Africa that were once under Western imperial rule or domination. A century ago a quarter of the world was under the British, and Western empires expanded further after 1918. We now live in a very different age from the 'age of imperialism'. The contemporary climate is all about emerging economies and a possible 'Asian century'. Nations once at the bottom of the heap are seen as on their way up.

The political, economic, and cultural transformations that have led from one kind of world to another have received much attention.[1] The wider consequences—including the environmental shifts in a major Asian society and polity that are the focus of this

Citations provide author surname, abbreviated title, and wherever required page numbers. The list of references at the end provides the full bibliographical details of all works cited.

[1] For instance, see Pomeranz, *The Great Divergence*; Mahbubani, *The New Asian Hemisphere.* For a restatement of a classical economic nationalist view with fresh evidence, see Parthasarathi, *Why Europe Grew Rich.*

book—have also come under closer scrutiny, even if only over the last three decades. Each essay in this collection was first published between 1998 and 2012. The work as a whole thus explores diverse themes, and it would be a help to show their collective existence within a wider context of political shifts and intellectual changes. There is active debate on when, why, and how these specific shifts took place, but there is little doubt that they occurred. The issues connected with these changes are of global significance not only because of altered power relations across nations, but also because of the ecological and environmental dimensions of the transformations. Economy and ecology, state-making and identity, nature and nation have all converged and cohered to form the centre of analyses of change in this new century.

Writing of Germany's water and landscape history, David Blackbourn observes that all history is about unintended consequences, the story of the human relationship with nature even more so.[2] He is writing of a time when Germany seemed set to dominate Europe and the world, but his words are pertinent when reflecting on environmental histories in general and large Asian polities in particular. It is critical to stress the words 'unintended' and 'consequences', for there is always a danger of collapsing stories with twists and turns, contested spaces and competing visions, into a single narrative of empire, nation, and nature. The established metanarratives or big-picture stories had a place and purpose, but it is time to step around and beyond them, or tell them in new ways. Ideas and shifting entities are integral to the story but should not overwhelm the many patterns and hues of a mosaic.

Historians of India's environment, in particular, have to account for irony and paradox. A landscape in which over half the land is under permanent tillage, and which has more people in its towns and cities than the population of Europe, is also one with a still extant and even teeming array of birds and plants, animals and fish, reptiles and insects. Large vertebrates that have vanished from much

[2] Blackbourn, *The Conquest of Nature*, p. 1.

of Asia are often to be found in larger numbers in India than in any other country: these include the tiger and elephant.[3] The country is host to a diversity of regional climates and topographies, which means that, though the Tropics may dominate our imagination of Indian ecology, Central Asia—with its wild goats and sheep—too has much in common with the Trans-Himalaya and Himalaya of northern India. Similarly, north-east India has much in common, ecologically, with areas in South East Asia as well as southern China. And the 8000 km coastline is a reminder of the many ways in which the ecologies of India are closely connected with the wider world of the Indian Ocean.

While millennia of animal husbandry and agriculture, long centuries of trade, and the rise and decay as well as founding and unsettling of towns have transformed the country's waterscape and land, the continuities are manifest in a rich, living tapestry of life and production. Environmental decline is only one thread within this tapestry. We also have to ask why and how many such places have remained habitable and productive. Perhaps crisis is not only about collapse but also about reorientation and creative response. On the other hand, there is no doubting the clear evidence of the collapse or decline of ecosystems at other points in time and/or other places. When, where, and why are the pertinent questions in confronting polluted zones, and areas of decline and decay. How recent are the processes that have caused these changes? And how recently has the frequency or intensity of extraction/production changed? These issues are not unique to India, but the archival and material record here, as much as the mosaic of life and experience, suggests not one but many facets.

This being so, it follows that writing about environmental change and continuity also involves looking at contrasts. How the historical processes of, for instance, colonialism and capitalism,

[3] Sukumar, *The Living Elephants*. The tiger became national animal in 1972, the elephant national heritage animal in 2010. To complete a trio, the Gangetic dolphin was declared national aquatic animal in 2011.

or those arising from geographic specificity, did or did not affect specific terrains need close examination, as do the ways in which people did or did not make use of the opportunities opened up by lands, waters, animals, and plants. The imperial or colonial interlude, or the era of Western dominance of the globe, whether direct or indirect, has often been seen as a point of departure, or alternatively one of 'soft' continuities. The latter refers to the notion that Company and imperial rule simply completed the business of denuding forests and settling itinerant groups, processes begun by Indian elites and state-makers. There is still deep interest in and engagement with the idea that colonialism constituted an ecological watershed, a time of unprecedented and far-reaching changes in the human equation with the environment. But, quite apart from historical specificities, this idea of a colonial watershed took shape prior to, or in the very early phase of, the quickening pace of economic growth in Asia. Since then, perhaps concurrent with the growth trajectory of Asia, more attention has begun to be paid to longer-term trends that antedate the colonial era. Once seen as decisive—and still seen as crucial in many respects—there is also much more acknowledgement that the centuries or millennia prior to colonialism require more critical engagement.

Given the pace and rate of economic expansion since around the end of the 1970s in China, Vietnam, and India, the geophysical, hydrological, and in the widest sense biological consequences of these processes, by no means unilinear and in many ways contested, are another critical dimension with which all contemporary histories of the environment must contend.[4] These are all countries with large populations and relatively fast-growing economies, but they also have in common large areas with tropical ecosystems and monsoon ecologies. Rich in biological diversity, they are in a phase

[4] Watts, *When a Billion Chinese Jump*; Biggs, *Quagmire*. I am also grateful to the comments and insights at a panel of the American Historical Association, 2 January 2013, most so to the co-panellists, Ken Pomeranz, David Biggs, and K. Sivaramakrishnan, for discussion of these issues.

of history in which rapid growth not only creates opportunity but, if not well planned or thought out, can obliterate whole landscapes and waterscapes in short timespans.

But beyond these issues and questions, we might ask if it is merely environmental history in the narrow sense that we seek to reflect upon and explore. Perhaps what we really mean to do when we write such history is to provide a wider sense of how history and the environment, or how histories and environments, relate to one another. When doing this it is possible to see the transformation of the debate to a more nuanced and multifaceted reading of complex processes, both in the longer term and the immediate.

There is one other issue in this preliminary outline of vital questions: we have to understand that India's environmental history has to a large measure been shaped by the concerns of the present, with issues in the public space often foreshadowing the concerns of scholars. In turn, papers and books that might otherwise have had a select academic audience have often been echoed in larger debates. It is no coincidence that the early 1980s saw a two-part essay on the colonial roots of India's forest policy written at a time when a proposed law would, if enacted, have given forest officials even more punitive powers over local forest users. A pioneering citizen's report similarly sought to provide an alternative vision drawing on science-based critiques as well as grassroots action.[5] Similarly, the anti-dam protests against projects in (the exquisitely named) Silent Valley on the Kuntipuzha river in Kerala, against dams on the Narmada river in Central India, and against those on the tributaries of the Ganga and Brahmaputra, have found counterparts in studies of when and why large projects became the rage among decision-makers.[6] Contests over spaces secured for nature preservation, and the coercive removal of slums for beautification

[5] Guha, 'Forestry in British and post-British India'; Agarwal, Chopra, and Sharma, *State of India's Environment*.

[6] Baruah, 'Whose River is it Anyway?'; Dharmadhikari, *Mountains of Concrete*.

and urban redevelopment, have likewise found place in scholarly study. The arrival in India of the politics of cultural identity—in myriad, often mutually contradictory, forms—has also been studied in diverse settings.

Such parallels are not one-on-one in a specific way. But the vibrancy of democracy, in its multiple forms and at different levels has, especially over the last three decades, seen issues of resources and living spaces becoming central to politics and public debate. These issues include livelihoods *vis-à-vis* making space for nature, the use or misuse of new technologies, sharpening contests over land and water, pastures and wetlands. If history as academic discipline was a latecomer, it has more than made up by the breadth of these new concerns and diverse views of why we came to be where we are.

The Chronology of Indian Environmental History

There is little doubt that many present-day conflicts over forest and coastline have precedents. But it is from around 1980 that environmental concerns merge with historical ones. This should not occasion surprise: it is from this time also that the pace of expansion of the Indian economy moved from 3.5 to over 5 per cent. The pace of the creation of wealth was to pick up further, with the growth rate reaching 8 per cent over 2003–11, an acceleration without precedent in the previous two centuries.[7] This feature had no parallel in a universal suffrage democracy of similar size and scale. A concomitant shift, especially from the end of the 1980s, was the greater volatility of India's voters: not only did more vote, they tended to vote parties out of office. Since the 1960s voter turnouts of 60 per cent-plus, once a feature restricted to southern India, have become the national norm. It is in this context of economic

[7] Subramanian, *India's Turn*; Damodaran, 'Economy, No Muqabla'. For another view, see Bhagwati and Panagariya, *India's Tryst*.

and political-democratic expansion—with the attendant ecological costs spread out very unevenly across different sections of society and in varying regions—that environment and politics have intersected more than ever before. The biophysical, geomorphological, ecological, and wider environmental consequences of the expansion of townships and modern manufacture, of deeper market links for meat, hides, wool, and dung, the extraction of ores to smelt, and the extension and intensification of agriculture have all combined to stress the physical and material environment, again on a scale with no precedent. The surge in human numbers is outdone by the pace and scale of the expansion of the economy. When and where these changes began is a point of dispute.

The multiple strands of movements in India that one might label 'environmental' find deep resonance not only in politics but also in the approaches of historians to the past. The observation needs qualification: studies of river systems and anthropologically informed accounts of forest peoples or pastoralists long pre-dated 'environmental history'.[8] Similarly, archaeological works on wet/dry cycles pertaining to the decline of the Harappan culture were conducted in the early 1970s and anticipated many twenty-first-century concerns with climate change.[9] And it could be said that the writings of nature enthusiasts such as Jim Corbett and M. Krishnan, early conservationists and protectionists, anticipated some of the more professional directions of the later discipline of ecology. Sálim Ali went even further, applying systematics and ecology to bird classification and taxonomy from the 1940s on.[10] Yet the precursors were just that: precursors. It was really in the framing of alternatives to the dominant model of development that environmental history found its moment of active and self-aware genesis.

[8] Mukherjee, *River Systems of Bengal.*

[9] Climates have rarely been stable, and earlier pathbreaking work had suggested a dry spell around 2000 BCE: Singh, Joshi, Chopra, and Singh 'Late Quaternary History of Climate'.

[10] Rangarajan, 'Five Nature Writers'.

An early essay by Madhav Gadgil (a mathematician who became an ecologist) and Ramachandra Guha (a sociologist who became a historian), published in 1989, appeared in that unforgettable year of the fall of the Berlin Wall. In Asia at this time the Mujahidin took over Kabul and there were the Tiananmen Square protests in Beijing. In New Delhi, a single-party government bowed out, making way for a new era of coalitions, multi-party ministries, and minority governments. These larger political events were the backdrop to the Gadgil–Guha essay which set out themes that these early historians of Indian environmentalism were to expand upon in two full-length works. Their synthesis—the insights of an ecologist and a historian—reveal two key features in common with the popular grassroots environmentalism best symbolized by the Citizens' State of India's Environment reports. (Interestingly the senior author, Gadgil, was among the principal contributors to those reports.[11]) The first theme was that the colonial–imperial era was a watershed inasmuch as it unleashed newer levels of exploitation of nature as well as new, more intrusive systems of resource control. Second, local systems of resource use and renewal were, on careful examination, found to be capable of prudence and repair. This twin theme, of a centralizing state with roots in the pre-1947 Raj and the unearthing of a longer lineage in movements for local control—often by and of marginal people—was a key feature of such works.[12] This summary naturally cannot do justice to complex and multi-layered arguments; it suffices to say that they

[11] Agarwal and Narain, *State of India's Environment: The Second Citizens' Report*, and *Towards Green Villages*; and Gadgil and Guha, *This Fissured Land*, and *Ecology and Equity*.

[12] A larger corpus of work arose at the time and much of today's work is in constant, often critical, dialogue with the insights generated. Agarwal, *Cold Hearths*; Shiva, *Staying Alive*; Sangari and Vaid, *Recasting Women*. At a policy level, Singh, Pande, Kothari, and Variava, *The Management of National Parks*. Alongside biologists, mention may be made of Raman Sukumar's work that included a historically acute and sociologically sensitive section on animal–human interactions through history and into the present: *The Asian Elephant*.

laid out an ecological–historical field which soon saw massive expansion.

A feature of the 1970–90 decades in the writing of such history that requires more sustained critical enquiry involves the ways in which ecological themes found resonance in the world of fiction and art as much as in academic scholarship. A snapshot choice would include an English novel on the displacement of a coastal village by a fertilizer factory near the great coastal city then called Bombay. Another recounts the clash of wills in the forest between bauxite mining and Adivasis. A third is a play that narrates the quest for water in a semi-arid land, leading to altercation between a poor rural settlement and a government department.[13] Such writings were forerunners of more environmentally grounded novels and other writings that evoke deep sensitivity to hitherto neglected peoples, lives, and landscapes. One feature in common then and now to such writings, and to much environmental history, is their focus on marginal peoples and ecologies.[14]

The perils and promise of scientific forestry in the foothills of the western Himalaya was the subject of a monograph by Ramachandra Guha in which he found hill peasant power at odds with foresters and officials.[15] A similar subject was equally well explored in a journalistic study by Darryl D'Monte of contemporary conflicts

[13] In English, on the fertilizer plant, Desai, *A Village by the Sea*; in Bengali, Mahasweta Devi, *Chhoti Munda*; in Tamil, Swaminathan, *Water!* The rural denudation of thorn forests and its links to commercialized agriculture was the Tamil novel by Kaa Subramanian *Saya Vanam* (1998), translated by Vasantha Surya as *The Defiant Jungle*. Special mention must be made of the corpus of writings, both reportage and commentary, collected by Mahasweta Devi, *Dust on the Road*.

[14] For a fine later instance, see Amitav Ghosh, *The Hungry Tide*. While Ghosh brings to life the Sundarban mangroves, another important intervention on the forested Gangetic plains was the translation of a classic by Bibhutibhushan Bandyopadhyaya, translated from the Bengali by Rimli Bhattacharya, *Aranyak of the Forest*. A more recent exploration of the forest is of the Himalayan foothills and memories of the legendary Jim Corbett in Anuradha Roy's *The Folded Earth*.

[15] Guha, *The Unquiet Woods*.

between industry and environment.[16] By the mid 1990s such themes of conflict found expression in an anthology of studies that widened the canvas to include herders and inland fishers, swidden farmers and irrigation engineers. The last two centuries of clearing and cultivating, canal building, river 'taming' and town expansion, of smoke in the city and the mapping of hill and mountain, all became part of the tapestry of a new kind of history.[17]

The polymath Richard Grove, from 1995 onward, sketched out a more nuanced and internally heterogeneous picture of, especially, the East India Company era. Apart from unearthing intellectual influences and concerns that may have shaped the official mind—to, for instance, promulgate regulations pertaining to private property so as to forestall ecological ruin and consequent political disorder—Grove also placed India in the wider frame of the world of the Indian Ocean. In an unpublished paper, 'Surgeons, Forests and Famine', he pointed to the need to ask more about science and its pasts.[18] A distinctive aspect of his work is the highlighting of fissures among Company officials. Grove shows that there were diverse, often contradictory, ideas and interests at work. The last decade has seen aspects of all the above approaches being challenged and revised.[19] Just as there were diverse strands in the Company polity, there were fragmented and colliding

[16] D'Monte, *Temples or Tombs?*

[17] Arnold and Guha, *Nature, Culture, Imperialism*. For a recent review, see Rangarajan, 'Colonialism, Ecology and Environment'. A synthesis acknowledging the regional heterogeneity of the ecological impact is provided in Sarkar, *Modern Times*, pp. 72–105.

[18] Grove, *Green Imperialism*; and Grove, Damodaran, and Sangwan, *Nature and the Orient.* Also see Kumar, Damodaran, and D'Souza, *Imperial Encounters.*

[19] A short list of works would include: Baviskar, *In the Belly of the River*; Rangarajan, *Fencing the Forest*; Buchy, *Teak and Arecanut*; Sundar, *Subalterns and Sovereigns*; Saberwal, *Pastoral Politics*; Sivaramakrishnan, *Modern Forests*; Vasavi, *Harbingers of Rain*. A more holistic view also looked well beyond forests and rivers to the larger agrarian setting, the special volumes on forests and pastures of *Studies in History*, New Series, 14, 2, 1998; *Environment and*

interests in the late imperial era in the forests of British India: in Bengal, in forested upland and plateau, in the mangroves of the Ganga–Brahmaputra delta.[20]

Since the late 1990s there has been a significant shift in the way histories of the environment have been researched and told. There is less emphasis than earlier on the sharpness of the break with the past in the colonial era. There are now accounts which go well beyond forest, hill, and mountain to cultivated lands, riversides, and borderland pastures.[21] There is a relatively new realization of how diverse and complex forms of engagement often blunted the edge of intrusive and grid-like patterns of land, water, and forest management. Controlled sheep grazing was seen as critical to regenerating conifers in the Himachal Himalaya and strict curbs were attempted on shepherds. But the shepherds managed to evade them and renegotiate terms of access, so, though their lives got more difficult, their practices and livelihoods persisted. Similar stories unfolded in the great deciduous forests of central and eastern India, where the ban on lighting fires was more often practised in the breach than the observance. The reliance on local labour gave peasants as well as tribals room to manoeuvre, short of outright rebellion. Such day-to-day tugs of war typified relations in forest and pasture, and at the jungle's edge; pictures of successful denial and outright exclusion are simplifications.

Much more is now known about the adaptive and complex systems that emerged, many of which defy easy labels like 'modern' and 'traditional'. For instance, in his widely read essay, 'The Tiger and the Honeybee', Savyasaachi recounts how certain Adivasis

---

History, Special Issue on South Asia, 2, 2, 1996; and Cederlof and Rangarajan, 'Predicaments of Nature and Power in India'.

[20] Jalais, *The Forest of Tigers*.

[21] The wider agrarian setting of environmental shifts in socio-ecological terms was given sharper focus by essays in Agrawal and Sivaramakrishnan, *Agrarian Environments*; Lahiri-Dutt and Samanta, *Dancing with the River*; and Kothari, *Memories and Movements*.

in the Mayurbhanj hills of Odisha categorize forest blocks by the quality and abundance of honey, not the number of tigers. A pollinator, not a predator, and the harvest of sweetness rather than the presence of a mega-carnivore, is here the measure of success; cohabitation instead of separateness is the hallmark of this forest. Securing the forest need not mean locking all local users out; ensuring its viability in ecological terms can be attempted short of total state control, or command of human activity and presence in the landscape. He points out that the sal forest of Simlipal could maintain its ecological integrity via a partnership with its human residents and users while making space for the tiger and the honeybee.[22] Such spaces have survived, helped by the fact that India has been largely a peasant society, and that it did not, for the most, experience settler colonialism, as did Algeria or South Africa.[23]

By the end of the twentieth century, debates on ecological alternatives moved in new directions. Differences on a host of issues emerged more explicitly than in the past. As contributors to an issue of the journal *Seminar* argued, there were, and are, not one but many shades of green.[24] This was an argument about the present, where even those who saw the ecological question as central to public life differed on how best to approach it. The divisions among the communities of conservation were becoming as acute as those between advocates of protection versus those arguing for faster growth.[25] Part of this developing new contestation arose from

[22] Savyasaachi, 'The Tiger and the Honeybee'.

[23] Beinart and Hughes, *Environment and Empire*.

[24] *Seminar*, 'Shades of Green', September 2003. At the workshop of 6 December 2001 that preceded the issue, Dr Sharad Lele made the insightful remark that in 1982 there had been a wheel of 'alternatives' in environmentalism, but the spokes have by now come apart (6 December 2002, Hindu College, University of Delhi, Delhi). Yet, this coming apart also led to greater plurality and, as we shall see, new currents.

[25] For instance see the issue of *Seminar*, 'The Tribal Bill', August 2005, and the Debate in *Economic and Political Weekly*, 19 November 2005. Or the very different views on the ecological crisis in Kothari and Shrivastava, *Churning Global India*; Roy, *Field Notes on Democracy*; Thapar, *The Last Tiger*; and

the very diversity of situations and contexts in a country with 800 agro-climatic zones, 18 national languages, and a society where even the simple act of shaking your head (which almost universally means no) can, deciphered in a different zone, connote a 'yes'. This diversity is now very considerably reflected in ecological studies of the past.

Unpacking the 'Pre-Colonial'

Most scholarship on India has focused on the colonial era, mainly the imperial period post-1857 and independent India. There has been far less work on the longer-range history. This contrasts with scholarship on the other large Asian country, China.[26] Consequently, even sophisticated scholarship, let alone political and ecological advocacy, has often been built on the premise of a long period of harmony upset by colonialism. A careful sifting of the evidence should be a corrective to the idea that there was any 'long stasis' in economic and thereby ecological terms from 320 BCE to 1600 CE. Of course the pace at which human population and settlement expanded over this long term was far slower than in the last century, but it can be asserted there was no time of equilibrium. To place things in perspective, the present-day population density in India is over 350 to a sq km, whereas it was less than 80 in the nineteenth century, and 35 to a sq km about 400 years ago. The phenomenon of islands of mature tree forest within a vast ocean of cultivated and permanently tilled fields is a historically recent development.[27] In historical time it is part of the recent human domination of the earth's ecosystems.

Thapar, *Ranthambhore*. A sociologically nuanced and historically informed analysis by a biologist is Shahabuddin, *Conservation at the Crossroads*. Also see Rangarajan, Madhusudan, and Shahabuddin, *Nature without Borders*.

[26] Elvin, *The Retreat of Elephants*; Bao, 'Environmental Resources'.

[27] Guha, *Health and Population in South Asia*, p. 31; Lal, *The Hindu Equilibrium*, pp. 2–3, 33–4. The present population density of India is 354 to a sq km or ten times the level of 1600 CE. The so-called Hindu

The idea of a long era of relative stability was integral to the notion of the colonial watershed. The emphasis on intrusive, rapid, and unprecedented transformation in the imperial era drew on, even required, a contrasting picture for the preceding centuries. Significantly, the idea of a long equilibrium, though at a somewhat different time—in the later part of the first millennium of the Common Era—was implicit though never articulated explicitly in the work of Gadgil and Guha. Though of this there is scant evidence, their claim of a long equilibrium was vital because they posited a 'major resource crunch' around 1000 CE, leading to restraints on customary resource use.[28] Similarly, the longer history of state-making and remaking of landscapes pre-1800 cannot be ignored. It would be going too far to say that colonialism simply amplified pre-existing trends and practices, that it did not mark a qualitative break from the past.

There is, of course, little doubt of the epochal and significant shift in the late-nineteenth-century regimes of exploitation and control of resources, yet the long tapestry of past change is important as history, not as mere backdrop.[29] This represents, in brief, a different emphasis, namely that longer-term perspectives are essential when studying landscapes and waterscapes that are connected to millennia of human presence. My own skills and expertise pertain to the colonial period and its aftermath. The essays in this collection focus almost wholly on these eras and argue the

---

Equilibrium *a la* the economist Sanjay Lal never existed. In fact the population density in the second century CE, about 1800 years before the present, was 5 to a sq km. The total population of what is now India was at that point about 20 million in all. This was to rise twelvefold by 1850, when it was 250 million. The expansion over a period of some 1600 years was still significant, even though it did not take place in a direct unilinear fashion.

[28] Gadgil and Guha, *This Fissured Land,* pp. 91–2.

[29] For a forceful and lucid argument on the latter, see Morrison, *The Human Face of the Land.* I am indebted to Kathleen Morrison, Mudit Trivedi, Nayanjot Lahiri, and Raman Sukumar for continued engagement on these issues.

case that it saw not one but multiple, and interconnected, shifts in policies towards and relationships with the wider environment. This is an acknowledgement of the need to explore more fully and integrate more seriously the rich insights provided by scholars who draw the material evidence as well as textual sources from earlier epochs of history; the opportunities and challenges have been explored elsewhere.[30]

When looking at India's ecological history we need to be clear that a host of contingent factors often determined the fate of particular families, villages, and their networks of kin, dependents, and allies. The ways in which particular landscapes were imagined helped transform and shape outcomes. An instance from southern India can illustrate this. The changing etymology of the word for 'forest' in Tamil provides a clue to the extent of elasticity in land use change and shifting cultural meaning. Two millennia ago the Tamil word *kadu* was used to describe a burning ground. It then came to be an omnibus term for uncultivated lands that were counterposed to the settled, tilled lands of the Kaveri delta. Then the word *kadu* came to denote unruly thickets of the interior, as a place of unruly folk. *Kadu* or 'untamed space' is now viewed as against *nadu*, which denotes the civilized countryside.[31]

Such terminological shifts speak of the displacement of mobile groups by settlers, at least in the core of the complex agrarian states, often in the fertile river valleys. But this was by no means a one-way street. Scholarship drawing on vernacular sources shows

[30] Eaton, *The Rise of Islam*. For instance, in the 1520s Babur saw the river Indus as a line dividing lands that were distinct in climates, cultures, and peoples: Thackston, *The Babarnama*, pp. 332–3. For further discussion on the so-called pre-colonial epoch, see M. Rangarajan and K. Sivaramakrishnan, eds, *India's Environmental History, from Ancient Times to the Colonial Period*. Also see Kathleen D. Morrison, 'Conceiving Ecology and Stopping the Clock: Narratives of Balance, Loss and Degradation', in M. Rangarajan and K. Sivaramakrishnan, eds, *Shifting Ground: People, Animals and Mobility in India's Environmental History*, pp. 39–64.

[31] Ludden, *Agrarian History of South Asia*, pp. 149–51.

a long-term set of processes of acculturation and reinvention in which the tribe-caste or the farm-forest frontier showed enormous fluidity and flexibility. The point about such local-language sources needs some emphasis: too many premises and assumptions about the past prior to colonialism deny these lands and peoples a history. Such denials often depend on a paucity or absence of historical sources from the era before the nineteenth century. If this is true of documentary sources, it is even truer of material remains—despite the rich corpus now of ecologically sensitive archaeological studies. To put it simply, the very term 'pre-colonial', besides being tautological, consigns not just centuries but even millennia to a past sans history. In recent years, however, it has been the crisscrossing of pre-history and history, and of trespassers ranging freely over ancient/medieval/modern/contemporary history, that have begun to yield rich dividend and insight.[32]

For instance, recent work on pastoral and agricultural relations and contexts in the medieval and early modern period shows ample evidence of the role and place of state-making in pastoral and agrarian production.[33] Similarly, late-eighteenth-century eastern Bengal (now the North East) has been shown as the scene of a close and complex interweaving of climate change, political contest, and legal enactment by a newly expanding East India Company polity.[34] Such works on the north-west and eastern edges of India are reminders that patterns of change crisscrossed the boundaries of the subcontinent.

This evocation of a longer view emerged clearly in scholarship by around 2000. Parallel to this was a more measured reassessment of the imperial impact in the nineteenth century.[35] The work of Sumit Guha was a useful corrective to the widespread view of the

[32] For more on this theme, see the Introduction in Rangarajan and Sivaramakrishnan, eds, *Shifting Ground.*

[33] Devra, *Environmental Crisis*; Kumar, *Monsoon Ecologies.*

[34] Cederlof, *Founding an Empire.*

[35] See Rangarajan, 'Polity, Ecology and Landscape'. This paper (2002) took a view on the colonial transition, that was reiterated with greater emphasis on sedenterization in another paper: Mahesh Rangarajan, 'Environment and

arcadian ruralness of forest peoples remote from history. Guha argued that fluidities gave way to fixity only in the late nineteenth century, with the emergence of a forest sub-proletariat.[36] The mobilities and fluidities, which were features of many societies and landscapes till into the Company era, came under severe strain. Despite the enormous power exerted by the modern colonial state in the nineteenth century to tame and limit nomadism and other forms of movement, the fluidities remained a feature of Indian society well into the twentieth century, both at the margins of empires and in parts of its heartland.

This wider theme of settling the lands and trying to fix potential revenue payers to single plots is an important theme. Though not eliminated, the attempt to control fluid movement was much more intense and sustained than ever in the past. This was despite a major remaking of the polity which saw an intensification of control over forests (with well over half a million sq km having been converted to government forests by 1904), the reclassification of wild animals as 'game' or 'vermin' (with over 500 elephants captured for sale and 1500 tigers killed every year over half a century for bounty), and the setting up of a canal network in the Indus and Ganga basins that has bequeathed Pakistan with the highest per capita irrigated land on earth. Many of these shifts and disjunctures are taken up in the essays that follow. They help us assess how the perceptions of historians, and the histories of the environment they crafted, have taken shape, and where they now stand. [37]

Contested Landscapes, Changing Polities

Even as the longer-term history nuances and qualifies the view that the imperial era constituted a watershed, all neat two-way

---

Ecology under British Rule', in Douglas M. Peers and Nandini Gooptu, eds, *India and the British Empire*, pp. 212–30.

[36] Guha, *Environment and Ethnicity in India.*

[37] These shifts are taken up in Rangarajan, 'Environmental Histories of South Asia'.

state–society polarizations, and sharp fissures in science–local knowledge, begin also to look like just-so stories. For instance, there was earlier a great fascination with sacred groves and ponds, both in popular literature and scholarly writings. These holy features of the landscape seemed rooted in custom and sanctified by practice, not imposed by bureaucratic fiat or imperial diktat. Sacred groves (or haunted forests) are in fact the products of human choice. People wanted to retain or foster particular plants to enable the worship of certain associated gods, saints, and miraculous events. Those who tended a grove also 're-natured' it, making the whole a humanized landscape. By no means could one say now that a sacred grove is the remnant of a primeval forest. It is akin to cultivated or re-natured space.

Not only are such sites limited in their extent and acreage, in many cases they are controlled by the locally dominant social strata. The more extravagant claims of their value in securing nature for posterity have been questioned even by those who acknowledge the value and role of such refugia.[38] Custom- and faith-based interventions do matter, but are being assessed far more critically today. Similarly, taking swidden cultivators' or herders' knowledge of their ecological milieu seriously could (often but not always) be a short step from seeing their culture as nature. Many such deeply ahistorical views come apart when subjected to rigorous investigation.[39]

There are similar cracks within state systems as well, and not only in the era of imperial rule. The tensions were often present even at the highest level in the processes of state-making and environmental transformation. The fissures, within the state system as also in society, are not simply a coming apart of the spokes of the wheel of either the government or of social movements. The high noon of the developmentalist state, 1950 to 1980s, is seen

[38] For a critique, see Garcia and Pascal, 'Sacred Forests'.

[39] See the Introduction in Cederlof and Sivaramakrishnan, *Ecological Nationalism*, p. 7. A fine journalistic account of local cultures of production, livelihood, exchange, and consumption is Subramanian, *Following Fish*.

as the time of large projects, with Nehru's speech praising dams as the temples of modern India singled out for mention by critics and admirers alike.[40] A closer look shows that the speech in fact extols what was a peaceful civilian engineering enterprise in Punjab, the state having had no peace at all during Partition. So, it was not a Big versus Small debate at all. In fact, the now-published correspondence of Nehru and Indira Gandhi shows, from the 1930s on, keen awareness of the problems with an overly technocratic form of development—aesthetic, scientific, and humane issues being discussed at some length. In a little-known letter by Nehru written a decade after Independence, he urges state chief ministers to assess how large projects might impinge on 'the economy of nature, established through the ages', with which they must tamper but prevent any possible 'evil consequences' to: 'We have many large scale river valley projects that are worked out by engineers. I wonder, however, how much thought is given before the project is launched to have an ecological survey of the area and to find out what effect it would have on the drainage system and the flora and fauna of that area.'[41] The words, penned on 15 August 1957, remain relevant. Such thoughts and ideas also go some way towards explaining the limits of power.

After 1947 India did not experience any wholesale uprooting and destruction of land, pasture, and forest-based production, as happened in post-Revolution China after 1949. Nor did India experience the kind of relentless agricultural extension of the variety promoted in the Soviet Union. In fact, Nehru's 1957 letter came between the Virgin Lands Campaign of Khruschev in the USSR (1956) and Mao's Great Leap Forward in China, launched in 1958. Both failed partly on account of the hubris involved in every deep

[40] He may have been on stronger historical ground than was then realized given the long history of rulers in southern India investing in reservoirs that, in some cases, endure to this day. See Morrison, 'Dharmic Projects'.

[41] Nehru, 'No. 67. Letter to Chief Ministers', pp. 543–4. Such doubts as Nehru expressed need to be set in the context of his wider record of promoting such projects. See D'Souza, 'Damming the Mahanadi River'.

faith convinced of its ability to conquer and subjugate nature.[42] Such policy-related dilemmas in the early years after Independence call for further study: part of the ambivalence and hesitation came from the longer history of debates among Indian nationalists before 1947.[43]

The succeeding period of Indian political history from around the end of the 1960s saw major political shifts in the ruling party, government, and polity. Concomitant with this was a new emphasis on a kind of ecological patriotism. The preservation of nature as heritage was a part of wider transformations: the expansion of government became in some measure the means of securing natural heritage. Shikar companies, hoarders and traders, ex-princes, and large landholders were seen as inimical to the public good. This may go some way in explaining why the long Indira Gandhi period (1966–84) saw wildlife protection becoming a key element of government policy. Even though it often entailed new, intensified regulation for marginal peoples, the democratic process also opened up, creating checks and balances that remain important. This was clearest in the case of the proposed Forest Bill in 1982, with stringent punishments for usufruct right holders. Because of protest, especially by Adivasis, the bill was never even tabled.[44] Some of the shifts of the period from 1969 to 1989 have had a lasting impact: environmental regulation bearing on capital and government, dating back to the enactments of the 1970s and the 1980s (on forests, wildlife, air and water pollution, and environmental protection), remain anathema to pro-growth advocates. Such laws and rules were a

[42] Schapiro, *Mao's War against Nature*; Taubman, *Nikita Khruschev*, pp. 262–3 and 266–7.

[43] The short essay on Gandhi and the longer engagement with Nehru's practices and ideas is attempted in Rangarajan, 'Gandhi's Notion of *Ahimsa*', and Rangarajan, 'Nature and Nationalism'.

[44] Rangarajan, 'Nature and Nationalism', and Rangarajan, 'Striving for a Balance'. Some fascinating details are in Divyabhanusinh, *The Story of Asia's Lions*, esp. pp. 166–75. For the correspondence of Indira and Jawaharlal 1922–64, see Gandhi, *Freedom's Daughter*, and Gandhi, *Two Alone*.

product of awareness both 'above' and 'below'. This emerges clearly in the much neglected but rich corpus of letters and speeches by Indira Gandhi (1917–84), and even more so from the emergence of new policies in her first spell in office, 1969–77.[45]

A broader political consensus on nature as heritage (even if often 'breach not observance') has been in place since the early 1970s. It might explain why India, somewhat singularly in South Asia, has resisted the drive, mainly from China, to regard legalizing the tiger trade as the best way to end threats to the animal. It is not an irony that a democracy with a mixed economy resists a neo-Smithian view that was adopted as policy by one of the last one-party Communist states on earth.[46] Nature and nation, and the story of technology and the environment in independent India, may as issues be as complex as ecology and empire.[47]

Environmental concerns, both elite and popular, are now more deeply politicized than ever before and, given the fierceness of the competition for living spaces, water, and fertile as well as marginal lands, they are more intense as well. In turn, the growing consciousness of gender and justice concerns has made a difference to the nature of scholarship. Given the rapidity of the economic transformations under way, the historian's task is all the more daunting. The enormity of the impact of mining and dam-building, urban expansion and rural technological transformation, is more undeniable than ever before. Therefore, ensuring peace with nature is part of the challenge of working in a democratic polity with a fast-expanding market economy. Though much is taken, much abides.

Nations and Animal Icons

Despite the centrality of nationalism as a theme in historical enquiry, few historians of India have explored the changing ways in

[45] This issue is explored in some depth in Rangarajan, 'The Politics of Ecology'.

[46] Meacham, *How the Tiger Lost its Stripes.*

[47] See D'Souza, *Environment, Technology and Development.*

which nature may be seen to define a nation. In this, they are very different from scholars elsewhere in the world who have explored these interconnections and overlaps. When moving beyond the imperial age, and by asking how nationalists of various hues and stripes had differing, even mutually contradictory, approaches, it proves useful to explore the nature–nation dynamic and observe how it has changed over time. Positioning these changes within a larger backdrop also helps place Indian experiences in context, as well as in identifying directions for further research.

'Settler' nationalism and European nationalism have both been investigated with rigour in this broad arena. Through a literary sleight of hand, the green hills of England—where the New Jerusalem would rise—seemed by their very existence and sighting to clothe utopia in the core colour of nature and bring it a step closer to the believer. American nationalism, similarly, drew on the idea that its canyons and mountains were older than the biblical texts, and gave these historical moorings. By making the canyon on the river Colorado 'Grand', nationalists ensured that those who visited or visualized it saw their nation gain legitimacy, extra mileage, a place in the sun.[48] White settler claims on the land were reinforced by valorizing nature's heritage, which also helped stigmatize other peoples and cultures as lazy and reckless. And, in one Australian case, a desert that was to be 'developed' for a township spurred a protest that helped redefine the outback as part and parcel of a larger national identity.[49]

All this is of special significance to South Asia, where cultural and material changes in state-making often saw rulers draw on animals as icons. In this they were not unique. Nationalism could tap into older lore and legend, epic and narrative. After all, birds and animals that commanded human attention had also played key roles in tales people had told each other down the ages, both here and in Europe. Ravens in the Tower of London are still

[48] Schama, *Landscape and Memory*, p. 5; Pyne, *How the Canyon became Grand*.

[49] Robin, *Defending the Little Desert*.

fed at midday by the Beef Eaters: their absence, it is said, would indicate that the Crown is unsafe. A French scholar tells of a time in early medieval Europe when the bear was the king.[50] Similar is the story of the Greater One-horned Rhinoceros, a lynchpin of Vedic and post-Vedic ritual till some time in the eighth century CE, when its symbolism vanished.[51] When and why such shifts away from these great beasts as symbols—the brown bear in Europe and the one-horned rhino in India—happened is what these studies investigate. Perhaps as tastes and fashions changed, shifts in human relations with animals were mirrored in part by new symbols replacing the old.

Not all such changes were abrupt. Schoolchildren in India are familiar with the fifth CE triad of the Gupta rulers, who used titles such as 'tiger slayer', 'lion slayer', and 'rhino slayer'.[52] Conquest and valour could be evoked by mortal combat with these megafauna. The dividing line between the hunt and war, between bravery and cruelty, or what set apart raw power from its modulated use, was not always clear. Ambivalence rather than clear logic was the norm. This emerges clearly from Indian and Asian accounts of a mega-herbivore that has long fascinated and awed humans: the elephant. Mughal rulers were new to the animal in the 1520s, but in half a century adapted and incorporated the animal into their armies. Elephants were vital as war booty and tribute: male tuskers or females could be given as gifts as well as celebrated in lore and portrait. The power and destructiveness of the animal on fields of battle were celebrated alongside its gentleness and intelligence.[53]

[50] Pastoreau, *Bear: History of a Fallen King*, reviewed by Jonathan Sumption, *Wall Street Journal*, http:// online.wsj.com/ article/ SB10001424052 9702045 2460457660 94434549 65846.html.

[51] Bose, 'From Eminence to Near Extinction'.

[52] *Vyagra bala parakrama* (Samudragupta), *simha bala parakrama* (Chandragupta), and *khadaga bala parakrama* (Kumaragupta) were all celebrated in the coins of their realms.

[53] Nath, 'From Mocking to Becoming'. The elephant far more than any other animal was widely depicted as an emblem of power in early India (Professor Upinder Singh, University of Delhi, personal communication).

Such invocation of animals as emblems of clans, rulers, and states was not new. More research is required on whether the evolution and growth of nations in Europe and elsewhere entailed qualitative shifts in attitudes to nature. One scholar has suggested this was the case in the move to a more compassionate view of nature in a three-century-long era in England by 1800.[54]

But it is still worth asking if those at the helm of states needed to connect with age-old manifestations of political power, and whether they did so to gain legitimacy. This has been suggested, though not quite so explicitly, for the Mughals. Megafauna were critical emblems of early modern kingship. From the late sixteenth century, Babur's successors saw the lion as the equal of the sovereign. This was no coincidence, for the animal had a long association with royalty in pre-Islamic India as well as Iran.[55] For Mughals and other such, therefore, the hunt was integral to war—a domination of the countryside. There were other ideas too, such as that of the lion and lamb lying side by side in peace, the suggestion being that the emperor, himself a slayer of lions, could simultaneously maintain peace between recalcitrant groups of subjects and conflicting symbols. Equally well known was the late-eighteenth-century Mysore ruler Tipu's invocation of the tiger, an animal that was critical to many communities in his realm—in forest, pasture, and settled village alike.[56]

In this respect, the British imperial era broke with the past. Wild flesh-eating beasts, especially those that could prey on people, were now viewed much more antagonistically. The war against 'dangerous beasts' waged with such ferocity in the late nineteenth century (the subject of one of the essays herein) drew on earlier British notions of animals like the tiger being ferocious and unruly. The savagery of the British imperial campaign, and of its many Indian partners and participants, against 'dangerous beasts and

[54] Thomas, *Man and the Natural World.*

[55] Brittlebank, *Tipu Sultan's Search for Legitimacy.*

[56] Divyabhanusinh, 'Lions, Cheetahs and Others'.

venomous snakes' was without precedent. In common with the bid to sedentarize itinerant peoples, the drive to wipe out whole species such as the tiger bound the ideology of empire with that of economic improvement.[57] Only by the 1920s was there an easing of the depredation, and the reason was, ironically, that the animals targeted for extermination had become something of a rarity in need of preservation.

There was also by 1900 the growing scientific concern that humans were driving their faunal wealth to extinction. Strong state action to rescue endangered species was now served up as a sign of benign statecraft. The very megafauna that had been targets for elimination a generation or two earlier were now seen as worth bringing under the umbrella of imperial or princely protection. By the late 1920s there were signs that the war against the tiger was past its peak. Depletion levels helped create conditions in which slaughter gave way to a degree of tolerance. In this, the tiger's case was by no means unique.

Conquest and domination began to pave the way for a new kind of dominance, expressed by allowing large and increasingly rare animals to remain within pockets of their former range. India was not alone in this respect. The American bison emerged in the late nineteenth century as the signifier of a wilderness that had vanished. Some of the very hunters who had aided its demise helped breed and restock small parts of its range. Its survival was deemed essential for the founding legends of a white settler nation.[58] Three decades later, Poland's rulers viewed the European bison (or wisent) as emblematic of the rebirth of the Polish state. Individual specimens were brought in from various collections so that they could once again wander and browse the great forest of Bialowieza.[59] The pioneering environmental

[57] See Rangarajan, 'The Raj and the Natural World'.

[58] Eisenberg, *The Destruction of the Bison*, pp. 164–92.

[59] Weisman, *The World without Us*, pp. 9–14, 21–7. I am grateful to Professor Ewa Domanska, Adam Mickiewicz University, Warsaw, Poland, for this reference and discussions on the subject.

historian Jane Carruthers has similarly shown how the creation of the vast Kruger National Park was, exclusively for white South Africans, living proof of their supremacy over the land. It also reaffirmed white unity *vis-à-vis* 'coloured' peoples, especially Africans, as also a sanctuary for the veld, where they could renew their pioneer spirit as settler state.[60]

Such exclusion was not the preserve of any one people or nation. In a poignant piece on birding in the West Bank, a birder writes of how the skies are divided up, with places set aside for the Israeli Air Force.[61] Conservation, much like extermination, was often a project driven by small but evolving elites. What was new was the willingness to let nature (or key animals or plants) live on, but the means and intent for doing so were not so universal or benign. Yet the birder finds places of quiet and sanctuary where Palestinians and Israelis can come together simply to watch, admire, and observe birds that live or breed in, or migrate to, a land divided by strife. Nature here reflects both the state of strife and the yearning for peace.[62]

Not all such symbols were exclusive. India was among the many newly independent countries in Africa and Asia after the Second World War that faced deep dilemmas. The leaders of such emerging nations saw nature as a unifying force, both as resource and heritage. India's new rulers were among many to respond to divisive forces by appealing to a deeper sense of topographical unity. In the mid-twentieth century the snows of Kilimanjaro had a mystic appeal for the leader of the Mau Mau rebel leader and later

[60] Carruthers, *The Kruger National Park*.

[61] Platt, 'Birding in Palestine'. Also see Tal, *Pollution in a Promised Land*.

[62] In the wake of the 1967 war, a group from a kibbutz came upon a grove of eucalyptus and thought these had been planted by the Jewish National Fund. A meticulous historian later found this indeed to have been the case, the plantations dating back to the 1940s: Segev, *1967*, p. 512. An early organizer of the Fund was none other than Golda Meyerson, later Golda Meir, Israel's first woman prime minister. I am grateful to Adi Inbar, Pnina Motzafi Haler, Shomen Mukherjee, and most of all Alon Tal for discussion on these issues.

President of Kenya, Jomo Kenyatta. That fire on the mountain mattered; so did the mountain itself. The leader of neighbouring Tanzania, Julius Nyerere, saw in the giraffe (or Twiga as it was named) an emblem that could help cohere the various tribes and ethnic elements of his vast and diverse nation into a whole. Their contemporary Nehru was also drawn to the mountains: he wrote in his *Autobiography* in 1936 of how he found, 'a strange satisfaction in these wild and desolate haunts of nature'. They left him 'full of energy and a feeling of exultation'.[63] Each of these politicians was in a sense doing something that, in the field of poetry, had been done in Virgil's Eclogues, in pastoral elegies, and in Milton's 'Lycidas', namely deploying what literary critics term 'pathetic fallacy', the trope by which physical features and landscapes are endowed human attributes, an emotional character, a new meaning. In the modern version the attempt is to bind men and women together in search of a political dream by making their surroundings come alive. Even more than mountains and rivers, apt for this purpose were animals and birds.

So, enlisting animals for modern state-making was not unique to India. Schama shows how the very elements in Polish society that admired the bison of the oak forest also saw Jewish foresters in the same habitat as alien.[64] Even before the Nazis and the Holocaust, many European societies had powerful currents of thought that held the land to be home for the many and only a habitat for the few. This may not be and certainly is not the case with all invocations of lineage that draw on natural symbols. But it has in more than one case been part of the Janus-faced nature of nationalism and nation-state-centred politics that celebrating nature includes some humans

[63] Nehru, *An Autobiography*, p. 37. More recently, the new leaders of post-genocide Rwanda have seen the rare mountain gorilla and wagtail, unifying symbols that transcend ties of tribe and ethnicity: see Weber and Veder, *In the Kingdom of the Gorilla*. For a different incorporation, this time of a wild ungulate into state-making in ex-Portuguese West Africa, see Walker, *A Certain Curve of Horn*.

[64] Schama, *Landscape and Memory*.

and excludes others. Future changes, specially in the notion of royal power as divine, may give a different place to the iconic role of the lion and the tiger. Some icons are extremely modern inventions: the Greater One-horned Rhino, now mostly found in Assam, had no role in Ahom state imagery over the six-century-long rule of the Ahoms. In the twentieth century the animal became a symbol of regional nationalism, its rarity and uniqueness playing a part. Therefore, precisely when the rhino became 'Assamese' requires engagement with processes of history, with the coalescing of linguistic identity, with the remaking of landscape, animals, rivers and all of nature as aspects of a homeland for a distinct people.[65] In settings as diverse as central Europe and north-east India, conservation has become part of a nationalist project. Just as the architects of nations defined bounds in space and time, so too did they appropriate key animals as their nation's icons.

In mobilizing people around the project of nationhood, key actors sought to imbue nature with nationalist colours as well. Aspects of the natural world were worked into the narrative of the nation. By doing so, the nation could be seen as inhering in nature, the intent being to remove all doubts about its historical legitimacy.

This leads to a larger question, for any definition of who is within a nation also acknowledges who is left out. Identifying an icon or animal as 'natural' to a nation also means indirectly marking other icons and animals as alien or external to it. Ideas of nationalism can, however, be both exclusive and inclusive. This is illustrated by the role of two great cats in the political and historical imagination in Asia: the tiger and the lion. The tiger is simultaneously the national animal of no less than six countries in

[65] Saikia, 'Dynamics of Social and Political History'. Saikia points out how as early as the 1930s the rhino was seen as distinctively Asomiya and how 'outsiders/non-Assamese' were blamed for its decline. The rhino has been claimed as symbol by a sub-regional group, the Bodo Area Autonomous Council. The same species is enlisted as mascot for Assamese regionalism and Bodo sub-regional aspirations.

Asia. In India it became—as for Subhas Chandra Bose's army in the 1940s—a sign of courage and freedom. What is significant is the way in which certain animals come to embody qualities that are politically and culturally vital to those who appropriate them. The history of the lion as a sign of royalty in India is one such tale (explored later in this volume).[66] It is intertwined as well as contrasted with that of the tiger. The challenge for the historian is to tell not one but both tales, the story of the encounter in real life as much as the history of shifting, changing, and contested imageries. The power and hold of these animals is such that, just over four decades ago, the lion lost its throne as India's national animal to the tiger. Around the same time it also became the 'state animal' of Gujarat, which is a linguistic state with a distinct regional nationalism that sees the lions of the Gir Forest as uniquely its own. Tracing past lineages and presence may be critical to the present. Plans to reintroduce lions into a forest in Central India have been opposed by the state of Gujarat. The iconic animal is a metaphor for humans who seek moorings in the past and for the future. But equally, metaphor as well as literal presence are often contested by different sets of people.

They are also implicitly if not explicitly questioned in a recent study that suggests the species itself is only present in India on account of being introduced by kings and rulers of the past.[67] Even the presence of lions in the Gir Forest has been traced in recent work to African-born animals being set free.[68] Without entering

[66] See Rangarajan, 'From Princely Symbol to Conservation Icon'; also Rangarajan, 'Animals with Rich Histories'.

[67] Thapar, Thapar, and Ansari, *Exotic Aliens*. For a critical review, see Divyabhanusinh and Ranjitsinh, 'Lion and Cheetah in India'. The authors' response was in press and I am grateful to Valmik Thapar for sharing it with me. It is evident that these animals excite curiosity and imagination both as symbol and in real life. See Thapar, *et al.*, 'Response to the Review', pp. 95–104.

[68] It is notable that Divyabhanusinh, 'The Junagadh State and its Lions', is about *in situ* conservation. The author found no archival record of any introduction of any live specimens from any part of Africa.

into the merits of the case, it is significant that nature is being recast in more ways than one here. And this is only one case out of many in which nature is manifest in royal, imperial, or republican power. So too is the idea that animals, like cultures or peoples, can be assessed by their origins. When and what is native or exotic, indigenous or alien, intrinsic or part of an external ecosystem, is always up for debate. As with immigrant humans, an issue raised as a corollary is the question of when and how an entity ceases to be alien. In a sense, the idea of a nation and certain kinds of ideas of nature may be enmeshed in ways we are barely aware of. Does the tiger (or the lion) become more indigenous because it arrived earlier in the areas that now constitute India? Given that these mammalian radiations perhaps occurred 30,000 to 100,000 years ago (roughly when humans also appear in the fossil record), does such a long past lend itself to such evocations of indigeneity or its denial?[69]

What is fascinating to a historian is the renewed debate on origins and indigeneity, these being seen as markers critical to the future of not only the denizens of the forest but about the role humans should now play. When and where did the original state of nature lie, and how far back in time ought one to go to draw a line between the human presence and the world of nature as *tabula rasa*? The issue is in fact even wider. Give that humans were part of the larger evolutionary drama, it is unclear when and how nature was pristine. It is best to avoid, or be deeply sceptical of, terms that classify humans as the only agents of change (and outside of or beyond nature). In the specific case of big cats, their origin and historic spread is the subject of active study. The lion, no less than the tiger, was long in India before human agency brought any of them.[70] These matters of debate are addressed

[69] Barnett, Yamaguchi, Barnes, and Cooper, 'The Origin, Current Diversity and Future of the Modern Lion'.

[70] Johnsingh and Manjrekar, *Mammals of South Asia*. The notion of 'original' inhabitants was advanced from the 'aboriginal' or 'tribal' peoples in late-nineteenth-century India, a twist to the idea of original dwellers as opposed to latecomers to the land.

in the essays that follow. It is worth noting the intertwining, in many of them, of nature and nation, of the fact that emblematic animals cannot claim rights but that humans can and do speak for or against them.

The rarity or uniqueness of an animal may get enmeshed with people's claims to their being distinct as a people. Nature conservation is in this sense an often deeply political project, specially in many formerly colonial countries where the ethic of the hunt gave way to preservation. Yet the idea of diversity in and of nature may not include adequate space for the very people reliant on nature. This remains the case in India, despite the fact that the acreage of its parks and sanctuaries even now is a bare 6 per cent of the land mass. Also, the administrative legacies of the imperial era remain evident in the way that wildlife parks in India are administered: new ideas drawing on science and community participation make far less headway on the subcontinent than in many emerging economies and former colonies.[71]

State diktat, even in a democracy, can often be harsh: it can be the price paid to serve a future for nature as part of a larger process of resource transfer away from the underprivileged. Forest bureaucracies, tourist interests, a growing middle class, and local rural elites are among those who powerfully shape preservation to suit their interests. The tiger and its fellow denizens are seen by administrators abstracted from the humans who share their living space and as often in conflict with them.[72] Jalais shows how the idea of peace with people, in this case the 'nimno vargo'—those constituting the lower social orders—did not matter to foresters, administrators, and political leaderships that displaced them from the mangroves of the Sundarbans in Bengal. This leads to the issue of who speaks for nature as much as who leads or speaks for the nation.

[71] For a review of key works on conservation histories in Africa and contrasts with India, see Rangarajan, 'Parks, Politics and History'.

[72] Jalais, 'Unmasking the Cosmopolitan Tiger'. On similar lines, see the meticulous and lucid study of displacement of Maasai herders from a park in Tanzania: Brockington, *Fortress Conservation*.

This is specially relevant in the context of India, which is still a country of landscapes in which people, livestock, and large wild animals cohabit. Even though conflicts are recurrent, there is scope for a reconciliation falling well short of the annihilation of wild vertebrates (as attempted in the imperial era), or the displacement of human settlements (as taken up in strict nature reserves since the 1960s). The 'cosmopolitan tiger' can mask a hard-edged attitude to local resource users, but all forms of intervention need not be so painful.[73] Many of the essays that follow focus on 'nature's future' to explore the challenges and potential of democratizing nature and nation.

Nature's Future

The dilemmas in securing a future for nature lie partly in the specifics of the body politic which defines the ways in which competing claims are to be settled or contested. Ever since the promulgation of the Constitution in January 1950, India has faced the larger question of pursuing equality in a society steeped in hierarchy. For our purposes the question can be simplified: can nature and nation relate to one another in a more just way than under the empires of the last few centuries and more? Does the nation need to annex and monopolize nature *in extremis* to save it, or are there better ways?[74] There was no simple 'Western' model of nature transplanted into India (as indeed of nation). Princely rulers held certain totem-like animals in high esteem but did not extend such sentiments to their subjects. 'Akin to leopards in gardens, Kings were no Strangers in the forest'—meaning that there was no basic or fundamental division between human and wild space. Culture and nature were not separable but interwoven,

[73] For a critique, see Ghosal, Athreya, Linnell, and Vedeld, 'An Ontological Crisis?' On leopards (though not the larger cat, the tiger), and overlaps of humanized zones and carnivores, see the evidence cited by Athreya, Odden, Linnell, Krishnaswamy, and Karanth, 'Big Cats in Our Backyards'.

[74] For instance, the late Kenyan Green Wangari Mathai suggested trans-border cooperation and inclusive governance as the means to save the Congo basin forests: Mathai, *The Challenge for Africa,* esp. pp. 260–74.

the prerogative of those in power being to remake the mosaic.[75] Are we living through a remaking of the mosaic or a tearing apart of the ecological fabric? Time will tell. This longer-term sensibility needs to be integrated into thinking much more critically among those engaged in directing environmental change.

The past also matters in relation to nature because of citizenship rights and issues of equality between segments of the citizenry. A question that needs to be asked is whether there were informal gradations of subjecthood in the past—in princely as much as British India—and the extent to which these continue into the present. Such legacies may hinder, delay, and impinge on the way towards full democratic citizenship in contemporary times. Some segments of citizens tend to be viewed by dominant elites as 'different', for instance when they seem closer to nature or to particular landscapes. It is commonplace to see itinerant or tribal peoples as part of nature, but also as needing to be enumerated, sedentarized, disciplined, and made productive. Such notions of centralizing state power in British India often resurface in the process of state-making as a nationalist project. What is crucial is that securing nature too may engender a collision of nature and such peoples; so it is important to emphasize the intertwining of the dual claims made on nature and nation. Nationalisms, as suggested above, entail organizing humans collectively as in/outside the nation. Both nature and nation are contested products of a history that is still unfolding.

This larger trope of ecological nationalism is in turn open to varying and even mutually conflicting interpretations. Can 'development' be opened up in an inclusive manner, and what does inclusion mean for the underclasses and non-human entities? The dams on the Narmada in Gujarat and bauxite mines in the Niyamgiri hills of Odisha have been opposed on environmental

[75] See the lucid argument on this point in Hughes, *Animal Kingdoms*, pp. 5–6. Such logic strongly refutes the argument in the well-known essay by Cronon, 'The Trouble with Wilderness', in Cronon, *Uncommon Ground*. For a similar, nuanced view of a Mediterranean culture, see Nabhan, *Songbirds, Truffles and Wolves*, esp. pp. 121–44.

grounds. It is easy to miss that these very projects are seen as harnessing the wealth of nature to create a prosperous economy. Language-based identity and economic growth also have deep ecological consequences and significant environmental components. In both cases the opposition took up not only the issues of forest loss and damage to ecological integrity, but also Scheduled Tribe life and livelihood. In the latter case there is often a complex process of re-negotiation before projects are allowed to begin, involving agreements on providing modern medicine and education, alongside collective access and individual farming rights in the forest, to those likely to be dispossessed.[76]

The legal enactment securing rights for Scheduled tribals and related others is thus a critical landmark in the realization of democratic citizenship. It marks a step away from the erosion of such rights from the forest acts onwards; it is the equivalent of the Bengal Tenancy Act of 1859, which first put curbs on rent receivers *vis-à-vis* tenants. One of the most significant dimensions of India's larger agro-ecological history has been that the process of the downward movement of rights-of-the-tiller on cultivable land, from as long back as the 1880s, has been paralleled by the reverse current on forest land, first for imperial development and after the 1940s to secure resources for industrial growth. The Forest Rights Act (FRA) not only provides for recognition of rights of tillage under specific conditions, but also accords space for pastoralists, and in clauses—observed so far more in their breach—for collective rights to forest protection. It is part of a larger process of the political assertion of Scheduled Tribes across many states, and marks a widening of the cast of actors in the larger frame of landscape change. Such shifts have also come about against the backdrop of more intense controversy over the expansion of mining for

[76] On the Narmada, see Fisher, *Toward Sustainable Development*, and also Sangvai, *The River and Life*. On the controversy, see the essays in Mehta and Mehta, *Gujarat beyond Gandhi*. For a reading that sees the project as vital for inclusive growth, see Wood, *The Politics of Water Resource Development in India*. On Niyamgiri, see Ramanathan, 'Unpublished Report'. On the Odisha contest, see Mishra, 'Goodbye Stormy Year'.

coal in key sal forest areas of East and Central India, much of which are critical wildlife habitat. Whether this will open up more spaces for cohabitation in parts of these tracts, or whether attempts at involving local councils or Gram Sabhas will fail, is yet unclear.

There have been notable shifts. One scholar offers a word of caution: 'From a policy perspective the problem villagers face is not one of legal literacy or access to justice; even if people were keen and able to act on their rights, it is extremely difficult for an ordinary person to know what his/her rights are.'[77] It is worth remembering that the FRA of 2006 preceded and fore-ran the 2013 Act which sought to protect the interests of cultivators *vis-à-vis* cultivable land. The evolution of such rights-based legislation is still at an early stage but may portend a new and more inclusive process of decision-making, with long-term implications for bureaucracy, knowledge, and power. Such legislation indicates the space wherein public debate and agenda are reshaped by local, sub-regional, and regional experience in new ways. Constitutional spaces via peaceful agitation and discussion are expanding the spaces for citizens, and in this case for the property rights of small holders. The long historical record of the intensive control of forests by British India and the princely states, and later independent India, means the process of recognition of rival right holders will be protracted and complex.[78]

Economic development as the means of fulfilling national or regional aspiration may itself be fractured, with competing visions of how to relate to the land, waters, and non-human entities that inhabit the same spaces. Increasingly, such controversies are central within political debate and contest. There is more than one road to development, each with differing ecological outcomes. This is a new and distinctive feature of modern states, especially of the

[77] Sundar, *Legal Grounds*, p. 15. The reference is to the Forest Rights Act (2006). It is significant that in 2012 Parliament enacted a new law to replace the Land Acquisition Act of 1894.

[78] Dasgupta, *Adivasis and the Raj*, esp. the conclusion on p. 200, where she writes of how the Ho people lost control of forests to outside superior interests.

democratic process within them, and therefore revealing and with no counterpart in the ages of kingly or imperial power.[79]

Peace with nature, howsoever defined, has to be concomitant with and underpinned by peace among people. There is ample reason for hope given the corpus of initiatives from peaceful protest to constructive attempts at repair, renewal, and restoration. Such hope springs not only from the grey of theory but also the green shoots of real-life practice. Predictions of doom as well as of nature's untapped bounty abound, the reality is full of twists and turns.[80] Unintended consequences often arise from the clash of wills of different actors with competing visions of the nation, as much as from the unpredictability of the natural world. The environmental imagination, as well as control of and relations with the material world, are contested, dynamic, and as yet unfolding.

This ever-changing dynamic of nature and nation promises fresh insights. The major gap in the literature on India's environmental history is the limited engagement in the interwoven histories of nature and nationalism. This the present book seeks to redress in a small way. Closely related is the question of when, how, and why states and societies can make spaces for ecological renewal and regeneration. These two larger issues—of nature and nation, and making spaces for nature—bring past and future together, but in highly focused historical enquiry and reflection. Environmental histories of nature and nation can hopefully help guide us to 'a land of sunlight and shadow where nature and history merge, and where a once familiar past seems new.'[81]

[79] Jayal, *Citizenship and its Discontents*. One might paraphrase Jayal, who argues that citizenship is an aspiration with no past; but it could be argued that contemporary developments do hold hope for full democratic citizenship and civic community for marginal peoples—far more than ever. The Forest Rights Act began as a Scheduled Tribe Act but was extended to cover other categories of citizens. 'Markers' of citizenship are both contested and negotiable.

[80] See Guha, 'Year of the Locust', pp. 258–66.

[81] Fiege, *The Republic of Nature*, esp. pp. 318–58 on the colour line, quality of life issues, and racial segregation.

References

Agarwal Anil, and Sunita Narain, *Towards Green Villages*, Delhi: Centre for Science and Environment, 1992.

———, *State of India's Environment: The Second Citizens' Report,* Delhi: Centre for Science and Environment, 1984–5.

Agarwal, Anil, Ravi Chopra, and Kalpana Sharma, *State of India's Environment: A Citizens' Report,* Delhi: CSE, 1982.

Agarwal, Bina, *Cold Hearths and Barren Slopes: The Woodfuel Crisis in the Third World,* London: Zed Books, 1986.

Agrawal, Arun, and K. Sivaramakrishnan, eds, *Agrarian Environments: Resources, Representations and Rule,* Durham: Duke University Press, 2000.

Arnold, David, and Ramachandra Guha, ed., *Nature, Culture, Imperialism,* Delhi: Oxford University Press, 1995.

Athreya, V.R., M. Odden, J.D.C. Linnell, J. Krishnaswamy, and K.U. Karanth, 'Big Cats in Our Backyards: Persistence of Large Carnivores in a Human Dominated Landscape in India', *PLoS One*, 8, 2013.

Bandyopadhyaya, Bibhutibhushan, *Aranyak of the Forest,* trans. from the Bengali by Rimli Bhattacharya, Calcutta: Seagull Books, 2002.

Bao, Maohong, 'Environmental Resources and China's Historical Development', in John McNeill, Augusto Padua, and Mahesh Rangarajan, eds, *Environmental History: As if Nature Existed,* Delhi: Oxford University Press, 2010.

Barnett, R., N. Yamaguchi, I. Barnes, and A. Cooper, 'The Origin, Current Diversity and Future of the Modern Lion (*Panthera leo*)', *Proceedings of the Royal Society*, 2006, doi:10.1098/rspb.2006.3555.

Baruah, Sanjib, 'Whose River is it Anyway? Political Economy of Hydropower in Eastern Himalayas', *Economic and Political Weekly*, 47, 2012.

Baviskar, Amita, *In the Belly of the River: Tribal Conflicts over Developments in the Narmada Valley,* Delhi: Oxford University Press, 1995.

Beinart, William, and Lotte Hughes, *Environment and Empire*, Cambridge: Cambridge University Press, 2007.

Bhagwati, J., and Arvind Panagariya, *India's Tryst with Destiny: Debunking Myths that Undermine Progress and Addressing New Challenges,* Delhi: HarperCollins, 2012.

Biggs, David, *Quagmire: Nation-building and Nature in the Mekong Delta,* Seattle: University of Washington Press, 2012.

Blackbourn, David, *The Conquest of Nature: Water, Landscape and the Making of Modern Germany*, London: Pimlico, 2007.

Bose, Shibani, 'From Eminence to Near-extinction: The Saga of the Rhino in India', in Mahesh Rangarajan and K. Sivaramakrishnan, eds, *Shifting Ground*, Delhi: Oxford University Press, 2014.

Brittlebank, Kate, *Tipu Sultan's Search for Legitimacy: Islam and Kingship in a Hindu Domain*, Delhi: Oxford University Press, 1998.

Brockington, Dan, *Fortress Conservation: The Preservation of the Mkomazi Game Reserve*, London: James Currey, 2002.

Buchy, Marlene, *Teak and Arecanut: Colonial State, Forest and People in the Western Ghats (South India), 1800–1914*, Delhi: INTACH, 1996.

Carruthers, Jane, *The Kruger National Park: A Social and Political History*, Pietermaritzburg: University of Natal Press, 1995.

Cederlof, Gunnel, *Founding an Empire in India's North Eastern Frontiers, 1790–1840*, Delhi: Oxford University Press, 2013.

———, and K. Sivaramakrishnan, eds, *Ecological Nationalisms: Nature, Livelihoods, and Identities in South Asia*, Ranikhet: Permanent Black, 2006.

Cederlof, Gunnel, and Mahesh Rangarajan, 'Predicaments of Nature and Power in India', *Conservation and Society*, 6, 3, 2009.

Cronon, William, 'The Trouble with Wilderness, or Getting Back to the Wrong Kind of Nature', in William Cronon, ed., *Uncommon Ground: Rethinking the Human Place in Nature*, New York: W.W. Norton, 1995.

D'Monte, Darryl, *Temples or Tombs? Industry versus Environment: Three Controversies*, Delhi: CSE, 1985.

D'Souza, Rohan, 'Damming the Mahanadi River: The Emergence of Multi-purpose River Valley Development in India', *Indian Economic and Social History Review*, 40, 2003, pp. 81–105.

———, ed., *Environment, Technology and Development: Critical and Subversive Essays*, Hyderabad: Orient BlackSwan, 2012.

Damodaran, Harish, 'Economy, No Muqabla', *The Hindu Business Line*, 21 July 2013.

Dasgupta, Sanjukta, *Adivasis and the Raj: Socio-economic Transition of the Hos, 1820–1932*, Hyderabad: Orient BlackSwan, 2011.

Desai, Anita, *A Village by the Sea*, London: Heinemann, 1982.

Devra, G.S.L., 'Environmental Crisis and Social Dismemberment in North-west India during the Pre-colonial Period', *Occasional Paper, History and Society*, New Series, no. 3, Delhi: Nehru Memorial Museum and Library, 2013.

Dharmadhikari, Shripad, *Mountains of Concrete: Dam Building in the Himalaya,* Berkeley: International Rivers, 2008.

Divyabhanusinh, *The Story of Asia's Lions,* Mumbai: Marg, 2005.

———, 'The Junagadh State and its Lions, 1879–1947', *Conservation and Society,* 4, 2006, 522–40.

———, 'Lions, Cheetahs and Others in the Mughal Landscape', in Mahesh Rangarajan and K. Sivaramakrishnan, eds, *Shifting Ground,* Delhi: Oxford University Press, 2014.

———, and Ranjitsinh, 'Lion and Cheetah in India: The Reality', *Journal of the Bombay Natural History Society,* 110, 2013, 3–21.

Eaton, Richard, *The Rise of Islam and the Bengal Frontier 1204–1760,* Delhi: Oxford University Press, 1995.

Eisenberg, Andrew C., *The Destruction of the Bison: An Environmental History 1750–1920,* Cambridge: Cambridge University Press, 2000.

Elvin, Mark, *The Retreat of Elephants: An Environmental History of China,* London: Allen Lane, 2005.

Fiege, Mark, *The Republic of Nature: An Environmental History of the United States,* Seattle: University of Washington Press, 2012.

Fisher, William F., ed., *Toward Sustainable Development: Struggling over India's Narmada River,* London: M.E. Sharpe, 1995.

Gadgil, Madhav and Ramachandra Guha, *This Fissured Land: An Ecological History of India,* Delhi: Oxford University Press, 1992.

———, *Ecology and Equity,* Delhi: Penguin, 1995.

Gandhi, Sonia, ed., *Freedom's Daughter: Letters between Indira Gandhi and Jawaharlal Nehru 1922–39,* London: Hodder and Stoughton, 1989.

———, *Two Alone, Two Together: Letters between Indira Gandhi and Jawaharlal Nehru 1940–1964,* London, Hodder and Stoughton, 1992.

Garcia, Claude, and J.-P. Pascal, 'Sacred Forests of Kodagu: Ecological Value and Social Role', in Gunnel Cederlof and K. Sivaramakrishnan, eds, *Ecological Nationalisms: Nature, Livelihoods, and Identities in South Asia,* Ranikhet: Permanent Black, 2005.

Ghosal, S., V. Athreya, J.C.D. Linnell, P.O. Vedeld, 'An Ontological Crisis? A Review of Large Field Conservation in India', *Biodiversity and Conservation,* 22, 2013, 2665–81.

Ghosh, Amitav, *The Hungry Tide,* Delhi: HarperCollins, 2004, rpnt. 2012.

Grove, Richard, *Green Imperialism: Colonial Expansion, Tropical Island Edens and the Origins of Environmentalism, 1600–1860,* Delhi: Oxford University Press, 1995.

———, Vinita Damodaran, and Satpal Sangwan, eds, *Nature and the Orient: The Environmental History of South and Southeast Asia,* Delhi: Oxford University Press, 1998.

Guha, Ramachandra, 'Forestry in British and post-British India: A Historical Analysis', *Economic and Political Weekly,* 18, 29 October and 5 November 1983, 1169–81 and 1882–16.

———, *The Unquiet Woods: Ecological Change and Peasant Resistance in the Himalaya,* Delhi: Oxford University Press, 1989; expanded edition Berkeley: University of California Press, 2000; new edition Ranikhet: Permanent Black, 2009.

———, 'Year of the Locust', in McKinsey and Co., ed., *Reimagining India: Unlocking the Potential of Asia's Next Superpower,* Delhi: Simon and Schuster, 2013.

Guha, Sumit, *Environment and Ethnicity in India, 1200–1991,* Cambridge: Cambridge University Press, 1999.

———, *Health and Population in South Asia from Earliest Times to the Present,* Delhi: Permanent Black, 2001.

Hughes, Julie, *Animal Kingdoms: Hunting, the Environment and Power in the Indian Princely States,* Ranikhet: Permanent Black, 2012.

Jalais, Annu, 'Unmasking the Cosmopolitan Tiger', *Nature and Culture,* 3, 2008, 25–40.

———, *The Forest of Tigers: People, Politics and Environment in the Sundarbans,* Delhi: Orient BlackSwan, 2009.

Jayal, Niraja Gopal, *Citizenship and its Discontents: An Indian History,* Ranikhet: Permanent Black, 2013.

Johnsingh, A.J.T., and Nima Manjrekar, *Mammals of South Asia, Vol. 1,* Hyderabad: Orient BlackSwan, 2013.

Kothari, Ashish, and Aseem Shrivastava, *Churning Global India,* Delhi: Penguin, 2012.

Kothari, Rita, *Memories and Movements: Borders and Communities in Banni, Kutch, Gujarat,* Hyderabad: Orient BlackSwan, 2013.

Kumar, Deepak, Vinita Damodaran, and Rohan D'Souza, eds, *Imperial Encounters: The British Empire and the Natural World,* Delhi: Oxford University Press, 2011.

Kumar, Mayank, *Monsoon Ecologies,* Delhi: Manohar, 2013.

Lahiri-Dutt, Kuntala, and Gopa Samanta, *Dancing with the River: People and Life on the Chars of South Asia,* New Haven: Yale University Press, 2013.

Lal, Sanjay, *The Hindu Equilibrium, Vol. 1,* Delhi: Oxford University Press, 1988.

Ludden, David, *Agrarian History of South Asia*, Cambridge: Cambridge University Press.

Mahasweta Devi, *Chhoti Munda and His Arrow* (Bengali original, 1980), trans. Gayatri Chakravorty Spivak, Kolkata: Seagull Books, 2002.

Mahasweta Devi, *Dust on the Road: The Activist Writings of Mahasweta Devi*, Kolkata: Seagull Books, 1980.

Mahbubani, Kishore, *The New Asian Hemisphere: The Irresistible Shift of Global Power to the East,* New York: Public Affairs, 2008.

Mathai, Wangari, *The Challenge for Africa,* New York: Arrow Books, 2010.

McNeill, John, Jose Augusto Padua, and Mahesh Rangarajan, eds, *Environmental History: As if Nature Existed*, New Delhi, Oxford University Press, 2010.

Meacham, Cory, *How the Tiger Lost its Stripes: An Exploration into the Endangerment of a Species*, New York: Harcourt, 1997.

Mehta, Nalin, and Mona Mehta, ed., *Gujarat beyond Gandhi: Identity, Conflict and Society*, New Delhi: HarperCollins, 2012.

Mishra, Asutosh, 'Goodbye Stormy Year: State Would Hope for Less Controversies in 2011', *The Telegraph*, 1 January 2011.

Morrison, Kathleen, 'Dharmic Projects, Imperial Reservoirs and New Temples of India: An Historical Perspective on Dams in India', *Conservation and Society*, 8, 2010, 182–95.

———, 'The Human Face of the Land: Why it Matters for India's Environmental Future', *History and Society Occasional Paper,* New Series, no. 27, Delhi: Nehru Memorial Museum and Library, 2013.

Mukherjee, Radhakamal, *River Systems of Bengal*, n.p., 1937.

Nabhan, Gary Paul, *Songbirds, Truffles and Wolves: An American Naturalist in Italy*, London: Penguin, 1993.

Nath, Pratyay, 'From Mocking to Becoming the Lords of the Elephants: War-elephants and the Mughals, 1526–*c.*1590', unpublished paper, workshop on 'Environments and Histories', New Delhi: Nehru Memorial Museum and Library, 5 May 2012.

Nehru, Jawaharlal, *An Autobiography*, London: The Bodley Head, 1936.

———, 'No. 67: Letter to Chief Ministers, Independence Day, 15 August 1957', in S. Gopal, ed., *Letters to Chief Ministers, Volume 4, 1954–1957*, Delhi: Oxford University Press, 1988.

Parthasarathi, Prasanan, *Why Europe Grew Rich and Asia Did Not: Global Economic Divergence, 1600–1850,* Cambridge: Cambridge University Press, 2012.

Pastoreau, Michel, *Bear: History of a Fallen King*, Cambridge: Harvard University Press, 2011.

Platt, Edward, 'Birding in Palestine', *The New Nature Writing, Granta 102,* Summer 2008.

Pomeranz, Ken, *The Great Divergence: China, Europe and the Making of the Modern World Economy,* London: Allen Lane, 2000.

Pyne, Stephen, *How the Canyon became Grand: A Short History,* New York: Viking, 1998; Penguin, 1999.

Ramanathan, Usha, Unpublished Report on Niyamgiri to the Forest Advisory Committee, Ministry of Environment and Forests, Government of India, New Delhi, May 2010.

Rangarajan, Mahesh, *Fencing the Forest: Conservation and Ecological Change in India's Central Province 1860–1914,* Delhi: Oxford University Press, 1996.

———, 'Environmental Histories of South Asia: A Review Essay', *Environment and History*, 1, 1996, 129–44.

———, 'The Politics of Ecology: The Debate on People and Wildlife in India 1970–1995', *Economic and Political Weekly*, 31, 1996, 2391–410.

———, 'Wildlife in India: Two Essays', *Occasional Papers*, No. 52, Delhi: Nehru Memorial Museum and Library, 1996.

———, 'The Role of Administration in Extermination: Fresh Evidence on the Cheetah in India', *Journal of the Bombay Natural History Society*, 95, 1998, 328–32.

———, 'The Raj and the Natural World: The Campaign against "Dangerous Beasts" in Colonial India', *Studies in History*, 14, 1998, 266–99.

———, 'Troubled Legacy: A Brief History of Wildlife Preservation in India', *Occasional Papers in History and Society*, No. 34, New Delhi: Nehru Memorial Museum and Library, 1998.

———, *India's Wildlife History: An Introduction*, Delhi: Permanent Black, 2001.

———, 'Five Nature Writers: Jim Corbett, Kenneth Anderson, Sálim Ali, Kailash Sankhala, and M. Krishnan', in Arvind Krishna Mehrotra, ed., *An Illustrated History of Indian Literature in English*, Delhi: Permanent Black, 2001.

———, 'From Princely Symbol to Conservation Icon: A Political History of the Lion in India', in Mushirul Hasan and Nariaki Nakazato, eds, *The Unfinished Agenda: Nation-building in South Asia*, New Delhi: Manohar, 2001.

———, 'Polity, Ecology and Landscape: Fresh Writing on South Asia's Past', *Studies in History*, 17, 1, 2002, 135–48.

———, 'Striving for a Balance: Nature, Power, Science and India's Indira Gandhi, 1917–84', *Conservation and Society*, 79, 4, 2009, 299–312.

———, 'Nature and Nationalism: Rethinking India's Nehru', in William McNeill, Jose Padua, and Mahesh Rangarajan, eds, *Environmental History: As if Nature Existed*, Delhi: Oxford University Press, 2010, 211–29.

———, 'Nations, Nature and Environmental History', in *The Future of Environmental History: Needs and Opportunities*, ed. Kimberly Coulter and Christof Mauch, *RCC Perspectives*, no. 3 (2011).

———, 'Colonialism, Ecology and Environment', in Douglas Peers and Nandini Gooptu, eds, *Oxford History of the British Empire, Companion Volume V*, Oxford: Oxford University Press, 2012, pp. 212–30.

———, 'Environment and Ecology under British Rule', in Douglas M. Peers and Nandini Gooptu, eds, Oxford: Oxford University Press, 2012, pp. 212–30.

———, 'Animals with Rich Histories: The Case of the Lions of Gir Forest, Gujarat, India', *History and Theory*, 52, December 2013, 109–27.

———, and Ghazala Shahabuddin, 'Relocation from Protected Areas: Towards a Historical and Biological Synthesis', *Conservation and Society*, 4 (2006), 359–78.

———, eds, *Making Conservation Work: Securing Biodiversity in this New Century*, Ranikhet: Permanent Black 2007.

Rangarajan, Mahesh, and K. Sivaramakrishnan, ed., *Shifting Ground: People, Animals, Mobility in India's Environmental History*, Delhi: Oxford University Press, 2014.

———, eds, *India's Environmental History, Vol. 1: From Earliest Times to the Colonial Era*, Ranikhet: Permanent Black, 2012.

———, eds, *India's Environmental History, Vol. 2: Colonialism, Modernity, and the Nation*, Ranikhet: Permanent Black 2012.

———, M.D. Madhusudan, and G. Shahabuddin, eds, *Nature without Borders*, Hyderabad: Orient Longman, 2014.

Robin, Libby, *Defending the Little Desert: The Rise of Ecological Consciousness in Australia*, Melbourne: Melbourne University Press, 1998.

Roy, Anuradha, *The Folded Earth*, Gurgaon: Hachette, 2011.

Roy, Arundhati, *Listening to Grasshoppers: Field Notes on Democracy*, London: Hamish Hamilton, 2009.

Saberwal, Vasant, *Pastoral Politics: Shepherds, Bureaucrats, and Conservation in the Western Himalayas*, Delhi: Oxford University Press, 1998.

———, and Mahesh Rangarajan, *Battles over Nature: Science and the Politics of Conservation*, Ranikhet: Permanent Black, 2003.

Saikia, Arupjyoti, 'Dynamics of Social and Political History: Kaziranga National Park', *Conservation and Society*, 7, 2009, 117–29.

Sangari, Kumkum, and Sudesh Vaid, eds, *Recasting Women: Essays in Indian Colonial History*, Delhi: Kali for Women and New Brunswick: Rutgers University Press, 1990.

Sangvai, Sanjay, *The River and Life*, Mumbai: The Other India Press, 2000.

Savyasaachi, 'The Tiger and the Honeybee' (1994), in Mahesh Rangarajan, ed., *Environmental Issues in India: A Reader*, Delhi: Pearson, 2007.

Schama, Simon *Landscape and Memory*, London: Allen Lane, 1995.

Schapiro, Judith, *Mao's War against Nature: Politics and the Environment in Revolutionary China*, Berkeley: University of California Press, 2004.

Segev, Tom, *1967: Israel, the War, and the Year that Transformed the Middle East*, London: Abacus Books, 2007.

Shahabuddin, Ghazala, *Conservation at the Crossroads*, Delhi: Permanent Black, 2010.

Shiva, Vandana, *Staying Alive: Women Ecology and Development*, Delhi: Kali for Women and London: Zed Books, 1989.

Singh, Gurdip, R.D. Joshi, S.K. Chopra, and A.B. Singh, 'Late Quaternary History of Climate and Vegetation in the Rajasthan Desert, India', *Philosophical Transactions of the Royal Society of London*, Series B 286, 1974, 467–501.

Singh, Shekhar, Pratibha Pande, Ashish Kothari, and Dilnavaz Variava, *The Management of National Parks and Wildlife Sanctuaries in India*, New Delhi: Indian Institute of Public Administration, 1989.

Sivaramakrishnan, K., *Modern Forests: State-making and Environmental Change in Colonial Eastern India*, Delhi: Oxford University Press, 1999.

Subramanian, Arvind, *India's Turn: Understanding the Economic Transformation*, Delhi: Oxford University Press, 2009.

Subramanian, Kaa, *Saya Vanam* (1998), trans. Vasantha Surya as *The Defiant Jungle*, Chennai: New Horizon Books, 2010.

Subramanian, Samarth, *Following Fish: Travels around the Indian Coast*, Delhi: Penguin, 2010.

Sukumar, Raman, *Asian Elephant: Ecology and Management*, Cambridge: Cambridge University Press, 1989.

———, *The Living Elephants: Evolutionary Ecology, Behaviour and Conservation,* New York: Oxford University Press, 2003.
Sundar, Nandini, *Subalterns and Sovereigns: An Anthropological History of Bastar 1854–2006,* Delhi: Oxford University Press, 1997.
———, ed., *Legal Grounds: Natural Resources, Identity and the Law in Jharkhand,* Delhi: Oxford University Press, 2009.
Swaminathan, Komal, *Water! A Tamil Play,* trans. S. Shankar, Kolkata: Seagull Books, 2005.
Tal, Alon, *Pollution in a Promised Land: An Environmental History of Israel,* Barcelona: Altamira Books, 2005.
Taubman, William, *Nikita Khrushchev: The Man and His Era,* New York: W.W. Norton, 2004.
Thackston, Wheeler, ed. and trans., *The Babarnama: Memoirs of Babur, Prince and Emperor,* New York: The Modern Library, 1992.
Thapar, Valmik, *The Last Tiger,* Delhi: Oxford University Press, 2008.
——, *Ranthambhore: Ten Days in the Tiger Fortress,* Delhi: Oxford University Press, 2010.
Thapar, Valmik, Romila Thapar, and Yusuf Ansari, *Exotic Aliens: The Lion and Cheetah in India,* Delhi: Aleph, 2013.
———, 'Response to the Review of Exotic Aiens', *Journal of the Bombay Natural History Society,* no. 110 (2013), pp. 95–104.
Thomas, K.V., *Man and the Natural World: Changing Attitudes in England, 1500–1800,* Harmondsworth: Penguin, 1983.
Vasavi, A.R., *Harbingers of Rain,* Delhi: Oxford University Press, 1996.
Walker, John F., *A Certain Curve of Horn: The Hundred Year Quest for the Giant Sable Antelope of Angola,* New York: Atlantic Monthly Press, 2002.
Watts, Jonathan, *When a Billion Chinese Jump: How China will save Mankind—or Destroy It,* New York: Scribner, 2010.
Weber, Bill, and Amy Veder, *In the Kindgom of the Gorilla: Fragile Species in a Dangerous Land,* New York: Simon and Schuster, 2001.
Weisman, Alan, *The World without Us,* New York: St Martin's Press, 2007.
Wood, John R., *The Politics of Water Resource Development in India: The Narmada Controversy,* Delhi: Sage, 1997.

2

The Raj and the Natural World

The War Against 'Dangerous Beasts' in Colonial India

South Asia has been a major arena of conflict between people and predators, but unlike England and North America its history has hardly been told.[1] The focus has mainly been on the changing attitudes and practices of the imperial rulers.[2] This is inevitable given the extent of the literature available on shikar, or hunting for sport. Useful as this may be in understanding the culture of empire, it is only a small part of the picture. The decline of wildlife raises broader questions about the nature and impact of colonial rule.

Hunting for sport was integral not only to the lifestyle of officials but also to their self-image as men who believed in fair play. The Raj was seen as powerful enough to contain danger.[3] Yet,

This paper was written as part of a larger research project I worked on at the Nehru Memorial Museum and Library, New Delhi. I am grateful to the editors of *Studies in History* for publishing a longer version of this paper (1998). Dr John Knight, Peter Boomgaard, Professor R. Kumar, Ravi Chellan, Professor M. Gadgil, and R. Guha helped enormously with their suggestions. The usual disclaimers apply.

[1] Worster, *Nature's Economy*; Thomas, *Man and the Natural World*.

[2] MacKenzie, *The Empire of Nature*; but see Rangarajan, *Fencing the Forest*, esp. pp. 138–98.

[3] See MacKenzie, ibid.

the self-regulatory character of colonial power is blamed for the increase of population and the breakdown of norms after 1947 for general ecological decline.[4] This is in a sense a double bind, for British officials in the past often assumed that they alone were brave enough to face large and hostile beasts. Fair play meant that strength was tempered by mercy. Such attitudes are not confined to the past.[5] This view of imperial stewardship needs to be tested against the evidence. The question can be posed at another level. The disappearance of free-ranging wildlife could have simply been a byproduct of the expansion of agriculture. Greater mobility and better weapons for the hunter may have been incidental to the decline of the Bengal tiger (*Panthera tigris tigris*). In that case, the fate of wildlife becomes simply part of a larger drama, and specific drives against particular species are incidental to the general impoverishment of a region's ecology. The killing of tigers or leopards (*Panthera pardus*) for bounties depended on Indian co-operation but the their reasons for doing so—or not doing so—have hardly been looked at. The schemes to wipe out 'dangerous beasts' offer insights into the interaction of government and rural land-users.

Indian Legacies

It is essential to get a perspective on the relationship between large mammals and people in the pre-colonial era. This may elide over and tend to flatten out the significant shifts over time, such as changes in technologies of warfare and production. But there is sufficient reason to assert that the dynamics of people–nature relations in the pre-colonial period were very different from what was to follow the consolidation of British power, especially after 1857. The agrarian frontier had long been the site of intense conflict, with people working out various ways to minimize contact with or even

[4] Vernede, *British Life in India*, emphasis added; Elliot, *Field Sports in India*, p. 4.

[5] Davidar, 'Wildlife Conservation in Tamil Nadu', pp. 65–6.

to retaliate against carnivores. Further, the tiger and the Asiatic lion (*Panthera leo persica*) were more than just the embodiment of ferocity, they also had religious and even magical attributes.

The relationship with large predators was multifaceted. Animals like the lion and tiger were often metaphors for power even as they were a source of danger.[6] The importance of the lion in the Ashokan pillar (third century BCE) is well known. The Valmiki *Ramayana*, possibly dating to the fourth–sixth centuries CE, refers to Dasratha as a 'lion among kings' but also describes Rama and Lakshmana as 'tigers among men'.[7] Even at a much later date, the killing of large mammals was a sign of the prowess of a warrior. Farid's slaying of a tiger earned him the name Sher Khan (1540–5) and the fact that it was killed with a spear on foot was a mark of bravery.[8] Akbar (1556–1605) was on a pilgrimage to the Chishti shrine at Ajmer in July 1572 when he hunted down a man-eating tiger.[9] The religious dimensions of perceptions of the natural world were often significant. Mughal chroniclers cited how Akbar stared at a tiger which 'cowered down from that divine glance'.[10] A European account in 1670 about the mangrove swamps of eastern Bengal, an area notorious for man-eaters, refers to a place where 'every Thursday night a tiger comes out and salaams a fakeer's tomb there.'[11] Islam had clearly co-opted and assimilated older traditions of tiger worship into a new framework.

The religious dimension should not detract from more prosaic

[6] The wolf is less prominent in lore than either the lion or the tiger. See Gandhi, *The Penguin Dictionary of Hindu Names*, pp. 389–90, 504–5, and 506–7.

[7] Pollock, ed., *The Ramayana of Valmiki, Vol. 1: The Balakanda*, p. 18; *Vol. II: The Aranyakanda*, p. 184; The lion motif was not an Islamic import, as suggested in Bayly, *An Illustrated History of Modern India*, p. 156.

[8] Sherwani, *Tarikh-i-Sher Shahi*, p. 316.

[9] al Fazl, *The Akbar Namah*, vol. II, p. 539. Subsequent research indicates such Persian references are to lions. See Chapter 3 below.

[10] al Fazl, *Ain i Akbari*, vol. II, p. 294.

[11] Eaton, *The Rise of Islam*, p. 209; for a later period, see Bhattacharya, 'The Tiger Cult', pp. 44–56.

ways of dealing with threats. Buchanan found villages in Kanara that had been 'formerly much infested with tigers' now devoid of them due to forest clearance.[12] Animal attacks could also limit the use of forests. The collection of lac and sandalwood had been given up in some woodlands in Kanara due to loss of lives to tigers. Cattle were carefully penned in at night to protect them from big cats.[13] Soldiering and hunting went hand in hand. The Bedas recruited into the army by Tipu Sultan of Mysore (d. 1799) were skilled marksmen who also pursued tigers.[14] Nor did Indians necessarily lack a notion of agrarian 'improvement'. Bishop Reginald Heber met a zamindar who exulted that tigers had given way to 'better things like corn fields, villages and people'. Nature retreated before the advance of the plough.[15]

There was no innate contradiction between such notions and a religious awe of wild animals. The Raja of Maihar near Panna, Central India told William Sleeman that there were two kinds of tigers: ordinary ones that turned man-eaters could be tracked and shot, but the ones along the Jabalpur–Mirzapur road were 'tail-less tigers' with magical properties. The only recourse was to pay a Gond tribal 10 to 20 rupees to conduct a sacrifice and placate the beasts.[16]

The long exposure to carnivores made it inevitable that various cultures and rulers in the subcontinent would perceive the animals in a multitude of ways. There were mutually contradictory strands, with the same animal being simultaneously revered and feared, hunted and worshipped. It would be anachronistic to see the past in terms of the easy coexistence of people and predators, but the dynamics of that interaction were about to undergo a very significant shift.

[12] Habib and Raychaudhuri, ed., *The Cambridge Economic History of India*, vol. I, p. 48.

[13] Buchanan, *A Journey from Madras*, vol. III, p. 75; ibid., vol. I, p. 383.

[14] Ibid., vol. I, pp. 178–9.

[15] Heber, *Narrative of a Journey*, vol. II, pp. 14, 148.

[16] Sleeman, *Rambles and Recollections*, pp. 126–7.

European History

In contrast with South Asia, the British had a very different history of relations with large wild mammals. In common with much of Europe, there had been concerted campaigns against specific animals.[17] In the 1620s, tenants in parts of Scotland were still paying an annual tribute in iron to their lairds to forge weapons against wolves.[18] The extermination of the species in the British Isles preceded its elimination in large parts of continental Europe.[19] The animal vanished in areas of intensive human settlement on the North Sea shores of the continent.

But the other dimensions of extermination were significant. As game became an object of leisure, landed groups sought not only to exclude the lower classes, they also trained their guns—literally as well as metaphorically—on wild animals that lived on birds and fish. Otters and wild cats were explicitly excluded from protection under the Game Act of 1671. They were vermin to be killed.[20] In the eighteenth century the king had an official rat-catcher, whose embroidered uniform showed figures of mice devouring wheat sheaves.[21] Some carnivores were seen as lawless beasts. The tiger was seen as especially ferocious even among other flesh-eaters due to its fondness for people as prey.[22] The broadly negative attitude to carnivores was to acquire a new significance in the subcontinental context.

South Asia must have seemed like a menagerie of fierce free-ranging wild animals.[23] The death of a young army officer, Munro, eaten by a tiger on Saugor island, was assimilated into British folk-lore: Staffordshire potteries even had a chimney ornament showing

[17] Braudel, *Civilization and Capitalism*, vol. I, p. 67.
[18] Smout, *A History of the Scottish People*, p. 131.
[19] Zimen, *The Wolf*, p. 296.
[20] Ritvo, *The Animal Estate*, p. 13.
[21] Thomas, *Man and the Natural World*, p. 274.
[22] Ritvo, *Animal Estate*, p. 28.
[23] N. Courtenay, *Tiger, Symbol of Courage*, p. 47.

a tiger with the head of the hapless officer.[24] As British power expanded into the subcontinent, the tiger loomed even larger in the consciousness of the conquerors. When Tipu Sultan was eventually defeated in 1799, the victory was commemorated with a special medallion which showed the imperial lion of Britannia overpowering a tiger.[25]

The predator known within Europe but with an extensive range in the subcontinent was the wolf. In Kanpur cantonment wolves were such a menace that they 'frequently' carried off children and attacked sentries.[26] Buchanan found them common in Shahabad, but they were elusive.[27] Such deep fears were not limited to large beasts of prey. The civet cat, for instance, is a small mustelid the size of a domestic cat and often reared in captivity—for its musk and to control mice. But to Williamson it was an insensate marauder, 'killing as it were, merely for sport.'[28]

In the Company Raj, different remedies were tried out in areas where the depredations of carnivores were seen as a threat to human life or as a barrier to cultivation.[29] Wild creatures that harmed humans violated what the conquerors held to be the order of God's creation. Their affinity to human rebels was all too obvious. There were two options. One was to pay bounties for the heads of animals. In Madras these were paid out for a variety of beasts from 1815 by the Board of Revenue. There was a larger bounty for the female of a species.[30] In Indore the bounty on a tiger's head

[24] Ibid., p. 52.

[25] Bayly, *Illustrated History*, pp. 156, 159.

[26] Forbes, *Oriental Memoirs*, vol. IV, p. 81.

[27] Buchanan, *An Account of the District of Shahabad*, p. 229.

[28] Williamson, *Oriental Field Sports*, vol. II, p. 109.

[29] Heber, *Narrative of a Journey*, vol. II, p. 15.

[30] National Archives of India, New Delhi, India (hereafter NAI), Home (Public) (hereafter H (P)), December 1890, A, nos. 360–407, 'Results of the measures adopted for exterminating wild animals and poisonous snakes in British India during the year 1889', no. 363, pp. 37–9; J. Grose, Board of Revenue, Madras to Sec., Home Dep., GOI, 8 May 1890 (hereafter Vermin 1890).

was the equivalent of four months' pay of a court officer.[31] The other option was to use military force to curb errant animals. Such instances were less common and the offer of rewards and incentives was the main instrument of policy.[32] Such efforts were mainly at a local or provincial level. It was only after 1857–8 that such schemes became more systematic.

The War against Vermin

Provincial-level schemes were sought to be extended after a debate on the ravages of wild beasts. The wider context of the debate was the disarming of Indians after the Rebellion of 1857–8. There were fears that the denial of modern firearms to people in rural areas was indirectly contributing to 'serious depredations' of cattle and crops. In the Madras Presidency there were frequent complaints of increased damage by tigers, wolves, and other animals.[33] In Bombay the authorities went a step further and even distributed arms in certain localities.[34] But such efforts were sporadic at best. An image of Indians as people incapable of self-defence meshed well with the kind of distrust that became the norm in the aftermath of 1857.

The discussion itself was in response to a bizarre proposal from a former army officer, B. Rogers, who wanted the entire campaign against carnivores placed on a war footing. In each district the local shikaris ('native hunters') were to be organized into a corps under the command of a civil or preferably military officer. The sole task was to eliminate large carnivores. He first won some support but eventually it came to naught.[35] Most officials agreed that

[31] NAI, Foreign (Political), 19 September 1845, no. 72: 'Reward for killing tigers in Indore', Sec., Govt NWP to Assistant to Gov., Nimar, 29 July 1845; Sec. Govt, Bombay to Foreign Dep., 19 September 1845.

[32] Campbell, *Gazetteer of the Bombay Presidency*, p. 30.

[33] NAI, H (P), 16 May 1864, B nos. 86–7: 'Orders regarding arms to be retained by villages suffering from the ravages of wild beasts', C. Wood, India Office, to Gov. Gen. (GG), 26 March 1864.

[34] Ibid., Home Office, GOI to NWPs and Presidency Govts, 16 May 1864.

[35] NAI, H (P), July 1875, nos. 151–2: 'Proposal of Major B. Rogers

something ought to be done, but they disagreed on the line of action. Dr Joseph Fayrer explicitly saw the Thugee Department of Colonel William Sleeman as the model. The affinity of human and beast outlaws was stretched to a point when even the remedies proposed against the latter began to mirror those used against the former.[36]

Parallels were also drawn between vermin control in the home country and the tasks at hand in India. Major Tweedie wanted to employ tiger-killers 'just like' the mole-catchers and rabbit-killers in England.[37] But senior officials frowned upon ambitious programmes that could involve more government spending. Alfred Lyall opposed the creation of an 'asphyxiating department'.[38] Rogers' proposal was aimed at his 'own nourishment', not the destruction of beasts.[39] In Madras a police officer, Col. Caulfield, was paid an extra stipend to kill tigers in the Coimbatore district.[40] He killed seven tigers using traps made by Toda tribals and was then dispatched to the Vizag region in the Eastern Ghats, an area known for tigers.[41] But it all cost too much.[42] The experiment was not a success. In contrast, the use of poisons to kill carnivores in

regarding the organization of a system of spring guns for the destruction of wild animals in India', August 1869; also H (P), September 1871, A no. p. 6: Captain Rogers, August 1869.

[36] Fayrer, *Destruction of Life*.

[37] NAI, H (P), January 1875, A nos. 286–311, no. 297, no pagination, 'Destruction of noxious beasts in India', Major Tweedie, First Assistant Resident, Berar to Sec., GOI, Home, 5 June 1874 (hereafter Vermin 1875).

[38] NAI, H (P), June 1876, A 127, 'Use of aconite for destroying tigers', A.C. Lyall, Note, 26 October 1876.

[39] NAI, H (P), October 1873, nos 287–9, pp. 2457–8, 'Measures taken for the destruction of wild animals', A.C. Lyall, Home Dep. Resolution, 25 August 1873.

[40] NAI, H (P), Vermin 1875, no. 307, R.A. Dalyell, Offg Chief Sec., Madras, 4 August 1873.

[41] Ibid., Lt. Col. W.S. Drewer, Acting Inspector General of Police to Chief Sec., Madras Govt, 17 November 1873.

[42] NAI, Vermin 1890, no. 365, p. 46; C.A. Galton, Sec. Board of Rev., 12 June 1890.

Coimbatore won encomiums from officials.[43] The poisoning of carcasses was in any case fraught with dangers and was 'perilous' even in England.[44]

The criticisms of a special force led to a focus on the comparative advantages of drawing on local hunters who would function more autonomously. Mobile corps of hunters would move from one tract to another. The village shikari was the best bet against 'both evils'—crop-raiding deer and man-eating tigers—on a beat with which they were familiar. In general, the existing system of bounties was seen as effective.[45] The idea of the temporary deployment of 'men from outside' remained an option. However, it was not imposed on the various provinces.[46] In Dinajpur in north Bengal zamindars shared the cost of hiring specialist tiger-killers from outside the district. This significantly increased the numbers of tigers slain in the dry season.[47] In the North West Provinces and Awadh, district officers employed Kanjers to kill snakes, paying a regular salary as well as 2 annas a snake in excess of twenty specimens. It cost much less than a special corps and allowed flexibility at the local level.[48]

Others contended that the expansion of agriculture would automatically resolve the issue by destroying the habitat of wild beasts. All the same, the protection of new settlements often entailed vigorous measures to exterminate wildlife. In the plains region of the Bombay Presidency, 'dangerous animals' had became rare in

[43] Vermin 1875, no. 307, W.S. Whiteside, Magistrate, North Arcot, of D.F. Carmichael, Sec., Bd. of Rev., 17 July 1874.

[44] Ibid., note by A.C. Lyall, pp. 1–2, 26 October 1874.

[45] NAI, H (P), December 1882, A nos 32–70, 'Results of the measures adopted for exterminating dangerous beasts and poisonous snakes in British India in 1881', no. 38, p. 13: C.A. Galton, Board of Rev., 4 March 1882, Extract from Procs, Board of Rev. (hereafter Vermin 1882).

[46] NAI, H (P), December 1882, A nos 32–70, no. 68, p. 82: GG to A. MacKenzie, 8 November 1882.

[47] Ibid., no. 38, p. 4, Note, JM, 19 October 1882.

[48] Ibid., no. 54, p. 47, Resn., NWP and Oudh, 2 June 1882.

areas where they had been common a few decades earlier.[49] Officials in Assam and Berar were confident that clearing the jungle would ensure that animals would 'gradually but surely disappear'.

The Princely States

Much of India not directly administered by the British was under princely rule. There were also several regions, such as Bengal, Bihar, and Orissa, where the Permanent Settlement made the zamindar the key player in the countryside. Hunting was a way of life for the landed gentry and princes, but their reactions to the programme to wipe out vermin were diverse. The responses in princely India offer an insight into contrasting attitudes to the programme.

Most rulers in Rajputana in western India either denied that carnivores were a major problem or claimed that sport-hunting was adequate as a means of control. The ecology and forms of land-use in these areas were often crucial in defusing the intensity of conflict between people and predators. Alwar included excellent tiger habitat in the thorn forests of the Aravallis, but rewards were only given for man-eaters.[50] In Bikaner it was reported that wolves 'do not hunt people'.[51] Large herds of blackbuck (*Antelopa cervicapra*), gazelle (*Gazella gazella*), and livestock probably provided an adequate prey base. Elsewhere, carnivores had been eliminated with the extension of agriculture. Some forests were already largely bereft of game.[52] In three years not a single tiger had been found by sportsmen in Sirohi.[53] Sport-hunting was often

[49] Ibid., no. 292, F.C. Chapman, Chief Sec., Bombay Pres., to Sec., GOI, 2 October 1873, no pagination.

[50] NAI, Vermin 1875, no. 301, Captain T. Cadell, Pol. Agent, Alwar, to Agent to GG, Rajputana, 30 December 1873.

[51] Ibid., Col. C.W. Burton, Asst. Agent, Soojangarh, to Agent, GG, Raj., 26 November 1873.

[52] Ibid., Capn W.A. Roberts, Pol. Agent, Eastern States, to Agent, GG, Raj., 26 November 1873.

[53] Ibid., Lt. Col. W. Carnell, Supt., Sirohi, to Agent, GG, Raj., 27 November 1873.

seen as an adequate defence against predators.[54] Captain Walker, British Agent in Marwar, was confident that the Rajputs were 'more or less true sportsmen' and could keep a check on animals.[55] This was also an expression of confidence in what was then considered a 'martial race'. Alwar's ruler, Sheodan Singh, claimed that he was willing to wipe out tigers from the state if only government would 'have the goodness to cause masonry "odeys" to be built at the shooting places.' Odeys were small fortresses and included a place where the hunter could wait in safety several feet above a buffalo tied up as bait.[56] This was clearly a bid to use the programme to satisfy the raja's hunger for trophies.

It is possible that predators were a threat to livestock in certain areas.[57] Some princes had already initiated or were willing to follow through with a scheme of rewards for killing vermin. Mysore and Hyderabad were prominent in their extensive system of bounties for wild animals and snakes.[58] Religious beliefs may have been crucial in resisting such measures in Marwar, where the raja refused to help in 'any organised attempt' to get rid of venomous reptiles.[59] In Jhallawar the Raj Rana was already giving out rewards for tigers

[54] Ibid., J.C. Berkeley, Pol. Agent, Harrowtee and Tonk, to Agent, GG, 30 December 1873, quoting the Nawab's letter to the former dated 1 November 1873.

[55] Ibid., K.M. Walker, Offg. Pol. Agent Marwar and Jaisalmer, to Agent, GG, Raj., 20 October 1873.

[56] Ibid., no. 301, Capn T. Cadell, Pol. Agent, Alwar, to Agent to GG, Raj., 30 December 1873, quoting a letter from Raja Sheodan Singh to the former, 4 October 1873. Emphasis added.

[57] NAI, Vermin 1877, no. 289, A.C. Lyall, Offg. Chief Comm., Ajmer-Mhairwara, to Sec., Foreign Dep., 2 May 1877.

[58] NAI, Vermin 1875, no. 303, Captain G.H. Trevor, Offg. Ist Asst. Resident, Hyd., to Sec., Foreign Dep., 10 March 1874; H (P), December 1877, A nos. 269–92, no. 284, p. 1829, Mjr T.G. Clarke, Sec., Chief Comm., Mysore, to Sec., Home Dep., GOI, 16 November 1877 (hereafter Vermin 1877).

[59] NAI, Vermin 1877, no. 301, L. Pelly, Pol. Agent, GG, Raj., to C.I. Aitchison, Sec., Foreign Dep., 21 February 1874.

and Bundi was ready to follow suit.[60] Kotah had a comprehensive system of bounties, with 10 rupees for a tiger and 5 for bears, wolves, and leopards. The state was unusual as perhaps the only princely house that still rewarded the killing of lions—which were already very rare. The bounty was as high as 25 rupees.[61] What is important is that such instances were still exceptional until the 1870s when the schemes were promoted by the British.

The Tiger: Ally or Enemy?

While there was broad accord on the need to control carnivores, even at its zenith the project did not have universal support. G.P. Sanderson was emphatic in his condemnation of the policy of eliminating large predators. Tigers lifted cattle but the advocates of 'a war of extermination' ignored a simple fact. The tiger was entitled to 'present his little account for services rendered in keeping down wild animals which destroy crops.'[62] There was no easy answer to the question raised by such objectors: was the tiger a foe or a friend? The tolerance for the tiger was qualified and was within the logic of agrarian expansion and consolidation. The Commissioner of Rajshahi explained that a tiger that killed game was fine but, 'when he travels outside the forests and seeks his prey in the neighborhood of villages, he becomes destructive.'[63]

Sportsmen became more critical of extermination as a policy with the decline in numbers of trophy-worthy specimens. The zamindar of Punganur in North Arcot was concerned that increased

[60] Ibid., no. 301, Capn J.C. Berkeley, Pol. Agent, Harrowtee and Tonk, to Agent, GG, 30 December 1873, quoting letter of the Raj Rana, Jhallawar, 10 Decmber 1873; Berkeley, letter again, 17 January 1874.

[61] Ibid., Berkeley, 10 April 1874. The scheme was endorsed by the Foreign Dept on 11 May 1874.

[62] Sanderson, *Thirteen Years among the Wild Beasts*, pp. 307, 312.

[63] NAI, H (P), March 1908, A 27–53, no. 29, p. 228, 'Game law for India', Annexure II, Bengal, C.R. Maridin, Comm., Rajshahi Div., to Sec., Bengal, Rev., 9 January 1905 (hereafter Game 1908).

movement of traffic on roads had driven tigers away from their age-old haunts.[64] Similarly, the veteran big-game hunter Captain A.E. Wardrop favoured the abolition of rewards for tigers.[65] As the range and availability of large carnivores declined, there was also a move to classify the tiger as a game animal instead of as vermin. Lord Curzon was concerned that 'foreign sportsmen not resident in India were bagging too many trophies.'[66] He warned against making forest reserves 'into a sort of sanctuary' where animals enjoyed protection. This would be 'indefensible and immoral'. There was no doubt that the war against the tiger was far from over.[67]

Anxieties over the availability of tigers did not prevail over the deeper concern with controlling predators with an extensive range. The idea that they were evil because of 'the fear they spread than the damage they do' was not going to die down quickly.[68] The worth of a species as trophy became crucial in enabling or thwarting the change of status from vermin to game. Advocates of the conservation of carnivores referred to the plight of the Asiatic lion.[69] But it was doubtful that tigers would be seen in the same light.[70] Three decades earlier, when the lion was already vanishing across much of its range in northern and central India, the Foreign Department had approved of rewards in Kotah.[71] The

[64] NAI, Vermin 1875, no. 307, W.S. Whiteside, Magistrate, North Arcot, to D.F. Carmichael, 17 July 1874.

[65] NAI, Game 1908, no. 30, p. 374: Captain A.E. Wardrop, Commanding Officer, European Battery, Royal Horse Artillery, Meerut, 23 July 1904.

[66] NAI, H (P), Aug. 1904, A 266–78, 'Preservation and protection of game and fish', p. 45, Note by Curzon, Keep-with section, no date (hereafter Game 1904).

[67] NAI, Game 1904, no. 266, Notes, Letters from local Govts, Curzon, 1 August 1902.

[68] NAI, Vermin 1890, C.J. Lyall, Note, 19 October 1890, p. 27.

[69] NAI, Game 1908, no. 30, p. 329, G. Bower, Collr, Saharanpur, to Chief Sec., UP, 21 July 1904.

[70] Ibid., no.30, p. 155, Conservator, Central Div., Bombay Pres., to Comm., 27 July 1904.

[71] NAI, H (P), January 1875, nos 286–311, no. 304, no pagination,

debate was shifting from efforts at examination to the applicability of protection. Protection was motivated by an ethic of use.[72] Protection of the cheetah was sought to be justified due to its rarity.[73] The idea that a carnivore could die out forever was now seen, at least by some, as a matter of regret. But they remained a vocal and powerless minority.[74]

Hunting for sport and fishing for leisure pitted forest officers in particular even against smaller carnivores. The forest was sought to be made an ordered landscape that could yield trophies and meat to sportsmen. Civets were dubbed 'active game-destroyers'. Owls and eagles were 'egg-thieves' and 'chick-destroyers'.[75] In the Konkan, sportsmen were worried about the large increase in the numbers of birds of prey.[76] Anglers feared their sport was in danger due to otters (*Lutra lutra*).[77] Three peons were set to work to kill freshwater crocodiles (*Crocodilus parustrius*) and destroy their eggs in the Tulsi and Virar lakes near Bombay. H.M. Phipson of the Bombay Natural History Society blamed the 'loathsome reptiles' for destroying fish and wild fowl.[78] Scientific expertise, aesthetic concerns, and sporting interests broadly concurred on this issue.

The critics of extermination often shared the values of its proponents. They saw carnivores as allies in the drive to transform jungle into farmland. But game destroyers were still marginal to

Capt. J.C. Berkeley, Pol. Agent, Harrowtee and Tonk, to Gov. Gen, 10 April 1874.

72 Wilson, *Letters to Nobody*, p. 137.

73 NAI, Game 1908, no. 30, p. 329, G. Bower, Collr., Saharanpur, to Chief Sec., UP, 21 July 1904.

74 NAI, Game 1911, no. 197, no. 106: Lt Gen. W. Osborn, to Asst. Comm., Kulu, 20 October 1908.

75 Stebbing, 'Review of W.S. Burke', pp. 220–3.

76 Anon., 'The Proposed Introduction', pp.119–23; Hodgson, 'Preservation of Harmless Wild Animals in Malcompeth', pp. 530–3.

77 OC, 'Notes on the Otter', pp. 34–5.

78 Barrow, 'Crocodiles in Artificial Reservoirs', p. 144; Phipson, 'The Crocodiles in Our Reservoirs'.

official efforts. It was animals like the tiger and wolf that were a threat to domestic stock and human life.

Tiger versus People

Tigers were in a very different category from mere game destroyers. It was unlikely that a case for their protection would win enough support to bring about a change of policy in general. Schemes for their elimination continued without modification in most parts of British India. There is little doubt that there were problems in the coexistence of people with the striped cat in many areas. Given the diversity of habitats and land-use systems, the intensity of conflicts varied.

In general, the species vanished from the plains areas: extermination and the extension of agriculture were complementary. But vermin slaughter gave the process an added impetus. For example, the Bombay Presidency witnessed a serious diminution in the range of the big cat. Tigers were still found in the Sahyadaris in the first half of the 1870s. About twenty tigers were killed each year not far from Bombay. By 1900 it was claimed, though inaccurately, that the tiger was confined to the Dangs, the Satpuras, and the Hatti hills. They were still found in Trombay in 1907.[79] Tigers swam across from the mainland.[80] The Amir of Bahawalpur shot thirteen specimens in Sind. It soon became extinct in these galley forests.[81] A similar picture emerges in Punjab, where the species was 'almost extinct', only rarely found even in the hilly parts of Ambala district. H. Maude recalled how in 1866–9 no less than 84 had been killed, of which as many as 50 were in Pindi and 22 in Ambala.[82]

The 20 per cent of the land area of British India that was government forest by 1900 could have helped the tiger. However, the existence of Reserved Forests was in itself no guarantee of

[79] Campbell, *Gazetteer of the Bombay Presidency, vol. XII, Part ii*, pp. 44 –5.

[80] Prater, 'On the Occurrence of Tigers', pp. 973–4.

[81] Roberts, *The Mammals of Pakistan*, pp. 144–5.

[82] NAI, Vermin 1890, no. 379, p. 81, H. Maude, Offg. Jr. Sec., Punjab, to Sec., Home Dept, GOI, 28 April 1890.

survival. Foresters oversaw special efforts to exterminate or at least limit the numbers of carnivores. This had a pincer-like effect: if the prey base and tree cover outside government forests was reduced by agrarian extension, the forests offered limited shelter on account of the killing of vermin. Smaller predators could still survive in patches of dhak (*Butea frondosa*) and scrub forest, but not the tiger.[83] The Forest Department rules allowed access into fire-protected forests for killing carnivora even when such tracts were normally closed.[84] In Nainital Division, tigers could be shot at waterholes and salt licks.[85] Nor were such rules in any way specific or unique to the province.

Elsewhere, predation on human beings was evidently in decline. Among the places where its incidence declined sharply was the Madras Presidency.[86] Even in the mid-1920s Madras topped the country in lives lost to tigers, with two out of every three fatal attacks. But predation was highly localized.[87] In general, there was a decline in the tiger's range in the south. But it is possible that, in the short run, increased human intrusion into forests exposed more people to the possibility of confrontation. In Vizag, for instance, the construction of the East Coast Railway opened up the country and increased the demand for wood for sleepers.[88] Despite the scepticism about rewards, Vizag and Ganjam were the districts with most tigers killed.[89] By 1945 an experienced sportsman could

[83] NAI, Game 1908, 30, WHL Impey to Sec., Home Dept, 2 February 1905.

[84] NAI, Game 1904, no. 269, J.O. Miller, Chief Sec., NWP and Oudh, 28 March 1895, Misc. Forest Dept, 15 March 1895.

[85] NAI, Dep. of Revenue and Agriculture (Forests), December 1909, A nos 1–2, 'Proposed rules to regulate hunting, shooting and fishing for Naini Tal and municipal forests which it has decided to make Protected Forests'.

[86] NAI, Vermin 1890, p. 13, Home Dep. Res., December 1890.

[87] NAI, H (P), 1926, file 126, no. 16, Board of Rev., Madras, 25 March 1926.

[88] NAI, Vermin 1890, no. 363, p. 39, J. Grose, Board of Rev., 8 May 1890.

[89] NAI, H (P), December 1885, A nos. 69–101, no. 69, Board of Rev. Procs., Madras, 19 June 1885.

argue that there were very few instances of man-eaters south of a line drawn across the peninsula at Bombay.[90] The pieces in the story point to a pattern. Increased market integration of forest areas led to a higher level of conflict in the short term, but these were resolved with the extinction of tigers outside very small parts of their former range. In turn, a region once known for man-eaters now became renowned for the absence of attacks on people.[91]

The reverse phenomenon was taking place in the United Provinces where man-eating, relatively rare till the 1920s, increased sharply. But the species as a whole fared better than in the West and the South, possibly due to the nature of the habitat. The combination of sal forests and open grasslands with large ungulate populations resulted in the presence of many big cats. As late as 1904, in the hill areas of Kumaon, where two-thirds of all money on tiger bounties was spent, three people were killed the previous year.[92] But in the 1920s and 1930s the area became synonymous with man-eaters. Corbett himself stressed 'the stress of circumstances' including disability and wounds as being a major factor for the spurt in man-eating. The other factor was possibly that leopards began living on human flesh in the aftermath of epidemics of cholera and influenza, the latter in 1918.[93] The destruction of individuals in one area simply opened up opportunities for others to move in from adjacent forests.[94] This was a resilient species, capable of making a comeback and even of modifying its behaviour as it came under intense pressure. Tigers seem to have become more nocturnal and secretive in their habits as hunting pressures increased.[95] These populations could survive as long as cover and prey were adequate in the area.[96]

[90] O'Brien, 'Where Man-eating Tigers Occur', pp. 231–2.

[91] Sankhala, *Tiger!*

[92] NAI, Game 1904, no. 266, 'Letters from Local Governments', John Hewett, Notes, 19 August 1902.

[93] Corbett, *Man-eaters of Kumaon*, pp. x–xiii.

[94] Prater, 'The Number of Tigers Shot', pp. 881–8.

[95] McDougall, *Face of the Tiger*, pp. 155–9.

[96] Singh, *Legend of the Man-eater*, pp. 81–2.

The scarcity of wild prey could compel carnivores to turn on cattle and even human beings.[97] The dry and moist deciduous forests that comprise much of tiger habitat in India have an extensive prey base, including large animals like the sambar (*Cervus unicolor*) and gaur (*Bos gaurus*). The wet grasslands of the Indo-Gangetic plains had an even higher concentration of prey species including the wild buffalo (*Bubalis*) and great one-horned rhino (*Rhinoceros unicornis*). Their steady retreat to small portions of their erstwhile range by 1900 may have led to increased preying on cattle or people. Interestingly, in Java, with a long history of habitual man-eating by tigers, the most common prey species was the much smaller wild boar.[98] But many observers in India linked tiger predation on cattle to human-induced scarcity of wild prey. In the Santhal-inhabited areas of Chhotanagpur, officials believed the tribal hunts had left vast stretches of sal forests with no deer or wild boar.[99] This factor should not be seen in isolation.[100] The decline of prey species may also have been due to increased sport-hunting with modern weapons. Cattle may have been killed for opportunistic reasons as they were easily available in forest tracts at certain times of the year.[101] Tigers in many areas probably had a long history of preying on cattle, slow-moving in comparison with most wild prey species. But decreases in deer and increases in cattle numbers in the home range of a tiger could lead to greater predation.[102] Many man-eaters shot by Corbett were probably sub-adult or mature individuals edged out by rivals into marginal habitats.[103] The territorial behaviour of the species often led to

[97] NAI, Game 1904, no. 277, p. 281, H.H. Risley, Sec., Home Dept, to Local Govts, 23 May 1904.

[98] Boomgaard, 'Man-eating'.

[99] Game 1904, no. 29. p. 257, J. Taylor, Sett. Officer, Burdwan, to Chief Sec., Bengal, 20 September 1904.

[100] NAI, Game 1904, no. 269, Notifications by the Bengal Govt, 'District Offficers' power in the Protected Forests of Santhal Parganas, Chotanagpur, Khurda and Rohtas', 24 September and 16 December 1895.

[101] Forsyth, *Highlands*, p. 95.

[102] Shahi, *Backs to the Wall*, pp. 13–14.

[103] McDougall, 'The Man-eating Tiger', pp. 435–48.

their dispersal, sparking off fresh conflicts in areas with a higher human population.

Bengal was the only province with a long history of predation on humans by tigers; in specific regions of it conflicts were very sharp. In 1901–5 over a third of all deaths caused by tigers in British India were in Bengal.[104] It was not so much a question of attacks in villages and cultivated fields as in the Sundarban mangroves, which had a distinctive ecology. Unlike elsewhere in tiger country, chance encounters were more common and the prey base quite narrow. Attacks were likely to continue in Khulna as the Sundarbans were 'more and more opened up'.[105] Similarly, in the 24 Parganas large numbers of the poor who collected fuel and thatching reeds were especially vulnerable.[106] These two districts accounted for the major increase in levels of tiger predation on people. Such 'tiger-plagues' were highly specific in their timing and occurrence even in the one region notorious for man-eaters. The time for gathering forest produce coincided with the time of year when tigresses had cubs.[107] Woodcutters in the Sundarbans ventured out into the mangroves in large parties accompanied by a fakir, who propitiated wild animals with offerings to the presiding deity. The system was not foolproof. The fakir decamped if any of the party was carried off by a tiger.[108] In the 24 Parganas, woodcutters worked only on specific sites sanctified by a fakir whose prayers were meant to scare away tigers. 'Gazi Sahib and his brother Kalu', were guardian deities 'venerated' by both Muslims and Hindus.[109]

[104] NAI, Vermin 1905, no. 269, Home Dep. Resn., 23 September 1905 (hereafter Vermin 1905).

[105] NAI, Vermin 1905, no. 67, HWC Carduff, Offg. Sec., Bengal, to Sec., Home Dept, GOI, 3 May 1904.

[106] NAI, H (P), September 1902, A nos 281–8, 'Measures adopted with a view to destroying wild animals and poisonous snakes in India during the year 1901', no. 285, p. 23, J.A. Bourdilon, Chief Sec., Bengal, to Sec., Home Dept, 21 April 1902.

[107] The phrase is from Boomgaard, 'Man-eating'.

[108] Hunter, *A Statistical Account of Bengal, Vol. I*, pp. 36–7, 312.

[109] O'Malley, *Bengal District Gazetteers, 24 Parganas*, pp. 74–5.

These were not expressions of fatalism as much as responses to a large predator in a harsh environment.[110] Going out in large parties was a way of scaring away all but the most determined of tigers.[111] The paucity of wild prey species in comparison to other habitats and the vulnerability of gatherers of forest produce and fisherfolk may explain the frequency of fatal attacks by tigers in the Sundarbans.[112]

The Sundarbans were exceptional: conflicts of tigers with people were common in some areas but virtually unknown in others. It is possible that changes in the colonial period contributed to increased man-eating in the short run. Tigers wounded by sport-hunters could turn to human prey as they were unable to chase wild animals. Prater estimated that as many as one in five tigers shot at in the late 1930s escaped wounded.[113] Given the sheer scale of hunting, this may have contributed to man-eating on a major scale. One estimate of the number shot as trophies over 1860–1960 is 20,000 and a fifth of that would mean a total of 4000 tigers![114] Moreover, the reduction of the prey base was partly related to sport-hunting. It was easy to blame the cultivator and the native shikari, but many officials felt that the 'the common ground' in the decline of game throughout India was 'the depredations of European sportsmen'.[115] Even a slight decline of the prey base would affect a large carnivore like the tiger.

The ecology and behaviour of the tiger gave it both strengths and weaknesses. Due to the diversity of habitat, it could weather the onslaught much more successfully than the lion or the cheetah, which, at least in India, were primarily animals of open plains and scrub country. Nevertheless, the tiger was a large predator,

[110] This view is very different from Boomgard's in 'Man-eating'.

[111] O'Malley, *Bengal District Gazetteers, Khulna*, pp. 20, 121.

[112] See Rishi, 'Man Mask, and Man-eater', pp. 9–14.

[113] Prater, 'The Number of Tigers', *Journal of the Bombay Natural History Society*, 1940.

[114] Thapar, *The Tiger's Destiny*.

[115] NAI, Game 1908, no. 30, p. 22, W.S. Morris to Chief Sec., UP, 2 August 1905.

weighing 200–230 kg and a stable population required adequate large prey. The bounty system had funded the killing of 16,573 tigers in 1879–88 alone. By computing the numbers killed between 1875 and 1925, the total works out to over 80,000 tigers. The files for thirteen years are missing, but even this is probably a conservative estimate.[116] The numbers are notoriously unreliable, and observations on man-eating tigers in Kumaon suggest, though not conclusively, that males were more prone to be aggressive.[117] Still, it is revealing that the bounty system in general was weighted against tigresses. Further, even if the number killed for rewards was assumed to be less than reported, there were several cases where kills were not reported or rewards refused for lack of evidence. The conclusion is inescapable: bounty killing was far more important in the decline of the feline than was realized until recently by most observers.

Contrary to the picture suggested for Java, there was no inherent conflict between people and tigers across the Indian subcontinent. Tigers may have survived partly because attitudes to them could range from unremitting hostility to tolerance. Some urban Indians already saw the elimination of wild animals as both necessary and desirable. In April 1880 the *Maharashtra Mitra*, a newspaper of Satara, asserted that tigers were 'creating havoc' in the district. The government was criticized for not allowing people to obtain modern firearms for self-defence. The newspaper went so far as to allege that it would be better if the British government were to kill its native subjects itself instead of allowing them to be devoured by animals.[118] The issue of marauding predators also provided a means to condemn the iniquities of the Arms Act.

[116] Vermin 1890, 'Keep-with Notes', J.P. Hutchins, 30 September 1890. The totals are computed on the basis of the Home (Public) documents for the succeeding years, 1873–1926. The missing years are 1891–5, 1905–11, and 1917–18.

[117] Of the eleven man-eaters taken by Corbett, six were male. See Sukumar, 'The Management of Large Mammals', pp. 93–102.

[118] NAI, H (P), May 1880, B nos. 67–8, p. 4, 'Allegation in Maharashtra Mitra about the inability of residents of Valva taluka, Satara district, to

The Indian-language press expressed resentment at the disparity between the conquerors and the conquered. The rural poor lacked weapons to defend themselves from 'dacoits' or wild beasts'.[119] The Bengal landholder Govind Charan Das blamed the absence of guns in the village. This enabled big cats to hunt without any great danger or trouble to themselves.[120] Critics agreed with the objective of curbing tigers but wanted people equipped with the requisite weaponry. But differences often went further especially in the forest regions where tigers were seen by inhabitants as part of the landscape. Some groups had religious qualms about killing certain animals. The Bengal Rajputs claimed descent 'from a royal' tiger' and protected them 'whenever' they could. They even refused to provide baits for white hunters.[121] But religious beliefs could change over time. The Khonds of Ganjam dragged their feet when it came to setting traps for carnivores 'for fear of destroying their ancestors'. But they overcame this impulse when officials increased the amount of the bounty.[122] The Mikirs of Nowgong in Assam made no attempt to kill or net tigers for fear of offending their deity.[123] There were differences also of the extent of opposition for tigers and people had often lived in close proximity without

---

defend themselves from attacks by tigers for lack of the arms', G.W. Kulkarni, Reporter, Native Press, 20 April 1880.

[119] NAI, H (P), June 1881, A nos. 10–13, 'Amendment of Arms Act (IX of 1878)', Note by the Sec., Viceroy, 14 January 1881.

[120] NAI, Game 1908, no. 29, p. 288: Govind Chandra Das, Sec., Eastern Bengal Land-Holders Association, to Sec., Rev., Bengal, 24 September 1904.

[121] Forsyth, *Highlands*, p. 28.

[122] NAI, H (P), December 1885, A nos. 69–101, 'Results of measures adopted for exterminating wild animals and poisonous snakes in British India during the year 1884', no. 69, Procs., Board of Rev., Madras, 19 June 1885 (hereafter Vermin 1885).

[123] NAI, H (P), December 1884, A nos 109–40, 'Results of measures adopted for exterminating wild animals and poisonous snakes in British India during the year 1883', no. 130, p. 61, Sec., Chief Comm., Assam to Sec., GOI, Home Dept, 16 May 1884.

threatening each other. Sanderson knew of a male tiger which lived close to a village and only lifted cattle, never mauling a cowherd. This tiger, known as Don, knocked down and killed a man when a group of people surrounded him with nets. But he still 'lost nothing in public esteem'. His effigy was in the precincts of the Koombappa temple. When Don was finally killed, a tracker recalled how he had 'never hurt any of us'.

Even those who lived in the haunts of man-eaters refuted the idea that all tigers were dangerous.[124] An affinity with the animal may also have stemmed from a realization of its role as a controller of deer and wild boar.[125] The Nawab of Rampur in the North West Provinces objected to the elimination of tigers, because they 'do no harm to crops and keep down the numerous animals that do'.[126] Pioneer cultivators in the forest 'trust to the tigers' to hold down the deer.[127] True, the bulk of killing for rewards was done by Indians but the impulse to exterminate the striped cat was not shared by all. Many dragged their feet. Others were indifferent. For some, strategies of avoidance seemed a better bet.

Overall, these strategies may have made the difference between extinction and survival. The absence of a uniformly negative image in cultures of the subcontinent stood the tiger in good stead. The war against the tiger had its moments of peace.

The Wolf as Unseen Predator

This was not so with a different animal with a wider range: the wolf. Only an excessive reliance on shikar literature and our own cultural disposition to the big cats has obscured the significance of the wolf as co-predator and victim of human intervention. Until its decline under human pressure over the last century, the

[124] Sanderson, *Thirteen Years*, pp. 307, 312.

[125] Forsyth, *Highlands*, p. 259.

[126] NAI, Vermin 1875, no. 302, no pagination, C.A. Ellison, Sec., NWP, to A.C. Lyall, 20 March 1874.

[127] Sanderson, *Thirteen Years*, pp. 237–8.

grey wolf was the most widespread large carnivore in the world. The Indian sub-species of the wolf (*Canis lupus pallipes*) is much smaller than its North American and weighs about 20–22 kg.[128] Wolves preyed on smaller domestic animals than did the tiger and were pre-eminently not inhabitants of the forest. Their habitat is described vividly in some hunting memoirs. In the Bombay Presidency, the greatest numbers of grey wolves were killed in Sind, Pune, and Ahmadnagar. On the other hand, tigers were mainly reported from Kanara, Kolaba, and Thana, all in regions with higher rainfall and dense tree cover.[129] This simple fact points to a very significant feature of wolf ecology in the subcontinent: it was 'extremely common' in areas with gazelle and blackbuck but 'very seldom' seen in forested patches.[130] Major Ray found them in large acacia (babool) plantations that were several hundred acres large. The country was 'absolutely flat' with only a few nullahs (dry stream beds), and a few stones here and there, crops down, and 'not a bush or anything' to obstruct the view.[131] Waddington speared wolves in flat, open country near the sea shore.[132] A pair of wolves was found harrying railway labourers in the 'low jungles' outside Jabalpur. In Damoh, 'low-caste' villagers helped a forester track down and shoot a female and a sub-adult male that were lifting children.[133] It was these two kinds of terrain—undulating open lands and hill-dotted rocky jungle—that were the main habitat of the wolf in the peninsula and the West.[134]

[128] Zoological Survey of India, *The Red Data Book of Indian Animals, Part I: Vertebrata*, pp. 45–9.

[129] NAI, H (P), September 1915, nos 100–16, 'Results of measures adopted for exterminating wild animals and poisonous snakes in British India during the year 1914', p. 18, J.L. Rieu, Bombay Govt., 14 June 1915.

[130] Forsyth, *Highlands*, pp. 68–70; also see Adams, 'Jungle Memories', pp. 652.

[131] Ray, 'Wolf-hunting', pp. 145–8.

[132] Waddington, 'Wolf hunting', pp. 554–5.

[133] Forsyth, *Highlands*, pp. 68–70.

[134] Krishnan, 'The Plains Wolf'.

The regional spread of the conflicts between people and wolves requires careful attention. Figures can convey only a partial view of the scale of conflict but in 1875 more people were killed by wolves than by tigers.[135] The North West Provinces and Bihar were among the worst affected by wolf attacks. In 1876 in the former as many as 721 lives were lost to wolves and in turn 2825 wolves were slain for bounties.[136] The loss of lives to wolves was also heavy in Bihar. In 1876 all but a dozen of the 185 deaths were from Patna and Bhagalpur Divisions. In turn they accounted for over half of the wolves killed.[137] In north-western, central, and southern India the main conflict with the species was not so much to do with attacks on children as depredations on livestock, especially sheep and goats.[138] Similarly, the animal was common in many parts of the Deccan but human casualties were rare or unknown.[139]

The extermination of wolves remained a priority in the NWP and Awadh (later UP) right into the 1920s. The Lieutenant Governor singled out the elimination of the wolf as 'the single most important part' of measures for destroying wild animals.[140] Wolves in the NWP accounted for 'twenty to fifty times' the human lives lost to other beasts of prey. Their persistent efforts to carry

[135] Fayrer, *Destruction of Life*, p. 14

[136] NAI, H (P), May 1877, A nos 60–85, 'Results of measures adopted for exterminating wild animals and poisonous snakes in British India during the year 1876', no. 66, B.W. Colvin, Offg. Sec., NWP, 29 May 1876 (hereafter Vermin 1877).

[137] NAI, Vermin 1877, no. 274, S.C. Bayley, Sec., Bengal, 6 August 1877.

[138] Vermin 1877, no. 69, L Griffin, Offg. Sec., Govt of Punjab and its dependencies, to A.P. Howell, Sec., GOI, Home, 12 May 1876; 4 people and 431 head of stock were killed by wolves that year.

[139] NAI, Vermin 1877, no. 274, S.C. Bayley, Sec., Bengal, 6 August 1877.

[140] NAI, H (P), December 1882, A nos 32–70, 'Results of measures adopted for exterminating wild animals and poisonous snakes in British India during the year 1881', no. 54, p. 46, Resn., Gen. Dep., NWP and Oudh, 2 June 1882 (hereafter Vermin 1882).

off children were 'almost incredible . . . If cubs are perseveringly destroyed, which they would be for good rewards, the race would be perceptibly diminished in a few years.' The bounty for a female wolf cub was as high as 12 annas, as compared to only 8 annas for a male. The cubs could be located in their dens in the breeding season and smoked to death. The Commissioner of Jaunpur favoured even higher rewards of 5 rupees for an adult animal and a rupee for each cub. Higher bounties, with larger amounts for females and cubs, were one way to encourage the destruction of the carnivore. In Gorakhpur, fatalities were highest in summer, 'when people are in the habit of sleeping in the open air.' The reward for a wolf was therefore fixed at 4 rupees, in contrast to only 3 rupees for the former.[141] In 1883 the Allababad district paid as much as 8 rupees for a female cub, twice that for an adult male.[142] The question of whether to give more incentives to local shikaris or deploy special forces often arose with respect to wolf-killing measures. Cash prizes were considered insufficient in areas where attacks on people and stock were common. Nats, Kanjers and Musahirs, 'low-caste' hunters who caught small mammals and reptiles, were paid a retainer in Fatehpur in the North West Provinces to ensure the killing of wolves. The scales could be tilted against the animal if it was possible to support anyone who made a business of wolf-catching.[143] But such steps were often not a success.[144] Groups like the Pardhis were still better equipped against a wary carnivore than a soldier as they had a deep knowledge of its habits and the

[141] NAI, Vermin 1875, no. 302, C.A. Ellison, Sec., NWP, to A.C. Lyall, 20 March 1874.

[142] NAI, H (P), December 1883, A nos 29–64, 'Results of measures adopted for exterminating wild animals and poisonous snakes in British India during the year 1882', no. 56, p. 52, Resn., Gen. Dep., NWP, 1 August 1883 (hereafter Vermin 1883).

[143] NAI, Vermin 1882, no. 54, p. 47, Resn., Gen. Dep., NWP and Oudh, 2 June 1882.

[144] NAI, Vermin 1883, no. 56, p. 52, Resn., Gen. Dep., NWP, 1 August 1883.

local terrain.[145] They often hunted wild boars and wolves and the rewards were added incentive.[146]

The fact that wolves could take shelter in fields is testimony to their adaptability and versatility. Even a large male was about 65–75 cm tall. This would explain its continued survival in the Indo-Gangetic plains well into the twentieth century.[147] When the NWP government sent Gorkhas to kill the packs, they were asked to hunt 'when the crops are off the ground' in order to obtain good results.[148] Until the harvest, wolves could take cover in the standing crop. In Badaun, Gorkha troops were unsuccessful as they went out after the animals in the first three months of the year. Local shikaris (village-based hunters) did not bother to try shooting wolves until the harvest and were more successful.[149] The breeding cycle of the species coincided with the time when the winter crop was still uncut. The wolf mates after the end of the monsoon and cubs are born around December.[150] Recent research suggests that single-crop cultivation of millets such as bajra or jowar provides ideal cover for cubbing.[151] Cubs could also be born in scrub jungle that adjoined cultivation.

There were doubts on the need to kill off wolves but arguments were utilitarian rather than aesthetic or ethical. The District Magistrate of Hamirpur was sceptical of the claim that wolves were killing people on a large scale. In all, seventeen lives had been lost

[145] Hurst, 'Pardhis', p. 51.

[146] Hobbart, 'Pig-rearing Pasis', pp. 22–8.

[147] Prater, *The Book of Indian Animals*, pp. 121, 125–6; R.W. Burton, 'Weights and Measurements', p. 16.

[148] NAI, H (P), September 1902, A nos 281–92, 'Results of measures adopted for exterminating wild animals and poisonous snakes in British India during the year 1901', no. 287, pp. 32–3: W.H.L. Impey, Chief Sec., UP, to Resn., Gen Admin., 20 May 1901.

[149] NAI, Vermin 1903, no. 241, p. 29, Resn., Gen. Admin., UP, 20 May 1902.

[150] Prater, *Indian Animals*, pp. 121, 125–6.

[151] Jhala and Giles, 'The Status', pp. 476–83.

in less than three years but he felt that several deaths were due to hyenas (*Hyena hyena*). Over 450 wolves had been killed for a sum of over 700 rupees disbursed as rewards. But this idea was rejected by his superiors who shared the commonly held view that hyenas were eaters of carrion and would 'never' attack human beings or children. There was also a realization that particular individual wolves may have 'tasted human flesh' and become dangerous to people. In Rae Bareli special parties of hunters were deployed to eliminate the marauding pack.[152] Attempts to blame hyenas or stigmatize particular individual wolves made little headway.

Programmes to wipe out the species had to contend with unforeseen obstacles. Local shikaris in Berar obtained licenses on condition they would shoot the carnivores but rarely used the guns for this purpose.[153] In several provinces the carcasses of wolves that had been paid for were dug up and turned in again for a fresh bounty. In Gonda the wolf-killers discovered where the ears were buried and sewed them back neatly. They managed to get a second reward for the same beast.[154] Often, the golden jackal (*Canis aureus*) was killed and produced to claim the bounty on the grey wolf.[155] Officials poorly versed in natural history were hard put to tell the difference. The young Phillip Mason in Saharanpur in UP certified that thirteen animals produced before him by Kanjers were wolves

[152] NAI, H (P), December 1899, nos 272–85, 'Results of measures adopted for exterminating wild animals and poisonous snakes in British India during the year 1898', no. 276, p. 37, Chief Sec., NWP, to Sec., GOI, Home, 19 May 1899.

[153] NAI, H (P), November 1893, A nos 1–43, 'Results of measures adopted for exterminating wild animals and poisonous snakes in British India during the year 1892', no. 11, p. 26, K.J.L. Mackenzie, Comm., Hyderabad Assigned Districts, to Sec., Berar, 11 March 1893.

[154] NAI, Vermin 1885, nos 176–7, J.W. Reid, Sec., Govt., NWPs, 18 August 1885.

[155] NAI, H (P), October 1891, nos 316–53, 'Results of measures adopted for exterminating wild animals and poisonous snakes in British India during the year 1890', no. 350, p. 93, Chief Sec., Bengal to Sec., GOI, Home, 29 July 1891.

and had the tail and ears cut off and burnt to prevent fraud. Only later did he realize that the Kanjers had sun-dried the carcasses of wolves and inserted a freshly killed jackal inside the rib cage, 'as the chef of a Victorian duke would stuff a quail inside an ortola and sewn on ears and tails manufactured from hessian and smeared fresh blood.'[156] Such evasion frustrated official campaigns.

It is not easy to assess the impact of the slaughter on the wolf as a species. Over 100,000 were killed for rewards in British India between 1871 and 1916. The records for as many as nineteen years (1877–9, 1889–95, and 1905–15) are incomplete. The total number killed for bounty by 1925 was probably over 200,000.[157] As several of the so-called wolves killed were actually jackals, the figures are less useful as an index of status than they could have been. But there is little doubt of a decline in some areas.[158] Around Delhi, where as many as three hundred wolves were killed for rewards over 1878–83, only three bounties were claimed in 1913.[159] Factors working in favour of the wolf were absent in the case of the tiger. Excluding the Tibetan sub-species, their pelts were not valuable.[160] The smaller body size of the Indian wolf also enabled it to survive in areas with a high degree of human activity, often in low jungle and scrub on the outskirts of villages. This did not confer on them any kind of immunity. A shift to double-cropping with irrigation could probably reduce breeding sites. Above all, the wolf retained a negative image in the eyes of most herders, who would not hesitate to kill it. Evidence of private vendetta is limited, but Le Mesurier referred to the sheep-owners of Chunar paying a rupee for a she-wolf. This was in addition to the reward of 6 rupees given by the authorities.[161] Despite this, there

[156] Manson, *A Shaft of Sunlight*, p. 72.

[157] These are from the totals given in the Home (Public) records.

[158] Vermin 1914, no. 7, pp. 51–2, 57: Procs., Lt. Gov., Punjab, 4 May 1914.

[159] Ibid.; W.M. Hailey, Chief Comm., Delhi, 18 March 1914.

[160] E.D. (pseudonym), 'Tiger skins', p. 69.

[161] Le Mesurier, 'Wolves', p. 185.

were substantial areas where the species could survive. In much of western India, the blackbuck (*Antelopa cervicapra*) survived in large numbers well into the 1930s.[162] The clearing of forests for cultivation has often been cited as a major threat to the survival of the tiger. But the wolf, weighing a bare 20 kg, could eke out an existence where the 230 kg big cat could not. The former was 'a difficult animal to exterminate'.[163] It could become increasingly nocturnal to avoid detection.[164] It is possible that its absence from timber forests was a blessing in disguise, for the Forest Department's writ in such areas included intensive programmes to kill off carnivores. But the pressure on the wolf could also have been more intense on account of cultural biases and prejudices against it. The 'vigorous campaign' against the wolf was stepped up at precisely the time when the tiger began winning a reprieve.[165] S.H. Butler, who favoured abolition of a general reward on the tiger, lobbied for a higher bounty for grey wolves.[166] If shepherds were not positively disposed to the species, officials and princes were no great fans. In the Punjab hills, princes gave a bounty of 3 rupees for a wolf, using not only villagers but also only armed Gorkhas to hunt them down. The objective: to build up stocks of game birds for sport-hunting.[167] The value of a wolf skin may have been low, but conversely there was no great sporting merit in maintaining its population. The wolf was seen not only as a killer of goats and

[162] Jhala and Giles, 'The Status'.

[163] NAI, H (P), November 1914, A nos 1–19 no. 10, p. 75, DC Jabalpur, quoted in the CPs Misc. Dep. Resolution,14 May 1914 (hereafter Vermin 1914).

[164] Dunbar Brander, *Wild Animals*, p. 27.

[165] NAI, H (P), September 1905, A nos 255–70, 'Results of measures adopted for exterminating wild animals and poisonous snakes in British India during the year 1904', no. 241, pp. 29, EPL Winter, Chief Sec., Gen., Admin., to Resn., UP, 19 May 1905.

[166] NAI, H (P), March 1907, A nos. 122–31, 'Results of measures adopted for exterminating wild animals and poisonous snakes in British India during the year 1906', no. 126, p. 21, S.H. Butler, Sec., UP, 1 April 1905.

[167] Ellison, 'Game Preservation', p. 124.

sheep but as a marauder against children. Its survival was a tribute to its own capacity to remain an unseen predator.

Dissenters and Defenders

The revulsion against the slaughter of predators was more marked by the 1920s and 1930s. The tiger and leopard now found articulate defenders. The early revulsion had often to do with the killing of cubs and pregnant females. Keeping wild animals as pets did not make their owners admirers of them in the wild. But it was in contrast with the general policy of slaying cubs. In the 1880s, a military officer kept a pet leopard in the Bundelkhand cantonment. He would turn it loose in his garden, where he enjoyed watching it 'stalking ponies in the long grass'.[168] Lady Curzon recounted how a pregnant tigress 'was skinned and cut up. They found three little ones inside her nearly ready to be born. Isn't it sad?'[169] Lord Reading shot a maned lion in the Gir Forest, Kathiawar, but was moved by the sight of a lioness and her six cubs playing around the base of a tree. All the more so because 'The cubs played like kittens.'[170] Big cats were seen in a more favourable light than reptiles. 'Such things', writes Vernede, 'are repulsive to man. The cat tribe is not. Between us there is not the same cold-blooded element.' [171]

The idea that watching animals in the wild was better than shooting them on sight was gathering ground. Jim Corbett, who would later win renown for his accounts of man-eaters in Kumaon, expressed his admiration for the tiger. He had sat up 'with the most modern rifle across my knee' as he watched 'a tigress and two fully grown cubs eat up the sambhar stag they killed and counted myself no poorer for having taken no trophy.'[172] Aesthetic sensibilities were

[168] Birdwood, *Khaki and Gown,* p. 51.

[169] Bradley, ed., *Lady Curzon's India,* p. 76.

[170] Butler, *The Viceroy's Wife,* p. 151. The letter is dated November 1924. Emphasis added.

[171] Vernede, *An Ignorant in India,* p. 85. Emphasis added.

[172] Corbett, 'The Pipal Pani Tiger', pp. 61–2.

evident in the defense of raptors as well. The first attempts to rein in tiger shooting had admittedly been 'unpopular' but there was really no alternative.[173] Part of the new tolerance was also a response to the advances in technology that made hunting down the tiger much easier than in the past. The keen sport-hunter was now assisted by 'good motor roads and even telephones in places.'[174] The revised Game Rules began to take note of the scarcity of tigers, though this was only true at a regional level. In the United Provinces, a favourite hunting ground of the official elite and a major battle ground in the struggle for survival of the species, limits on the bags came into force in 1921.[175] In Mysore the 'fear of total extinction' led to controls on shooting.[176] There were glimmers of a more nuanced understanding of the relationship between prey and predators. Champion blamed the elimination of tigers for the rapid growth of populations of wild boar and deer in the forests and on the borders of cultivated lands. He rebutted the idea that tigers were cruel beasts and instead upheld them as 'merciful' in comparison to 'man, the avowed hater of cruelty.'[177]

The transformation of the deadly hunter of humans into an animal-citizen endowed with the quality of mercy was not going to be easy. Corbett's own writings were to help reinforce the image of marauding man-eaters that could only be curbed by a hunter with superhuman qualities.[178] It is difficult to see how readers would remain unmoved by the descriptions of the cunning of errant and devious predators on the rampage in village India.[179] There was, of course, no shortage of opponents of empire and Mason explicitly compared some of them to tigers. Officials in the 1920s and 1930s hoped they would not have to do to Pathan tribes of the frontier

[173] Champion, *With a Camera in Tigerland*, p. 45.
[174] Champion, *The Jungle*, p. 45.
[175] Stracey, *Wildlife in India*, p. 103.
[176] Rao, *Mysore Gazetteer, Vol. I*, p. 78.
[177] Champion, *The Jungle*, p. 36.
[178] Sankhala, *Tiger!*, p. 138.
[179] Mukherjee, *Forster and Further*, p. 212.

what they did to disobedient tigers. 'They (the tigers) could kill what deer they liked in a park', wrote Mason, 'but they risked a bullet if they came outside and took village cattle.'[180] A tiger that knew and kept to its place was allright. This was a shift from seeing all tigers as potential man-killers. The view also encapsulates in kernel a major change that had come about in the previous fifty years. Instead of being presumed guilty, it was now possible for tigers not to be on parole. A victor could afford to be magnanimous. The domain of mercy was not very far removed from the world of blood and gore.

Conclusion

The programmes to control vermin provide insights into the wider process of imperial intervention in rural India. The Indian legacy of dealing with carnivorous animals was rich and diverse. In contrast to Britain and Western Europe, there was no long history of state-sponsored projects to eliminate carnivores. Rulers did kill man-eaters and help in the process of agrarian expansion. But a degree of tolerance was perhaps easier in the context of relatively dispersed rural settlements with a large proportion of the land area under forest cover. There is evidence of recourse to religious and magical methods to ward off tigers. But there were also a variety of other means of self-defence, ranging from avoidance to the simple elimination of marauding animals. British attitudes were not static. Initially, the extermination of these creatures was left to local authorities. Curbing the tiger seemed the logical corollary to the campaign against human outlaws and as essential for agricultural extension. But it was more than just that. The 'improvement' of India under the Raj could only proceed if such obstacles were removed. In the aftermath of the Rebellion of 1857, Indians were not to be trusted with modern firearms. Some officials felt that only a white man would be resourceful enough to oversee the hunting

[180] Mason, *The Men Who Ruled India*, p. 292.

of predators. 'Martial races' like the Rajputs and Gorkhas were seen as capable of standing up to dangerous beasts as much as in war. Village headmen and cultivators were sometimes even issued guns for self-protection. But the main thrust of policy was to get villagers to eliminate carnivores without using modern firearms. The general policy of denying them such weapons was retained, except in special cases. Bounties for females and cubs aimed at more than control: the 'elimination' of species was seen as an index of success.

Princely states varied in their responses to the programme, but many followed suit. Cattle-lifting was cited as a brake on the expansion of agriculture. Cattle were the prime source of draught power. Tigers had to be sacrificed in the interest of land revenue. However, there was no unanimity on how much damage predators actually caused to the economy. A few officials argued that control of herbivores by leopards and tigers actually assisted cultivators. It was more than a simple case of identifying barriers to expansion of the plough. The grey wolf rarely threatened cattle, but often preyed on sheep and goats. In this case, the conflict was with animal-rearing rather than cultivation. Sportsmen saw carnivores as competitors for game. Elite hunters carried the war against vermin into the heart of the forest.

There was a strong cultural bias against an animal like the tiger with its alleged liking for human flesh. But there is little evidence that tigers in all areas habitually consumed people. The Sundarbans in Bengal were exceptional in having a very high degree of man-eating by tigers throughout our period and beyond. Elsewhere, man-eating was situation-specific and not a general phenomenon. The factors that led to man-eating included a paucity of natural prey, opportunities for attacks on cattle, wounds inflicted by sport hunters and the dispersal of younger tigers into areas with high intensities of human use. There is little evidence of an irreconcilable conflict of existence between people and tigers. The inter-regional disparities are also clear with the wolf. After all, tigers and wolves had shared their habitats with people for centuries. Bounty-hunting aided in decline but its impact was uneven, depending on the region and species. Its impact on the tiger cannot be seen in isolation from hunting for sport. Sportsmen often saw elimination as their great 'achievement'. Far from simply being an adjunct to expanding cultivation, vermin-killing carried the battle well beyond the borders of the cultivated arable. Any tiger anywhere was better dead than alive. For a time, no place in British India was sanctuary for such vermin. Preliminary figures indicate that far more tigers were killed for reward than were shot for sport. This does not minimize the latter as the two were inseparable for a long time. But the extension of agriculture, as in the Indus basin, also exerted a powerful influence on the fortune of the species. Given its large body size and need for forest cover, even an animal as resilient as the tiger found it difficult to survive. Unlike the tiger, the wolf could survive in scrub jungle and switch to living off smaller prey. The carnivore managed to survive in many areas by remaining elusive.

The strategies of avoidance and self-defence at the local level meant that people often stopped short of a desire to wipe out the tiger. Religious and cultural objections slowed vermin-killing but were perhaps specific to certain regions and cultures. What was more widespread was a willingness to coexist with the animal. It would be misleading to romanticize such situations, especially when many people turned up to claim bounties. The extent to which specific kinds of land-use enabled or hindered coexistence is worth detailed study at the micro level. Tolerance and 'good-will' were not universal. Middle-class Indians opposed to the Arms Act cited the need for self-defence against wild animals. Often the discord in village and forest hamlet was over how much should be paid out as reward. Specialists in wolf-killing and snake-catching also took advantage of the opportunity to earn extra cash. This also brought them under government control to a greater extent than in the past. With the growth of market linkages and the quickening pulse of economic interaction there were new pressures. Despite such extensive changes, there is enough to suggest that there were alternatives to extermination. Certain forms of land-use could coexist with wild animals. The animosity of the Raj to the feline was not shared by all. Many zamindars and some princes did much less than the British to wipe out dangerous beasts. Clearly, a romanticized view, however attractive, would be as misleading as a picture of all-out conflict.

The shift in attitudes by the 1920s was in part a consequence of the success of vermin extermination operations. Though the number of lives lost and the beasts killed for rewards was still high in the mid-1920s, a decision was taken to stop collating any information at the all-India level.[181] Provinces were free to pursue their own line of action. If the tiger found breathing space, the wolf did not. The former won admirers, who saw it as an embodiment of gentlemanly virtue. Others acknowledged the positive role of predators in controlling herbivores in forests and on the fringes of cultivated arable. But such views were still held by a minority. Programmes to wipe out vermin continued for much longer.[182] Yet the era of branding a species as vermin was drawing to a close. It was the tragedy of the tiger that it was winning small battles but losing the war.

References

Adams, Lt. Col. E.G. Pythian, 'Jungle Memories', *Journal of the Bombay Natural History Society*, vol. 48 (1949).

al Fazl, Abu, *Ain i Akbari*, trans. and ed. H. Blochmann, Calcutta: Asiatic Society of Bengal, rpnt. Delhi, 1972.

———, *The Akbar Namah*, trans. and ed. H. Blochmann, Calcutta: Rpnt., 1972.

Anon., 'The Proposed Introduction of Game into the Neighbourhood of Bombay', *JBNHS*, vol. 6 (1891).

Barrow, H.W., 'Crocodiles in Artificial Reservoirs', *Journal of the Bombay Natural History Society*, vol. 10 (1895).

[181] NAI, H (P), 1926, file 126.

[182] Adams, 'Jungle Memories', pp. 646–55; Stracey, *India's Wildlife*, pp. 168, 181.

Bayly, C.A., *An Illustrated History of Modern India, 1600–1947*, Bombay: Oxford University Press, 1991.

Bhattacharya, A., 'The Tiger Cult and its Literature in Lower Bengal', *Man in India*, vol. 27 (1947).

Birdwood, Field Marshall, *Khaki and Gown: An Autobiography*, London: Lock and Co., no date.

Boomgaard, P., 'Man-eating: The Deadly Encounters between People and Tigers/Leopards in Indonesia, 1650–1950', paper presented at the Conference on the Environment in South East Asia, School of Oriental and African Studies, London, 28–30 March 1994.

Bradley, J., ed., *Lady Curzon's India: Letters of a Vicerine*, New York: Beaufort Books, 1985.

Braudel, F., *Civilization and Capitalism, 15th to 18th Centuries: The Structures of Everyday Life*, London: Collins, Fontana, 1981.

Buchanan, F., *An Account of the District of Shahabad in 1812–13*, rpnt. Delhi: Usha Jain, 1986.

Buchanan, Hamilton, *A Journey from Madras through the Countries of Canara, Mysore and Malabar*, London: W. Bulmer and Co., 1807.

Burton, R.W., 'Weights and Measurements of Game Animals', *Journal of the Bombay Natural History Society*, vol. 24 (1915).

Butler, Iris, *The Viceroy's Wife: Letters of Alice, Countess of Reading, from India, 1921–25*, London: Hodder and Stoughton, 1969.

Campbell, J.M., *Gazetteer of the Bombay Presidency, Vol. XII: Khandesh*, Bombay: Government Central Press, 1880.

Campbell, J.M., *Gazetteer of the Bombay Presidency, Vol. XII, Pt ii,* Thana, Bombay, 1882, rpnt, Pune: Government Press, 1984.

Champion, F.W., *The Jungle in Sunlight and Shadow*, London: Chatto and Windus, 1933.

———, *With a Camera in Tigerland*, London: Chatto and Windus, 1927.

Corbett, J., 'The Pipal Pani Tiger', *Hog Hunters Annual*, no. 4 (1931).

———, *The Man-eaters of Kumaon*, Bombay: Oxford University Press, 1944; rpnt. Delhi: 1995.

Courtenay, N., *Tiger, Symbol of Courage*, London: Quartet Books, 1980.

Davidar, E.R.C., 'Wildlife Conservation in Tamil Nadu', *Journal of the Bombay Natural History Society*, vol. 83 (1986).

E.D. (pseudonym), 'Tiger Skins', *Indian Forester*, vol. 19 (1893).

Eaton, R., *The Rise of Islam and the Bengal Frontier, 1204–1760*, Delhi: Oxford University Press, 1994.

Elliot, Gen. J.G. *Field Sports in India, 1800–1947*, London: Gentry Books, 1973.

Ellison, B.C., 'Game Preservation and Game Experiments in India', *Journal of the Bombay Natural History Society*, vol. 33 (1928).

Fayrer, J., *Destruction of Life by Wild Animals and Venomous Snakes in India*, London: Society of Arts, 1878.

Forbes, J., *Oriental Memoirs*, London: William, Constance and Co., 1813.

Gandhi, M., *The Penguin Dictionary of Hindu Names*, Delhi: Viking Penguin, 1992.

Habib, I. and T. Raychaudhuri, ed., *The Cambridge Economic History of India, Vol. I: c. 1200–1750*, Delhi: Macmillan, 1982.

Heber, Reginald, *Narrative of a Journey through the Upper Provinces of India from Calcutta to Bombay, 1824–25*, London: 1827, rpnt. Delhi Low Price Publications, 1993.

Hobbart, C., 'Pig-rearing Pasis and Kindred Clans', *Hog Hunters Annual*, no. 5 (1932).

Hodgson, H., 'Preservation of Harmless Wild Animals in Malcompeth (Mahabaleshwar)', *Journal of the Bombay Natural History Society*, vol. 7 (1893).

Hunter, W.W., *A Statistical Account of Bengal, Vol. I: 24 Parganas and Sundarbans*, London: Trubner and Co.,1875; rpnt Delhi: D.K. Publishers, 1973.

Hurst, G., 'Pardhis', *Hog Hunters Annual*, no. 4 (1931).

Jhala, Y.V. and R. Giles, 'The Status and Conservation of the Wolf in Gujarat and Rajasthan, India', *Conservation Biology*, vol. 5 (1991).

Krishnan, M., 'The Plains Wolf', *The Statesman*, Calcutta, 15 July 1984.

Le Mesurier, Henry P., 'Wolves', *Murwala*, 21 January 1865.

MacKenzie, J.M., *The Empire of Nature: Hunting, Parks and British Imperialism*, Manchester: Manchester University Press, 1988.

Manson, P., *A Shaft of Sunlight: Memories of a Varied Life*, Delhi: Vikas, 1978.

Mason, P. *The Men who Ruled India: The Guardians*, London: Jonathan Cape, 1954; rpnt. 1974.

McDougall, C., 'The Man-eating Tiger in Geographical and Historical Perspective', in R.L. Tilson and U. Seal, eds, *Tigers of the World*, New Jersey: Alfred Noyes, 1987.

———, *The Face of the Tiger*, Delhi: 1978.

Mukherjee, S., *Forster and Further: The Tradition of Anglo-Indian Fiction*, Hyderabad: Orient Longman, 1993.

O'Brien, Lt. Col., 'Where Man-eating Tigers Occur', *Journal of the Bombay Natural History Society*, vol. 45 (1945).

O'Brien, Stephen, 'The "Exotic Aliens" Controversy: A View from Afar?, *Journal of the Bombay Natural History Society*, 110 (2013).

O'Malley, L.S.S., *Bengal District Gazetteers, 24 Parganas,* Calcutta: Bengal Secretariat, 1914.

———, *Bengal District Gazetteers, Khulna*, Calcutta: Bengal Secretariat, 1908.

OC, 'Notes on the Otter', *Indian Forester*, vol. 19 (1893).

Phipson, H.W., 'The Crocodiles in Our Reservoirs', Letter to the Editor, *The Times of India*, Bombay, 16 January 1892.

Pollock, S.E., ed., *The Ramayana of Valmiki, An Epic of Ancient India, Vol. 1*: *The Balakanda*, Princeton: Princeton University Press, 1984.

———, ed., *The Ramayana of Valmiki, An Epic of Ancient India, Vol. II*: *The Aranyakanda*, Princeton: Princeton University Press, 1991.

Prater, S.H., 'On the Occurrence of Tigers on the Island of Bombay and Salsettee', *Journal of the Bombay Natural History Society*, vol. 33 (1929).

———, 'The Number of Tigers Shot in the Reserved Forests of India and Burma during the Year 1937–38', *Journal of the Bombay Natural History Society*, vol. 41 (1940).

———, *The Book of Indian Animals*, Bombay: Oxford University Press, 1948; rpnt. 1965.

Rangarajan, M., *Fencing the Forest: Conservation and Ecological Change in India's Central Provinces, 1860–1914*, Delhi: Oxford University Press, 1996.

Rao, Hayavadana, *Mysore Gazetteer, Vol. I: Descriptive*, Mysore: 1927; rpnt. Delhi: B.R. Publishing Co., 1984.

Ray, Major J.W., 'Wolf-hunting in Southern Maratha country', *JBNHS*, vol. 8 (1893).

Rishi, V., 'Man-mask and Man-eater', *Tiger Paper*, vol. 15 (1988).

Ritvo, H., *The Animal Estate: The English and Other Creatures in the Victorian Age*, Harmondsworth: Penguin, 1990.

Roberts, T.J., *The Mammals of Pakistan*, London: Ernst Benn, 1976.

Sanderson, G.P., *Thirteen Years among the Wild Beasts of India,* 1874; rpnt. Delhi: Mittal, 1983.

Sankhala, K.S., *Tiger! The Story of the Indian Tiger*, London: Collins, 1978.

Shahi, S.P., *Backs to the Wall: The Saga of Wildlife in Bihar*, Delhi: East-West Affiliated Press, 1978.

Sherwani, Abbas Khan, *Tarikh-i-Sher Shahi*, in H.M. Elliot and J. Dowson, *The History of India as Told by Its Own Historians*, Allahabad: Kitab Mahal, 1979 edn.

Singh, A., *The Legend of the Man-eater*, Delhi: Ravi Dayal, 1993.
Sleeman, W., *Rambles and Recollections of an Indian Official*, 1844; rpnt. Karachi: Oxford University Press, 1980.
Smout, T.C., *A History of the Scottish People, 1560–1830*, London: Collins, 1969.
Stebbing, E.P., 'Review of WS Burke. "The Indian Shikar Field Book"', *Indian Forester*, vol. 32 (1906).
Stracey, P.D., *Wildlife in India—Its Conservation and Control*, Delhi: Manager of Publications, 1963.
Sukumar, R., 'The Management of Large Mammals in Relation to Male Strategies and Conflicts with People', *Biological Conservation*, vol. 55 (1991).
Thapar, V., *The Tiger's Destiny*, London: Elm Tree Books, 1994.
Thomas, K.V., *Man and the Natural World: Changing Attitudes in England, 1500–1800*, Harmondsworth: Penguin, 1983.
Vernede, R.E., *An Ignorant in India*, London: William Blackwood, 1911.
———, *British Life in India*, Delhi: Oxford University Press, 1995.
Williamson, T., *Oriental Field Sports*, London: Edward Orme, 1807–8.
Wilson, Sir Guy Fleetwood *Letters to Nobody, 1908–12*, London: John Murray, 1921.
Worster, D., *Nature's Economy: The Roots of Ecology*, New York: Sierra Club Books, 1977.
Zimen, E., *The Wolf: His Place in the Natural World*, London: 1981.
Zoological Survey of India, *The Red Data Book of Indian Animals, Part I: Vertebrata*, Calcutta: 1994.

3

From Princely Symbol to Conservation Icon

A Political History of the Lion in India

Appointment with a Lion

One March evening in 1973, arriving in the Gir Forest—the last abode of lions in the wild outside Africa—a veteran Indian journalist, Saeed Naqvi, penned this thought: 'We would have to be off within minutes to keep a date with a lion who had been kept waiting for us about five miles away. This intrigued me. However publicity-minded the beast, I could not for the life of me understand how a lion could be kept waiting to keep an appointment with the Fourth Estate. I mean I would have understood if it were a zoo or a circus lion. But in the Gir Forest?'[1] Naqvi's bafflement was far from singular. In the Gir Forest, visitors can still view lions on foot: until recently, baits were put out to entice the big cats towards tourists.

In our ecology-conscious age, experiencing the wild as a spectacle over an evening visit to the forest may seem perfectly logical to

This paper is part of a larger study. I am obliged to Romila Thapar, A. Srivastava, R. Sukumar, Ullas Karanth, Divyabhanusinh, Dunu Roy, R. D'Souza, M.K. Ranjitsinh, Ravi Chellam, and Valmik Thapar. I owe a special word of thanks to the staff of the National Archives of India, particularly Dr Pradeep Mehra and Mr Rajmani, who went out of their way to help me. I am grateful to all of them. The usual disclaimers apply.

[1] Naqvi, 'Hard Life and Mean Death'.

many. But such intimacy between a huge forest predator and his human viewers is a relatively recent development. The 'friendly Gir lion' is a product of developments since 1947.

Things had not always been like this. Earlier, a few lions were shot every year by the local ruler, the Nawab of Junagadh, and his guests. A century ago, the idea of lion conservation would have sounded fanciful to princes and officials. The extermination of carnivores across the Indian countryside was seen as a proof of progress. From a creature to be feared, the lion became a princely symbol, and finally a conservation icon. These changes can provide insights into the problems of coexistence of people with a great terrestrial carnivore. The species' near-total extermination in the nineteenth century raises questions about who played the prime role—officials or herders. Similarly, few have asked how far princely models of conservation have left an imprint on practices in independent India. The big cat's relations with those who shared its forest home can reveal if local forms of land-use helped it survive in the Gir Forest. This history is more than backdrop to the present predicament: it can guide the shape of the future. What lions mean to people has changed in profound ways. With the decrease of its number, the animal and its habitat have become the subject and site of conflicts.

'The King of the Deer'

The lion became a symbol of power early in human history. The mane of males who roar virtually every night made the animal hard to miss and easy to be impressed by. But its presence in large parts of South Asia in cultural artifacts was more extensive than its physical range in the subcontinent. It was perhaps only rivalled in its power over the human imagination in India by the tiger. The earliest signs of the lion as a species go back to the Pleistocene era, with remains having been found in Bankura in western Bengal.[2]

[2] Sahu, *From Hunters to Breeders,* pp. 72–3. Recent DNA-based work has shed new light on the origins and diffusion of the lion from southern Africa

The Asian sub-species (*Panthera leo persica*) probably branched off from the African lion (*Panthera leo leo*) 100,000 years ago and was present in India by about 40,000 years ago. The lion was probably a later arrival in the region than the tiger: even after the colonization of habitat reached its apogee, the tiger had a more extensive range. Lions were not found east of Bihar or south of the river Narmada. Given that the two species are roughly the same size and weight, it is likely that, even if they lived in adjacent tracts, their ranges did not fully coincide.

The imagery of the lion in human history was more complex. It was not as prominent five millennia ago in Harappan culture as its striped cousin. The depictions of tigers in Harappa are widely known but there are also two-headed lion figurines.[3] The tiger lived in the galley forests along the Indus river, but lions were in the drier hinterland, not so far away. The lion was described in Sanskrit lore as *mrigaraja* or the king of the deer. Man was at the apex of the inhabitants of cultivated spaces, or *grama*, the lion held sway over the *aranya* (the forest). Descriptions of the lion in literature suggest a greater familiarity with it than its depictions in stone. The latter were often highly stylized, not only in southern India, where there were no lions, but even in the north. Buddhist traditions compare the first sermon of the Enlightened One to the roar of a lion and indicate a sense of awe at that most unmistakable trait of the great cat, its roar. Ascetics used the same lion symbolism as kings but for very different ends. By the time three lions figured in the famous capital of the Mauryan ruler Asoka in the third century BC, they were closely associated with power and royalty.[4] Dating Sanskrit or Pali texts is more difficult than putting a firm time to material evidence. But there is little reason to suppose that the imagery of

---

into Asia, and on to Iran and India. See Barnett, *et al.*, 'The Origin, Current Diversity'.

[3] Iyer, *Animals in Indian Sculpture*, p. 65.

[4] Divyabhanusinh, *The End of a Trail*, p. 23; Monier Williams, *A Sanskrit–English Dictionary*, pp. 1036, 1217.

the animal was simply a Western import, from Hellenic or Roman influences.

At a time when hunters used bows, arrows, and spears, encounters with wild animals were seen as proof of valour. This was all the more so given the frequency of its conflict with livestock. Tigers and lions were both markers of royalty. After his conquest of Kathiawar, Chandragupta (d. AD 414) issued coins bearing the title 'lion slayer'. His father, Samudragupta, assumed a similar title, 'slayer of tigers', soon after his conquest of the Ganga valley.[5] The maned big cat was found in the Kathiawar peninsula, where there were no tigers.

The lion's fondness for cattle could be its undoing. Hunters shot poisoned arrows from platforms mounted on trees near fields or waterholes. It was even easier to kill them 'by placing the carcass of a cow in a suitable position.'[6] Such literary references were added to by Afghan and Mughal rulers in northern India. A Rajput prince saved the life of Jahangir (r. 1605–27) in the hunting reserve of Madari Bagh near Agra. The latter wrote of how Anoop Rai 'was heading the men who were with him in the hunt when he saw a half-eaten bullock. Near it a powerful lion got out of a clump and went off . . .' For saving the emperor's life at great personal risk he was given the title of *Ani rai singh dalan*, or commander of an army and slayer of lions.[7]

Two things are clear from a brief foray across the ages. Lion–human relations had their points of tension. Preying upon milch or draught cattle led to friction. Still, no single region in India had a history of man-eating lions in quite the way in which the Sundarbans of the Bengal delta were known for harbouring

[5] Majumdar and Altekar, *The Gupta-Vakataka Age*, p. 168.

[6] Chand, *Syainkyasastra, Rudra Deva of Kumaon*, pp. 186–8. The sixteenth-century text is based on older traditions and lore of the hunt.

[7] Welch, *India, Art and Culture*, pp. 187–8. The illustration of the hunt in 1610 clearly shows a lion and not a tiger. The usual translation of a tiger is incorrect. See Rogers and Beveridge, *Tuzuk i Jahangiri, Volume I*, pp. 185–8.

dangerous tigers. The lion was the scourge of domestic animals rather than people. Besides, the tiger was never entirely out of the picture. The lion was ubiquitous as a symbol of royalty and was given a pride of place in lore and text—Sanskrit and Tamil, Pali and Persian. Tigers were probably more prominent in southern India, where lions were not to be found. Tipu Sultan (d. 1799) actually sat on a tiger throne, the only Indian ruler ever to do so. This has even been seen as a bid to bind his kingdom more closely with worshippers of tiger-riding deities. In virtually every other case on record it was lions that decorated the ruler's seat. The word *simhasana* (seat of the lion) was meant quite literally. Even in Tipu's Mysore, his favourite shrine in Penukonda was said to have been guarded by a tiger. Yet the deity within was one of a *baba* (holy man) riding a lion.[8] Perhaps the sheer presence of the latter in the Indian landscape, its prominent mane, and its roar made it overwhelmingly emblematic. But the very visibility of the species was to become the key to its rapid eclipse. It was ironic that this coincided with the rise to prominence of the British, whose emblem too was a lion.

'The Ardour of Sport'

India was at the eastern edge of the lion's global range and it vanished once modern weapons magnified the ability of people to hunt it down. Its very preference for more open habitat, low scrub jungle, and open plain made it highly vulnerable. The contrast with the tiger was lucidly explained in the diary of a surveyor, Thomas White, in May 1809. The hills north of Ambala in the Punjab were 'covered with brushwood, bamboo and the high grass jungle . . . elephants, bears, wolves and tigers inhabit them but no lions, from whence it is conjectured that those seen at Patialah must have come up from the south.'[9] Lions had never been

[8] Brittlebank, *Tipu Sultan's Search*, p. 143.

[9] Phillimore, *Historical Records of the Survey of India, Vol. II*, p. 68: Francis White, 28 May 1809.

common in the great sal forests to the east. When a lion was killed in Palamau in the Chhotanagpur plateau five years later, none of the villagers could even identify it. The British magistrate of Ramgarh identified it as a straggler from the west.[10] The animals moved in from adjacent tracts with breeding populations. Where there were so few, they were quickly wiped out. The rough rule of thumb of tigers in the wooded hills and lions in the plains works, but only up to a point. Even in the hills it was easier to shoot lions than wary tigers.[11] The former was also easily shot in the plains. Along the river Sabarmati, Benjamin Howe was amazed at how 'antelopes are by the thousands in every direction and foxes, jackals and hyenas innumerable. I saw several skins of lions but did not see one alive . . . I understand there are an abundance (of them).'[12] In dry grasslands they could be bagged from elephant back. Villagers joined in beats seeking lion meat to 'become strong'. Lion fat was used to cure rheumatism and Wagri tribals relished its flesh.[13] Cattle-lifting made them unpopular where herding was the main livelihood. A companion of Bartle Frere recalled how 'We brought four lions on our cart as a result of the day's sport to the great admiration of the villagers.'[14]

Hunters with better rifles gunned down whole prides. Andrew Fraser alone killed eighty-four lions.[15] A bag of 300 lions was the all-time Indian record. George Acland Smith shot fifty of these in the Delhi region in 1857–8.[16] Tigers were killed in even greater numbers,[17] but their relative shyness was to be a great asset in the

[10] Hamilton, *East India Gazetteer, Vol. II*, p. 359.

[11] Forbes, *Oriental Memoirs, Vol. II*, 1813, pp. 91–5.

[12] Government of Bombay, *Selections from the Records*, p. 79.

[13] Dewar, *Beasts of an Indian Village*, pp. 72–4; Forbes, *Memoirs, Vol. II*, p. 95.

[14] Martineau, *The Life and Correspondence of the Rt. Hon. Sir Bartle Frere, Vol. I*, p. 33.

[15] Mundy, *Pen and Pencil Sketches*, p. 329.

[16] Kinnear, 'The Past and Present Distribution of the Lion', p. 38.

[17] Ibid.

struggle for survival. The last lion in Sindh was killed in 1842, while the tiger lingered till the eve of World War I. Much of the lion habitat lay within princely states like Bahawalpur, where the maharaja shot the last specimen in 1800.[18] Ranjit Singh's soldiers bayoneted big cats near Lahore.[19] The Patiala hunt was a warlike campaign in which 400 horsemen beat vast plains teeming with antelope and nilgai.[20] Such large hunts would have had little impact if the population had had time to recover.

Decline was uneven but inexorable. By the 1870s there were lions only in Gwalior, Mount Abu, and Gujarat, all in hilly country. The animal vanished with agrarian extension and the coming of the railways. Its rarity only whetted the appetite of hunters. Hills were safer for the lion than plains, but only for a while. Ten lions were shot in Kotah in Rajasthan in 1866. One fell to railway engineers in Rewa in Central India. The railway helped hunters strike the last blow against the few prides that remained in the highlands.[21] Bounties were now given by the British and some Indian rulers to wipe out 'dangerous beasts'. Villagers sometimes refused to help hunt the tiger, but not the other great cat, probably due to its fondness for cattle.[22] The regional names by which lions were known show they were once common across a wide swathe. The terms used include the Harriana lion (in the 1820s) and 'the lion of Gwalior and Rajpootana' (1885). But it was the Gujarat or Kathiawar label that stuck.[23] It was to be more than just that, for by the end of the 1880s there were none alive elsewhere in India. Though some survived in parts of Iraq and Iran till later, the populations were not viable.

The lion vanished in the plains before it did in the hills, and in British India before the princely states. It survived longest in the

[18] Roberts, *The Mammals of Pakistan*, p. 156.

[19] Vigne, *A Personal Narrative, Vol. I*, pp. 13–14.

[20] Jacquemont, *Letters from India, Vol. II*, pp. 202–3: Letter, May 1830.

[21] Blanford, 'Zoological Notes', pp. 189–97.

[22] Kinnear, 'The Past and Present Distribution of the Lion'; on bounties, see Rangarajan, 'The Raj and the Natural World'.

[23] Balfour, *The Cyclopedia of India*, p. 719.

forests of western and central India. The prides were wiped out in a matter of decades, being confined to one small part of a once-vast range. Herders assisted British officials and Indian princes in the extermination. Only one small forest remained where its roar still echoed across the land.

'Mountains and Stony Regions'

When Prince Victor Albert visited India in 1890, the only place where he could hunt lions was the Gir Forest in Kathiawar. Also known as Saurashtra, the peninsula was easily accessible by sea. It was easy to land at Veraval on the shores of the Arabian Sea and journey to the hills, where the big cats still roamed. Senior officials vied with each other to be granted a lion. The prince's host, the Nawab of Junagadh, left no stone unturned, this being the first visit to his kingdom by anyone from the British royal family. No lion fell to the royal rifle, but not for want of effort.[24] The transformation of the Gir hills into a royal hunting ground was itself a recent development. Even a few decades earlier, it had been a marcher area, keenly contested between rival rulers and seen as a source of disorder.

The peninsula was a mainly pastoral region even in Mughal times. The Persian chronicler of the *Mirat i Ahmadi* described it accurately. 'There are', he wrote, 'mountains and stony regions. A slight drizzle makes the soil slippery which makes passing over it very difficult. But some of the mountains and places have mango trees, rayan trees, tamarind trees and forests of acacia. It is a mine of Kathi horses.' In Akbar's day the Mughals knew of the Gir Forest and trapped cheetahs in Nawanagar, also in the peninsula. Interestingly, through all this time, the term Kathiawar was applied to one of the subdivisions of the peninsula, which as a whole was called Sorath. The faujdar (administrator) of Sorath was stationed at Junagadh, an old centre of power from pre-Mughal times. The

[24] Fenton, 'The Kathiawar Lion', p. 744; Wilberforce-Bell, *History of Kathiawad*, p. 244.

Babi Pathans, who founded the dynasty of Junagadh after the break-up of the Mughal empire in the eighteenth century, inherited the dream of dominating the entire region that had once been the Mughal province of Sorath.[25]

A former British Political Agent had complained of 'not having a map to refer to, of at least one half of the territory.'[26] Yet, it was not maps that were a major source of anxiety in the region. Rival states contended for territorial control. The founder of Junagadh, Sher Khan Babi (d. 1758), and his successors had to contend with the territorial expansion of the Gaekwads of Baroda. Junagadh had to pay a double tribute to the Baroda rulers and to the Peshwas of Pune. But in 1808 the British imposed their own terms, putting an end to military expeditions by powers not based in the peninsula. The Peshwa's rights lapsed after his defeat in 1817, and the Gaekwad's tribute was collected and paid to him by the Bombay government. The nawab, in any case, ruled the largest state in Kathiawar, and many of the smaller feudatories paid him a tribute called *zortalabee*.

Among other rulers of some importance was Bhavnagar, under the Gohel Rajputs. The nawab collected tribute from the smaller state of Nawanagar, and from a host of vassals. The peninsula was divided both vertically, in territories of the princely states, and horizontally, with several layers of intermediaries between the ruler of a state and the ruled. Borders could not be changed through war once the British asserted their hegemony but princes could petition the Raj. Gir was a central bone of contention between the nawab and the Gaekwads. Neither had ever fully controlled the forest. The first Dewan (chief minister) of Junagadh, Amarji, had led military expeditions into the hills in the 1780s. Four decades later, Kathi raiders found refuge in the forest after raids on nearby

[25] Lokhandwala, *Mirat i Ahmadi, Vol. II*, p. 153; for a Mughal reference, see Habib, *An Atlas of the Mughal Empire*, Sheet & B, Gujarat, Economic and Notes, p. 25.

[26] Commissariat, *A History of Gujarat, Vol. II*, pp. 435, 552–3; Wilberforce-Bell, *History of Kathiawad*, pp. 139–40.

Bhavnagar. The Gaekwads gained sole control of the Korinar Gir, but no settlement was made of the territories to the north. Dewan Vittal Rao encouraged 'his subordinates to work to clear the jungle and make a road through the Gheer' and bring in settlers. This would reinforce the Gaekwads' claims to the area. Even in the 1800s, the area was not really controlled by either party and was 'an impenetrable jungle and a notorious asylum for robbers and outlaws.'[27] Junagadh, in turn, claimed that 'the Gaekwar *sarkar* has already taken control of some of our villages.'[28]

Gir remained a refuge for raiders till as late as the 1860s, when a major military expedition was mounted involving local princely troops led by a British colonel. A military garrison was permanently stationed at Rajkot. This creation of firm lines of territory on the ground was itself a necessity for the British, who had to settle disputes between the subordinate powers. But the Gir case kept simmering for a long time. The nature of the dispute changed as the border laid down by the British had to be accepted by the tributary powers. Instead, the parties to the dispute each claimed the other had trespassed on its lands. This itself was significant: dual or triple sovereignty was drawing to an end. Earlier, some smaller feudatories paid dues to the Peshwa, to the Gaekwads, and to Junagadh. Most of the Gir Forest was in Junagadh, with Baroda in charge of a small area in Amreli. Smaller tracts were under the Kathi rulers of Jetpur and Bilkha. The Raj preferred to freeze the claims and recognize the rights of the possessor: in general this was to Junagadh's advantage.

The extension of the agrarian frontier was a matter of concern. The British distrusted itinerant groups, wishing to bind them down to a fixed abode whenever feasible. But the Gir area had long been a

[27] National Archives of India, New Delhi, India (hereafter NAI), Foreign Dept, Internal A, June 1888, nos 121–37, 'Memorial from HH the Gaekwar of Baroda regarding the Gheer boundary case': Memo, Dewan, Baroda, Qazi Shabuddin, 3 April 1886; Keep-With Notes, No. 1: Captain Evans-Gordon, 22 February 1888. This file is hereafter referred to as the Gir Case.

[28] Gir Case, Appendix 31, p. 109: Govindji, Junagarh, 14 April 1852.

region of 'pastoral character', breeding valuable plough and milch cattle. Cattle-breeding was linked to wider market economies: a pair of Gir cows cost as much as forty pound sterling even in 1820. Significantly, even tribute was paid in the form of honey and hides; the skins, fat, and claws of lions; and soap nuts. Of course, the largest chunk of revenues came from grazing fees, often farmed out to revenue contractors (*ijaradars*).[29] Farm produce was not the main form of wealth and the surplus was skimmed off in other ways. During droughts cattle 'from many miles round' grazed in the forest.[30]

Livestock and wild game were among the major products of the Gir hills. Frontiers were fluid, resulting in conflicts. The nawab and the Gaekwad claimed that the other ruler was illegally harvesting grass or wood. The border had been defined, but who would use which lands was often unclear on the ground. In fact, a more fixed and absolute notion of property was congealing via such disputes. The nawab alleged that cattle from Korinar grazed in his fields. His watchman even 'took away the clothes of the herdsmen' to discourage entry. There were problems within the territories and Makrani and Sindhi intermediaries found it hard to get the semi-nomadic herders to pay taxes.[31] The British pressed for tighter control. Colonel Lang warned the Amreli officials: 'The Rabris and Charans live in your limits in scattered neyses, where the outlaws find shelter, which leads to the commission of more crimes. These neyses should therefore be removed and one or two big neyses should be built for them there or near a village, and a thana should be placed there.'[32] Though the proposal was not

[29] Tod, *Travels*, pp. 324–5; for collection of tribute, Desai, *The Forest of Gir*, pp. 18–20.

[30] Le Grand, Report upon the General Condition of Kateewar in 1842, p. 10.

[31] Gir Case, App. 46, p. 127: Nawab to Political Agent, 21 September 1854; Desai, *Forest of Gir*, p. 21.

[32] Gir Case, App. 26, p. 87: Col. Lang to the Vahiwatdar of Amreli, Baroda Gir, 20 December 1848; on Gir and raids, see Wilberforce-Bell, pp. 198–216.

acted on, this was the first time a regrouping of graziers had been suggested on strategic grounds. Progress on this count was far from smooth. Permanence of abode mattered to the British: cultivation meant revenue and villages as opposed to mobile settlements meant 'order'.

There was some commonality of interests between the nawab and the British. With 300 nesses in the Junagadh Gir, he had not been able to found too many permanent villages.[33] But things were changing. By 1899 the forest generated as much as Rs 100,000 annually. A fresh revenue settlement of the Junagadh Gir now aimed at populating arable patches in the forest. Survey Officer Harprasad Desai demarcated lands to be retained under tree cover to provide timber, grazing, and game. Cultivators from Gondal and Nawanagar were encouraged to colonize thinly forested lands. Forest and farm were being demarcated as different landscapes, each with a distinctive role to play in productive terms. New settlers like Kunbi Patels, Lohana Muslims, and Ahirs established thirty-two new villages. They were regarded as more productive than the Maldharis (graziers), Labadis (woodcutters), and Siddis (descendants of Abyssinian slaves).[34] A grant of revenue-free land was made to a group of Siddis to help provide for the *dargah* (shrine) of Jambur Pir, the saint of Jambur. They sowed fresh lands and prayed for the ruler's success.[35]

Agrarian expansion could have led to irreconcilable conflict with the lion and the graziers. But there was a change in the perception of the animal—from a pest to a game species to be nurtured for

---

The neysses (or nesses) were stockaded settlements; they were transient in nature until very recently—since the 1960s—when they became permanent. They were and are inhabited by buffalo-keeping pastoralists known by the generic term 'maldharis'.

[33] Gir Case, Col. Lester, January 1867, quoted in Memo, Dewan, Baroda, 3 April 1886.

[34] Desai, *Forest of Gir*, pp. 24–5, 34–5.

[35] Trivedi, *Census of India, Vol. V, Part V-B, No. 1*, pp. 7–9.

princely hunts. This was to have major implications for the herders of the Gir Forest, though of course the change did not happen overnight.

There were tensions between carnivores and both cultivators and herders. Rulers in Kathiawar rewarded the killing of lions till around 1870. Sixteen lions were killed in three years, bounties being paid to their hunters.[36] Given the depredations on cattle, this may have been welcomed by herders. Prides mostly lived off wild prey: the nilgai, sambar, and wild boar, but lions also often killed stray buffaloes. Locally the predator was called *sawaj*, 'the one who makes flocks bleat'. Herders stockaded cattle at night to minimize attack. Though individual lions continued to be shot, their growing rarity made them worth more alive than dead to the nawab. Lions as a species had to survive if only a few were allowed to be shot for sport. Most of Gir had been decisively assigned to the nawab. Anyone who wanted to hunt in the forest required the ruler's nod. Access to the forest meant a prized trophy for British officers, and Junagadh's rulers were too canny to let a trump card slip out of their hands. Even the nesses had their uses for sportsmen. It was easiest to shoot a big cat by sitting up over a kill or by using a buffalo calf as bait.[37] The day of bounty-hunting was at an end. This was not conservation for its own sake; it was clearly self-interest at work.

[36] NAI, Home (Public), September 1871, A, nos 43–72, no. 47: 'Statement showing the amount of rewards granted for destruction of wild beasts from the Kattywar Political Agency Treasury, Krishnagee Luximon, Asst to Pol. Agent, 10 June 1870'. Despite the contention that lions were imported, captive-bred, and released into the Gir Forest, there is no documentary or pictorial evidence to support this hypothesis: Thapar, 'The Last Lions'. In fact a detailed study of the Junagadh archives and sources found evidence of protection but none of captive release: Divyabhanusinh, *The Story of Asia's Lions*. This issue of their genetic character is well argued in a paper that synthesizes evidence that Asia's lions descended from ancestors in Africa. The Asian and North African populations are closely related. See Barnett, *et al.*, 'The Origin, Current Diversity', pp. 2119–25.

[37] Campbell, *Gazetteer of the Bombay Presidency, Vol. VIII*, pp. 100–1; Rice, *Indian Game*, p. 139.

The value of the feline as a trophy aided its survival, just as it had earlier hastened extermination. The presence of prides also helped save the Gir from axe and plough: the forest was of more value to the ruler if it continued to harbour lions.

Lions had a brush with extinction in their last stronghold. There were only a dozen by the mid-1880s, though the court may have understated the actual numbers to keep sportsmen at bay.[38] Areas like Chotilla, Than, and Baranbor had too little cover for large wild animals. The 1800 sq mile Gir was a malarial tract, visited by hunters from winter till the monsoons. Watersheds of several rivers lay in the highlands, and were seen as the key to productive agriculture in the plains.[39] The lion's survival still hinged on the restraint of sportsmen and the will of the nawab. Given the contentious history of the Gir Forest, till so recently a disputed territory, the nawab had his work cut out. Unlike the tiger, the lion did not have a uniformly negative image in British eyes. When Curzon visited the area as viceroy in November 1900, preparations were made for a big shoot. But he demurred. He was aware that 'Up till the time of the Mutiny, lions were shot in central India. They are now confined to an ever-narrowing patch of forest in Kathiawar. I was on the verge of contributing still further to their reduction in numbers but fortunately I found out my mistake in time, and was able to adopt a restraint which I hope that others will follow.'[40]

The lion's fate was now linked to that of the Babi dynasty. Intent on guarding their hunting estate they drew on viceregal support. Captain Carter laid the foundation stone of a hunting lodge at Malkana and was presented with 'a silver trowel, square and plummet weighing 80 tolas.' The Bombay governor, Lord Lamington, enjoyed shikar in Gir. A forest officer from the Bombay

[38] Gee, *The Wildlife of India*, p. 79.

[39] Campbell, *Gazetteer of the Bombay Presidency, Vol. VIII*, p. 94; Wilson, 'A Run through Kathiawar', p. 217.

[40] NAI, Home (Public), August 1904, C, no. 15, 'Gov. Gen. Reply to the Memorial of the Burma Game Preservation Association', no date.

cadre was deputed to help in 'the preservation and development on scientific lines' of the forest.[41] The wheel had come full circle. Two generations earlier, the forest had been a refuge for outlaw and rebel, a place beyond the reach of the new imperial power. Now it saw hunts of a very different sort, with the nawab's guests indulging in a ritual within which a royal beast was the quarry. Junagadh seemed to have got its way by using the lion as a bargaining chip. His neighbours and underlings had other plans. Prides often crossed state boundaries. It was not easy to determine who had rights over them. Due to the older rivalry over Gir, lions became pawns on the political chessboard.

'A Rare Treasure of His Estate'

Protection could not have begun at a worse time. Rains failed in both 1899 and 1900. All living lions were royal game. But they now became a major menace to cattle and even humans. Protection spurred resentment when people suffered losses, and to complicate matters Junagadh's neighbours used the issue to question his claims to ownership over wild animals. Carnivores wandered out of the forest in search of food. There were anxieties that their numbers had increased due to 'strict protection'. A more complex set of changes lay behind the escalation in attacks. The forest staff poached wild prey like the chital, sambar, and wild boar. Even cattle in the forest perished in the drought. Lions did not recognize man-made administrative boundaries and moved out of Gir.[42] They had imposed a virtual 'reign of terror' in Ghantawad district. Junagadh's subjects were in line: 31 people were mauled and 3 killed by lions in 1902 alone. In 1904 lions mauled 11 and caused the death of another 29 people. Rasulkhanji now allowed the shooting of animals, though the effort was to kill as few as possible. His men beat drums and let off firecrackers to drive 'errant'

[41] NAI, Foreign Dept, July 1902, Internal B, nos 166–7: S.W. Edgerly, Chief Sec., Bombay, to Sec., Foreign Dept, 14 June 1902; Copland, *The British Raj*, p. 237.

[42] Fenton, *The Rifle in India*, p. 7.

animals back into the forest. Losses of goats, cows, and buffaloes were compensated in the Junagadh Gir.[43] The nawab refused to compensate losses outside his territories, even as he protested efforts to eliminate lions. These were mutually contradictory claims. All lions were claimed as the exclusive property of the dynasty, but the consequences of their actions were not to be redressed except in the home state. So, lions became mobile royal markers of Junagadh whom no one else was to harm. The viceroy was backing the nawab. But when a number of goats were killed in Jetpur, its ruler demanded 'That Junagadh should stock his own forests with goats to attract lions back to it.' No compensation was paid and, needless to add, no goats were raised in the forest! In the Korinar Gir, which was under Baroda, things took a turn for the worse. Two men were killed when defending their herds of cattle from attack. The maharaja reserved the right to specify which individual specimens could be destroyed to safeguard the lives of people and stock. But the immediate provocation for conflict between the rival rulers disappeared as wild prey recovered and the annual cycles of the monsoon returned to normal. The crisis passed as quickly as it had arisen. Looking back, Wynter-Blyth would remark how 'it was during these years that the habits of the lions underwent a profound change for never again are they heard of as a menace to human life.'[44]

There was no end to disputes over the ownership of lions. The shoot that provoked the most strident protest involved the cricketer prince Ranjitsinhji of Nawanagar. In March 1906 he tracked and shot two lions in a dry stream bed in Gir. Edward Stebbing, the influential forester, did not mince his words when he said these were not the acts of sportsmen but of 'slayers'. All zoologists and sportsmen had to unite 'to preserve the few that remain from the hand of the butcher.' [45] The Gir lions were the first wild carnivores in the world to win protection. Yet the assertion of royal right to a

43 Wynter-Blyth, 'The History of the Lion', p. 468.

44 Ibid., p. 469.

45 Stebbing, 'The Gir Forest Lions', pp. 159–60.

large wild animal was not new and was known in several princely states with wild tigers.[46] What made the Gir different was its uniqueness: nowhere else in the world was there perhaps such a close link between hunting interests and the survival of a wild carnivore. Not at this time.

Controversy could be amusing. The prince of Bikaner, Sadul Singh, had shot thirty-three tigers and forty-one panthers but 'only one lion'. He had sought to 'make up' by bagging African lions, but his record book was incomplete. Since Junagadh refused him an invitation, he went lion hunting in the Jetpur Gir. His quarry vanished as Junagadh men fired off blanks 'to frighten away the lion if he was anywhere near us.' Forest guards even mutilated the body of a leopard shot by another visitor.[47] Still, there was no better place to go than the nawab's dominions. The accession of Mahabat Khan (1900–49) in 1922 enabled the Bikaner prince to wangle an invitation to Junagadh. Sadul Singh grumbled about the attitude of his guides: 'I rather think they did not try very hard for a lion today as father and I are allowed to shoot only one lion each. If I had shot one today, they were afraid I would go off and bag another in Jitpur . . . it is all for the best, I think, because we are now on good terms with the Junagarh people.' [48]

Strict quotas made a lion trophy a mirage for most sportsmen. The Gohel Rajput rulers of Bhavnagar took a leaf out of the nawab's book. The last lions in their state had been shot out in the Sihor hills in 1857. Occasional stragglers still wandered across into the Mytiala hills at the eastern edge of the Gir highland system much

[46] Ranjitsinh, *Beyond the Tiger*, p. 32. For instance, in Udaipur, only the Rana and the sixteen major noble families were allowed to shoot tigers.

[47] Big Game Diary of Sadul Singh of Bikaner, unpublished, p. 35: entry on the shoot in Jetpur Gir, June 1921; Wynter-Blyth, 'The History of the Lion', p. 470.

[48] Sadul Singh, Diary, p. 38: 21 March 1922. Neighbouring states such as Junagadh, Bhavnagar, and Baroda, and the smaller principalities had 'turf wars' over who had prior right to shoot the lions. But protection to peripatetic animals was accorded priority only by Junagadh and Bhavnagar.

later. 'Since the forest was so poor and lacking in water', they rarely stayed on. In the 1920s the ruler Krishna Kumarsinhji began serious efforts to attract lions into the area. 'Strict preservation' of the forest made it an 'ideal resort' for lions. This was well within the rubric of a shikar ethos and the rewards were rich: twenty-three lions were shot in the area by 1946. Hunters after 1929 spared lionesses. Bhavnagar beat Junagadh at its own game. The British Army officer Col. A.E. Mosse and the big-game hunter W.S. Burke bagged trophies 'without recourse to the Nawab'. When asked where Bhavnagar's lands began, visitors pointed to the border 'where trees and game could be seen'. Expert *pagis* (trackers) assisted in hunts in the Mytiala Lion Reserve.[49]

But this was a sideshow to Junagadh, where lions were a powerful cultural and political icon. The Sunni Muslim dynasty had chosen its symbol well. The lion had a deep symbolic significance in local lore, syncretic and orthodox, caste Hindu and nomadic. Nor was the local imagery of the lion always negative. The forest included the temples of Tulsishyam and Kankeshwari. In the latter case, the Maldharis believed of the goddess that 'she holds an ox in one hand and a lion in the other/ none can dare cross the line drawn by the mother.'[50] Maldhari was a generic term for herders. One group of cattle-keepers who called themselves Charans had also been the bards of Rajputs. They worshipped the goddess Bhavani, whose mount was a lion.[51] The Siddis, who were Muslims, sang of how their children were as brave as lions.[52] Animosity towards lions had its limits. Gir was still only lightly administered and the ruler had to appeal to those who lived within the bounds of the forest. The lion was a link with those who saw the Gir as a living space.

[49] Dharamkumarsinhji, 'The Lion in Bhavnagar State', p. 693; NAI, WISA (Western India States Agency), f. no. D/2-1, 1944, 'Annual Administrative reports of Indian states': *Report on the Administration of Bhavnagar state for the year 1936–37*, State Printing Press, 1939, p. 39.

[50] Desai, *Forest of Gir*, p. 59.

[51] Desai, *Maldharis of Saurashtra*, p. 52.

[52] Trivedi, *Siddi*, p. 33.

Most, though not all, communities in the forest were vegetarian, and there was no direct conflict over the hunting rights exercised by the nawab. Though relations were not idyllic, conflicts were largely confined to the payment of taxes.

'A Good Deal of Work to be Done'

By the late 1920s Gir was famous as the lion's last home. Threats to their survival did not vanish. The lion was now to become a matter of wider concern with the advent, for the first time, of imperial conservation lobbies based in London. The efforts to limit hunting and safeguard their existence gained further support from the Raj just as British rule itself was threatened with extinction. Mahabat Khan even used lion imagery to advance his regional aspirations. The first postage stamp in India featuring a wild animal was that of a Gir Forest lion. Significantly, the Junagadh stamp had the words 'Sorath sarkar' (Government of Sorath) inscribed on it. This was the only princely state in the region to lay claim to the entire peninsula. It was a dream that could not be realized in life but was hinted at in art.[53] The royal seal approved of by the Western India States Agency in 1931 showed a lion in the foreground. Behind the royal beast lay two mountains and ships sailing in the sea.[54] Both the seal and the stamp were modern innovations, but they expressed older claims of the house of the Babis.

Junagadh faced serious problems with adjacent states when it equated its own interest with that of the lion's survival. Improved rail and road links had made travel to and from the forests much easier. A narrow gauge rail line reached Talala by the end of the First World War. A hunting party drove down from Sasan, the main hunting lodge, to Jetpur in just forty minutes in a Model T Ford:

[53] Divyabhanusinh, 'Asiatic Lion on a Postage Stamp'. The same year saw Junagadh issue a stamp of another distinctive local breed, the Kathi horse.

[54] NAI, WISA, serial no. 9, file no. 8a, 1931, 'Grant of dignity to the Thakur sahib of Limbdi and GIC to the Nawab of Junagarh': Amir Shaikh Mohammad Bhai to Asst to Gov. Gen., 2 June 1931.

the automobile had reached the land of the lion.[55] Sport remained a priority. The lions, in turn, were increasingly wary. If they sensed the approach of hunters, they 'gave vent to depart'. It required all the skills of the *pagis* to lead sport-hunters to their quarry. Often, they commenced work in the pre-dawn darkness, locating lions by their roars. The pug marks were then tracked through forest paths. Coming across a sleeping lion, a tracker would dissemble and 'emit the loud wail or yodel-like sound' of buffalo graziers, this being familiar to the big cats. Lions were rarely bothered by the movements of graziers, who seldom troubled them.[56] So familiar were the *pagis* with individual lions that, even before his shoot, the Earl of Ronaldshay heard of the chosen target, 'a well known, unusually big, old and grey lion'.[57]

There were fresh anxieties for the future of the species. A prescient sportsman had expressed his anxieties in the early 1920s. Col. Fenton went so far as to write that 'I am afraid the day is not far off when the Indian lion will become extinct.' He had little faith in the efficacy of protection. The Rabaris killed cubs; their cattle numbers were far too high and a lot of hunting was done on the quiet. The remedy: a sanctuary for all wild animals, a 600 sq mile tract freed of hunters and graziers.[58] Fenton's fears were soon being expressed by far more influential figures. A member of the English aristocracy got a London-based lobby for fauna involved in favour of lions. In 1936 the Earl of Onslow wrote to the Secretary of State on the matter of the 'Asiatic lions of Junagadh state'. Aristocrats who sought a role as the moral conscience of empire on wildlife matters dominated the Society for the Preservation of Fauna in the Empire (SPFE), which the earl headed. It was more influential in Africa than in India. Ironically, a class losing its political clout within the United Kingdom was taking up the lost cause of fauna overseas. Onslow's title and kinship ties made

[55] Ronaldshay, *Letters to Nobody*, p. 138.

[56] Dharamkumarsinhji, *Reminiscences of Indian Wildlife*, pp. 74–7.

[57] Ronaldshay, *Letters to Nobody*, p. 140; Sadul Singh, Diary, p. 38.

[58] Fenton, *Rifle*, p. 8.

him a man hard to ignore. He was the brother-in-law of Lord Irwin, viceroy over 1926–31.[59] The Society appreciated Junagadh's conservation-oriented measures. Lions were shot when they strayed outside the state, 'being often enticed by baits for this purpose'. Political officers ought to take up the matter and ensure all local rulers protected the now-rare creature. Zetland replied within a week. 'There was', he confessed, 'a good deal of work to be done.' He hoped for more co-operation between component units of the proposed all-India federation on wildlife matters. The princes and the British could be allies working for the cause of Indian fauna.[60] Any actual intervention was going to be difficult. The Raj rested on getting a degree of co-operation from the various states in the region and its political officers had to tread carefully.

The men on the spot were more confident. However, a closer look shows that inter-state discord was a serious problem. Junagadh had just conducted a rough count of the big cats. Numbers were said to be at an all-time high for the past few decades, with 150 lions in the Junagadh Gir alone. Contrary to fears, even the ruler's guests were taken shooting outside the sanctuary area. In fact, the nawab's men were apt to underestimate the number of lions to be able to resist pressure for hunts from trophy-crazy princes and officials.[61]

Attempts to broker an accord with the other rulers ran into rough weather in 1934. Bhavnagar had agreed not to shoot lionesses, sub-adult males, and cubs. No lions were to be shot within a mile of the inter-state border. Baroda did not even reply. The Maharaja of Gondal flatly refused to 'surrender his rights of shooting lions in his territory.' To make matters more complicated, the Gir Forest

[59] Neumann, 'Dukes, Earls', pp. 79–98.

[60] NAI, Political Dep., Internal A Branch, file no. 33-IA/1937, p. 1: 'Protection and preservation of the wild ass of Cutch state and the last remaining Asiatic lions of Junagarh state': Earl of Onslow to Zetland, 5 November 1936; the reply, 11 November 1936 (henceforth, Lion 1936).

[61] NAI, Lion 1936, Col. Harvey, for the Resident, State of Western India to Sec., Crown Representative, Pol. Dept, Delhi, 12 April 1937.

itself was a patchwork quilt of territories controlled by various ruling houses. In addition to the larger states, there were a number of minor figures: Pithadia, Jetpur, Bilkha, Waghania, Manpur, and Khijadia, to name but a few. These minor chiefs zealously prevented their subjects from hunting lions but organized shoots of their own. The former exemplified the dilemma facing the British. Its chief often called in guests into this fifteen-square-mile enclave in the Gir Forest. There was 'much ill-feeling' between Mahabat Khan and the chief of Pithadia, Vala Mulu Surag. Junagadh asserted that lions were decoyed across the border while the Pithadia chief retorted that the lions bred 'within his limits'. In this case, the Raj simply took over the lease of the patch of forest after the chief's death.[62]

More serious problems arose when prides moved into 'cultivated and inhabited areas' on the perimeter of the forested zone. As many as twenty-eight cattle were killed each year between 1928 and 1936 by big cats outside the reserve. Junagadh was prompt in compensating losses incurred by its own subjects, provided there was no negligence on the part of the cattle owner. Eventually, a broad accord was hammered out. If any lions harmed cattle on a managed estate, 'every endeavour should be made to drive them over the border back into Junagadh territory.' Only if all such attempts came to naught were they to be shot, and that too only on the orders of the local Thanadar or manager.[63] In more than one instance, the Raj backed Junagadh. It was in the nawab's dominions that the lion found refuge. It was a balancing act, but the tilt was very clear.

For the first time, the prey base of the carnivores became a factor taken into account. But an expert who toured the Gir Forest and reported back to the SPFE did not share the optimism of the officials. The East African Game Warden, Keith Caldwell had accompanied the Prince of Wales and his wife on a hunting

[62] Ibid., p. 4: Harvey to Sec., Crown Rep., 16 April 1937.

[63] Ibid., pp. 8–9: Harvey to CCB St John, Pol. Agent, Western Kathiawar Agency, 16 April 1937.

tour of East Africa in the mid 1920s. By drawing on his skills the Society drove home its claim that it had at its disposal a 'body of experience' about fauna and subject peoples. His report was significant, being the first to place the predator's prospects in the context of its prey base. Caldwell estimated there were 200 lions in the jungle, of which 15 were shot annually, two-thirds outside Junagadh. The prides were well protected by 150-odd guards in the reserve, but this was not enough. The crux of the lion question was 'food supply'. The equation was a simple one. 'Two hundred lions need a lot to eat. Even allowing for occasional meatless days, I think I am safe in saying they must kill at least 8,000–10,000 times a year . . . The more they live on a game diet, in lieu of a cattle diet, the better . . . The game in the Forest is being extensively killed . . . In addition such game as I saw seemed quite terrified of cars. The sight of a motor sent everything away at full gallop. So far as I know this always means that game is regularly shot from cars.'[64]

The future of the royal beast hinged on adequate wild prey; or else, conflicts with cattle would intensify. Caldwell's equation was not wide off the mark but he may have been unduly pessimistic. A local naturalist felt the sambar and wild boar were 'rapidly increasing'. Poaching was rare, the cover adequate. What matters of course is not so much the actual situation of the wild herbivores as the fact that their fate began to be seen as crucial to that of the lion.[65] The nawab soon controlled exports of 'lion, lion cubs, lion skins and lucky bones' and 'the horns and antlers' of deer and antelope.[66]

Junagadh pioneered protection to large carnivores and ungulates, in comparison with both contemporaries and beyond India. At

[64] Caldwell, 'The Gir Lions', pp. 63–5; on Africa, see Neumann, op. cit., p. 89.

[65] Dharamkumarsinh, 'The Changing Wildlife of Kathiawar', p. 640.

[66] NAI, WISA V-II, D Branch, no. 195, D-12-2, 1941: 'The preservation of wildlife in India': Dewan, Junagarh to Resident, States of Western India, 24 February 1942.

this time lions were still being killed as dangerous vermin in the Kruger National Park in South Africa, with their skulls lined up for photos outside the park headquarters. Conversely, in the Serengeti game reserve in British East Africa, lions were protected as a tourist attraction—visitors were encouraged to shoot zebras.[67] The princely mode of protection was also more inclusive than the British in terms of animal life. Junagadh's motives were not entirely selfless. The nawab and his guests were at the apex of the food chain. Like any predator, he needed enough 'prey' for the future and had a vested interest in the survival of the population of lions. So that a few could be shot, many more had to live. But the aristocratic or princely model had its limitations. Other rulers in India were not as concerned with deer that were not subject to royal privilege. In Dungarpur, the ruler guarded 'his' tigers but not their prey, the deer.[68] Further, there were often sharp conflicts with local forest users. In the 1920s Madhav Maharaj of Gwalior released African lions brought in from the Sudan in a 1000 square mile reserve in the Sheopur–Shivpuri forest range. They began preying first on cattle and then on 'the inhabitants of hamlets (who) possessed no firearms.' Some lions were shot dead and others moved out of the reserve.[69] Authoritarian conservation could menace tribal and caste Hindu peoples living on the forest edge. Of course, the failure to re-establish the species in Central India only made Gir all the more important for aspiring hunters.

By the 1930s Junagadh acquired a new political import as 'one of the leading Muslim-ruled states in India.'[70] For the first time, the dewan was not a Nagar Brahmin but a Muslim. Abdul Kadir,

[67] Lions were killed as vermin even in the 1920s within Kruger Park. See Carruthers, *Kruger National Park*, p. 110; on the Serengeti of the 1930s and 1940s, Adamson, *Bwana Game*, p. 68.

[68] NAI, Southern Rajputana Agency, serial no. 225, file no. 261, 1928: 'Game reserves in Indian states': Col. Field, note on file, 20 October 1928.

[69] Singh, *The Tiger of Rajasthan*, p. 157.

[70] Anon., *Speeches of the Earl of Willingdon, Vol. II*, p. 169: speech at Junagadh, 10 January 1936.

a Gujarati Muslim, was eventually to be replaced by the Sindhi landowner Shah Nawaz Bhutto. Pakistan, only an idea in 1940, seemed to the dewan and the nawab to be an imminent dream by the coming of Partition. With a Hindu-majority population, the growth of Congress-aligned nationalism, and a territory surrounded on all sides by India, the nawab's bid to join Pakistan was doomed to failure. He went across the border in October 1948. Indian forces soon crossed the border and *arzi hukumat* (people's rule) was proclaimed. The danger to the lions was all too real. After all, there was no dearth of big-game hunters who wanted a trophy on their walls. The lynchpin of protection was the nawab, who had guarded them like 'a rare treasure of (his) estate'.[71] With the protector gone, they could fall prey in a free for all.

'The PM's Personal Interest'

The SPFE now opened a line to India's new rulers. The Duke of Devonshire appealed to the prime minister of India, Jawaharlal Nehru, to save the lions. The letter struck a deep chord. On 26 February 1948 the prime minister warned the administration of Saurashtra to take all steps necessary to protect the species: 'I have long been interested in the preservation of lions in India. They exist only in Kathiawar now in the Gir Forest and it would be a great pity if they were shot or otherwise allowed to suffer extinction. In the past, he took strong exception to occasional expeditions by Viceroys and other officials to the forest for the purpose of shooting lions.'[72]

Junagadh's power had crumbled and the new regime was unable to enforce rules on hunting. Older rivalries over access to lions

[71] Cadell, 'The Preservation of Wildlife in India', pp. 162–6; Mosse, 'The Lion of the Gir', pp. 568–76.

[72] NAI, WISA, Part II, D-12-2/1949: 'Preservation of lions and wildlife in the Gir Forest', pp. 1–2: Duke of Devonshire to J. Nehru, 13 January 1948; J. Nehru, signed minute, 26 February 1948 (henceforth Lions 1949). A wider assessment of Nehru and nature is taken up in a separate paper.

came to the fore. Responding to queries, the Chief Forest Officer mouthed platitudes: the preservation of 'this noble animal' was a matter of the highest priority. A census was planned shortly. But S.W. Shiveshwarkar, a senior civil servant in Saurashtra, painted a very different picture.[73] Lions were being shot outside the territory of Junagadh: Jetpur had 'taken' two and Waghania four. The former's hunters had struck twice in April, weeks after the prime minister's letter. By May, Waghania's men had set up a machan in Bilkha and were waiting for a lion. Only in late June did local officials reply that no lion had been shot and all killing had ceased.[74] The new regime soon faced the acid test. The Jam Saheb of Nawanagar was proclaimed Rajpramukh (governor) of the United States of Saurashtra. Princes from other parts of India now pestered him for invitations.

Ramanuj Saran Singh Deo of Sarguja in Central India was the pick of the lot. Already famous for his record of shooting a thousand tigers, his main regret was that he had so far taken only one Asiatic lion. He told V.P. Menon, the influential civil servant in Delhi, 'I have been anxious to shoot two good lions.' Then came the punchline: 'I shall be grateful if you can do something for me.'[75] The hint from New Delhi first worked wonders. N.M. Buch was most obliging and lobbied Sarguja's case, but in vain. The latter had already bagged a trophy in the past and could not be given another chance. Sarguja was disappointed but quoted precedents of guests who had held two lion shoots.[76] The Rajpramukh was

[73] Lions 1949, pp. 8–9: Note by A.K.B. Kazi, Chief Forest Officer, 29 March 1948; S.W. Shiveshwarkar to V.V. Baxi, Regional Commissioner, 9 April 1948.

[74] Lions 1949, p. 10: Shiveshwarkar to N.M. Buch, 4 May 1948; telegrams from V.T. Dehejia, Junagadh, to V.V. Baxi, Sec., Western India, 4 May 1948 and 21 June 1948.

[75] Lions 1949, Maharaj Ramanuj Saran Singh Deo, Maharaja of Sarguja to V.P. Menon, Political Adviser, Ministry of States, 11 October 1949.

[76] Lions 1949, Buch to V. Ishwaran, Chief Sec., United States of Saurashtra, 29 November 1949, and to Sarguja, 11 January 1950.

unwavering. In a confidential note, he was scornful of Ramanuj's records in big-game shooting but felt 'This is not a thing to be proud of. He has denuded his own state of game and I know that at one time he used to get lions in Junagadh by poaching.'[77] There was no total ban on lion hunting. The culture of shikar did not die out. In fact it received a new lease of life under a new regime, which brought the Amreli and Junagadh Gir under one authority for the first time. Three years later, lions were declared protected—but the notification permitted a limited number to be shot annually. Four were 'taken' every year. This was in accordance with the broad pattern of accession to India: princes retained some privileges.[78]

The lion was now a subject of new kinds of symbolism. Stripped of association with Junagadh, it struck a chord at a wider regional level. Even the Rajpramukh evoked the rights of the people of Saurashtra against the claims of Sarguja.[79] The Gujarat Natural History Society of Ahmedabad urged Nehru to declare the Gir Forest 'a national lion sanctuary'. The prime minister responded positively and asked the Ministry of States 'what exactly' it proposed to do about the matter.[80] By now, the animal was already part of the national emblem, which reworked the Asokan pillar with its three lions.[81] The lion had just became the national animal of India in 1952, with the chairman of the newly constituted Indian Board for Wildlife declaring it 'more indigenous to India than the tiger'.[82] When the board met in the Gir Forest, members discussed

[77] NAI, WISA, D-8-6-1950,'Gir Lions': Maharajah of Sarguja to Rajpramukh, 13 January 1950; Rajpramukh, Jamnagar, to Buch, 12 January 1950 (henceforth Lions 1950).

[78] Dharamkumarsinh, 'Wildlife Preservation in India', p. 867. Notification number DP/F/1118-7/157, 25 July 1953.

[79] Lions 1950, Rajpramukh to Buch, 12 January 1950.

[80] Lions 1949, p. 82: Principal Private Secretary to the Prime Minister to Sec., Min. of States, 16 May 1949, quoting a telegram from the Gujarat Natural History Society to the PM, n.d., and PM's minute.

[81] Gandhi, *Rajaji*, p. 295.

[82] Government of India (henceforth GOI), *Proceedings of the Inaugural Session*, p. 14: Maharaja of Mysore, Inaugural Speech.

a proposal to transfer a few specimens to another reserve. Having 'all the eggs in one basket' was not a prudent policy. The species could be wiped out by an epidemic or natural disaster. The Rajpramukh was quick to praise the lion's qualities in terms that subtly played on regional pride. The lion was 'the noblest animal throughout the length and breadth of India.' But a hasty relocation that failed would 'give it a name'.[83]

The race to find a second home for the Gir lions saw other provinces lobbying their case. The Inspector General of Forests felt the dry scrub jungles in Tungabhadra in the Deccan were 'more or less like the terrain in Sasan Gir'; not surprising, given he himself was from southern India. The forests of Vindhya Pradesh, where the Sindhias had tried to bring back African lions, had their champions. Eventually, the powerful chief minister of Uttar Pradesh (UP), Dr Sampurnanand, won the day. He was keen on having lions in the Chakia Forest, where they would be a tourist attraction close to the pilgrim city of Varanasi. As the most populous state in India, UP had its way.[84] A lion and two lionesses were released into the forest reserve, which had been renamed Chandraprabha (radiance of the moon) in December 1957. This did not stop voices of dissent. Among them was K.S. Lavkumar's: he was from the princely family of Jasdan in Saurashtra as well as being an ornithologist and wildlife expert. His objections were grounded in terms both scientific and regionalist. 'Now where is there a place where antelopes can be found in the concentrated numbers that are sufficient to support a pride of lions?' he asked. Gir was 'a fine home' for lions and would suffice 'unless it is intended to give another state the pride of being the possessor of Asiatic lions. This privilege is, however, fraught with danger.'[85] The subtle play on the words used to describe the species should not be missed.

[83] GOI, *Proceedings of the Fourth Executive Committee Meeting*, pp. 9–11 (henceforth IBWL 1956).

[84] IBWL 1956, pp. 9, 25, 54–6: C.R. Ranganathan was the IGF.

[85] Lavkumar, 'Transferring of the Indian Lions', pp. 173–4; see in the same issue, Gee, 'Reply', pp. 174–5.

Widely called the Gir lion or the Indian lion, it was here referred to, perhaps quite intentionally, as the Asiatic lion. Earlier in the century it had the appellation 'Kathiawar' lion, and there was a frankly regional dimension in the Lavkumar warning. Saurashtra could pride itself on being the only abode of the species in Asia. The loss of this unique privilege rankled at least as much as the feasibility of the scheme for transferring a few animals.

As it turned out, the relocation scheme was a failure and the Gir Forest soon won back its singular status. Though the lions appear to have bred in their new home, they either wandered out of the sanctuary or turned on cattle. As its critics had feared, the area chosen was too small, being barely a fifth the size of the Gir. It had 'vast herds of domestic cattle all over the place', even within the bounds of the sanctuary. This was regarded as adding variety to the big cat's diet but there was no arrangement for compensation of losses.[86] A central part of the forest was fenced in with barbed wire to 'keep out domestic cattle'. One lioness escaped from the enclosure, which was soon broken down. Two years later the forester S.S. Negi showed signs of overconfidence when he claimed that the experiment had been a success. Fears that they would move outside the sanctuary were groundless as the area had 'sufficient food, water and cover'.[87] By 1965 it was clear no lions were left in the new second home and its most strident advocate, the very same S.S. Negi, admitted that the area had been too small and lacked enough wild herbivores. Cattle-owners probably poisoned the big cats in retaliation for stock losses that ought to have been indemnified. Hunters killed some lions, a cub being taken in the early phase.[88] To compound the incompetence that marked the entire enterprise, the claims were dubious. The three lions released had been in the Junagadh zoo for ten months, which may have habituated them to a diet of cattle. N.D. Bachketi, Conservator of Forests in charge of the area, found little sign of any lions in

[86] Gee, *Wildlife*, p. 90.
[87] Negi, 'Release of the Indian Lion', p. 60.
[88] Negi, 'Transferring of Indian Lion in UP', pp. 98–101.

1966. The record of births of lions in the previous years 'were too exact to be believed . . . The monthly birth and death statement is more like a statement that is possible in a zoo or a farm.' Forest guards assumed every kill or pugmark in the area to be that of a lion, though the forest still had tigers. Bachketi investigated the whole experiment in 1974 but his report was not made public. It was only many years later that he summarized his findings in a journal article![89] The fairytale had turned sour. This only reinforced the uniqueness of Gir.

The first decades after Independence saw major changes. Controlled hunting did continue till the end of the 1950s. But the new political class was largely indifferent or hostile to it: in this respect, Nehru was not alone. Even regional rivalries were markedly different from the rumpus over shikar rights in the princely era. The conflict was over the ownership of live wild animals, not over rights to shoot them dead. The living lion was now more a prize than the trophy version. An emerging urban middle class, as in the case of the Ahmedabad naturalists who championed the lion's cause, would now become increasingly influential. But if the heyday of the landed gentry and princes was over, they were not entirely out of the picture. In the Gir the Rajpramukh stepped into the nawab's shoes. This was one of the few powers that the princes had after signing treaties of accession. Further, the advisory boards on wildlife, both in the Union and the states, had a disproportionately large share of former royalty. As with the British aristocrats in the twilight of empire, but with less effect, they stepped out for a last bow. The ethos of the hunt was on its last legs, though it did not quite die out. But to understand the ideas and practices that would influence the future of the forest, one has to look beyond it.

Competing Visions

There were bound to be sharper conflicts on what to do in and about the Gir than in the past. But the same patch of land could mean

[89] Bachketi, 'Introduction of Lions in Chandraprabha Sanctuary', pp. 11–14.

very different things to different people. The twilight of the hunting epoch did not lead directly to the notion of total preservation of wild lands. Soon after Partition the forester in charge of the area wrote that lions, deer, and antelope were safe. But panther-shooting was encouraged in order to reduce the competition for food facing lions![90] The same practices were endorsed in independent India. The Board for Wildlife opposed rewards for killing wild boar, a prey species. Panthers, however, were vermin because of the damage they inflicted on 'deer, antelope and pig'.[91] Of course, the idea that the forest was mainly a lion sanctuary itself had the impress of the hunting era, when forests were identified by the major big-game animal they contained. The Gir Forest was to provide sanctuary for wild animals but all of them were not equal. Those that were more equal, in this case the lionesses, lions, and their cubs, got preferential treatment. Potential rivals, in this case panthers, were to be eliminated when possible. One option was to protect the Gir Forest as a lion sanctuary, but support for the idea lacked unanimity. In particular, there were rival platforms, one endorsing forestry, the other championing wildlife interests. To complicate matters further, both had to frame a response to the presence of large numbers of herders and their cattle within the forest perimeter. Though none of their proposals were fully implemented, the clash of competing visions did matter.

Foresters' plans for the Gir gave primacy to improvement of growing stock of teak trees by removing 'old, fire-injured, cracked, hollow and unsound trees.' S.R. Pandya, the new Conservator of Forests of Junagadh, arrived in February 1948 and pointed out the missed opportunities of the previous few decades.[92] Working Plans

[90] Lions 1949, pp. 8–9: note by A.K.B. Kazi, Chief Forest Officer, 29 March 1948.

[91] Gee, 'The Management of India's National Parks', pp. 14–15.

[92] NAI, WISA, F 2/12-1948: 'Deputation of Rao Bahadur S.R. Pandya to Junagadh State': S.R. Pandya, Preliminary Report for the Re-organization of the Forests of Junagadh State, 29 November 1948, pp. 3–4 (hereafter Pandya Report).

prepared in 1908 and in 1920 had never been implemented, and only in the mid 1930s had the foresters laid down fair-weather roads and started clear-felling trees in some tracts. Pandya was crystal clear on what he wanted done: the woodland was to be divided into blocks and the trees clear-cut on a forty-year felling cycle. Gir was to be divided up into 80 Felling Series of 4000 acres each. Clear-cutting of all trees was the best bet. 'It is easy to manage', he assured his superiors. 'There will be rapid removal of the bad quality teak crop. Even though the area of the coupe will be small, the prices for the material will be high.' The land would be intensively ploughed and seeds of teak and bombax, khair, and haldu broadcast.[93] The prime objective of protecting the forest was to generate adequate quantities of small timber, Minor Forest Produce, charcoal, and firewood. The needs of graziers were secondary: though they could not be excluded, it would be ideal to locate them 'in such places where the forests are not likely to suffer.' The Gir was a compact block with no rights and only about a hundred nesses. The 'heavy incidence' of cattle grazing near their settlements damaged saplings, reduced humus, and eroded soil cover. Each ness had 50 to 300 buffaloes: there was a conflict of interest between enhancing the timber production and cattle grazing. But to accomplish his dream of increasing production, he preferred to establish Forest Settlement Villages peopled by the Koli tribals of western India. Twenty such villages with each settler in them being given a patch of twenty acres to cultivate as a tenant-at-will of the Forest Department would provide 'timely labour' for forestry operations. In the nearby forest of Girnar, the main aim was to protect the water sources of the city of Junagadh. Here, it was not the human inhabitants but the native flora that would make way for exotic species that would grow fast enough to meet the fuel demands of the nearby urban areas. In particular, he recommended a Mexican tree, the *Prosopis juliflora*, that grew quickly and was not eaten by cattle. Fast-growing fuel plantations were preferable to trees being

[93] Pandya Report, pp. 15–16.

cut and carted away on the heads of woodcutters and the backs of donkeys.[94] Pandya hoped to increase the revenue generated by the Gir Forest and the Girnar reserve to about a million rupees a year. Yet he disclaimed any obsession with increasing cash flows or simply maximizing output. Forests in the whole of Kathiawar clothed less than a fifth of the land area. Most of this was within Gir, and his aim was to replace 'the ruinous policy of former days' with modern forest techniques.[95] Despite his disclaimers, he saw the forest itself as a vast potential manufactory, the wildlife in it being incidental. About the only specific proposal he had on the fauna fitted well with his production-centred view of the landscape as a whole. The Devalia Block was to be managed for licensed hunts. Lion and panther numbers had to be trimmed. Licensed shoots would 'keep down the population of big game'.[96]

K.S. Dharamkumarsinh (1917–86) of the Bhavnagar royal family had a very different vision for the forest. Whereas little is known of Pandya's life, the naturalist in the prince left enough in the form of articles, papers, and books to gain an insight into the experiences that shaped his perceptions of the lion forest. He had surveyed the area for the Education Department of Saurashtra in October 1948. Little action was taken and a revised report written four years later. By 1952 the princely interest in game protection had gone for good. But there are notes of nostalgia about an older social order that was on the way out. He had grown up in a Kathiawar where 'prowess was judged by the number of duck you shot out of the winter skies.' Game meant venison for the table and tame cheetahs to hunt down antelope.[97] 'Don't let the name scare you', he once wrote to two American naturalist-photographers, who then spent a few months with him in Bhavnagar. Dharma Bapa, as he was known, was one of the first princes whose interest in wildlife

[94] Ibid., pp. 14, 16–17.

[95] Ibid., p. 14.

[96] Ibid., pp. 17–18.

[97] Khacher and Khacher, 'R.S. Dharamkumarsinh (1917–86)', pp. 186–8; much more comprehensive is Divyabhanusinh, 'A Brief Biography', pp. vii–xi.

went beyond the gun to the study of creatures in the wild. His small Bhavnagar study group had spoken out in favour of protecting endangered species as early as 1944, mentioning the Asiatic lion, cheetah, and one-horned rhino.[98] His life marks the transition from the days when prince and *pagi* followed up game towards an age when wild animals were to be watched, not shot.[99]

His priority was the opposite of the one suggested by foresters: what remained had to be preserved, if not wholly, at least in large measure. A Gir national game sanctuary would help 'preserve and perpetuate the lion and its habitat *without* interfering with a reasonable forest or grass income to the state.' The centrepiece of his plan for the wildlife of the region was the eventual creation of a national park in the Gir Forest under the central government. Initially, the area would be a sanctuary for five to ten years, with only game wardens permitted to shoot any lions in self-defence. Later it would become a world-class national park.[100] Not surprisingly, he saw the Gir yielding annual revenue of not more than Rs 400,000, less than half that suggested by foresters like Pandya. He did not mince words: the forest area was shrinking each passing year. Farmers and woodcutters were encroaching on areas under departmental control. If this continued 'The forest shelter canopy of the Gir will be reduced and wild game will tend to find shelter in smaller forest areas and thus its natural habitat will be reduced'.[101]

What makes Dharma Bapa's ideas noteworthy is his attempt to blend elements of the old order with the new. He welcomed the

[98] Craighead and Craighead, 'Life with an Indian Prince', pp. 235–72; NAI, Lions 1949, KS Dharamkumarsinhji of Bhavnagar, Bhavnagar Study Group, no. 3, Wildlife and its Preservation.

[99] Dharamkumarsinh, *Reminiscences*, pp. 67–70; also idem, 'An April Day in the Gir Forest'.

[100] NAI, WISA/Office of the Regional Commissioner of Saurashtra, serial no. 382, file no. A 66/2/52, 1952: 'Preservation of wildlife: Report on rapid survey of wildlife conditions in Saurashtra and schemes for the preservation of wildlife and game', no date, submitted in 1952, pp. 2, 32. Quote from p. 12, emphasis added (hereafter Wildlife 1952).

[101] Wildlife 1952, p. 11.

unified administration over all of Gir under a forest officer. But he was sharply critical of the new regime for turning a blind eye to or acquiescing in the depletion of wildlife. Officials were themselves contributing to the attrition of the faunal heritage. Police harassed the Maldharis and disturbed wildlife in the Gir, making lions shelter in smaller patches of woodland. Policemen searching for bandits shot game! Officials were often corrupt and 'none' had any knowledge of the fauna or flora. Forestry was blind to wildlife needs. He warned of the impending extinction of the grey hornbill, a species that required old and hollow trees for nesting. Forest officers cut down nesting trees during the bird's breeding season. Its feathers were of medicinal value and they were being killed off 'in the same way as the killing of the rhino in Assam for its horn'. His view of the forest went well beyond large game animals—the lion and the sambar, the chital and the leopard—to embrace the array of bird species that inhabited the Gir hills. 'A chorus of sweet avian music' was as much part and parcel of the experience of the forest as the roar of the lion.[102] Similarly, the forest itself was of great importance for its role in binding the soil, protecting water sources, and maintaining rainfall levels. All forestry operations ought to be subject to the approval of the Chief Wildlife Warden. The lion–human relationship was at the core of his concerns and he feared that most killings were not really in self-defence. Dharamkumarsinh laid down strict criteria to identify which lion was a menace to humans. These were only to be shot by foresters; the norms for panthers were more lax. Not being as rare, the animal could be shot once the Forest Department gave the nod. The lion remained a privileged species, as in princely days.[103]

Despite the deep discord between the maximum programmes of forester and naturalist, they did have key common elements. Both hoped to retain the area as a woodland where forestry, grazing, and wildlife conservation would all be pursued simultaneously. Neither contested departmental control of the forested tract: this

[102] Dharamkumarsinh, 'Some Interesting Birds', pp. 187–90.
[103] Wildlife 1952, pp. 9–11.

had clearly come to stay. Though neither asked that graziers be removed, each had their own grouse against herders. But attitudes could harden as the naturalist, no less than the forester, turned from narrower issues of lion-killing to the capacity of the flora to recuperate after grazing.

Two botanists from Bombay sounded a note of alarm. The Reserved Forest was physically distinguishable from adjacent tracts. 'When we came to the Revenue areas', they recalled, 'the look of the country changed completely.' Gir could maintain 5000 cattle but had ten times as many. Teak trees and saplings were rare near the nesses and 'spiny shrubs or small trees' abundant.[104] From this prognosis to advocating the separation of herders from the forest was but a short step. By the mid 1950s Dharamkumarsinh too praised the Saurashtra Forest Minister D. Dave's plan to relocate graziers outside the forest's bounds. This would 'seclude Maldharis and afford them greater safety from the lions, and also give the lion and its habitat rest and relief.' A 350-square-mile area freed from grazing could instead be used for recreation, conservation and sport.[105] The project of relocating the grazier could also be part of their integration into wider society under nationalist aegis. This meshed very well with the dominant nationalist idea of the time, especially in Gujarat, with the notion of the settled peasant with a fixed plot of land as the ideal citizen in the new polity. In other parts of Saurashtra, over 5000 Maldharis adopted a sedentary lifestyle. Separation would give the people a new start and the forest a chance to recover. The botanists, Santapau and Raizada, observed how the inhabitants of Jumwania ness were 'dying out due to low birth rate combined with high infant mortality.' The headman complained of losses of 200 stock a year to lions.[106]

In terms of wildlife conservation, the time was not ripe for such ideas. The seeds of future changes were being sown at the time. Fresh legislation in Saurashtra provided for no rights of residence in

[104] Santapau and Raizada, 'Contribution to the Flora', p. 383.
[105] Dharamkumarsinh, 'Wildlife Preservation in India', pp. 868–9.
[106] Santapau and Raizada, 'Contribution to the Flora', p. 382.

such a park except for purposes of 'study, health (and) recreation'. The Collector would notify the creation of a National Park and all objections had to be made in writing within two months. The law, the Saurashtra National Parks Act, remained a dead letter.[107] In the IBWL, members drew solace from the experience in East Africa, where 2000 Maasai herders and over 300,00 cattle lived in the Serengeti park. The villages in Gir were to be 'restricted, regulated or controlled', not moved out. The Gir Forest was still a Reserved Forest with a large number of human settlements within it and not a national park.[108] Still, the acceptance of the presence of the nesses was a grudging one. In effect, they were on probation. The main criterion was still the number of lions and not the quality of the habitat. By the early 1960s there were reports of several lions, 'half a dozen to a hundred', being poisoned by disgruntled villagers. The pugmark census of 1963 laid such fears to rest but portents of the future were all in place. As for the Maldharis, they remained within the Gir but their actions were now subject to close scrutiny. They were not excluded but there was a shift in the terms of the debate and, for the first time, the idea was in the air.[109]

Foresters and naturalists agreed on whose writ would run in the forest but differed sharply in how best to use the wooded estate. Neither won a decisive victory. Forestry operations expanded but not to the level hoped for by the proponents of higher production. Wildlife did get protection, but the tract was not upgraded to a sanctuary till 1965. Foresters mostly focussed on the regeneration of the tree cover, naturalists on lion numbers. Once these two currents of concern coalesced, the Maldharis would face a fresh offensive.

'An Ecologically Sound Model'

Middle-class wildlife enthusiasts soon came round to back harsh measures against local people. Before this, Gir had to evolve from

[107] NAI, Regional Commissioner, Saurashtra, file no. C 13-38/52, 1952, 'Saurashtra National Parks Act', pp. 4–5, 8–9.

[108] Gee, 'The Management of India's National Parks', p. 10.

[109] Gee, *The Wildlife of India*, pp. 82–3.

an exclusive princely preserve into a tourist destination. In 1955 Jawaharlal Nehru and his daughter Indira Gandhi visited the Gir Forest. Impressed by the lions, they favoured increased access for tourists. To ensure lion sightings, forest guards tied up buffalo baits. A goat was often used to attract a lion, its bleats serving as 'a sort of live dinner bell', as visitors watched on foot. Even kills by the big cats were secured with ropes to enable easy photography. By the end of the 1960s thousands of tourists went out on 'lion-shows' every year.[110] So famous and photo-friendly were the huge beasts that when a well-known male called Tilyar died, it was announced on All India Radio as the death of the 'king of lions'.[111]

This re-naturing of the lions was to be of great significance: the lions were friendly wild animals, shorn of savagery and wildness. At this time, tiger hunting was still legal and often on the itinerary of the Western tourist visiting India. Hunting the lions was a thing of the past and a wide audience now learnt how harmless they could be: the lion was acquiring a new image as a sort of large tawny cat. Anyone who endangered the survival of these magnificent creatures would find it difficult to garner support.

As it turned out, the same period saw a fresh set of crises. Some cattle owners began poisoning carnivores by putting insecticide on their kills.[112] Initially, the lion censuses showed little impact. But in 1968 a new system of counting them by sight was adopted. Live baits were tied out in several sites and officials counted up the numbers: a bare 177, a decline of over a hundred in just five years. What mattered was not the validity of the census figures but the perception of imminent extinction.[113] One is tempted to add that it was no more just the death of a species but of the extraordinary individual lions and lionesses that were winning an audience across India.

[110] Ibid., p. 84; the figures are from Joslin, 'Conserving the Asian Lion', pp. 24–32 (hereafter IUCN 1969).

[111] Bedi, *Simha*, pp. 51–2. Tilyar died in March 1965.

[112] Stracey, *Wildlife in India*, p. 98.

[113] Even this figure included fifteen animals captured and kept in captivity for treatment in the Junagadh zoo. Dalvi, 'Gir Lion Census, 1968'.

The crisis in Gir formed the backdrop for the initiation of a large research project aimed at devising effective strategies to save the forest and its chief predator. It also marked a new external influence in the form of American-funded ecological research. Far more than ever before, the lobbying of Indian authorities by international organizations and their local allies would draw on the findings of scientific research. The School of Forestry at Yale University teamed up with the Bombay Natural History Society to fund a crop of fresh studies. Funded under PL 480, this represented, at the time, the most ambitious policy-driven wildlife research project in Asia. Unlike in the past, when nature photographers or princes had written about the forest, these were not gentlemen naturalists but scientists. This gave their word a ring of authority, which was echoed in deliberations of global bodies like the International Union for the Conservation of Nature (IUCN). The question asked by the various biologists was simple: What were 'the requirements and the current status' of key species of wildlife in the Gir? These were to include studies by specific scholars: American and British, with one Indian researcher. They included the Scottish biologists Paul Joslin (working on the lion), T.B. Hodd (on vegetation), Stephen Berwick (on ungulates), and Robert Grubh from Bombay, India. Their work did not include a full-length sociological study though William Burch, an eminent Yale social scientist, was associated with setting up the project. The Yale Project set out by defining the problem in terms of biology.[114] The Tenth General Assembly of the IUCN in New Delhi in November 1969 gave the delegates a chance to draw the attention of the Union government to the plight of the Gir.

The research changed the terms of debate about the forest forever. In place of older debates about lion numbers came new equations, often quantified, of prey and predator, domestic and wild herbivores, primary producers or green plants and their direct consumers, the ungulates. In qualitative terms too there was a huge

[114] Berwick and Jordan, 'Final Report', pp. 412–13.

shift, with impressionistic visits replaced by detailed field study. Though none of them suggested all-out exclusion of herders from the forest, they had serious doubts about the ability of the land to withstand high levels of cattle density in the long run. Joslin's work collecting lion scats for analysis covered villages both within and outside the sanctuary. Lions everywhere mainly lived on domestic cattle. Year round 20,000 to 25,000 head of stock lived in the Gir, and an equal number grazed there for a part of the year. Even the resident herds far outnumbered the six species of wild herbivores. Yet Joslin felt the sudden expulsion of all domestic cattle would create fresh problems. 'If all the cattle were to be removed suddenly', he admitted, 'with the objective of allowing the wild herbivores to recover, the lions might emigrate or starve.'[115] Scholars working on the herbivores sounded a similar note of caution. Buffaloes and cows did not directly compete with all wild herbivores: the former preferred grass, the latter often browsed off shrubs and trees. But to ensure that lions survived, Berwick had a novel idea: to reintroduce feral cattle into the forest. No scientist doubted that the Maldharis and the owners of migrant cattle were 'destroying the Gir. This is a long-term process and not immediately evident but progressing and virtually irreversible.'[116] A botanist was struck by the degradation of plant productivity and the harm done to the 'integrity' of the ecosystem. He even found the structure of the plant community changing in favour of thorny species that alone could withstand heavy grazing.[117] Cattle made up most of the 350,000 kg of meat consumed annually by lions, lionesses, and cubs. Relations between herders and foresters were often bitter. Schemes to compensate the loss of stock were so complicated that two of three herdsmen did not even bother to apply for the money. Anyone with over twenty

[115] Joslin, IUCN 1969, pp. 25–32. Quote from p. 31; also see his unpublished PhD: Joslin, 'The Asiatic Lion'.

[116] Berwick, 'The Gir Forest', p. 37; Berwick and Jordan, 'An Analysis of Herbivory'.

[117] Hodd, 'The Ecological Impact', pp. 259–64. Hodd was much more negative in his assessment of the cattle on wild ungulates than Berwick.

animals was not even eligible. Nor were those who owned cattle but lived outside the forest perimeter allowed to stake a claim.[118] To make matters worse, most kills outside the sanctuary yielded very little meat. No sooner had a lion made a kill than leather working members of the Scheduled Castes drove them away and took the hide for making leather. Hide collectors took away two of three carcasses of animals killed by the carnivore. Though they consumed only a little of the meat, the removal of the skins gave vultures easy access to food. They consumed more meat than the lions. The relationship between predator and scavenger was unwittingly tilted in favour of the latter by the most underprivileged group in village society.[119]

The challenge was in reconciling people's needs with those of wildlife. Officials went much further than scientists in wanting to exclude local people. Woodcutting and minor forest produce were valued at Rs 500,000 a year. No scientist called for closure of the entire forest to livestock. They wanted 12 to 16 per cent of the land free of all cattle. Restrictions on the activities of hide collectors would help lions get more meat per kill. Cultivated areas were to be reforested and the blackbuck reintroduced. Biologists advocated an end to forestry in a part of the Gir Forest.[120] The State Wildlife Advisory Board also wanted a national park where commercial forestry would cease.[121]

Many of these proposals were soon implemented. Wildlife conservation outweighed forest revenues in the new national park. Further, a larger wildlife sanctuary was declared under a new central law, the Wildlife (Protection) Act of 1972. All outside cattle were to be barred entry and Maldharis from the entire forest resettled

[118] Joslin, IUCN 1969, p. 31.

[119] Grubh, 'The Griffon Vultures', pp. 1058–68. Also see his unpublished PhD: 'The Ecology and Behaviour of Vultures'.

[120] Joslin, IUCN 1969, p. 31; Berwick and Jordan, 'The Ecology of the Maldhari Grazier', p. 17.

[121] Desai, 'The Gir Forest Reserve', pp. 193–8. The relevant resolution of the State Wildlife Advisory Board, 1968.

outside its bounds. 'The area', said the Ecology Council, 'was to be set free of the local inhabitants at a greater pace.' Protection of Gir from overgrazing was central to the task of making it a 'model of ecologically sound practices for other areas.' The Gir Forest case now fitted into a wider push for wildlife conservation, at both a regional and national level. Two major landmarks were crossed. In the struggle between production forestry and conservation, the latter had won the day. The state-level leadership had backed the new initiatives and influential sections supported exclusion. Digvijaysinh, head of the State Ecology Council, a former prince of Wankaner, was a Congressman from the region. Dr Amrita Patel, a veterinarian who drew up the project plan, worked with the BNHS and was the daughter of a senior civil servant, H.M. Patel. Clearly, there was a broad unity among the state authorities that something drastic had to be done. This was reinforced once the lion became the state animal of Gujarat, even as it was replaced as India's national animal by the tiger. There was a sense of pride that the Gir would soon become the 'largest biologically intact contiguous tract of land' in the country set aside for wildlife preservation.[122]

Changes were facilitated in no small part by the personal support extended at the highest level of the federal government. Guy Mountfort of the World Wildlife Fund (WWF) warned Prime Minister Indira Gandhi in January 1970 that the species would die out unless a comprehensive plan was implemented.[123] Yet external influences were limited to funding research and did not include funds for conservation which were entirely indigenous. This was in contrast to Project Tiger launched in April 1973. At the same time, the Gir Forest was a trendsetter in another sense. The effort here rested on the creation of a central zone free of both forestry and local resource users surrounded by a larger buffer that was less intensively policed. Given the historic emphasis on forests

[122] Government of Gujarat, *Gir Lion Sanctuary Project*, pp. 12–13. Orders were issued in January 1971: p. 115 (henceforth *Lion Sanctuary*).

[123] *Lion Sanctuary*, pp. 63–8.

as a source of hard cash, the closure of parts of the woodland for commercial forestry was a milestone. In Gir itself the government's annual loss of forest revenue was over Rs 250,000.[124] Conservation took precedence over revenue. Political upheavals in the state did not upset conservation plans. It is notable that the elected Congress state government (1972–4), a period under the Governor (1974–5), the short-lived Janata Front government (1975–6), and the successor Congress ministry (1976–80) all followed the same trajectory on protecting the Gir Forest. The lions and their future united leaders cutting across political divisions and party loyalties.

But the nub lay in the fate of the Maldharis. They were an impoverished group living close to the resource base, with only 'a thin line separating them from economic disaster.' In all, the Gir Forest had 137 nesses, and an average density of six people per sq. km. All the biologists wanted some curbs and many hoped for at least partial closure of the forest to cattle. Biologists and foresters ticked off the demands made on the forest: grazing was already too high, green fodder was lopped, thorn bushes cut to make fences, and dung sold off to cultivators. The Maldhari emerged as the prime competitor for living space with the lion and other wildlife. Earlier, most of the nesses were not sedentary, shifting every two or three years. As two out of three of the settlements became more rooted, their exploitation of the flora became more intense. With the control of smallpox and malarial mosquitoes by modern medicine and pesticides, respectively, the number of Maldharis increased. Their relations with foresters were not always amicable. Inhabitants of the Junwania ness were apprehensive that researchers were actually government agents. The Chodia ness had already been moved in 1968 from one site in the forest to another to help the regeneration of teak saplings.[125] Maldhari resettlement schemes had been discussed in the past but now steps were taken

[124] Narayan, 'Joint Management of the Gir National Park', pp. 212–25; *Lion Sanctuary*, pp. 23–6.

[125] Berwick and Berwick, 'The Ecology of the Maldhari Grazier'; idem, in Daniel and Serrao, *Conservation in Developing Countries*, pp. 81–94.

to remove them from the national park. In the rest of the area, grazing was controlled but not banned.

The relocation of 580 families and over 6000 cattle began in 1973. This was the first major resettlement of villages to make way for wildlife in independent India. The process was completed during the period of President's Rule in 1974–5. The absence of an elected state government insulated the authorities from discontent. Each family was given a grant, a loan, and a plot of land for cultivation. The Gir Forest still contained cattle but one enclave was free of all settlements.[126] The forest as a living space for the lion would ideally exclude the Maldhari. The first phase of exclusion was to have been followed up later in the rest of the forest, though this never came about.

The impact of these measures on the forest ecosystem was far-reaching. The advance of cultivation into the forest was halted. Fresh studies conducted by researchers from the Dehra Dun-based Wildlife Institute of India give an insight into the ecological changes in the quarter century since the Gir Project began. Virtually all the second wave of research was by Indians who studied foodchains in the forest. The lions were pegged at 180 in 1974 and a decade later at over 280. Though the numbers need not be taken at face value, the trend was very clear. Lions now mostly lived on wild prey. Only a third of their diet was livestock.[127] Relocation of nesses aided the forest-loving sambar. By contrast, the chital, a deer that preferred open spaces, could easily coexist with herders. Biologists appreciated the impact of past relocations of Maldharis but advised a more cautious approach. Provided there was a minimum distance of 8 km between adjacent nesses, the sambar would retain its living space. Biologists Sharma and Johnsingh suggested a gradual removal of half the nesses to aid the flora and fauna.[128] Their research findings indicated a possibility of regulated habitat use

[126] *Lion Sanctuary*, pp. 6–13.

[127] Chellam, 'Ecology of the Asiatic Lion'; Johnsingh and Chellam, 'Management of the Asiatic Lion', pp. 409–24.

[128] Sharma and Johnsingh, *Impacts of Management*, pp. 77–8; Chellam, 'Ecology of the Asiatic Lion'.

and, where necessary, of a carefully planned resettlement strategy. None disagreed with the principle of the exclusion of local peoples in the interests of ecological recovery, but they wanted a cautious response.

The caution sprang in part from a realization that ecological successes were not matched by successful relocation of the Maldharis. The entire premise of rehabilitation was to free the forest of grazing while enabling the Maldharis to take up settled agriculture. Half those evicted were Charans, traditional breeders of the famous Jaffrabadi buffalo and among the earliest settlers in Gir. Taking to the plough was itself a new experience for many of them. Charan Naranbhai Gadhvi, one of those forced to move would recall, 'We were driven out of Gir for no fault of our own. We were promised land and other facilities but did not get anything.' In the absence of effective irrigation, even those given eight acres of land were unable to raise an adequate harvest. The new controls on movement in and out of the Gir also made it impossible for those who had moved out of the forest temporarily in the drought of 1967–8 to return home.[129] Land was not given to families who owned revenue lands or those unable to produce evidence of residence prior to 1971.[130] After the relocation, an official survey found the incomes of oustees had declined. In many cases they had to sell their land at throwaway prices and take to wage labour. This transformation from relative self-reliance to penury was, of course, in stark contrast to the aim of giving Maldharis a new deal. The failure had other unintended costs as well. The Forest Department had hoped to reintroduce lions into a wildlife sanctuary in the Barda hills. In 1978–9 it was proposed that Maldhari herders be moved out from the hills to make way for a second home for the lions. The non-cooperation of the herders doomed the project. Perhaps the failures in the

[129] Abdi, *Maldharis*, pp. 53–4; Narayan, 'Joint Management of the Gir National Park', p. 217.

[130] Shrivastava, 'Maldharis and Biodiversity in the Gir' (hereafter *Gir Ecodev.*).

Gir weakened the claims of foresters that they would give buffalo herders a better life.[131]

In net, the landscape of the forest changed in very significant ways. Wildlife took precedence over forestry, preservation over the extraction of wealth. The expertise of biologists was drawn upon to further an official programme of exclusion. In the 1970s and 1990s scientists urged a cautious approach and not total exclusion. But as the lion became the flagship for saving the forest from ruin, administrators pushed ahead. Habitat recovery of the Gir was accompanied by the impoverishment of many herders. The premise that they could change their livelihood overnight was dubious, nor were they given effective assistance. Preservation was equated with the Forest Department's powers but policing was not backed by ameliorative measures. The Gir Forest was a forerunner of the relocation of villagers from many Indian tiger reserves.[132] Even with the Maldharis being marginalized, there were others laying claim on the forest.

'Lion of Gujarat'

In a sense, the Maldharis were a soft target in comparison with other users of forested space. The aftermath of relocation revealed how other threats loomed much larger over the land of the lion. Villages on the periphery made their own demands on forest biomass. More ominously, the increased pilgrim traffic to major shrines in the sanctuary brought in their wake modern perils, including motorized traffic and waste. Mining ate away not only the tree cover but even the topsoil at the edge of the sanctuary. In focussing mainly on the graziers, the administration had tried to isolate the lion's habitat from human use. Its success in this effort

[131] Rashid and David, *The Asiatic Lion*, pp. 116–17.

[132] By 1984, over 6000 people had been resettled outside the tiger reserves, mainly drawn away from Kanha, Ranthambhore, and Bandipur. See Panwar, 'What to Do', pp. 182–3.

could not insulate the forest from other more insidious influences that could undermine the ecosystem.

But the forest still had a variety of uses other than for wildlife conservation. Gir had within its borders various elements of a vigorous and active economy, of which herders were only one component. People still living both within and beyond Gir continue to draw on its wealth. The industrialization of Saurashtra has generated fresh pressures. The Forest Department as landlord relied on 14 Forest Settlement Villages whose 4500 inhabitants fell trees and cut fire lines. By the late 1980s even resettling them was proving difficult due to the paucity of fertile land elsewhere in the region. On the periphery of the 1400 sq km sanctuary are 150,000 people and 100,000 cattle. These mixed-caste villages included powerful landed groups like Ismailis and Brahmins, who were able to successfully resist foresters. Not that the herders had all been removed. The national park was closed to Maldharis but the rest of Gir still had 2500 herders and 10,000 cattle.[133] The forest remained a source of fodder and firewood, a place to graze cattle and collect kendu leaves and gum arabic for the market. In the conflict between different kinds of users, foresters and biologists established the primacy of wildlife in a part of the land. The contest over the rest of Gir continues. For Maldharis, the forest is not only a source of wealth, it is a living space. But other users are under less pressure than the graziers, who number less than the Forest Settlement villagers or those on the periphery. As the largest forest in Saurashtra, Gir also sustains cattle from elsewhere during droughts. One biologist even felt such cattle imperilled wildlife more than the herders did.[134]

Conservation was equated with hiving off the forest from the wider economy but networks of exchange broke through protective barriers. Limestone mines and stone quarries ate into the forest

[133] Narayan, 'Joint Management of the Gir National Park', pp. 215–16; Shrivastava, 'Stakeholders in Gir', in *Gir Ecodev.*

[134] Chellam, *Asiatic Lion.*

on the edge of the sanctuary. By 1995, as a Maldhari of Sadbeheda ness, put it, 'The forest will soon reverberate not to the roar of lions but to the sounds of pick axe and drilling machines. The land that sustains our cattle will turn bone white and the cattle will die.'[135] Despite strong objections from foresters, the District Collector allowed mining even in areas with over fifty trees a hectare. In one such patch near Babaria village in Una taluka, lions were losing living space, and villagers fodder and firewood. Mining was allowed even when in clear violation of court orders restraining such activity along the borders of sanctuaries.[136] Increasingly, a protective system geared to dealing with semi-nomadic herdsmen is under pressure from more influential groups. Controversies centre on growing pilgrim traffic to the shrines in the Gir. The number of pilgrims increased fivefold to 50,000 a year by 1997–8, in ten years. The temple at the Tulsishyam springs controls 12 sq km of forest estate. The Kankai Mata temple is in the eye of the storm. Responding to criticisms, a senior office-bearer claimed that 'Not a single offence has been recorded against any of our trustees, our staff or devotees . . . we are committed to maintaining peace and harmony but we must be allowed our right to worship.'[137]

But the issue is one of imposing new demands on the habitat. Temple complexes have been extended beyond the plots originally granted to them. Demolitions by authorities have prompted protest from the Vishwa Hindu Parishad (World Hindu Council).[138] The Kankeshwari temple is over 400 years old and was accorded rights in November 1974. This was around the time that the relocation of Maldharis was under way. The temples may become a population centre in the heart of the forest. Temple authorities harvest grass, pilgrims use firewood. In March 1998 the state government permitted several activities that disturb wildlife. Vehicles may enter

[135] Jain, 'The Problems Behind the Pug Marks', pp. 25–31.

[136] D.S. Chavda, IUCN, to Sec., Ministry of Forest and Environment, Gandhinagar, 18 October 1996.

[137] Kankiya, 'The Right to Worship'.

[138] Anon., 'Reconversion of Dalits and Backwards'.

from any checkpost even at night. In one case, a speeding vehicle knocked down and killed a lioness.[139] By the mid 1990s, 187,000 motorized vehicles brought in devotees every year.[140] Sacred sites have emerged as a focus of controversy, with their increased popularity and the ease of road transport. Further, temple authorities are politically well connected and can resist foresters. Increased vehicular traffic and the semi-urban lifestyles of pilgrims are new threats to the Gir.

The lion's home is also the subject of fierce controversy between the authorities and increasingly assertive local forest users. It is also a symbol that can be drawn upon for political ends. Foresters tap pro-lion sentiments for conservation. One official asked villagers to guard lions like their family jewellery. They replied they wanted to be consulted on matters affecting the forest. Notification of the Maldharis as Scheduled Tribes in 1990 has given them some bargaining power. Even officials have had to concede that any resettlement will now be voluntary, not coercive. The links with marginal groups and middle-class sympathizers elsewhere in India have also been used skilfully by local groups.[141] Maldhari leaders now interact more closely with politicians, even complaining to ministers against the Forest Department.[142] The issue of access to the woods for meeting livelihood needs has led to tensions. Shepherds have confronted forest guards at checkposts, wood-collectors have won political support for their demands. Villagers have clashed with foresters over the removal of teak logs from the Gir.[143] Its forest

[139] D.S. Chavda, Member, Cat Specialist Group, IUCN, Letter to Suresh Prabhu, Minister of State for Environment and Forests, New Delhi, 12 August 1998.

[140] Shrivastava, *Gir Ecodev.*, Annexure V.

[141] Anon., 'Maldharis Being Evicted?', pp. 1–2; *Phulchab*, Rajkot, 16 September 1994. This Gujarati daily from Rajkot regularly reports on the Gir Forest. I am grateful to Divyabhanusinh for translating and making this source available. Divyabhanusinh is working on a history of the lion in Gujarat: it will be the definitive account.

[142] *Phulchab*, 21 August 1994.

[143] Ibid., 4 August 1993, 16 July 1993, 18 January 1994.

home may be under new pressures but the lion is now a symbol not only of Saurashtra but also of all Gujarati-speaking people. Biologists have proposed, and the federal government has accepted, a plan to relocate a few lions in a reserve in Madhya Pradesh. A small pride of six to eight lions is to be set free after a prolonged period of habitat protection and the build-up of herds of deer and antelope. But this has led to considerable resentment within Gujarat. In April 1997, Chief Minister S.S. Waghela told journalists that 'not even a single cub' would be allowed to leave the state. As if on cue, local wildlife enthusiasts even protested outside the Collector's office against the removal of 'our' lions. The issue was raised in parliament in New Delhi. A second home would act as insurance in the event of a calamity or disease wiping out prides in the Gir Forest. But the resurgence of regional pride has found an emblem in the lion, its uniqueness adding to its appeal. Waghela's regional party prominently displays a roaring lion on its posters.[144] Yet, the opposition to the plan has to do with more than just the issue of Gujarati *asmita* (the pride of Gujarati speakers). The Saurashtra Environment Protection Society voiced fears that the removal of lions from a patch of their habitat will 'expose the forest to destruction by those who are waiting for it.'[145]

None of these frictions are peculiar to the Gir Forest. What sets it apart is not just the presence of the lion in its last refuge in Asia. Far more than anywhere else in its once-extensive range in the subcontinent, it is integrated into local culture and idiom. Lions were wiped out across India as pests who preyed on livestock. In the Gir they survived in a mainly pastoral region, where even now losses are compensated and reprisals rare. The big cat has long been associated with royalty, but only here did it get a measure of royal protection. The coming of Independence eventually ended the era of huge shoots and trophy hunts, with the lion becoming an early emblem of the new nation's bid to break with imperial legacies.

[144] Ibid., 25 April 1997, 27 April 1997, 4 May 1994.
[145] Ibid., 21 March 1994.

In the succeeding period, the ethic of conservation itself powered fresh conflicts between those who saw the forest as a place for wildlife alone and human communities who had made it a home for centuries. As the pressures of modernization mount, and foresters and villagers face each other in more tense conflicts than in the past, there are clouds of uncertainty over the future of Gir. Even as there are anxieties about the fate of the forest, the last century has given us a legacy of lion–human interaction that may well endure. In Gir lions have been re-natured to a far greater extent than in other wildlife reserves. For instance, individuals who sustain injury are treated at the local zoo![146] The rarity of attacks on humans and the ability of lions to adapt to the presence of people make the Gir Forest a symbol of coexistence in a time of conflict.

Perhaps the last word should be left to an Indian schoolboy whose verse expressed both the uniqueness and the fragility of Gir: 'Lion, O Lion of Gujarat/ In Forest Gir, you roam free/ The tiger be no rival to thee/ Though he has usurped thy throne/ But your numbers have grown so small/ That it is possible to hold a roll call.'[147]

References

Adamson, G., *Bwana Game: The Life Story of George Adamson*, London: Collins, 1968.

Anon., 'Maldharis Being Evicted?', *Joint Protected Area Management (JPAM) Update*, Delhi, no. 10 (1996).

Anon., 'Reconversion of Dalits and Backwards', *Organiser*, 24 July 1996.

Anon., *Speeches of the Earl of Willingdon, Vol. II: From 29 June 1934 to 18 April 1936*, Delhi: Government of India Press, 1937.

Bachketi, N.D., 'Introduction of Lions in Chandraprabha Sanctuary', *Cheetal*, vol. 34 (1991).

[146] Ibid., 3 October 1993. The re-naturing of the lions is explored in detail in Rangarajan, 'Animals with Rich Histories'. The wider theme of the interactive, fluid, and contingent nature of wild animal–human relations requires wider study and reflection. A valuable collection is Divyabhanusinh, *The Lions of India*.

[147] Shankar, 'Lion, O Lion of Gujarat'.

Balfour, E., *The Cyclopedia of India and of Eastern and Southern Asia*, 2nd edn, London: n.p., 1885.

Barnett, Ross, N. Yamaguchi, Ian Barnes, and Alan Cooper, 'The Origin, Current Diversity and Future Conservation of the Lion (*Panthera leo*)', *Proceedings of the Royal Society*, B 273 (2006).

Bedi, R., *Simha*, New Delhi: Publications Division, Ministry of Information and Broadcasting, 1968.

Berwick, M.A. and S.H. Berwick, 'The Ecology of the Maldhari Grazier in Gir Forest, India', mimeo, Yale University, n.d.

Berwick, Mariane, 'The Ecology of the Maldhari Grazier in Gir Forest, India', in J.C. Daniel and J.S. Serrao, ed., *Conservation in Developing Countries: Problems and Prospects*, Delhi: Oxford University Press, 1990.

Berwick, S.H., 'The Gir Forest—An Endangered Ecosystem', *American Scientist*, vol. 64 (1976).

——— and P. Jordan, 'An Analysis of Herbivory and Predation in the Gir Forest, India: An Ecosystem Approach to Conservation Planning', mimeo, Morges: IUCN, n.d.

———, 'Final Report of the Yale–BNHS Studies of Wild Ungulates in the Gir Forest, India', *Journal of the Bombay Natural History Society*, vol. 68 (1971).

Blanford, H.R., 'Zoological Notes', *Journal of the Asiatic Society of Bengal*, vol. 26 (1867).

Brittlebank, K., *Tipu Sultan's Search for Legitimacy: Islamic Kingship in a Hindu Domain*, Delhi: Oxford University Press, 1997.

Cadell, P., 'The Preservation of Wildlife in India, No.5: The Indian Lion', *Journal of the Bombay Natural History Society*, vol. 37 (1934).

Caldwell, K., 'The Gir Lions', *Journal of the Society for the Preservation of Fauna of the Empire*, vol. 34 (1938).

Campbell, J., ed., *Gazetteer of the Bombay Presidency, Vol. VIII: Kathiawar*, Bombay: Government Central Press, 1884.

Carruthers, J., *Kruger National Park: A Social and Political History*, Pietermaritzburg: University of Natal, 1995.

Chand, Mohan, ed., *Syainkyasastra, Rudra Deva of Kumaon: The Art of Hunting in Ancient India*, rpnt. Delhi: Eastern Booklines.

Chellam, Ravi, 'Ecology of the Asiatic Lion', unpublished PhD thesis, Saurashtra University, Gujarat, 1993.

Commissariat, A.S., *A History of Gujarat, Vol. II: The Mughal Period from 1573–1758*, Hyderabad: Orient Longman, 1957.

Copland, Ian, *The British Raj and the Indian Princes: Paramountcy in British India, 1857–1930*, Delhi: Longman, 1982.

Craighead, John and Frank Craighead, 'Life with an Indian Prince', *National Geographic Magazine* (February 1942).

Dalvi, M.K., 'Gir Lion Census, 1968', *Indian Forester*, vol. 95 (1969), no pagination.

Desai, J.R., 'The Gir Forest Reserve: Its Habitat, Faunal and Social Problems', in H.B. Elliot, ed., *Second World Conference on National Parks*, Morges: IUCN, 1974.

Desai, R.A., *Maldharis of Saurashtra—A Glimpse into Their Past and Present*, Bhavnagar: Suchitra Offset Press, 1992.

Desai, S.H., *The Forest of Gir*, Junagadh: Prabhas Prakasan, 1995.

Dewar, D., *Beasts of an Indian Village*, London: n.p., 1923.

Dharamkumarsinh, 'An April Day in the Gir Forest', in Dharamkumarsinh, *Birds of Saurashtra, India*, Bombay: Times of India Press, 1951.

———, 'Some Interesting Birds of the Gir and Girnar Forests, Kathiawar', *Journal of the Bombay Natural History Society*, vol. 48 (1949).

———, 'Wildlife Preservation in India—Annual Report for the Western Region', *Journal of the Bombay Natural History Society*, vol. 52 (1955).

———, 'The Changing Wildlife of Kathiawar', *Journal of the Bombay Natural History Society*, vol. 75 (1978).

———, *Reminiscences of Indian Wildlife*, Delhi: Oxford University Press, 1998.

———, ed., 'The Lion in Bhavnagar State', *Journal of the Bombay Natural History Society*, vol. 49 (1951).

Divyabhanusinh, 'A Brief Biography', in Dharamkumarsinh, *Reminiscences*, Delhi: Oxford University Press, 1998.

———, 'Asiatic Lion on a Postage Stamp', in M.A. Rashid and R. David, *The Asiatic Lion*, New Delhi: Dept of Environment, Govt of India, 1992.

———, *The End of a Trail: The Cheetah in India*, Delhi: Banyan Books, 1995.

———, *The Lions of India*, Ranikhet: Black Kite, 2008.

———, *The Story of Asia's Lions*, Mumbai: Marg, 2005.

Fenton, F.L., 'The Kathiawar Lion', *Journal of the Bombay Natural History Society*, vol. 20 (1911).

Fenton, L.L., *The Rifle in India, Being the Sporting Experiences of an Indian Officer*, Berlin: August Scherl, 1923.

Forbes, J., *Oriental Memoirs, Selected from a Series of Letters Written during 17 Years Residence in India, Vol. II*, 1813, rpnt. Delhi: Gian Publications, 1988.

Gandhi, Rajmohan, *Rajaji*, Delhi: Penguin Books, 1997.

Gee, E.P., 'The Management of India's National Parks and Wildlife Sanctuaries—Part III', *Journal of the Bombay Natural History Society*, vol. 54 (1956).

———, *The Wildlife of India*, 1964; rpnt. Delhi: Indus, 1992.

Government of Gujarat, *Gir Lion Sanctuary Project*, Gandhinagar: Government Central Press, 1972; rev. edn, 1975.

Government of India, *Proceedings of the Fourth Executive Committee Meeting of the Indian Board for Wildlife held in Sasan Gir, Saurashtra, 18–20 January 1956*, New Delhi: Ministry of Agriculture and Forests, 1956.

———, *Proceedings of the Inaugural Session of the IBWL held at Mysore from 25 Nov. to 1 Dec. 1952*, Delhi: Ministry of Agriculture and Forests, 1952.

Government of Bombay, *Selections from the Records of the Bombay Government, no. 16, New Series: Tours for Scientific and Economical Research made in Guzerat, Kattiawar and the Conkans in 1787–88 by Dr Benjamin Howe*, Bombay: Education Society Press, 1855.

Grubh, R., 'The Ecology and Behaviour of Vultures in Gir Forest', unpublished PhD thesis, Bombay University, India, 1974.

———, 'The Griffon Vultures of the Gir Forest—Their Feeding Habits and the Nature of Their Association with the Asiatic Lion', *Journal of the Bombay Natural History Society*, vol. 75 (1980).

Habib, I., *An Atlas of the Mughal Empire*, Delhi: Oxford University Press, 1982.

Hamilton, W., ed., *East India Gazetteer of the Territories under the Government of the East India Company, Vol. II*, 2nd edn, 1982; rpnt. Delhi: Low Price Publications.

Hodd, K.T.B., 'The Ecological Impact of Domestic Stock on the Gir Forest', Morges: IUCN Publications, New Series, vol. 18 (1970).

Iyer, K. Bharatha, *Animals in Indian Sculpture*, Bombay: B.D. Taraporevala, 1977.

Jacquemont, V., *Letters from India, Vol. II*, 1834; rpnt. Delhi: Oxford University Press, 1979.

Jain, R., 'The Problems behind the Pug Marks', *Down to Earth*, 28 February 1995.

Johnsingh, A.J.T. and Ravi Chellam, 'Management of the Asiatic Lion in Gir Forest, India', in P. Joslin, 'Conserving the Asian Lion', *11th Technical Meeting of the International Union for the Conservation of Nature, New Delhi, 25–28 Nov. 1969, Vol. I*, Morges: IUCN Publications, New Series, vol. 18 (1970).

Joslin, P., 'The Asiatic Lion: A Study of Ecology and Behaviour', Edinburgh University, UK, 1973.

Kankiya, J.J. (President, Shree Mataji Kankeshwari Temple Trust), 'The Right to Worship', *The Times of India*, Delhi, 30 July 1996.

Kesri Singh, Col., *The Tiger of Rajasthan*, 1959; rpnt. Bombay: Jaico Books, 1967.

Khacher, S. and L. Khacher, 'R.S. Dharamkumarsinh (1917–86)', *Journal of the Bombay Natural History Society*, vol. 83 (1986).

Kinnear, N.B., 'The Past and Present Distribution of the Lion in South Eastern Asia', *Journal of the Bombay Natural History Society*, vol. 27 (1920).

Lavkumar, K.S., 'Transferring of the Indian Lions to an Additional Locality', *Journal of the Bombay Natural History Society*, vol. 54 (1956).

Le Grand, Jacob, 'Report upon the General Condition of Kateewar in 1842', *Transactions of the Bombay Geographical Society, 1843*, rpnt. Bombay, 1894.

Lokhandwala, M.F., trans. and ed., *Mirat i Ahmadi, Vol. II*, Baroda: Oriental Institute, 1965.

Majumdar, R.C., and V.S. Altekar, *The Gupta-Vakataka Age*, Delhi: Motilal Banarsidass, 1967.

Martineau, J., *The Life and Correspondence of the Rt. Hon. Sir Bartle Frere, Vol. I*, London: John Murray, 1895.

Monier Williams, M., *A Sanskrit–English Dictionary*, 1899; rev. edn Oxford: Clarendon Press, 1963.

Mosse, A.H., 'The Lion of the Gir', *Journal of the Bombay Natural History Society*, vol. 54 (1957).

Mundy, G.C., *Pen and Pencil Sketches, Being the Journal of a Tour in India, Vol. I*, London: John Murray, 1832.

Naqvi, Saeed, 'Hard Life and Mean Death of the Gir Lions', *The Statesman*, Calcutta, 4 March 1973.

Narayan, Shankar, 'Joint Management of the Gir National Park', in A. Kothari, N. Singh, and S. Suri, ed., *People and Protected Areas: Towards Participatory Conservation in India*, Delhi: Sage, 1995.

Negi, S.S., 'Release of the Indian Lion in the UP Forests', *Indian Forester*, vol. 85 (1959).

———, 'Transferring of Indian Lion in UP', *Cheetal*, vol. 12 (1969).

Neumann, R.P., 'Dukes, Earls and Ersatz Edens: Aristocratic Nature Preservationists in Colonial Africa', *Environment and Planning D: Society and Space*, vol. 14 (1996).

Panwar, H.S., 'What to do when You Have Succeeded: Project Tiger 10 Years Later', in J. McNeely and K. Miller, *National Parks, Conservation and Development: The Role of Protected Areas in Sustaining Society*, Washington: Smithsonian, 1984.

Phillimore, R.H., ed., *Historical Records of the Survey of India, Vol. II: The 18th Century*, Dehra Dun: Survey of India, n.d.

Rangarajan, M., 'Animals with Rich Histories: The Case of the Lions of Gir Forest, Gujarat, India', *History and Theory*, vol. 42, issue 4, December 2013.

———, 'The Raj and the Natural World: The War against "Dangerous Beasts" in Colonial India', *Studies in History*, New Series, vol. 14 (1998).

Ranjitsinh, M.K., *Beyond the Tiger: Portraits of Asian Wildlife*, Delhi: Brijbasi Publishers, 1997.

Rice, W., *Indian Game, From Quail to Tiger*, London: W.H. Allen and Co., 1884.

Roberts, T.J., *The Mammals of Pakistan*, London: Ernest Benn, 1977.

Rogers, A. and H. Beveridge, trans. and ed., *Tuzuk i Jahangiri, Volume I*, 1909; rpnt. Delhi: Munshiram Manoharlal, 1982.

Ronaldshay, Earl of, *Letters to Nobody, 1908–13*, London: John Murray, 1921.

Sahu, B.P., *From Hunters to Breeders: Faunal Background of Early India*, Delhi: Anamika Prakashan, 1988.

Santapau, H. and M.B. Raizada, 'Contribution to the Flora of the Gir Forest in Saurashtra', *Indian Forester*, vol. 80 (1954).

Shankar, Sachin, 'Lion, O Lion of Gujarat', *Environment and Wildlife*, no. I (1976).

Sharma, D. and A.J.T. Johnsingh, *Impacts of Management Practices on Lion and Ungulate Habitats in Gir Protected Area*, Dehra Dun: Wildlife Institute of India, 1996.

Shrivastava, A., 'Maldharis and Biodiversity in the Gir', in A. Shrivastava and R.L. Meena, *Ecodevelopment in Gir—A Status Report*, mimeo, Sasan, November 1996, no pagination.

Stebbing, E.P., 'The Gir Forest Lions', *Indian Forester*, vol. 32 (1906).

Stracey, P.D., *Wildlife in India, its Conservation and Control*, Dehra Dun: Manager of Publications, 1963.

Symposium of the Zoological Society of London, vol. 65 (1993).

Thapar, V., 'The Last Lions', in V. Thapar, R. Thapar, and Y. Ansari, *Exotic Aliens: The Lions and the Cheetah in India*, Delhi: Aleph, 2013.

———, Romila Thapar, and Yusuf Ansari, 'Response to the Review of *Exotic Aliens*', *Journal of the Bombay Natural History Society*, 110 (2013).

Tod, J., *Travels in Western India*, 1820; rpnt. Delhi: Oriental Publications, 1971.

Trivedi, R.K., *Census of India, Vol. V, Part V-B, No. 1, Ethnographic Series, Gujarat, Siddi, A Negroid Tribe of Gujarat*, Ahmedabad: Navjeevan Press, 1969.

Vigne, T.G., *A Personal Narrative of a Visit to Ghazni, Kabul and Afghanistan, Vol. I*, London: Whitaker and Co., 1840.

Welch, Stuart Cary, *India: Art and Culture, 1300–1800*, Delhi: Mapin, 1985.

Wilberforce-Bell, H.H., *History of Kathiawad*, 1916; rpnt. Delhi: Ajay Books, 1980.

Wilson, A., 'A Run through Kathiawar', *Blackwoods Magazine*, no. 10 (1876); rpnt. 1899.

Wynter-Blyth, M.A., 'The History of the Lion in Junagadh State, 1880–1936', *Journal of the Bombay Natural History Society*, vol. 49 (1951).

4

Gandhi's Notion of Ahimsa and the Human–Nature Relationship

The growth of environmental awareness has led to revaluating the relevance and significance of the legacy of Mahatma Gandhi (1869–1948). The focus has mainly been on the implications of choices of technology and scales of production on the environment and on the ethical underpinnings of an alternative notion of development. One important suggestion in Guha's perceptive cameo of a study is that Gandhi's ideas had more to do with the village than the forest or the city. The careful use of resources within cultivated settlements was much more important to the Mahatma than either the issues that concerned the Adivasis or other forest-dependent people or the inhabitants of growing cities and towns. It was caste-Hindu village India rather than millworkers or forest users that were the focal point of his concerns.[1]

The question examined here has a bearing on the wider debates but is focussed on his notion of non-violence *vis-à-vis* non-human life and how he as well as some amongst his followers tried to put

I am grateful to the late Professor Ravinder Kumar, Professor Tanika Sarkar, Professor Ramachandra Guha, and Mr Mahendra Vyas for their suggestions. The usual disclaimers apply.

[1] Guha, *Gandhi and the Environmental Movement*, pp. 111–28.

these out into practice. The impact of vegetarianism among the Vaishnavas in his native Saurashtra is too well known to require fresh recounting. These had not only Sanatan Dharma roots but also Jain antecedents. It was, however, in his student days in England that he began to develop a philosophy around such beliefs. The interaction with Henry S. Salt as a law student in London was as important as the imprint of the likes of Ruskin and Tolstoy. Salt, the former Eton schoolmaster who influenced Gandhi, was more than a champion of strict vegetarianism. He also opposed fox-hunting, which then as now was a major leisure pursuit among the landed gentry and their middle-class imitators. His campaigns for the conservation of wild flowers were later to win support from leading members of the political class.[2] Though Gandhi met Salt and was deeply impressed by his advocacy of animal rights, he did not draw upon the other concerns of the latter. This omission may have had a wider logic. Salt was to aggressively take up the issues of hunting and protection of wild flowers a little later than in the early 1890s, when he and Gandhi first met. More crucially, the young Mohandas saw the issue of vegetarianism in the light of a revaluation of religious teachings. It was no coincidence that he came across a copy of the Holy Bible for the first time in a vegetarian eating-house in London. The wider intellectual milieu of alternative modes of thought and living, of which vegetarianism was a vital and substantive element, informed the genesis of his political thought. Salt was a crucial figure, as was this wider milieu.[3]

Compassion extended beyond humans to animals but this did not lead to any sustained engagement with the conservationist concerns of some of his contemporaries. Yet the question of human–animal relations resurfaced in the very early stages of his

[2] Winsten, *Salt and His Circle*, esp. pp. 55–61, 118; on the milieu, see Leela Gandhi, *Affective Communities*, esp. 70–2.

[3] Nanda, *Gandhi: A Pictorial Biography*, pp. 12–13; Ramachandra Guha observes that the vegetarians in London gave the young Mohandas 'his first public platform' and transcended the barriers of race: Guha, *Gandhi Before India*, p. 50.

public life. The founding of ashrams where life would be organized according to an alternative set of principles greatly preoccupied Gandhi. These included Phoenix in Natal, and Sabarmati and Sevagram in India. The aesthetic dimensions of nature are in the background here by comparison with another Indian who attempted constructive work in a rural setting, namely Tagore. While Tagore shared Gandhi's apprehensions about the destructive impact of city life, the poet in him identified with features of the landscape with far greater sensitivity. In *Gora*, for instance, the protagonist walks on the riverside, entranced by its beauty, which 'had not been invaded by the ugliness which commercial greed has brought in its train.'[4] Despite this, Gandhi's later attempts to work out a way of applying his principles of tolerance in relation to the animal world require a closer look. The formulation of the concepts and practice of satyagraha (struggle for truth) first took place not in India but in South Africa. The Phoenix settlement in Natal province abounded in vipers and other poisonous species of snakes that were a potential threat to human life. Both here and in the ashram at Sabarmati near Ahmedabad, founded in 1927, the policy was to not kill reptiles. Gandhi also endorsed the superstition among inmates that by not harming the snakes they in turn were left alone.[5]

In his public interventions Gandhi was confronted with much more difficult choices. None was to be as controversial in this sphere as the case of the stray dogs of Ahmedabad. This was the only area in which Gandhi had sustained and long-term interaction with the urban working class. Though heterogeneous in religious terms, they were largely Gujarati speaking. The city also had a significant presence of trading castes—Bania, Marwari, and Jain. The spark came due to the actions of the millowner Ambalal Sarabhai, a close associate of the Mahatma.

In 1926, a number of rabid stray dogs that had become a menace to workers were shot dead in Ahmedabad, at the instance

[4] Tagore, *Gora*.

[5] Gandhi, *An Autobiography*, p. 46.

of Sarabhai. Unfortunately, the dead bodies of the dogs were taken in open carts through the market on a day when the bazaar was humming with activity. There was outrage among the traders, who staged a hartal (closure) in protest against the cruelty to the animals. The only point on which the two sides could agree was to have the Mahatma arbitrate. Sarabhai felt he was protecting the workers, his critics that he was being needlessly cruel to living beings.

What is notable is that Gandhi disappointed the traders.[6] His correspondence on the subject continued for a period of over two years in the pages of his journals, *Navjeevan* and *Young India*. In these articles he distinguished between his individual belief in ahimsa (non-violence) and the application of the principle in everyday life. The very existence of stray dogs was an indicator of the irresponsible nature of human society. He did not and could not advocate the wiping out of dogs or any other creatures as a class.[7] But if there was a choice to be made between a child and a poisonous snake, he would be with the child whose life was in danger. In an article entitled, 'Is this Humanity?' he asked if the *ahimsak* (practitioner of non-violence) did not even have the right to kill in defence of the weak. The reply was that he had. To simply preach coexistence was a luxury. Working out how to apply it was the acid test of a practitioner.[8]

The wider principle that emerged from the incident was that compassion for animals ought not to be seen in isolation. This could not exclude taking difficult decisions. There was ample room for coexistence. Aware of the conflicts in village India, where carnivorous animals could pose a threat to flocks of sheep or cattle, Gandhi responded with a sophisticated argument. Villagers often considered it necessary to kill tigers or lions in self-defence. But it was still possible to look forward to a future where life would

[6] Erickson, *Gandhi's Truth*.

[7] Gandhi, *Collected Works*, 11 November 1926, and 2 December 1926 in vol. 27, pp. 14–16, and vol. 28, p. 379, respectively.

[8] Ibid., 25 November 1926, vol. 27, pp. 72–3.

be different. All animals were our brethren, even the lion and the tiger. It was 'because of our ignorance' that 'We do not even know how to befriend them. Today, he does not even know how to befriend a man of a different religion or from a different country.'[9] In line with the parables of holy men being able to commune with the most ferocious of beasts, of Buddha and the raging tusker, or of St Francis of Assisi and the wolf of Gubio, Gandhi hoped to break even this last barrier between human and animal. The pure idealism was nothing short of utopian but fits quite well with his general belief in the ability to transform human nature through restraint, and to conquer an adversary with compassion. But his ideal worldview was tempered by calculations that might have appealed to those who lived in proximity to the great beasts of the forest, and who sometimes had to defend themselves or their livelihood from attacks. Yet, defence was to be a last resort, not a first response.

The criticisms that greeted such a stance were what led to the series of articles in the journals. But the repartee is also useful for another, more significant reason. Though Gandhi was widely seen as having carried forward older notions of ahimsa, as propounded by teachers such as Mahavira and other religious leaders, his own reading of the past was sophisticated, if innovative. If he could endorse religion to avoid the wholesale killing of snakes, he could be much more self-critical in other cases. A correspondent asked him how be could ignore the verse that one should not kill even a beast of prey, even if this saves the life of many.

Another critic, this time a Jain visitor, suggested he was violating the letter and spirit of non-violence. Refuting these ideas, he went well beyond invoking contingency and duty to curb dangerous beasts and poisonous snakes. Ahimsa, he felt, was not a monopoly

[9] Fischer, *The Life of Mahatma Gandhi*. Many of the issues on what is or is not an animal in Gandhi's view are taken up in a perceptive paper: Kumar, 'Satyagraha and the Place of the Animal', pp. 359–81. The issue of placing human life in danger requires further study and reflection.

of the Jains or any other group. In any case, the restraint on killing living beings was a critical but not sole part of the philosophy of ahimsa. While Mahavira was a genuine votary of this philosophy, he knew several Jains who fell short of such standards.[10] There was an all too real danger that ahimsa, instead of being a broad idea, was becoming the 'monopoly of a few timid Vaishyas.'[11] It would be easy for the mercantile communities to speak of non-killing as the *sine qua non* of ahimsa. But this would only evade the wider problem of their own actions in daily life that increased pain, suffering, and violence. By domesticating animals, men had already denied other beings their freedom. The question was of how the line could be drawn in such a way as to root out the desire to hurt other living things. This, and not the mere absence of killing, was ahimsa in action.

Such choices were indeed faced by the next generation of Gandhians. A diverse and mixed crew, their divisions and beliefs are beyond the scope of this essay. But an experience of his disciple Mira Behn in her ashram in the foothills of the Himalaya is illuminating. Gandhiji's own ashrams on the Sabarmati and in Wardha were in largely deforested countryside where plough and axe had replaced the jungle with villages and fields. Mira's choice of a site was different, being influenced by a love of the mountains. The awareness of nature's beauty was a constant and abiding feature of her life. But the process of founding a homestead was far from easy. In 1948, it was necessary in Pashulok Ashram to beat pots and pans at night to scare away wild elephants. She was happy that the forest had a resident tiger. When cattle-lifting by the tiger threatened the livelihood of the local pastoralist Gujjars, a hunter sat up on a machan and shot the animal. In her writings about the incident, she echoed Gandhi's view: 'You did us great wrong', she said (addressing the tiger!), 'I am very sorry about your death.

[10] 'Gandhi, *Collected Works*, 25 November 1926, and 25 October 1926, in vol. 7, p. 73, and vol. 31, pp. 505–7, respectively.

[11] Ibid., vol. 31, p. 524.

But we had to kill you because we were helpless.' Again, there was a choice between two evils, not an easy one.[12]

Conclusion

There is a simple but powerful way in which the Mahatma and some of his apostles attempted to address a dilemma of modern society. Conflicts often lead to intolerance, not only between different groups of people but also with respect to the natural world. Ahimsa was a credo that held the seeds of a solution. But in its application the practitioner had to be sensitive to the underprivileged, whether the millworker threatened by stray dogs or the cattle-keeper in conflict with tigers. The wider implications of this are significant. While development cannot be about economic growth alone, urban environmentalists and animal rights activists can do much more to emulate the Mahatma. A sensitivity to the animal world has to combine with attention to disadvantaged people if one is to make any headway. A narrow notion of coexistence can be as damaging as the consumerist notions of development that it seeks to displace.

At the same time, the ideological content of Gandhi's thought has to be assimilated more critically than is often the case. He was not simply drawing on tradition but was critically reinterpreting it. This process was not carried out in the abstract but was often shaped by his engagement with real problems on the ground. At times, these took him well off what most scholars see as the beaten track of his concerns with the village and the peasant. The stray dogs' case was a classic urban problem and he saw it as an index of the decay of life in the city. The breakdown of communitarian structures was itself responsible for the existence of stray dogs. He did not see any easy way out by letting the dogs live. That he drew an analogy with villagers confronted by carnivores was instructive. There was no easy choice. The practitioner of non-violence had to

[12] Gupta, *Mira Behn.*

evolve responses to real problems, not generate ideal solutions. The abiding relevance of this point in both the city and the forest in India today could provoke a more rigorous revaluation of Gandhian thought and practice than the very brief attempt made here.

References

Erickson, Eric, *Gandhi's Truth*, New York: Harper and Row, 1997.

Fischer, Louis, *The Life of Mahatma Gandhi*, New York: Harper and Row, 1950.

Gandhi, Indira, 'Address to UN Conference on the Human Environment', 14 June 1972, in *Peoples and Problems*, London: Hodder and Stoughton, 1982, 2nd edn, 1983.

Gandhi, Leela, *Affective Communities: Anticolonial Thought and the Politics of Friendship*, Ranikhet: Permanent Black, 2006.

Gandhi, M.K., *An Autobiography, or The Story of My Experiments with Truth*, Ahmedabad: Navjivan Press, 1927.

———, *Collected Works of Mahatma Gandhi*, Volumes 27–29, 31, New Delhi: Ministry of Information and Broadcasting, 1968–9.

Guha, Ramachandra, *Gandhi and the Environmental Movement: The Parisar Annual Lecture*, Pune: Parisar, 1993, rpntd in M. Rangarajan, ed., *Environmental Issues in India: A Reader*, Delhi: Pearson, 2007.

——, *Gandhi Before India*, Delhi: Penguin, 2013.

Gupta, K.M., ed., *Mira Behn, Gandhiji's Daughter Disciple*, Delhi: Himalaya Seva Sangh, 1992.

Kumar, Aishwarya, 'Satyagraha and the Place of the Animal: Gandhi's Distinctions', *Social History* 39 (2014).

Nanda, B.R., *Gandhi: A Pictorial Biography*, Delhi: Publications Division, 1972.

Tagore, Rabindranath, *Gora*, 1924; rpnt. Calcutta: Macmillan, 1965.

Winsten, Stephen, *Salt and His Circl*., London: Hutchinson, 1951.

5

Striving for a Balance

Nature, Power, Science, and India's Indira Gandhi 1917–1984

Indira Gandhi's engagement with environmental issues was strongly evident during both her tenures in office as prime minister of the world's largest democracy. Even a brief intellectual and cultural biography of India's most influential prime minister in recent times (the post-1967 era) provides a good vantage point to examine the broader questions of conservation and livelihoods, democracy and authoritarianism, and national sovereignty and international influence. It can also hinge on how one approaches the interplay of ideas and interests, of an awareness

I owe a debt to many people, but must above all record my appreciation to all my colleagues and students at the Department of History, University of Delhi. An earlier version of this article was presented at a workshop on, 'Nature, Knowledge and Power', held at the University of Uppsala, Sweden, 15–17August 2008. Many ideas in this article emerged from sustained discussions with three individuals who are no more: Professor Ravinder Kumar, R. Rangarajan, and Kailash Sankhala. I am also grateful to Gunnel Cederlof, Harish Damodaran, Leela Gandhi, Heather Goodall, Ramachandra Guha, Ullas Karanth, Aromar Revi, Valerian Rodrigues, Vijay Sanghvi, Dinesh C. Sharma, Aarthi Sridhar, Ajantha Subramanian, R. Sukumar, and Himanshu Thakkar. The usual disclaimers apply.

of a larger horizon as opposed to more prosaic issues of power. Environmental issues held a special place throughout her political career at the top. This was so from January 1966 to March 1977, and again from January 1980 till her assassination in October 1984. Key interventions took place even at times of mounting international tensions or domestic political crises. November 1969, for instance, was amidst the historic split of the ruling Congress party, reducing her government to a minority in the Lok Sabha. Yet it was the very month in which she made a major address to an international conservation body in the capital.[1] The first meeting of the newly created National Committee on Environmental Planning and Coordination (NCEPC) was on 6 December 1971, even as the war with Pakistan had begun. Similarly, her letter to the chief minister of Bihar asking him to halt the diversion of forest land for a development project was sent from Shimla in May 1972. She was at the hill station to negotiate with the Pakistani Premier Zulfikar Ali Bhutto in the aftermath of the Bangladesh war.[2] This should set at rest the idea, current among scholars of different hues, that environmental concern was largely aimed at wooing a Western audience, especially in times of a chill in Indo–US ties, during 1969–71, or indeed after the Emergency was imposed and the basic rights of expression suspended in June 1975.[3]

There was a larger consistency in her engagement with such issues. It is less of a surprise that most biographers and students of politics have paid little attention to this dimension. The former set of scholars sees it as a spin-off from her authoritarian ways and impulses, and the latter ignore it altogether.[4] These two sharply opposed views—one seeing her as intrinsically authoritarian and the other as a benevolent presence assisting nature's recovery—are not antithetical. But one is overly functional and the latter serves

[1] Gandhi, 'Preserving Wildlife', pp. 264–7 (hereafter *Speeches 1969*).

[2] Thapar, *The Last Tiger*, p. 65.

[3] Greenough, 'Pathogens, Pugmarks'; Guha, *How Much*, pp. 125–51 (appropriately titled 'Authoritarianism in the Wild').

[4] For instance Malhotra, *Indira Gandhi*.

to view political leadership in the abstract, almost in a vacuum, shaping but hardly touched by cultural and intellectual influences of the time.

Even more problematic is the role cast for her as a saviour. Over the last few years there has been a swirl of controversy over the fate of the tiger, with proponents and critics of the new, more people-friendly strategies revisiting the time in 1973, when Project Tiger was launched.[5] A close relative of a key figure in tiger conservation in her time recently recalled the 'good days' when the foundations of wildlife and forest conservancy were laid. Not unimportantly, Suraj, spouse of the late Kailash Sankhala, also mentioned regular calls from the PM at functions, both formal and informal, where the Director of Project Tiger could have the leader's ear.[6] The tiger conservationist and photographer Valmik Thapar goes so far as to assert that 'if we have any ecological security left, it is due to Indira Gandhi.' The laws enacted in her time are seen by him as a bulwark against anarchy, and their erosion is turning the tide against nature in India.[7]

That her legacy is significant is not in doubt. In 2006, parliament enacted the Scheduled Tribes and Other Traditional Forest Dwellers' (Recognition of Forest Rights) Bill, a legislative measure that allows for legal recognition of a title to the Adivasi or Scheduled Tribe cultivators on forest lands. This effectively reopens the question of where the frontier of farmland and forested land lies. A keystone of the arch from her time, the Forest (Conservation) Act (or FCA) of 1980, was thus remade in 21st-century India, twenty-six years after its enactment.[8] Scientists and ecological activists,

[5] Ministry of Environment, *Joining the Dots*.

[6] Sankhala, 'I Remember'.

[7] Thapar, *The Last Tiger*, p. 304. An earlier instance of such a view can be found in Sankhala, 'After the Carnage'. Of tiger poaching in Rajasthan he wrote: 'had *She* (Indira) been there, many heads will have rolled.'

[8] The Scheduled Tribes and Other Traditional Forest Dwellers' (Recognition of Forest Rights) Act, 2006. See the special issue of *Seminar*, August 2006, and the various articles in the debate section of *Economic and Political Weekly*,

both from India and overseas, found her a communicative and serious listener. The futurist Buckminster Fuller, designer of the geodesic dome and the tetrahedral city, counted himself as an old friend.[9] Over a decade and a half later the polymath and critic of high technology Fritjoff Capra felt, in a one-on-one meeting, that her silence was a signal for having 'a conversation of substance'.[10] She was as much at ease with the 'more with less technology' of Buckminster Fuller as with the more philosophical inclinations of Capra. This ease and familiarity with matters ecological had its local counterpart with the issue of the felling on the Ridge, the last outcrop of the Aravalli hills that was integral to the landscape of Delhi.[11] She took steps to secure the city forest in the summer of 1980, when petitioned by a student group. What the group was unaware of was her central role a few years earlier in getting a key Indian Air Force installation modified to preserve the skyline as well as the biophysical integrity of the forest.[12]

Neither an admirer nor a critic, therefore, did justice to the subject. Her engagement was part of a larger milieu of nationalist debates in late colonial India; and her legacy survived in part as its seeds fell on fertile soil. Part of the clue is provided by the fact that even a journalist and biographer who knew her quite well admitted to having simply 'gone along with the generally accepted view that not only was her formal education episodic and limited, but she had little interest in books or ideas.'[13] As the two volumes edited by Sonia Gandhi show, her correspondence with Jawaharlal Nehru from 1922 to 1964 contains a misperception: even the young

---

19 November, 2005, vol. 40. Unwittingly or not, the latter coincided with the 88th birth anniversary of Indira Gandhi.

[9] Gandhi, 'Science to Solve Man's Problems', pp. 411–12.

[10] Capra, *Uncommon Wisdom.*

[11] Krishen, *Trees of Delhi*, pp. 22–6. See especially the section 'Where Exactly is the Ridge?'

[12] 'Appeal to the Prime Minister to Save the Delhi Ridge, April 1980', unpublished, Delhi: Kalpavriksh; on the Ridge, see Parthasarathi, *Technology at the Core*, pp. 275–7.

[13] Malhotra, *Indira Gandhi*, p. 184.

Indira—and we will see some of this subsequently—could differ pretty sharply with 'Pappu' (as she called Nehru).[14] A second kind of evidence is the speeches at public fora. Although composed often with a team of writers, especially the polymath H.Y. Sharada Prasad, they still provide clues to a larger sense of engagement with issues not only of knowledge and power, but with the human–nature relationship.[15]

The major milestone in her appearance on the world stage with ecological overtones was undoubtedly the speech at Stockholm in the summer of 1972. This famous, if often misquoted, speech at the first UN Conference on the Human Environment at Stockholm in June 1972 came at the zenith of her political career. After a shaky start as the world's second woman prime minister, in January 1966 she had faced down a division in her own party and gone on to win a two-thirds majority in the general elections of 1971. War followed soon after, with victory in the battle to liberate Bangladesh placing her among the few leaders to have successfully stood up to the US president Richard Nixon. It was in the glow of victory that the invitation came. It held out for her 'the promise of a setting that would behove a world leader' who could use the stage to address a global audience.[16] The speech was marked by an awareness of the inequities across nation-states which could be a barrier to joint action to keep the earth habitable. Nations could not be 'preserved as museum pieces' in the name of diversity. One earth could work as a concept only if the ideals of humanity faced up to the inequities of access to wealth and knowledge. Her most oft-quoted line about poverty as an affliction acquires a different meaning when read as part of a longer epistle. She asked:

> Are not poverty and need the greatest polluters? The environment cannot be improved in conditions of poverty. Nor can poverty be eradicated without the use of science and technology. For instance, unless we are in a position to provide for the daily necessities of tribal

[14] Gandhi, *Two Alone*. The volume on the earlier period, while not used in this essay, is an equally insightful source: Gandhi, *Freedom's Daughter*.

[15] Sharada Prasad, 2005, p. 15.

[16] Parthasarathi, *Technology at the Core*, pp. 250–1.

> people and those who live in and around our jungles, we cannot keep them from combing the forests for their livelihood, from poaching and despoiling the vegetation. When they themselves feel deprived, how can we urge the preservation of animals?

Rejecting extreme views, she showed herself in favour of a more holistic view, blaming neither population growth nor economic affluence singly. The conflict was between conservation and reckless exploitation, not between progress *per se* and ecological values.[17]

Heralds of a New Dawn

Of course, speeches and interviews were but a small part of a long and tempestuous political life. Born in November 1917, at a time of war, upheaval, and revolution, she was the only daughter of Kamala and Jawaharlal Nehru. Her political and personal lives were intertwined from the start. Her life spanned much of the twentieth century, a time that witnessed a secular shift, a fourfold expansion of the number of humans on the planet. It is true that she was, for her first thirty years, more closely concerned with an equally crucial and historic change in politics, the emergence into freedom of new nation-states as the colonial era came to a close. A fourth of the world was under the Union Jack when she was born, but by the century's end there were four times as many nation-states as in 1914, when the Great War began.[18] How she reflected on and responded to these two major secular shifts had much to do with India's engagement with issues of nature and power in her time. As her Stockholm speech indicated, inequities within societies could have much to do with how the trade-offs of equity and ecology were made or unmade. An examination of her work cannot be delinked from her record in office and power, but a search must begin in the realm of ideas and influences in the early years. While a fuller

[17] Gandhi, 'Man and His World'.

[18] McNeill, *Something New under the Sun*; for nation-states, see Hobsbawm, *Globalisation, Democracy and Terrorism*.

treatment of the multiple engagements of Indian nationalism, with the problem of nature, lie well beyond the scope of this essay, Indira Priyadarshini Nehru is best seen against a larger backdrop.

A rare only-girl child in her generation and for her class, her familiarity with nature began early. Growing up in Allahabad, she was to be schooled at a variety of locations including Delhi and Santiniketan, Switzerland and Oxford. The Nehrus—and not just father and daughter—had a keen eye for natural beauty. This was indirectly reinforced by the Gandhian impact, for it forced a reassessment of lifestyles at a personal level. This had included an end to shikar, the ritual hunts that were a pursuit of middle-class Indians in smaller towns and cities on weekends.[19] The world of nature was instead a balm for non-violent soldiers against the Raj. At times, as political prisoners, they identified with animals that were victims. Writing of the Dehra Dun jail, Nehru was upset by the capture of a pangolin by a jail employee.[20]

There were compensations. The drongo, an elegant, and sprightly insect-eater were among the birds she identified in early 1943. *The Book of Indian Birds* by Sálim Ali, a German-trained ornithologist and the first Asian to be a Fellow of the Royal Society, was at her side on more than one occasion. In turn, her father identified the pangolin, an obscure small ant-eating mammal, by referring to F.W. Champion's *The Jungle in Sunlight and Shadow*, a pioneering work of natural-history photography of animals in the wild.[21] In solitary confinement in Ahmadnagar Fort, Jawaharlal wrote to his sister excitedly about the arrival of a pair of migratory wagtails, 'the heralds of a new season'.[22]

[19] Hasan, *The Nehrus*, pp. 46–7; a photo entitled 'On a Hunting Expedition' shows a dapper Jawaharlal leaning against a rifle.

[20] Nehru, *Autobiography*, p. 374. Nehru himself probably stopped hunting even before he came under Gandhi's spell—ibid., p. 33.

[21] Indira Gandhi (IG) to Jawaharlal Nehru (JN), 17 July 1943, in Gandhi, *Two Alone*, p. 240.

[22] JN to Vijayalakshmi Pandit, 19 October 1943, in Sahgal, *Before Freedom*, p. 284.

This went beyond harmless pursuits of leisure among a nascent English-educated middle class. It is difficult for us today to capture the sense of excitement about new developments, especially in physics and chemistry, in the years preceding and during the Second World War. This was the age of Einstein, Rutherford, and Bohr. Two letters from Switzerland in early 1940 testify to a fascination with modern technology and the new frontiers of discovery. Chemistry could provide humans with artifacts in every way 'superior to the natural product', she told Nehru. Every week saw a new discovery, with change a harbinger of new opportunities.[23]

It was never mentioned openly but her own health hinged on her vulnerability to tuberculosis, the disease that had claimed her mother's life. It was only as recently as 2001 when a perceptive biographer, Katherine Frank, herself a social historian of TB, uncovered Indira's long battle with what was always in her time referred to as 'the problem'. Her month-long stay in Leysin, in the upper Rhone valley, in the winter of 1939, was aimed at a cure. This 'white frozen world of sickness and death' did not work any magic and her departure from the mountain resort came soon after. It was only seventeen years later, with new post-war drugs, that she became 'an unusually healthy and fit woman'. However, it is important to note how a dangerous organism had claimed the life of a parent (Kamala) and threatened her with ill health till the age of forty.[24] In light of this it seems even more remarkable that she did not view science simply as a project of human dominance over nature. The American botanist D.C. Peattie gets her approving nod in a letter. He reminded all of how 'the life of all living things are bound together', but his *Flowering Earth* was not alone among the books she was familiar with.[25] In a rare essay during her prime-ministership, penned in a women's magazine, she recalled *The Faber Book on Insects* and Maeterlinck's books on bees.[26]

[23] IG to JN, 9 February 1940, in Gandhi, *Two Alone*, pp. 260–2.
[24] Frank, *Indira*, pp. 145, 146–64; and on her cure, pp. 239–40.
[25] IG to JN, 13 April 1940, in Gandhi, *Two Alone*, pp. 284–5.
[26] The article was published in *Eve's Weekly*, 2 November 1967; quoted in Bhagat, *Indiraji*, pp. 145–6.

Looking back, it seems only natural that technology was seen often as a Janus-faced phenomenon by these two Indians, who had travelled Republican Spain and heard accounts of the bombing of Guernica by the Condor Air Legion—dispatched by the Fuehrer to aid the royalists against a doomed democracy. Nehru and the young Indira were sure that science should be allied to life, and development to peace, not war. But how would the choices be made as freedom dawned in the middle years of the century? Nehru had cause to differ with Gandhi. Although known as the one who would speak the latter's language when he was gone, his views on modern technology and large industry were different in content and emphasis. In his *The Discovery of India* he was appreciative of Gandhi's distrust of technology as a cure-all. However, he himself was also clear that there was a choice between two paradigms, and one of the two would be 'dominating and paramount'. Planning would limit the evils of technology, while big machinery had to be accepted.[27] By this time, if not earlier, it was the younger man who was more in step with the Congress' mind. On freedom's doorstep the future seemed to lie with industrialization, not its alternatives. Steel mills and atomic power, not spinning wheels and village self-rule, would be the centrepiece of a new India. The latter could endure, but only as a complement to the former.

A Perfectly Entrancing Place

The coming of Independence and Partition in August 1947 was at a troubled time, but it opened up new horizons. Indira Gandhi became and remained till May 1964 the prime minister's hostess and confidante. They lived almost that entire time in Teen Murti House, a vast residence formerly occupied by the army commander-in-chief. With stately trees and flower beds, it also included an old hunting lodge (*shikargah*) built by the fourteenth-century ruler

[27] Nehru, *Discovery*, pp. 445–51. A careful reading of the chapter, especially pages 445–8, shows a critical view of farm mechanization in the densely peopled Ganga basin and sharp criticisms of the blocking of the natural drainage paths of rivers in the plains.

Feroz Shah Tughluq. Her sons Rajiv and Sanjay lived with their mother and grandfather. The love of animals continued. There were two tiger cubs, later gifted to a zoo, well before they had become adults, 'muscles rippling with power and grace'. More famous was a friendly and photogenic red panda, presented to them during a tour of Assam. Nobody in the entourage quite knew what the creature was and it was only identified using 'a book on Indian animals'. Soon joined by a mate, it was housed in a special treehouse. Fed bamboo shoots by Nehru each morning, the pair spent their winters in Shimla.[28] This was an India where the Raj habit of hunts was alive and well. On a visit to the Gir Forest, the lion's only home outside Africa, Indira Gandhi wore a khaki-coloured coat, to avoid alarming the big cats. Still-shot by special permission, the prides were wary of humans.[29]

Her exposure to peoples and cultures was also extensive. Preparations for the Republic Day pageant of 1952 found Indira Gandhi working closely with tribal dancers. Pupul Jayakar, close associate and keen cultural afficionado, felt this was her first contact with tribal people. In August 1961, she was virtually present as the old map of European rule folded up in Africa. Over a dozen of its nations were on the doorstep to independence. She met leaders of major Kenyan nationalist groups, and as always wrote home from the Indian High Commission. Meeting Jomo Kenyatta, the future president of Kenya, was not the only thing to report back to her father from Nairobi. The Amboseli game reserve, she wrote, was for her and her two sons a 'perfectly entrancing place' to view lions and lionesses. 'Unexpected frolic took place right in front of my hut in the pale hours of dawn—elephants, giraffes, zebras, gazelles were thoroughly enjoying themselves.'[30]

Horace Alexander, Quaker and sympathizer of the freedom struggle, had founded the Delhi Bird Watchers' Society, of which

[28] Gandhi, *My Truth*, pp. 72–3.

[29] Divyabhanusinh, *The Story of Asia's Lions*, p. 173. Nehru moved into Teen Murti House in August 1948 and lived there till his death in May 1964.

[30] IG to JN, 25 August 1961, in Gandhi, *My Truth*, p. 587.

Indira Gandhi briefly served as president. This was prior to her stint as Congress president in 1957. Malcolm MacDonald, the British high commissioner, was another enthusiast. To date, Indira Gandhi is the only Indian prime minister (there have been fourteen) to have headed a naturalists' society. An aide was amazed at how she and her colleagues had learnt to 'recognise birds by their sound'.[31] However, politics and public life never left much time for such privacy. She once complained to a friend of how, even nearing a glacier 16,000 feet above sea level, there were people with requests, all of whom 'come only to get or ask something'.[32]

Nehru had all along been drawn to rivers, but she felt closer to the mountains.[33] Her older son, Rajiv, was a budding photographer whose pictures include one of his younger brother Sanjay fording a stream.[34] It was the summer of 1960, and she was on vacation with her husband, the Member of Parliament Feroze Gandhi, and their two sons. They were in Daksum, 'a pleasant place, pine and fir forest and trout streams and all.' This was where bears came down from the wooded hills to gorge themselves on stores of maize and on the grain ripening in the fields.[35] Still, 'a kingfisher came right into our sitting room and a swift had perched on Rajiv's shoulder.'[36] Such joy was short-lived; two weeks later her husband was dead.

I Don't Ever Want Us to Beg for Food Again

By the early 1960s Indira Gandhi's role in public life was larger than before: it became more central as Nehru's health and political

[31] Anon., 'The Delhi Bird Watchers' Society'; Bhagat, *Indiraji*, p. 151.

[32] IG to Dorothy Norman, 13 October 1963, in Norman, *Indira Gandhi*, p. 96.

[33] Gandhi, 'Manali'.

[34] The photo is published in Gandhi, *Rajiv's World*, p. 9. This family holiday was a rare moment together in an estranged marriage, but foreshadowed tragedy. Feroze Gandhi died two months later, aged only forty-eight: Frank, *Indira*, p. 256.

[35] IG to JN, House Boat Argonaut, Nagin Lake, Kashmir, 27 June 1960, in Gandhi, *Two Alone*, p. 566.

[36] Ibid.

standing suffered after China's attack on India in October 1962. It was no surprise she was Union Minister of the Information and Broadcasting Ministry, earlier headed by Nehru's successor Lal Bahadur Shastri (1964–6). The latter's death and a bitter inner party succession struggle propelled her to the top in January 1966. She would soon draw on a range of new ideas about water and wildlife, forests and the environment at large. However, there was a more pressing matter at hand: food, or rather the lack of it in adequate amounts for those who needed it the most.

The India she came to lead in January 1966 was a country heavily, even excessively, reliant on the monsoon. Nature's wrath was more evident than its beneficence; and it was the food crisis that commanded immediate attention. Over 70 per cent of India lived off the land. Her visit to Washington DC two months later, as she confided to the veteran journalist Inder Malhotra, was aimed to 'get food, aid and foreign exchange *without* appearing to ask for it.'[37] Her visit to Washington was deemed a success. Charmed by the young premier, Lyndon Johnson asked the US Congress to double food aid to seven million tonnes. The World Bank increased lending to 1.5 billion dollars. Already embroiled in a land war in Vietnam, Johnson saw India as a bulwark of democracy in an Asia vulnerable to communism. India's grain imports in the next two years would total nineteen million tonnes. Over the first of those years alone, one out of every five kg of grain harvested in the US headed India's way. This was aid, not outright purchase. India was to devalue the rupee and accept economic measures the US saw as essential. Even as she phoned the White House for more food, she told an aide in that December of 1966, 'I don't ever want us to beg for food again'.[38]

The honeymoon was short-lived. There was a storm of protest awaiting the PM at home, not least within the ruling party.

[37] Malhotra, *Indira Gandhi*, p. 95.

[38] IG to H.Y. Sharada Prasad, December 1966, in Kux, *The United States and India*, p. 257.

Relations soured by July. Washington never came through with the quantum of assistance it had promised. India soon condemned the American bombing of North Vietnam. From 'understanding' America's anguish in Vietnam to 'condemning' the bombing, Indira Gandhi travelled a great ideological distance between March and July of 1966. That latter month saw her in Moscow, where the statement called for a halt of bombing of Hanoi and condemned 'imperialist and reactionary forces'.[39] Relations became bitter, even as Indian reliance on American largesse had, perforce, to continue. In 1967 she sent personal greetings to Vietnam's leader Ho Chi Minh on his seventy-fifth birthday. Three years later, speaking at a conclave of the non-aligned countries in Lusaka, she drew parallels between the nuclear peril and what was 'more insidious', daily pollution of the environment. What crossed the line was clear: the chemical contamination of animal and plant life in Vietnam.[40] Ecological warfare was a symbol of assault on nature as much as on freedom. Charming Washington had given way to standing up for Asia and Africa. Yet a strident stance abroad required serious reform at home. This was clear on the public platform. A year into her premiership, at a varsity convocation in Bangalore she sketched out connections between water scarcity and denudation of forest cover. Hydel projects and mines were imperative, but 'our building zeal is not accompanied by respect for the needs of conservation.' Nor was this a matter of choice. For there was a clear link between the widespread drought and deforestation. She rued the fact that 'We had cut down many forests.'[41] It was even clearer in the executive action on the farm front. The Green Revolution, focussed as it was on high yielding varieties and higher prices to cultivators in a few select regions, was the concomitant of such conservation.

Its roots, earlier, literally lay in the induction of C. Subramaniam into the agriculture ministry under her predecessor in 1964. 'CS',

[39] Frank, *Indira*, pp. 297, 299. By November she was in Moscow for the anniversary of the October Revolution.

[40] Gandhi, 'The Unfinished Revolution', p. 55.

[41] Gandhi, 'Tradition and Change', pp. 15, 17.

as he was known, made available the work of Indian scientists already in touch with Norman Borlaug and was a driving force at the very apex of the polity. Results were not long in coming. Speaking to a gathering of Asia's scientists in 1968, Mrs Gandhi was at pains to refute the image of peasant conservatism. Tobacco and groundnut farming had been transformed: 'similar changes' lay ahead for cereal crops.[42] The overall farm growth rate figures actually showed a dip from the previous period, falling from 2.9 per cent (1961–5) to 2.1 per cent in the succeeding four years. However, these were misleading. The output of grain increased by 5 per cent a year, from 1966 onward, for a period of fifteen years. At a time when Malthusian fears were the fashion, this was more than twice the rate of growth of India's population. More important was the food stock kept by the federal government which increased to nine million tonnes by 1971.[43] By then, the acreage of hybrid wheat varieties had increased to over four million hectares.[44]

It was ironical for the Rockefeller Foundation to be facilitating co-operation between American and Indian scientists. The aim was to get hybrid seeds for the farmer. President Johnson assisted this shift, seeing himself as a driving force for change. Subramaniam reflected years later that the president saw himself as a district nawab. Himself an agronomist from the cultivating community of Gounders in Tamil Nadu, CS was clear that the motive force for change came from Indians themselves, not the Americans. Looking back it is unclear if America was being used more by India than the other way round. Yet it was touch and go till late in the day, with shipments of food often held up when they were needed most.[45]

The transformation also had a critical political dimension. The rise of the Maoist insurgency at Naxalbari, a village in West Bengal,

[42] Gandhi, 'Tasks Before Asian Scientists', p. 27.

[43] Panagariya, *India: Emerging Giant*, pp. 71–3.

[44] Gandhi, 'Stimulate Economic Growth', p. 123.

[45] Swaminathan, 'The Green Revolution'; on Subramaniam's reflections, Kux, *The United States and India*, p. 247.

in May 1968 and later elsewhere in the country, made it imperative to raise agricultural production and generate rural jobs.[46] The Green Revolution did *not* put an end to food imports or indeed to hunger. What it did do was make India less reliant on the vagaries of the monsoon and US food aid. When food imports soared in 1976, India bought over 12 million tonnes, but paid for it. The aid era was at an end.[47]

Such a narrative cannot possibly do justice to the complexity of events, but the denouement does reveal two interlinked facets of Indira Gandhi's India. Agricultural intensification and nature protection went hand in hand. The two were complementary, or at least seen to be so. More than that, preservation was part of a larger nationalist enterprise, with the leadership throwing its weight behind innovators precisely at a time of maturing internal and external crises. There was more to saving forests and wildlife than the fates of the wild. Higher yields per acre meant more land did not have to be ploughed up in order to grow more food. There was a shift to intensive cultivation as opposed to government-sponsored colonization, as had been the case in the terai in North India in the 1950s.

An Abundance of Irony

Preserving nature was integral to the effort and has often been seen as a flagship. In a telling sign of the times, around 1972 the Bengal tiger began to be referred to as the Indian tiger.[48] It was a patriotic enterprise, with Indians being asked to rally round to save a heritage in peril, natural as much as national. The forester Kailash Sankhala had long exchanged his shotgun for a camera, getting the PM to even name two tiger cubs in the city zoo. As a Jawaharlal Nehru Fellow he submitted a research report detailing the decline of the

[46] See the penultimate chapter of Rao, *The Insider*.

[47] Panagariya, *India: Emerging Giant*, p. 72.

[48] The point is made in Greenough, 'Pathogens, Pugmarks'. For a more comprehensive treatment, see Rangarajan, 'The Politics of Ecology', pp. 189–239.

species due to overhunting, poaching, and loss of habitat.[49] Exports of big cat skins had already been banned. Sport hunting by safari companies, a valuable source of foreign exchange, also ended. When a Task Force reported in September 1972 that the tiger required safe havens where it could live and multiply with adequate cover and wild prey, a nationwide effort was launched the very next April. As Indira Gandhi said, Project Tiger abounded in irony. The species was in a struggle to survive in the land that had been its abode for millennia.[50] A major concomitant of these efforts was the widening of horizons of wildlife to extend to all uncultivated flora and fauna and not just birds and animals. Each tiger reserve, and there were nine in all, had core zones closed off from tree felling by foresters, grazing of cattle, and human habitation.[51] Radical preservation won advocacy from key opinion makers outside the government, such as M. Krishnan, the reputed naturalist and photographer.[52] Also a Nehru Fellow, he saw the project as a turning point in securing India's unique identity, no less linked to irreplaceable natural features as to monuments and cultures.[53] Saving the tiger was a route to a larger appreciation of landscapes, arid or wet, hillside or desert: they were not simply seen as raw material or potential arable or as waste.[54] Such ecological patriotism put pristine nature at the centre of a project for the nation-state.

This shift from an overly commercial view of nature to a more holistic appreciation of nature as a common heritage had a social and political context. November 1969, when the government

[49] Sankhala, *Tiger!*, pp. 141, 161. For tiger cubs, see idem, *Wild Beauty*; idem, *The Controversial Tiger*.

[50] Gandhi, 'Message for the Launch of Project Tiger', p. 112.

[51] For a detailed examination, see Rangarajan, *India's Wildlife History*, pp. 94–108.

[52] See his writings in Guha, *Nature's Spokesman*.

[53] This shift was authored mainly by Krishnan, himself a B.Sc. in Botany. See Indian Board for Wildlife, *Wildlife Conservation*, p. 1 (hereafter *Wildlife 1970*). The older view that wildlife equals animals is elaborated in Gee, 'The Management of India's National Parks'.

[54] Ishwar Prakash, 'The Amazing Life'.

banned tiger skin exports, was also the month when chief ministers came together for a conference on land reforms.[55] The end of sport-hunting companies was a blow to the owners, many of whom were former princes, a class whose privileges were now abolished for good. The abolition of the privy purses of princes, a holdover from the time of their accession after Independence, was a major battle cry of the Congress as it entered the general election campaign of 1971.

The campaign to 'Save our Skins' against the fur trade got under way around the same time as the finance ministry raided black marketeers and hoarders. Bank nationalization rallied those who had had little access to credit; nature protection looked like a similar defence of a common wealth against loot. These 'carefully chosen targets' were past oppressors, whether princes, bankers, or conservative judges. However, they gave Indira Gandhi legitimacy for larger schemes, including those that sought to 'make room for nature'.[56] Both Krishnan and Sankhala formed a part of the larger milieu that marked the early years of the new prime minister. This is not the place to go into detail, but a few parallels will suffice. Their call for sustained state action was in line with the wider political agendas of her left-wing advisers, once she took on the Old Guard or Syndicate in 1969. Her secretary and former Foreign Service diplomat, the erudite P.N. Haksar, provided ideological rationale for the government takeover of fourteen private sector banks. Crackdowns on smugglers and black marketeers were a hallmark of a minister of state, K.R. Ganesh. The coal minister and former communist Mohan Kumaramangalam piloted the bill to nationalize the coal sector. In all these cases there was a pitting of the interests of many versus the few, and an attack on privilege.[57]

[55] Gandhi, 'Science to Solve Man's Problems'; idem, Importance of Land Reforms, Chief Ministers' Conference on Land Reforms, 28 November 1969, in *Speeches 1969*, pp. 267–73.

[56] These points are forcefully made in a perceptive piece: Karanth, 'Making Room for Nature'.

[57] On K.R. Ganesh, see memoirs of the revenue service officer F.G. Gilani

The mood lasted till after the general elections of 1971, which the Congress won on the slogan of abolishing poverty. It carried over to the state assembly polls of 1972, after the Bangladesh war. Mrs Gandhi had faced down the party bosses, then the US, and now ruled via loyal followers both in New Delhi and in all but one state. As an astute observer later recalled, 'The poor man in the village began to walk with a bit of a swagger, because of a combination of naiveté and a genuine awakening of consciousness.'[58] 'Hands off' nature had its flip side. It was no coincidence that the term *sanctum sanctorum*, which has religious overtones, was used to describe the core zones of the tiger reserves.[59] Unlike in the 1950s, when Sálim Ali urged Nehru to save a wetland, or the late 1960s when studies by the Smithsonian informed efforts to secure the lions of the Gir Forest, science took a back seat. Indian foresters claimed prior and superior knowledge of 'their' tigers. The Smithsonian's director complained of 'an evolving nationalistic pride' and was not far off the mark.[60] Yet Indian relations with the United States were in the deep freeze from 1970 on, as Nixon tilted towards the military regime in Pakistan. India may have closed doors to America, but a leading UN agency got involved with efforts to save crocodilians. Soon after, the British naturalist Gerald Durrell's Jersey Wildlife Trust was allowed to advise on saving the pygmy hog, a rare small mammal in a sensitive border state in Assam. A leading European expert even researched the Kashmir stag in the Dachigam sanctuary to help evolve protective strategies.

Project Tiger itself was to get a million dollars from the World Wildlife Fund. It was significant that its key leaders were European.

---

under the pen-name Iqbal Masud: Masud, *Dream Merchants*, p. 106. All those named in this paragraph had been left-wing activists in their student days.

[58] This was, of course, P.V. Narasimha Rao. See Rao, *The Insider*, p. 623.

[59] See Krishnan, 'An Ecological Survey'; 'delimit sanctum sanctorum in national parks and wildlife sanctuaries and exclude all human disturbance including forestry operations', in Indian Board for Wildlife, IX Session, Delhi: Ministry of Food and Agriculture, pp. 20–3.

[60] Lewis, *Inventing Global Ecology*, pp. 235–6.

Prince Bernhard was Dutch royalty and Guy Mountfort a British advertising czar.[61] In fact, far from being nationalists with a blind spot, the Indians had played their wildlife wealth to advantage and wooed the Europeans in place of the Americans. In the early 1970s there was still a heady dose of nationalism. It was all the more heady as it evoked the spectre of a crisis. Just as agricultural scientists, long at work, were to be at the forefront of new techniques in the farm, so too were there new thinkers on the ecological front. Conservation, like agricultural innovation, was driven by a sense of crisis. Failure meant disaster, success was all. Indira Gandhi gave them an ear and much more, a milieu in which their ideas acquired force and momentum.[62] It also reached back into the past. The movement to have national parks in India was for a proponent 'as old as Indian history', and it was commonplace to cite Asokan edicts of the third century BCE.[63] This evocation of the tiger as a symbol of unity reached its apogee as Project Tiger got under way after 1 April 1973, barely a year and eighteen days before the nuclear tests at Pokhran. Later, in 1974, India launched a space satellite, appropriately named after the fifth-century astronomer Aryabhatta.

Getting out of one crisis did little to avert another. By 1972 the mood was changing. Narasimha Rao put it dryly: 'The more the euphoria', he wrote, 'the deeper and quicker the disillusionment.'[64] War had brought in 10 million refugees. Agriculture suffered under successive droughts in 1971 and 1972. The Arab–Israel war of October 1973 was accompanied by the oil-price shock.

[61] This point was first made by Lewis. See ibid., pp. 245–7. See Holloway and Wani, *Management Plan*; Oliver, *The Pygmy Hog*; Mountfort, 'International Efforts'.

[62] Parthasarathi, *Technology at the Core*, pp. 241–77. Among those involved with environmental policies were Pitamber Pant, M.S. Swaminathan, and public health specialist J.M. Dave. The issues taken up included diesel exhaust by Delhi buses, pesticide plant residues outside the capital, and the Mathura refinery close to the Taj Mahal.

[63] Anon., *Save Our Skins*; Sankhala, 'The National Parks', p. 1.

[64] Rao, *The Insider*, p. 647.

Finally, prices of consumer goods rose by over 20 per cent a year for two successive years. By mid 1974 the polity was heading towards breakdown. A year later the prime minister when unseated by a court in a disputed election advised the president to evoke Emergency powers. For the first time since Independence, India was no more a democracy. Yet the Emergency was built on notions of centralist governance, initially at least, with a large middle-class constituency. It had an appeal among advocates of conservation that was easy to miss.

One common rallying point among preservationists was the issue of the states' rights over forests. The country's top ornithologist had long advocated the leasing of wetlands by the Centre. State governments were also a target of attack for abetting forest conversion to farmland in a host of ways. Only 'an integrated authority', wrote the irrepressible Krishnan, could avoid the mantle of protection from being taken apart altogether.[65] They may not have been unaware that the prime minister too was thinking on similar lines.[66] The Forty-second Constitution Amendment carried into effect in January 1977 did much to weaken the democratic edifice, but it also placed 'Forests and Wildlife' on the Concurrent as opposed to the States' List. This meant that both the federal and state governments had jurisdiction. However, in the event of a difference, it was the Union whose will would prevail. It is significant that even after Mrs Gandhi lost power in March 1977, and the opposition Janata Party came to power, it did not undo this provision.

Conservation got a boost as its darker side became apparent. Ironically, while shutting out American wildlife biology, Indian

[65] On wetlands, Ali, 'Some Problems of Assessing Wildfowl', p. 233; IG had discussed the possibility in September 1971. On forests, Krishnan, 'An Ecological Survey', p. 531.

[66] Indian Board for Wildlife, 18 November 1972, Item no. 3, Proposal to Lease Parks of National Significance to the Union Government, Ministry of Agriculture and Forests, 1972, *Ninth Session of the Indian Board for Wildlife*, p. 17.

foresters also reinforced their own monopoly over wildlife watching and monitoring. Nowhere was this as stark as in the pugmark-based tiger counts, whose results became a subject of controversy. Greenough has drawn parallels of the smallpox eradication and tiger protection campaigns. Actually, there was a game of numbers, but it had to do with the multiplication of the striped beasts and the rising numbers of sterilized humans in the Emergency. By 1976, Project Tiger officials were claiming a surge in tiger populations. An expert team from Western conservation organizations questioned this, but the report was not known to anyone in India till well after the Emergency. The Mid Term Assessment did more than call for more science-based studies. It also asked for a far more accommodative approach for village-level livelihoods in the buffer zone of the Tiger Reserves.[67] It hardly caused a ripple. Although far from radical, it looked at the landscape as two biologists and a civil administrator would. It was at variance on key issues with the way foresters saw preservation simply as an issue of enforcement.[68]

The issue of sterilization by coercion was more explosive and at a human level far more serious. It did much to undermine the Congress' rock-solid support among the underclasses on whose strength it had won such a huge mandate only a few years earlier. It was estimated that the target of 23 million sterilizations would be met in thirty-six months. Three million sterilizations were carried out in just the first five months, from July to November of 1975.[69] Backed by her son and heir apparent Sanjay Gandhi, it also focussed neo-Malthusian fears on the poor, the Scheduled Castes, and the religious minorities. It was also closely linked to urban slum demolitions, especially in Delhi. This stands out, even with hindsight, as the one time when the number and population of slum dwellers actually declined due to coercive displacement.

[67] Leyhausen, Holloway, and Ranjitsinh, *Conservation of the Tiger*, pp. 18, 38–9, 48–9.

[68] This was true even of outstanding forester naturalists. See Deb Roy, 'Socio-economic Aspects of Preservation'.

[69] Frank, *Indira*, p. 407.

As with centralist impulses for preservation, the concept of unauthorized slums pre-dated the Emergency. The latter transmuted power into authority overnight, enabling coercion to be exercised out in the open.[70] There were limits to the process. An aide recalled an incident in late 1976: the PM was visibly shaken when shown a report about schoolteachers being coerced to get 'volunteers' for vasectomy. She began to search for ways to end the impasse.[71]

The Centre Cannot Hold

The Emergency era ended suddenly in January 1977 when the prime minister dissolved parliament and called for elections. Her party's rout was total and it was out of power for the first time in three decades. However, she was back in office in just eighteen months. The period of 1979–80 marked a turning point in political fortunes for the leader who was back at the helm, again with a massive two-thirds majority.

Where did all this leave preservation? In a way, now the sense of crisis was less on the wildlife front and more of a rapid expansion of the existing programmes. By the end of the 1980s about 4 per cent of the land area was under sanctuaries and parks, as compared to one-eighth that figure in 1970. The Wildlife Protection Act of 1972 remained the key legal instrument, but programmes such as Project Tiger were now routinized. Its director even wrote a paper entitled 'What to Do When You Have Succeeded'.[72] The tiger, like India, seemed to bask in success.

Yet, there was a cauldron of brewing conflicts. Some had their genesis in the first Indira period, but had taken time to crystallize. What had begun as a project of protection driven by the prime minister's office became an article of faith for political leaders of

[70] DuPont, 'Slum Demolitions'; Tarlo, 'Welcome to History'.

[71] Dhar, *Indira Gandhi*, pp. 343–4.

[72] Panwar, 'What to Do'. H.S. Panwar, then Director of Project Tiger, later became Director of the Wildlife Institute of India.

different parties. In February 1978 an International Symposium on the Tiger, held when she was out of power, was inaugurated by her former associate and now *bête noire*, Jagjivan Ram.[73] Protecting tigers for their own sake had once been a radical, even outlandish idea. It had become a new orthodoxy.

Looking back, what is striking is how far displacement of residents, by 1977, itself became the *sine qua non* of wildlife preservation. It was often the first rather than the last response. Initially, it had been confined to a few select habitats of rare species: the swamp deer (*Cervus duaveceli branderi*) in Central India or the Asian (or Indian) lion (*Panthera leo persica*) in Gujarat. A handful of tiger reserves followed suit, the issue of habitat contiguity and prey availability taking priority over continued human habitation. Those that moved out—whether pastoralists, Adivasi (or for that matter non-tribal) cultivators, or fishers—often found coping with new styles of production arduous.[74] Displacement from conservation areas for wildlife was not new: there were a few precedents. They became an ideal for foresters to strive for.

Conflict could be violent. There was serious, bloody confrontation in the buffer zone of the Sundarbans Tiger Reserve, where the forcible eviction of refugees led to violence and massacre. This incident in West Bengal, long forgotten, took place in 1978, and has been documented in detail by scholars. A Left Front government elected in 1977, and one with an enviable record of land reform and devolution, was responsible for such violent displacement. Yet, when it came to dealing with refugees settled on government forest estates earmarked for tiger habitats, its response was brutal.[75] There were other instances of closure of access, including one in

[73] J. Ram, Union Minister for Defence, 'Inaugural Address, First International Symposium on the Tiger', Delhi, typescript. The veteran minister was no newcomer to the issues, having held the Agriculture portfolio at crucial times in the 1970s.

[74] For a review of issues on relocation, see Rangarajan and Shahabuddin, 'Relocation from Protected Areas', pp. 359–78.

[75] Jalais, 'Dwelling on Morichjhanppi'; idem, *Forest of Tigers*.

November 1982, leading to police firing in Keoladeo Ghana, the waterfowl reserve in Bharatpur. Here, the issue was not eviction, but tightening of controls, as the site went from being a mere sanctuary to a national park. Deprived of grazing access overnight, the villagers broke the rubble wall and entered the park. Police firing followed. The government stood its ground. Eviction if possible and enclosure if not was becoming a norm.[76]

The fate of the forest was a keen subject of contest. As with the Emergency-era regulations, administrative fiat and coercion had the ear of officialdom. The Forest (Conservation) Act in 1980 made union government clearance mandatory for the clearance of forest areas of over ten hectares. This centralized powers, even as there were new pressures on forest land due to agricultural extension and large industrial projects. By October 1982 Indira Gandhi lectured state forest ministers on how the country needed some really 'hard measures' to halt denudation of hill catchments.[77] The difference was that in the India of the 1980s public opinion mattered a lot more. The Congress' victory had in part been enabled by a sweep of most parliamentary seats reserved for the Scheduled Tribes. By 1982 many Adivasi groups were up in revolt against a new proposed Forest Bill. A Delhi-based group put it simply, calling the legislation part of an 'undeclared civil war'. Forest officers were to be given magisterial powers of detention; customary access would be effectively criminalized.

The issue brought together a multi-hued coalition of opponents: liberation theologists and tribal mass organizations, as also urban ecologically aware youth and human rights groups. A fusion of ecological and justice themes emerged in the course of the campaign. The Bill was never tabled.[78] The multiple shades of green, or of green merging with other colours of a more radical or liberal hue, did not always lead to rejection or repression. In fact, it was

[76] Kalpavriksh, *Death in a Sanctuary.*

[77] Gandhi, Speech to the Central Forestry Board, pp. 53–4.

[78] People's Union for Democratic Rights, *Undeclared Civil War.*

striking to see how personal ties were central to Indira Gandhi's politics. This had been a marked feature of her first term. Now, even as her party lacked leaders of experience, as in the past she drew on a wider ecumene.[79] By 1980, protests against monoculture taken up by the Chipko movement in the Western Himalayas from 1973, had their counterparts elsewhere. In the Jharkhand plateau the cry against commercial forestry pitted the sal (*Shorea robusta*) against the sagwan or teak (*Tectona grandis*). Livelihood was in opposition to commerce. It was around this time that there was a shift in the policy. This did not end the clear-felling of mixed natural forests for monocultures, but at least it was no more a policy. A major project for pine plantation, for paper pulp in Bastar, Central India, was shelved after a review.[80] In 1982, even as it stepped back from the Forest Bill, the union government also passed orders against leasing out government forest land to private companies. Of course, state governments often went their own way, and leases such as those in Madhya Pradesh, the state with the most extensive forest acreage, were never cancelled.[81] The larger rubric of the conflicts was between rival resource users; increasing demand for biomass from industry was contending with usufruct rightholders.

If the government came down more clearly on the side of the forester, it was part of a larger secular shift in the politics of the Congress. Indira Gandhi's politics had edged away from socialist rhetoric and populism to a more 'pro-business' attitude. Critical changes in the licensing policy eased technology imports, and capacity expansion with wealth creation, not redistribution, was the focus of the policy. This was symbolized by a dinner in her honour in an elite Delhi hotel. The host was Dhirubhai Ambani, already India's largest producer of polyester, the synthetic fibre that would

[79] For instance, see veteran Chipko leader Sunderlal Bahuguna's warm memories of the late prime minister: S. Bahuguna, 'Interview: My Work will Go on Even if I Fail', *The Hindu*, 18 June 1995. For an analysis of the differences among various activists, see Guha, *Unquiet Woods*, pp. 179–84.

[80] Anderson and Huber, *Hour of the Fox*.

[81] Chambers, *et al.*, *To the Hands of the Poor*, p. 236.

over time displace cotton as the poor man's fabric.[82] New policies to assist private investment in electronics were integral to the larger economic changes. It was around this time that Wipro, a company known for its vegetable oil business, entered the software business, as did Infosys, and today's software giants were set up.[83] If silicon and not steel was to define the century up ahead, the beginnings lay here in the late Indira period.

The growth story was better than in her first stint in power and this was not just so for large industrial houses. Growth rates through the 1980s rose at a steady clip, coming close to 6 per cent, almost double that of the rocky decade of the 1970s. These changes were counterbalanced by higher rates of growth, especially in agriculture. Farm growth rates were high, as the Green Revolution spread beyond north-west India, helped by diesel pumpsets for drawing groundwater, and the growth of credit. In 1983–4 it was pegged at as high as 8.1 per cent.

These figures are dry, as figures can be, but they do indicate a very different context from that of the 1970s.[84] As with the politics of ecology, the economic scenario was a mixed one. The overall drift was clear, but there were checks and balances. It is plausible that more farm and non-farm job creation took some of the edge off natural resource-related conflicts and tensions.

This rapprochement with industrialists had its external counterpart. Despite the outbreak of a new cold war, especially around the Afghan issue, India entered into a closer dialogue with Reagan's America. Economics was never too far from either the US president's mind or the Indian PM's. This also helped cement Indo-American ties in biological research, with a bounty for new research programmes. A new generation of wildlife biologists outside the

[82] MacDonald, *Polyester Prince*, pp. 48–9. Reliance was among the top fifty industrial houses in 1980 but would be among the five largest by 1984.

[83] Sharma, *The Long Revolution*. I am grateful to the author for sharing his manuscript and ideas on the subject; on Wipro and Infosys, Subramanian, *India's Rise*, esp. p. 42.

[84] Panagariya, *India: Emerging Giant*, p. 84.

Forest Department, and working on a range of habitats, were beneficiaries of the thaw.[85]

Not Starting from Ground Zero

The storm over large dam projects soon found Mrs Gandhi at their centre. She was not an advocate of appropriate technologies. Her remark to Capra in 1983 is worth reflecting on: 'If I could start from zero, I would do things differently. But I have to be realistic. There is a large technological base in India which I can't throw away.' The issue, she told the physicist, was how to choose the technology appropriate to the task at hand. There was, she freely admitted, an issue of technology 'destroying the existing culture'. She might have added, not just cultures but the integrity of ecosystems was under threat.[86] She was part and parcel of a tradition of commissioning large projects. There is an uncanny echo of Jawaharlal Nehru—who used a similar idiom—in a closed-door meeting of Gandhi's closest associates only weeks after his death. Industrialization was not a matter of choice or simply of survival; it was imperative for the defence of India. Speaking as he was only weeks after the winter war of 1947–8 over Kashmir, his words had an urgency none of the senior Gandhians missed.[87] By 1980 the legacy of large projects was all too real. In just thirty years, ending in 1980, India had built nearly 900 large dams, more than any country after the US, USSR, Japan, and China.[88] Yet Indira Gandhi was aware of the larger debate on dams. Prior to her electoral rout in 1977, she had ordered a comprehensive environmental impact assessment of all large and medium irrigation projects. Although nothing came of this, it does show a keen awareness of larger issues.[89]

[85] Lewis, *Inventing Global Ecology*, p. 247; for an account of such interaction, see Sale, 'Reintroduction in Indian Wildlife Management'.

[86] Capra, *Uncommon Wisdom*, pp. 337, 338. Emphasis added.

[87] Gandhi, *Gandhi is Gone*, p. 64.

[88] Khagram, *Dams and Development*, p. 37.

[89] Ibid., p. 42.

By 1980 the senior civil servant B.B. Vohra, a Punjab Indian Administrative Service officer with a special interest in land and water issues, had honed a sharp critique of large multi-purpose river valley projects. Mrs Gandhi had given teeth to his ideas by creating Land Use boards, although these were but paper tigers.[90] In her case, there was more of a willingness to look at options, mainly for ecological rationale, as in the cases of Moyar and Silent Valley. Big dams were as integral to Indira Gandhi's worldview as they had been to her father's. Neither was an uncritical admirer, but both were advocates.[91]

In 1974 she inaugurated stretches of what would become the Rajasthan Canal, one of the largest man-made inter-basin water transfers in the country's history. The veteran actor Sunil Dutt's *Reshma aur Shera* also commemorated the canal in a memorable film. Fittingly, the hero loses his life in bringing waters to the parched land. Such projects were difficult to accomplish given that large rivers ran through more than one state. In 1974 and again in 1981 she got the chief ministers of the riparian states of the river Narmada around a table. Contrary to her image as an inveterate centralizer, she was often cautious about state-level aspirations, urging the two key states along rather than issuing a diktat to the two Congress chief ministers. On the second occasion, in 1981, much more than earlier, these were men who owed much to her politically. Arjun Singh in Madhya Pradesh and Madhavsinh Solanki were state leaders of the populist alliances of the 'so-called lower' castes and Scheduled Tribes. However, even here there was only so much the union government could do.[92] Larger critiques of the Narmada projects that combined displacement and ecological dimensions had been compiled by 1983, but were yet to reach centrestage.[93] Political leaders were faced with a prosaic question:

[90] Vohra, *Land and Water Policy*.

[91] Rangarajan, 'Of Nature and Nationalism'.

[92] See Khagram, *Dams and Development*, p. 239, n. 37. Khagram's account of the Narmada issue is a finely balanced one. On the Indira years, see esp. pp. 78–87.

[93] Kalpavriksh, *Death in a Sanctuary*.

How to divide the wealth of waters, not whether or not to dam their flow. The riparian states differed on who would get how much water or power. They were all at one as regards building a series of large dams.

All this did not mean that Indira Gandhi could not take a stand *against* such projects. She did; and this could make all, or much, of the difference. In 1973 (the same year as Project Tiger), power engineers set their sights on Silent Valley, to build a dam on the river Kuntipuzha. Prime Minister Morarji Desai initially cleared the 240 megawatt project for construction, in 1978. He agreed to the scheme in return for letting the left-wing state government go easy on his pet project: prohibition. Indira Gandhi, then in the Opposition, was unable to get her state Congress unit to distance itself from the proposed dam. The grassroots campaign of the mass people's science movement, the Kerala Shastra Sahitya Parishad gained impressive support; and scientists the world over appealed against the dam. A committee of experts, headed by naturalist Zafar Futehally, investigated the project; but, more importantly, the larger committee continued to lobby Desai's successor Charan Singh. In January 1980, as prime minister, Indira Gandhi had to devise a way out. Her sympathies clearly lay with advocates of preserving a site critical as a rainforest.[94] However, in her letters she admitted to being under pressure. There were, after all, legitimate regional aspirations for power and water. North Kerala, a backward region, had legitimate demands that could not be overlooked.[95] It took until 1983 for the M.S. Swaminathan Committee's report to secure the rainforest, while developing alternative sources for power and irrigation.

This was not the only such case where her intervention was critical to staving off a hydel project. The Moyar Dam that would

[94] This account owes much to D'Monte, *Temples or Tombs?* pp. 45–61. In neither of the other cases—the refinery near the Taj or the fertilizer plant near Bombay—was relocation even considered. An important early critique of large dams was Sharma and Sharma, *Major Dams.*

[95] Indira Gandhi to Mustafa Tolba, 13 August 1981, in Gandhi, *Selected Speeches and Writings, 1980–81*, pp. 306–12.

have inundated the Mudumalai wildlife sanctuary in neighbouring Tamil Nadu was also set aside.[96] This was even more critical as it formed part of a vast habitat of intact forest and scrub comprising as many as four large Protected Areas. If both Silent Valley and Mudumalai remain intact to this day, any assessment would have to give some credit to her openness to the idea of ecological integrity and species diversity. The NCEPC, to be superseded in November 1980 by the Department of Environment, had played a key role in the turn of events.[97] However, in the Silent Valley case, she had gone beyond the committee of the newly constituted Department of Environment. Any such lobbying had self-evident limits. Prime ministerial authority could only be invoked in exceptional cases. As in so much else, her personal role may have averted the crises, but it came at the cost of sound institutional mechanisms. The power of the office and the person who held it was central to her aura. It is tempting to ask if each such crisis really needed intervention at the highest level, and that too in a country the size of Western Europe and with well over half a billion people.

Much of her career at the top had been about the push and pull between populist development ideas and elite conservation agendas. There was little doubt that she espoused *both* very categorically. However, there was a pronounced and clear shift towards growth first than over redistribution. Already by the mid 1970s many of her left-wing advisers had gone from the scene. The easing of import restrictions for industry, although limited, was to be of great significance. These included initiatives for a more stringent legislation on forests and a much more successful enactment of the Forest Conservation Act that gave New Delhi a decisive say in the conversion of forest land to alternative use.

[96] D'Monte, *Temples or Tombs?* pp. 74–5.

[97] The Department of Environment was formed on the recommendation of a committee headed by senior union minister Narain Dutt Tiwari. Its first head was a marine biologist of repute, S. Zahoor Qasim; later it was headed by an eminent botanist, Triloki Nath Khooshoo. This convention was soon set aside in favour of civil servants, who soon ousted scientists from the top post.

By 1983 the political picture was fast deteriorating. This was helped in no small way by the crisis in her own party. The economy picked up pace. However, her party lost its hold on two southern states that had stood by it even in 1977, Karnataka and Andhra Pradesh. Furthermore, concomitant with her pro-business stance, she also began courting Hindu cultural nationalism, especially in handling sensitive issues of identity in two border states where Hindus were in a minority. The die was cast by the time of the army action in the summer of 1984 in Punjab. Her assassination in October ended a long and tempestuous life. When asked whether she was losing her grip, a journalist close to her publicly said she had never regained control after her return to office. In a private correspondence a year earlier, Indira Gandhi had quoted Yeats: 'Things fall apart. The centre cannot hold.'[98]

Room for All of Us

Historians of late-twentieth-century India can scarcely avoid the record or the legacy of its first woman prime minister. Her action and words counted even before she came to power and in the interregnum when she was out of office. In a speech to the heads of state and government gathered at the Non Aligned Summit in Delhi in 1983 she spoke of how the earth had 'room for all of us'. Of course, in the eyes of both critics and admirers, especially so of her environmental record, it looked rather different. There seems to have been room for only one of us.[99] Indira Priyadarshini Nehru Gandhi was a product of a vibrant and active nationalist awakening. It was one that engaged with issues of ethics and science, technology and nature to a far greater extent than we often give credit for. She was a statist, and, in her father's mould, a modernizer. But far more than him, she was deeply sensitive to more than just the call of the wild or the question of making room

[98] Malhotra, *Indira Gandhi*, p. 285.

[99] This is also true of my own earlier and very preliminary engagement with this subject: Rangarajan, 'Ideology, the Environment, and Policy'.

for nature in the world's second-most populous country. In fact, in the 1970s, as in the 1980s, there was close correspondence between her political turns and her environmental policies. If in the first she took a leftward course, there was a coinciding of targets in politics as in conservation. The 1980s saw a movement to the centre-right and there is no doubt at all that the authoritarian impulse of the Emergency was alive and well, although in homoeopathic doses. The absence of works of the timbre of *Discovery of India* may indicate less in terms of scholarship, but there is no doubt at all of the quality of intellect that grappled with dilemmas of development. By the 1980s it was more than the economy that had matured. As democracy struck deeper roots, new impulses came to the fore. This was as true of the forest as of the polity as a whole.

Institutional disarray and decay were masked by her sense of energy and engagement with crises. Nature was framed for her by the nation-state, for its birth and reinforcement were central to her life. In keeping with the shifting kaleidoscope of the Congress' ways, there was empathy for the underclass, but less of a recognition of rights than a careful dispersal of patronage. Looking back there is little doubt that the legacy is one that divides as much as it unifies. Contrary to the challenge of a contemporary history that is marked by detachment or distance, over time, there is only *more* to move the student of her record to empathy as much as outrage, admiration as much as criticism.[100] In common with other political leaders, her ideas and practices evolved over time. As her conservation initiatives collided with state powers, federal government structures, and the aspirations of the poor—especially rural and tribal people threatened by parks, forests, and reserves—she learnt to conflate her ideals and nationalism. Her personal inclinations and the demands of practical statecraft were an ever-changing mix. In general, there were two critical paradigm shifts in Indira Gandhi's approach to questions of conservation in the period after 1969. There was a growing affinity that developed between her autocratic approach to government and nature after 1972. This was concomitant with

[100] Guha, 'The Challenge of Contemporary History'.

her general deepening hold on power, both at the federal and state levels, to a degree unprecedented in independent India. Many of the initiatives were to outlast her defeat and even her return to office. However, equally significant was the fact that there was another shift, signs of which were evident in the mid 1970s, but which was to fructify fully after 1980, of a more authoritarian and centralized framework. This took time to mature and was never fully hegemonic, being locked in conflict with aspirations her earlier populism had been shaped by.

This still leaves us with a question with larger philosophical implications. Was Indira Gandhi an ecological nationalist by ideological conviction, or was she opportunistically nationalist to justify the expansion or arrogation of federal and statist powers in the area of nature conservation? As with all else, there is no easy way of unwrapping the puzzle. There was much that was driven by the impulse to centralize powers. It was no coincidence that the subject of forests and the environment was placed on the Concurrent List in the Forty-second Amendment, enacted during the Emergency. Similarly, there were major gains in terms of New Delhi's clout over forest areas and designated natural zones in the 1970s and 1980s. Yet, it was far too mechanical and simplistic to see the one as the outcome of the other. There was a larger drift towards centralization and also to the accretion of the power above, but this does not deny or detract from the depth of concerns that were often ecological *and* nationalist. This was clearest in Mrs Gandhi's emergence as a spokeswoman for a carefully crafted position, as an advocate of a Southern way of looking at planetary predicaments that emerged in 1972, and which was reiterated in 1980 at the world fora. More so, the efflorescence of nature reserves and the halting of specific dam projects had deeper roots in the notion of a nation where nature had a place. There seems no doubt that her initiatives were intensely and deeply political, but this does not detract from a significance going beyond her immediate political concerns.

She engaged more closely with issues of an ecological nature than any Indian prime minister and had a worldview far more nuanced, developed, and sophisticated than that of her father, Jawaharlal

Nehru. There is little doubt that there were authoritarian elements in her projects of saving nature and remaking the environment, but the shadow cast by them was not all-encompassing. The access to women and men of science, and the ability to engage with diverse activists, Gandhian or nature lovers, had roots in an older and more eclectic style of nationalism. This larger ecumene outlasted her left-wing advisers, supporters, and colleagues, whose influence had waned by the mid 1970s. It did not and indeed could not prevent her and the larger forces arrayed alongside her from coming up with strong radical and populist opposition by the early 1980s.

A quarter-century after her passing, the issues and legacies of the times she lived in are very much with us. It is a complex record that calls for critical reflection about the nature of power and knowledge, and the manifold ways in which they are intertwined in our world. In many ways it is a history that is very much part of the living present. It calls from moving on from mere condemnation or iconic acclaim towards historically informed reflection and debate.

References

Ali, Sálim, 'Some Problems of Assessing Wildfowl Numbers and Maintaining Wildfowl Habitat and Stocks', in IUCN, *IUCN Technical Proceedings Meeting, Wetland Conservation, Ankara, 9–16 October 1967*, Morges: IUCN, 1968.

Anderson, R.S. and W. Huber, *The Hour of the Fox: Tropical Forests, the World Bank and Indigenous Peoples in Central India*, Delhi: Vistaar Publications, 1988.

Anon., 'The Delhi Bird Watchers' Society', *Journal of the Bombay Natural History Society 49*: 595, 1950.

———, *Save Our Skins*, Bombay: World Wildlife Fund India, 1973.

Bhagat, U., *Indiraji, Through My Eyes*, Delhi: Penguin Viking, 2005.

Capra, F., *Uncommon Wisdom: Conversations with Remarkable People*, 1988; rpnt. London: Flamingo Books, 1989.

Chambers, R., N.C. Saxena, and T. Shah, *To the Hands of the Poor: Water, Trees and Land*, Delhi: Oxford and IBH, 1989.

D'Monte, D., *Temples or Tombs? Industry versus the Environment—Three Controversies*, Delhi: Centre for Science and Environment, 1985.

Deb Roy, S., 'Socio-economic Aspects of Preservation of Tigers', *Tiger Paper* (1979), 6.

Dhar, P.N., *Indira Gandhi, The 'Emergency' and Indian Democracy*, Delhi: Oxford University Press, 2000.

Divyabhanusinh, *The Story of Asia's Lions*, Mumbai: Marg, 2005.

DuPont, V., 'Slum Demolitions in Delhi', *Economic and Political Weekly* (2008), 43 (28).

Frank, K., *Indira: The Life of Indira Nehru Gandhi*, Delhi: HarperCollins, 2001.

Gandhi, G., ed., *Gandhi is Gone, Who will Guide Us Now? Sevagram, March 1948*, Delhi: Permanent Black, 2008.

Gandhi, I., 'Manali: A Place for Contemplation, *The Sunday Statesman*, 13 July 1958.

———, 'Science to Solve Man's Problems: Speech Welcoming Buckminster Fuller at the J. Nehru Memorial Lecture, 13 November 1969', in idem, *The Years of Endeavour: Selected Speeches of Indira Gandhi, August 1969–August 1972,* Delhi: Publications Division, 1975.

———, 'Value of Wildlife', speech inaugurating the Seventh Session of the Indian Board for Wildlife, New Delhi, 8 July 1969, in idem, *Selected Speeches of Indira Gandhi, January 1966–August 1969,* Delhi: Publications Division, 1971.

———, *My Truth*, Delhi: Vision Books, 1981.

———, 'Centenary Address', *Hornbill*, February 1983.

———, 'Man and his World, Speech at the UN Conference on the Human Environment, Stockholm', 14 June 1972, in idem, *On Peoples and Problems*, 1982; 2nd edn, London: Hodder and Stoughton, 1983.

———, *Selected Speeches and Writings, 1980–81,* vol. IV, Delhi: Publications Division, 1983.

———, 'Stimulate Economic Growth without Damage to Ecological Harmony, Address at the Fifteenth FAO Regional Conference', New Delhi, 10 March 1980, in idem, *On Peoples and Problems*, 1982; 2nd edn, London: Hodder and Stoughton, 1983.

———, 'Tasks before Asian Scientists: Inaugural Address to the Conference on the Application of Science and Technology to the Development of Asia', New Delhi, 9 August 1968, in idem, *On Peoples and Problems*, 1982; 2nd edn, London: Hodder and Stoughton, 1983.

———, 'Tradition and Change: Address to the Convocation of Bangalore University, 8 January 1967', in idem, *On Peoples and Problems*, 1982; 2nd edn, London: Hodder and Stoughton, 1983.

———, 'The Unfinished Revolution: Address to the Non Aligned Summit, Lusaka', May 1970, in idem, *On Peoples and Problems*, 1982; 2nd edn, London: Hodder and Stoughton, 1983.

———, 'Message for the Launch of Project Tiger', 26 March 1973, in *Indira Gandhi on the Environment*, Delhi: Indira Gandhi Memorial Fund, 1984.

——, Speech to the Central Forestry Board, 25 August 1982, in *Indira Gandhi on the Environment*, Delhi: Department of Environment, 1984.

Gandhi, S., ed., *Freedom's Daughter: Letters between Indira Gandhi and Jawaharlal Nehru, 1922–1939*, London: Hodder and Stoughton, 1989.

———, ed., *Two Alone, Two Together: Letters between Indira Gandhi and Jawaharlal Nehru, 1940–64*, London: Hodder and Stoughton, 1992.

———, *Rajiv's World*, Delhi: Viking Penguin, 1994.

Gee, E.P., 'The Management of India's National Parks and Wildlife Sanctuaries, Part V', *Journal of the Bombay Natural History Society* (1962), 59: 453–86.

Greenough, P., 'Pathogens, Pugmarks and Political "Emergency": The 1970s' South Asian Debates on Nature', in *Nature in the Global South: Environmental Projects in South and South East Asia*, ed. P. Greenough, P. Tsing, and A. Tsing, Delhi: Orient Longman, 2003.

Guha, R., *The Unquiet Woods: Ecological Change and Peasant Resistance in the Himalaya*, 1989; rpnt. Delhi: Oxford University Press, 1999.

———, *How Much Should a Person Consume? Thinking through the Environment*, Delhi: Permanent Black, 2006.

———, 'The Challenge of Contemporary History', *Economic and Political Weekly 43* (2008).

———, ed., *Nature's Spokesman: M. Krishnan and India's Wildlife*, 2000; Delhi: Penguin, 2008.

Hasan, M., *The Nehrus: Personal Histories*, Delhi: Lustre Press, Roli Books, 2007.

Hobsbawm, E.J., *Globalisation, Democracy and Terrorism*, New York: Little, Brown, 2006.

Holloway, C. and A.R. Wani, *Management Plan for Dachigam Sanctuary, 1971–75*, Srinagar: Forest Department, 1970.

Indian Board for Wildlife, *Wildlife Conservation in India, Report of the Expert Committee*, Delhi: Indian Board for Wildlife, 1970.

Ishwar Prakash, I., 'The Amazing Life in the Indian Desert', *The Illustrated Weekly of India*, Annual 1975.

Jalais, A., 'Dwelling on Morichjhanpi: When Tigers Became "Citizens", Refugees "Tiger-food"', *Economic and Political Weekly 40* (2005).

———, *The Forest of Tigers*, Delhi: Routledge, 2009.

Jayakar, P., *Indira Gandhi: An Intimate Biography*, Delhi: Penguin, 1988.

Kalpavriksh, *Death in a Sanctuary: Report of the Fact-finding Team*, Delhi: Privately published, December 1982.

Karanth, U., 'Making Room for Nature', Bangalore, *The Hindu*, 15 August 2007.

Khagram, S., *Dams and Development: International Struggles for Water and Power*, Delhi: Oxford University Press, 2005.

Krishen, P., *Trees of Delhi: A Field Guide*. Delhi: Dorling Kindersley, 2006.

Krishnan, M., 'An Ecological Survey of the Mammals of India', *Journal of the Bombay Natural History Society 68* (1971).

Kux, D., *The United States and India, 1947–1991: Estranged Democracies*, Washington, DC: National Defence Press, 1993.

Lewis, M., *Inventing Global Ecology: Tracking the Biodiversity Ideal in India, 1945–97*, Delhi: Orient Longman, 2003.

Leyhausen, P., C. Holloway, and M.K. Ranjitsinh, *Conservation of the Tiger in India—A Report to the Chairman of the Project Tiger Steering Committee on a Mid-term Study of Project Tiger*, Delhi: World Wildlife Fund–International Union for the Conservation of Nature, 1976.

MacDonald, H., *Polyester Prince: The Rise of Dhirubhai Ambani*, London: Allen and Unwin, 1998.

Malhotra, I., *Indira Gandhi: A Personal and Political Biography*, London: Coronet Books, 1989.

———, *Indira Gandhi*, Delhi: National Book Trust, 2006.

Masud, I., *Dream Merchants, Politicians and Partition: Memoirs of an Indian Muslim*, Mumbai: HarperCollins, 1997.

McNeill, J.R., *Something New under the Sun: An Environmental History of the Twentieth Century*, Harmondsworth: Penguin, Allen Lane, 2000.

Ministry of Environment, *Joining the Dots: Report of the Tiger Task Force*, Delhi: Ministry of Environment and Forests, n.d.

Mountfort, G., 'International Efforts to Save the Tiger', *Biological Conservation 6* (1974).

Nehru, J., *An Autobiography*, 1936; rpnt. Harmondsworth: Penguin, 2004.

———, *The Discovery of India*, 1946; rpnt. Harmondsworth: Penguin, 2004.

Norman, D., ed., *Indira Gandhi: Letters to a Friend, 1950–84*, London: Weidenfeld and Nicholson, 1986.

Oliver, W., *The Pygmy Hog*, Jersey: Jersey Wildlife Preservation Trust, 1980.

Panagariya, A., *India: Emerging Giant*, Delhi: Oxford University Press, 2008.

Panwar, H.S., 'What to Do When You've Succeeded: Project Tiger Ten Years Later', in *Conservation and Development: The Role of Parks in Sustaining Society*, ed. J. McNeely and K. Miller, New York: Smithsonian, 1984.

Parthasarathi, A., *Technology at the Core: Science and Technology under Indira Gandhi*, Delhi: Pearson Longman, 2007.

People's Union for Democratic Rights (PUDR), *Undeclared Civil War: Defend the Rights of Tribals, Oppose Forest Bill*, Delhi: PUDR, 1982.

Rangarajan, M., 'The Politics of Ecology: The Debate on People and Wildlife, 1970–95', in *Battles over Nature: Science and the Politics of Conservation*, ed. V.K. Saberwal and M. Rangarajan, Delhi: Permanent Black, 1996.

———, *India's Wildlife History: An Introduction*, Delhi: Permanent Black and Ranthambhore Foundation, 2001.

———, 'Ideology, the Environment and Policy: Indira Gandhi', *The India International Centre Quarterly 33* (2006).

———, 'Of Nature and Nationalism: Rethinking India's Nehru', in *Environmental History: As if Nature Existed*, ed. John McNeill, J.A. Jose Padua, and M. Rangarajan, Delhi: Oxford University Press, forthcoming.

——— and G. Shahabuddin, 'Relocation from Protected Areas: Towards a Historical and Biological Synthesis', *Conservation and Society 4.3* (2006).

Rao, P.V.N., *The Insider*, 1998; rpnt. Delhi: Penguin, 2000.

Sahgal, N., ed., *Before Freedom: Nehru's Letters to His Sister, 1909–47*, London: Weidenfeld and Nicholson, 2004.

Sale, J.B., 'Reintroduction in Indian Wildlife Management', *Indian Forester 112* (1986).

Sankhala, K., *The Controversial Tiger: A Study of Ecology, Behavior and Status, May 1970 to April 1972. Quarterly Report to the J. Nehru Memorial Fund, 1st Quarter, May–July 1970*, Delhi: Jawaharlal Nehru Memorial Fund, 1970.

———, 'The National Parks of India', in *International Union for the Conservation of Nature Country Situation Report*, Morges: IUCN, 1970.

———, *Wild Beauty*, Delhi: National Book Trust, 1973.

———, *Tiger! The Story of the Indian Tiger*, London: Collins, 1978.

———, 'After the Carnage', *Frontline*, 5 November 1993.

———, 'I Remember', in *Lest We Forget: Kailash Sankhala's India*, ed. B. Sahgal, Mumbai: Sanctuary Books, 2008.

Sharada Prasad, H.Y., *The Book I Won't Be Writing and Other Essays*, Delhi: Chronicle Books, 2003.

Sharma, D.C., *The Long Revolution*, Delhi: HarperCollins, 2009.

Sharma, L.T. and R. Sharma, ed., *Major Dams: A Second Look*, Delhi: Gandhi Peace Foundation, 1981.

Swaminathan M.S., 'The Green Revolution Can Reach the Small Farmer', in *Politics and Markets: The Real Issues in the World Crisis*, ed. Sartaj Asia, Food Forum chaired by Barbara Ward, Rome; New York: New York University Press, 1974.

Tarlo, E., 'Welcome to History: A Resettlement Colony in the Making', in *Delhi: Urban Space and Human Destinies*, ed. V. Dupont, E. Tarlo, and D. Vidal, Delhi: Manohar, 2000.

Thapar, V., *The Last Tiger: Struggling for Survival*, Delhi: Oxford University Press, 2006.

Vohra, B.B., *A Land and Water Policy for India: The Sardar Patel Memorial Lectures*, New Delhi: Manager of Publications, 1980.

6

Of Nature and Nationalism

Rethinking India's Nehru

Jawaharlal Nehru is often seen by large sections of the environmental movement as an environmental vandal. In contrast with Mahatma Gandhi, who symbolizes tradition as opposed to modernity and small technologies as against large, Nehru is seen as the architect of much that is wrong with the contemporary condition. Such a critique can often be misleading and only an obsession with Jawaharlal's larger historical role has obscured his critical engagement with an array of issues that would today qualify as environmental.

Drawing on a range of his writings and speeches, including well-known publications like *An Autobiography,* I will try to re-examine Nehru in the context of his own times. His passion for science was often matched by a deep concern about modern knowledge as a Faustian bargain. In the Europe and India of the 1930s, both the Congress leader and his daughter Indira combined deep awareness of nature with alertness to how science could change everyday life. There are often contradictory strains in Nehru's thought—as in his admiration of ancient humans for taming the wild and his love of mountains and rivers, forests and trees.

In independent India the well-known emphasis on dam-building and large public-sector units is best seen in its larger context. Neglected but critical features of Nehru's later life include a deep awareness of bird lore, a sense of the aesthetic far more developed than in his mentor Gandhi, and an openness to expertise from figures like Sálim Ali, E.P. Gee, and Verrier Elwin. On issues as diverse as town planning and the role of small projects as supplementary to large ones, he proved to be prescient. I also examine his interventions, in particular early conservation crises such as Gir and Bharatpur, in the immediate aftermath of Independence.

Nehru's stewardship as prime minister (1947–64) was marked by a far greater emphasis on increasing the rate of growth and far less on conservation. Planning rarely included an environmental component. The imperative to modernize could have adverse consequences for forest-dependent people as well as entire landscapes such as the terai. Modernizing industry and agriculture often came at costs that were unevenly distributed across different sections of society. Yet the developments of later years—even environmental awakening—often built on foundations in this early period. A careful reappraisal of the Nehru era and its legacies would be more useful than either condemnation of them or mere hagiography.

Many critical issues, such as the displacement of civilian populations on account of large projects, the clash of Adivasis and other forest users with modern industry and the larger crises that led to social and environmental unrest by the late 1960s, can indeed be traced to the Nehru years. Yet it would be misleading to ignore the space that democracy provided for dissent or to the new institutions of science created in this period. Similarly, the dilemmas were not specific to India but were part of a larger current of technological optimism of the post-World War II years. Nehru shared the strengths but also reflected the weaknesses of the dominant views of the times he lived in. Reassessing the legacy requires sober thought and reflection.

Jawaharlal Nehru has not been a poster boy of the modern environmental movement. His famous quote on Bhakra Nangal as an emblem of modern India is a good instance of how negatively he came to be viewed by the end of the twentieth century. Yet criticisms, significant and thought-provoking as they are, do little justice to the complexities of India's first prime minister. Radical ecologists are likely to see Gandhi as benign and Nehru as the antithesis of all that the former believed in and stood for. As Ramachandra Guha has remarked, far more than his mentor, Mahatma Gandhi, Nehru was attuned to environmental dilemmas in two landscapes that Gandhi had little do with. One was the city and the other the forest. It can in fact be argued that Nehru's ideas and thoughts were indicative of wider currents of his age. It would be anachronistic to see him anticipating the crises of the environment of the late 1960s and after. But it is possible to find in his writings and activities a wider aesthetic sensibility, disquiet about the direction of modern science, and early attempts to grapple with some of the ecological dimensions of development.[1]

Nehru's sensitivity to nature and natural surroundings is well known, but its larger environmental implications require more attention than is often the case. There were intimations of a wider kinship with nature even earlier. It is true that such sensitivity often saw nature as symbol of larger collective identities. A postcard sent by his father in 1905 showed the Jhelum flowing through the valley. 'The motherland', wrote a proud Motilal to his son in distant England, 'sends you her greetings.'[2] Landscape became a marker of memory and more crucially of identity. This was a trope Jawaharlal would often return to: the valley of Kashmir and the Himalayas would symbolize a sense of hope and renewal, a retreat from the chaos of modern civilization. His lyrical prose would recall 'the sense of exhilaration' on his return to the mountains. On a journey to Almora he found the sight of the snow-capped peaks had a 'cooling effect on the fever in the brain, and the petty conflicts and intrigues, the lusts and the falsehoods of the plains and the cities seemed so far away.'[3]

[1] Guha, *Mahatma Gandhi and the Environmental Movement*, esp. pp. 14–16.

[2] Akbar, *Nehru*, p. 30.

[3] Nehru, *Autobiography*, p. 569.

His accounts of jail life include sentimental bits about bird and small-animal life. This is clear in the first long spells in jail in the wake of the Non-Cooperation Movement of 1919–21. The beauty of the clouds as they changed colour was a stirring memory. A fourteen-month spell in the Dehra Dun jail he noticed pipal (*Ficus religiosa*) trees changing leaf: 'How wonderful is the sudden change from bud to leaf.' The longer jail spells in the wake of the Civil Disobedience Movement at the end of the 1920s were more memorable for the dabbling into natural history. Flocks of wild ducks would fly overhead. The long afternoons were marked by the call of the brainfever bird. The irritatingly repetitive call of common hawk cuckoos convinced him of the appropriateness of their name! Inmates shared food with mynahs and pigeons, which became quite tame. The threat was from jailers, who sometimes shot and ate pigeons. A monkey whose young fell into a crowd of men armed with lathis charged and rescued its young one.[4]

The naturalist in Jawaharlal was active in jail. In this he found the warders singularly uncooperative. In August 1935 in Almora jail, he watched a hawk (almost certainly a *shikhra*, a small sparrowhawk) swoop down, hunt, and kill a bird. He asked a jailer whether he knew the species in question. The terse reply: '*Hum to kaue koh pahchanat hain*' was all he got—the wardens only recognized crows.[5] Empathy came with deep curiosity about the natural world. When he saw an animal—'something of a cross between a lizard and a crocodile'—he was keen to identify it. The vernacular name *bo*, the jailer told him, meant but little, and it was only later, going through the pages of the forester-naturalist F.W. Champion's *The Jungle in Sunlight and Shadow*, that he identified it as a pangolin.[6]

In his *Glimpses of World History* (1934) he found the idea of 'conquest of nature' to be nothing but 'loose talk. It is far better to say that man has begun to understand nature and the more he has understood, the more he has been able to co-operate with nature

[4] Ibid., pp. 354–8.

[5] JN to IG, 16 August 1935, in Gandhi, *Freedom's Daughter*, p. 118.

[6] Nehru, *Autobiography*, p. 358.

and utilise it for his own purposes.' Yet he could also write about how the history of man was fascinating 'precisely because of the struggle though the ages against nature'. It was only by subduing the elements such as wild beasts and the jungle that human societies had been able to flourish.[7] Such ideas of a struggle with nature were confirmed during his extensive travels through India over the 1920s and 1930s. Though he never alluded to it directly, this was still a society slowly recovering from the ravages of the influenza pandemic of 1918. The advance of the agrarian frontier was widely accepted as signifier of human progress. Looking at the verdant green of the forest from a train in the Surma Valley in Assam, Nehru wrote of how forest trees looked 'with disdain on this human effort and were full of hostility of the forest against man.'[8] In the late 1930s, on a trip to Garhwal, he identified with the local demand for better roads. 'A motor road to Srinagar' seemed to him 'a legitimate wish. Another wish, rapidly taking forms and entirely right, is to develop electric power.' The mountain world of Garhwal was neglected and poor but a land of immense possibilities.[9]

Even in the 1930s he was sensitive to the destruction of tree wealth in the hills. When released from goal he spent time in a bungalow in Khali, Almora, where he was angry because Jamnalalji's (Jamnalal Bajaj, the nationalist industrialist) 'sole use' for deodar trees 'was to cut them down . . . The stumps of deodar were mute witness to the tragedy.' He was all praise for his own brother-in-law, Ranjit Pandit, who had cleared away shrubs and planted trees. There were flowers and fruit trees, nectarines and tangerines, all gaining from the care of a man who 'tends and watches it grow like a child'.[10] Such concerns are also evident in his letter to Indira from Madurai in Tamil Nadu, where he watched in awe as the deity was

[7] Nehru, *Glimpses*, pp. 58–60.

[8] Nehru, 'In the Surma Valley', *The Bombay Chronicle*, 21 December 1938, in Gopal, *Nehru: An Anthology*, p. 598.

[9] 'Letter to Indira', 4 May 1938, from Srinagar, Garhwal, in Gopal, SWJN, vol. 3, p. 468.

[10] 'Letter to Indira', 11 March 1938, in ibid., p. 458.

offered over 200 huge garlands a day. The agnostic in him was as aghast as the Fabian socialist: he found it 'a pity to waste so many flowers.'[11]

His disquiet was not with the world of nature as much as with human intentions and malign concerns. The ferocity of the jungle animal was aimed only at sustenance, he felt, 'not of the mass murder that man calls war.'[12] Such views echoed his disquiet with the violence of fascism in the Europe of the 1930s. Animals were often symbols of human achievement. Yet far too often it was the ferocity of a beast that was reason to celebrate it: the bulldog and the eagle were emblems, not gentle creatures.[13] It was no coincidence that the former is associated with aggressive English nationalism and that the latter is so prominent in fascist iconography.

Part of the affiliation to nature drew simply from a romantic association with wild places and things. Nehru's education at Harrow and then Trinity College, Cambridge, inculcated in him a love of outdoor sports and physical fitness, including a keen interest in swimming, rowing, walking, and mountaineering. In the mid 1940s a time of intense political manoeuvre and strife, he found the time to escape to Gangabal Lake in Kashmir. Writing to Mahatma Gandhi, he remarked on how he was tired by nightfall but rose fresh to greet each morning. He was ecstatic about the 'pure sensual enjoyment of the mountain air and the snow and forests and flowers.'[14] Four years later he wrote of the cold desert of Ladakh, of how it was a 'vast wilderness'. Its monasteries looked like they had grown out of the rocks in a part of India where 'nature was still dominant and triumphant'. This was in stark contrast to Calcutta, the city of five million where he went next, a place where 'nature [was] not very obvious and only man and his conflicts were evident.'[15]

[11] JN to IG, 15 October 1936, in Gopal, *Nehru: An Anthology*, p. 616.

[12] JN to IG, 'In the Surma Valley', in ibid., p. 598.

[13] Nehru, *Autobiography*, p. 359.

[14] JN to Mahatma Gandhi, 30 July 1945, *SWJN*, vol. 3, pp. 476–7.

[15] JN to Premiers of Provinces, 20 July 1949, *SWJN*, vol. 12, pp. 299–300.

By the 1930s he also had a companion with a keen interest not only in nature but also in the implications of science for the larger human predicament: his daughter Indira. His letters took on a new tone of passionate interest, reinforced no doubt by the availability of new literature on the subject. Mention has already been made of F.W. Champion. Both the forester-naturalist and the legendary sportsman Jim Corbett were part of a short-lived initiative, the early nature journal *Indian Wildlife*, of which Nehru was a subscriber. More significant was *The Book of Indian Birds* by Sálim Ali, an ornithologist from a distinguished business family of Bombay. In a letter where he says he cannot identify a species based on 'vague description', Nehru refers his daughter to Horace Alexander's book collection in the house. Her faith in his knowledge was touching but had little basis![16] Indira managed to identify the red-vented bulbul and white-breasted kingfisher in Panchgani.[17] Writing from Anand Bhavan in Allahabad, she commented on winter arrivals. There was the redstart, 'rather an amusing fellow the way he shivers his tail all the time.'[18] Indira's descriptions show a keen eye and felicity of phrase. For instance, the wagtail was 'extremely elegant in black and white'.[19] Interestingly, it was the father in Ahmadnagar Fort in Maharashtra who promised her the book. Her wait would be longer, he warned, as others in the jail were busy using it. His fellow freedom fighter Asaf Ali had been most helpful in supplying the Hindustani names of several birds.[20] The sense of excitement in this set of letters is obvious, and anyone who has ever been a birdwatcher can feel how the two correspondents felt when the winter migrants came in from the Caucasus and across the Himalayas. Her only regret was that she had not bought a good pair of binoculars from England. The old opera glasses were 'quite useless for longer distances'. The larger

[16] JN to IG, from Ahmednagar Fort Prison, 14 May 1943, in Gandhi, *Two Alone*, p. 200.

[17] IG to JN, Omara Hall, Panchgani, 17 July 1943, ibid., p. 240.

[18] IG to JN, 21 October 1943, from Anand Bhavan, ibid., p. 291.

[19] IG to JN, in Naini Central Prison, 25 April 1943, pp. 188–9.

[20] JN to IG, 29 February 1944, ibid., p. 351.

political situation was never too far away. England was at war and much of India was in the throes of 1942 movement. Binoculars 'were non existent from a civilian point of view.'[21]

The passion for nature-watching did not exist in isolation. By this time a new scientific and industrial revolution was well on its way. It would not be one of the dark satanic mills that had been emblems of the ire of Tolstoy, Ruskin, and Gandhi, but the transformation of fossil fuel-based derivatives. The petrochemical revolution would gather force across the world only after the end of the war that found Jawaharlal in jail and Asia either at war or in an uncivil peace. Mahatma Gandhi's travels across India famously saw him in third class railway carriages: later he too used the motorcar, usually lent him by a supportive industrialist.

But the change was much more epochal than simply one of transport being faster and easier. Nearly every week came with 'a new discovery' that would in the course of time 'change our way of living'. Indira in Switzerland wrote to Jawaharlal about new discoveries and inventions. It would soon be possible to photograph and study in detail all movements made on earth. She was most fascinated by the stroboscope and new nylon fabrics. Nylon was made from water, coal, and air, and was already in the market. 'Elastic, strong and transparent or opaque . . . it can be made into anything from toothbrush bristle to women's sheer stockings. The more it is pulled, the stronger it gets.'[22] She presciently observed that the issue was not so much to do with mastering nature as of articles that were 'in many ways superior to the natural product'. Nylon was just one small instance of the new world that was being brought into being by chemists. The new world had marvels about which she could go on forever.[23]

It is important to note how such receptivity to new technologies was combined with a deep awareness of new insights into the workings of natural systems. By April 1940, just a month after

[21] IG to JN, 21 September 1943, ibid., p. 272.
[22] IG to JN, 9 February 1940, ibid., pp. 16, 272.
[23] IG to JN, 3 March 1940, ibid., pp. 30–1.

her letter on nylon, Indira was writing to her father about D.C. Peattie's book, *Flowering Earth*. Her words found a receptive listener in Nehru, and read well even today. 'Is it not wonderful, the oneness of life?' she wrote. 'It is ever a source of marvel to me how intrinsically the life of all living things are bound together and how dependent they are on one another.' She identified with D.H. Lawrence's idea of a living organic connection that ought not to be undone.[24] Two weeks later Nehru replied in the affirmative but placed the issue in a wider context of the ethical role of knowledge, science in particular. Science must be 'allied to life, to flowers, and trees and mountains and rivers . . . Otherwise it is lifeless.'[25]

Nature and Nation after Independence

The close links of life with science and peace would continue as a key strand in his thinking in the aftermath of Independence in 1947. In these areas there were divergences between Nehru as a politician and as an individual with strong preferences. Yet the larger imperatives of state policy and the dynamic of the polity drew in substantial part from his impulses. In 1947–52 the horror of Partition, the resettling of refugees, and the integration of princely states preceded the first general elections of 1952. Many of the critical policy initiatives over the next two decades had their roots in developments in this period.

Few incidents were to be as remarkable as Nehru's intervention in the matter of the hunting down of Asia's last lions in the former princely state of Junagadh. Once their protector, the nawab, had fled to Pakistan, the lions of the Gir Forest were exposed to danger from trigger-happy sportsmen. Jawaharlal was petitioned by the Society for the Preservation of Fauna in the Empire, a body of ex-aristocrats—a vanishing species he had little sympathy with. The Duke of Devonshire who headed the Society appealed to Nehru

[24] IG to JN, 13 April 1940, ibid., p. 53.
[25] JN to IG, 26 April 1940, ibid., p. 58.

to step in and save the lions. From another part of the spectrum he also received telegrams from naturalists in Gujarat where the big cat was now seen as a symbol of regional nationalism. Nehru's wire to the local government minced no words. The case for the lions had been raised by the British historian Edward Thompson in the early 1940s. Thompson found Nehru far more sympathetic than Gandhi. Nehru now reminded officials that the lions were confined to one forest patch. 'It would be a great pity if they were allowed to be shot or otherwise to suffer extinction.'[26] What is notable is that this minute was dictated within four weeks of the assassination of Gandhi. Through a small but critical intervention, Jawaharlal helped secure an endangered species. It was not the last time his path would cross that of lions.[27] Yet the case showed up the potential and limits of the new India: the old princely order vanished but the princes with their privy purses remained a part of the Indian scene till the end of the 1960s. Among their privileges were their hunting rights. These now devolved to the Rajpramukh of Saurashtra, which included the former territory of Junagadh. Hunts for a chosen few continued till over a decade after Independence. The old order did change, but not with a body blow.

It is still significant that two men who did not hunt now ruled India. It is difficult to comprehend how important as a ritual the hunt was in British India, for the viceroys and military and civil officials and for their princely and aristocratic allies. Nehru had indeed shot dead a goat antelope (goral) on his honeymoon as far back as 1916, but that was perhaps the last time he lifted a gun. The head of state, C. Rajagopalachari, a lifelong Gandhian, chose not to exercise the governor general's shooting rights in the Shivaliks and the tract of Reserved Forests became an early sanctuary.[28]

Just as the carnage of the trenches in the Great War had reinforced an anti-hunting ethic, so too did the horror of Hiroshima

[26] JN, 25 February 1948, in Gopal, *SWJN*, vol. 5, 1987, p. 562.
[27] Rangarajan, 'From Princely Symbol', pp. 399–442.
[28] Gandhi, *Rajaji*.

and Nagasaki seem to reconfirm a belief in ahimsa. The artifacts made by humans and those handed down by nature were both viewed through the lens of promoting peace. Peace among men and women had been the ideal of Nehru's mentor, Gandhi. India's assertion of its place in the comity of nations was to be different from a raw affirmation of brute force. Receiving the relics of the Buddha's disciples, Jawaharlal evoked the message of the sage of the Sakyas to remind those around him of his modern counterpart. Gandhi had been dead less than a year when Nehru received the relics from the Victoria and Albert Museum.[29] The same imagery would recur in a message to children the following year. 'It is far more interesting and amusing', he wrote, 'to wander about without a gun or any other weapon and find that the wild animals are not afraid.' Love for the wild begat love, while only violence would provoke an attack. The forests and mountains were sites for discovery not places of danger.[30]

Nature too had a symbolic import in the evolution of India's relations with the rest of Asia. Nehru's sense of the importance of Asia in the coming period was evident in a little incident, the gifting of an elephant calf to Japan. The elephants in Tokyo zoo had been killed over the Allied bombing, and the Indian prime minister was presented an ingenious idea by the president of the Japanese Giant Salamander Association. Japan would gift a pair of giant salamanders, and India would gift the children of the island nation an elephant. Though the PM admitted he 'did not know what a giant salamander is', he gave the green signal. A calf named Indira reached Japan in October 1949.[31]

Benign attitudes to nature could also have critical scientific support. Dr Sálim Ali was Asia's first ornithologist, with a German

[29] JN, 4 January 1949, in Gopal, *SWJN*, vol. 9, pp. 101–3.

[30] Nehru, 'Children of the World', 3 December 1949, and 'This Beautiful World of Ours', 26 December 1950, in Nehru, *Nehru's Speeches*, p. 439. Both these were published in *Shankar's Weekly.*

[31] Gopal, *SWJN*, vol. 11, p. 412. Devonshire's letter dated 13 January 1948 had also referred to the shooting of prey from cars.

higher degree and bird guides that were the treasured possessions of not only Nehru but also colleagues like Abul Kalam Azad during their days in and out of prison. Ali's own research was often bankrolled by various princes. He was the first to study the nesting colonies of waterbirds in the Keoladeo Ghana, the wetland reserve of the Jat dynasty of Bharatpur. In the afterglow of Independence, demobilized soldiers as well as landless members of the 'Depressed Classes' (as Dalits were then called) pressed for opening up the reserve. Amelioration of poverty and the right to live with dignity were seen as the antithesis of the old princely order. Sálim Ali took the case to the PM and the food and agriculture minister, Rafi Ahmad Kidwai. His argument: the Ghana was a living laboratory to study the immense productivity and potential of wetlands. By keeping it intact, it could provide fuel and fodder for the nearby villages and the town of Bharatpur. Its loss would be irreparable. The Ghana was saved and survives to this day.[32]

Big Dams, Agrarian Extension, and Industry

As prime minister it was not all harmony. The wrath of nature was often on the agenda. There was a larger legacy of debates on the best technology and the ideal path for the new nation. Nehru's own difference of vantage point and programme with Gandhi has been discussed threadbare. These differing ideologies of change, for that is what they were, had been played out both within and beyond the Congress from the 1920s. What is often ignored is the larger geographical setting and historical context in which large projects were seen as a viable option in the early two decades after Independence.

The legacy of debates within the larger movement was fresh in memory. They found political antagonists turning into allies when it came to choosing models of growth. One of the great divisions in the 1940s had been between those who supported the British-led war effort and those who rallied to the Quit India movement

[32] Ali, *Fall of a Sparrow*, pp. 150–1.

of 1942. Dr B.R. Ambedkar was prominent in the former group and served in the Viceroy's Executive Council. He strongly backed the Damodar Valley project, which he saw as an exemplar of a new India, where bounds of caste would weaken and a new division of labour based not on birth but merit would prevail. The large dam was not merely a source of hydel power, a means to channel excess water or a flood-control measure. For Ambedkar as much as for Nehru it was the path to a new social order.[33]

They were not alone in seeing big as beautiful. There were other influential strands of thought. Modern chemical industry, steel, and fertilizers would provide the impetuses of economic growth, giving the polity strength in a world still dominated by industrialized countries, many with a colonial past.[34] The Gandhian economist Dr J.C. Kumarappa saw decentralized renewable energy as less destructive. Such critics of high technology were outnumbered. Much more credence was given to the idea of men like Dr Meghnad Saha.[35]

Ironical as it might seem in hindsight, there were other protagonists of big-as-beautiful. Diwan Visweswaraya of Mysore had led in the building of a dam on the river Kaveri. The Krishna Raja Sagara dam would ignite conflicts with downstream Madras Presidency in British India, which continues to the present day. Similarly, engineers working for the Nizam of Hyderabad drew up the first proposals for a dam on the river Krishna. Even the most celebrated big dams of the Nehru era, the Bhakra and Nangal, had a formidable earlier advocate, the former British Lieutenant Governor of Punjab, Sir Louis Dane.[36]

[33] Omvedt, *Ambedkar*, pp. 111–12.

[34] Guha, *Gandhi and the Environmental Movement*.

[35] Saha, 'A Scientist's Philosophy', pp. 145–9. Also see Chatterji, *Towards Freedom*, pp. 846–52. I am grateful to Dan Klingensmith for sharing ideas from his forthcoming paper on inter-war colonialism, nationalism, and ecological issues.

[36] Randhawà, *History of Agriculture in India*, pp. 114–15; also see Guha, *India after Gandhi*, esp. chapter titled 'The Conquest of Nature', pp. 225–60.

The extension of the agrarian frontier was a high priority, and again the new rulers began with the wartime legacy of the Grow More Food campaigns. To the north-west, where the monsoon tails off in semi-arid and desert country, a canal project found a champion in an influential ruler who was a pillar of the Raj: Ganga Singh of Bikaner.[37] The new irrigated and intensively cropped landscapes would sustain far higher numbers of people per square kilometre than the systems of production they supplanted. This was a fact not lost on decision-makers as the population growth rates went over the 1 per cent mark after 1921. No wonder that peasants and literati alike eulogized dam builders in the South Indian countryside.[38] The left-wing Congressman and labour-union leader V.V. Giri favoured the wholesale adoption of modern technology to utilize 'every acre' of land. Expansion of the cultivated arable was practicable, even if his estimates were far too optimistic.[39]

Land colonization was critical to settle the refugees of Partition in the north and in north-western India. The two major transformations of land, the irrigation of eastern Punjab and the clearance of the terai were both related to the aftermath of Partition. The terai, low-lying grassland that runs along the foothills of the Himalayas, was the destination for refugees displaced by Partition, mostly Sikhs from western Punjab. Govind Ballabh Pant, chief minister of UP, placed Harpal Singh Sandhu, Deputy Director of Colonization, in charge of the operation in 1947–8. 'A fleet of heavy tractors moved', he would later recall of early January 1948, 'in a bid to clear 76,900 hectares of virgin soil.' The settling of the terai put an end to some of the best tiger and barasingha (swamp deer, *Cervus duavaceli*) habitats in the subcontinent.[40] Similar land clearance in the South Indian highlands was facilitated by the use of chemical pesticides, especially a new chemical compound, DDT.

[37] Randhawa, *History of Agriculture.* Also see Farmer, *Agricultural Colonization*, pp. 40–5.

[38] Easvara Rao, 'Colonial Discourses on Dam Technology'.

[39] Giri, *Jobs for the Millions*, pp. 39, 41.

[40] Randhawa, *History of Agriculture*, pp. 54–9.

The advance of the farm frontier was a matter of celebration both for refugees who had a new start in life and for peasants in search of land.[41] The larger challenge lay in the north-west, where over half the irrigated lands of the Canal Colonies of the Punjab now lay in West Pakistan. The Nangal dam was completed in 1954 but its prelude lay in land consolidation in eastern Punjab, which had a fraction of the irrigated area of West Punjab.[42]

Flood control was another objective of the large projects. The Kosi, eastern India's river of sorrow, caused extensive flood havoc. A.N. Khosla, the senior engineer who headed a committee on the matter, outlined a complex scheme of control of the waters. To Nehru this looked like 'a very slow way of proceeding'. He urged engineers to work out canal systems that would disperse the water even before the dams were operational. In an aside he mused over the possibility of a huge dam some 750 feet high in the Nepal Himalaya, taming the waters, generating hydropower, and ending floods for all time.[43] Much more ambitious was the vast Damodar Valley Authority, modelled consciously on the Tennessee Valley of the USA. In a sense, the latter project captured the imagination of engineers and the political leadership in India.

Nehru was by no means alone among leaders of the world who favoured large projects of water diversion and control. India played a key role in dam-building. Between 1951 and 1982 it accounted for more dams than any other country after the USA, USSR, China, and Japan. In all, 883 were built, as against 202 before 1950.[44] Dams were a sign of progress not just for Nehru but also for Ghana's Nkrumah and Egypt's Nasser, not to mention other twentieth-century figures such as Mao, Franklin Delano Roosevelt, and Stalin.[45] Indian wheat output grew sevenfold and rice tripled in the four decades after 1950. Hydroelectric power output grew

[41] Farmer, *Agricultural Colonization*, pp. 40–5.

[42] Randhawa, *History of Agriculture*,, pp. 1–38.

[43] Gopal, *SWJN*, vol. 14, pt II, 8 April to 3 July 1950, pp. 204–5.

[44] Khagram, *Dams and Development*, p. 37.

[45] McNeill, *Something New*, pp. 157–92.

by a factor of twelve.[46] Such schemes in India had older, deeper roots. British engineers, Indian princes, and visiting American technical experts had prepared the ground for large projects of water diversion long before Jawaharlal entered the corridors of power. He drew these currents together and gave them all a fresh impetus and new legitimacy.

Reflections and Dissonances

At what cost was this huge expansion and how did Nehru reconcile with the underside of such growth? Before turning to this, it is essential to note that his fascination with large water storage projects was not exceptional. As argued, he gave lucid expression to ideas that were common currency in his day and age. Yet he might also have had a keener sense of the history of water storage in India's past, during which there were associations of culture and economy alike with tanks. This was most so in peninsular India, with its seasonal rivers, which did not have snowmelt—as the river systems of the Indus-Ganga Brahmaputra system did—and where dams had long been an attractive option. While India may not have had a long and active history of hydrology and river projects as in early China, it is plausible that Nehru was aware of earlier rulers and their attempts with water storage.[47]

However, it was not the patterns of the past but the tumult of the present that would raise questions about the legacy he was in the process of creating. Nehru had to deal with popular protest in one case and intellectual dissent in the other. Of the latter, prominent in the case of the Damodar Valley, there is no record of his own intervention. The former was a different story altogether. Kapil Dev Bhattacharya wrote extensively about the ills of the project. A technically qualified critic, his objections were rational. For instance, he drew attention to the silt load of the Damodar

[46] Mitchell, *International Historical Statistics*, p. 196.

[47] I am grateful to Kathleen Morrison for drawing my attention to this longer legacy of water storage in southern India, based on her continuing researches on the subject. See Morrison, *Daroji Valley*.

and argued the turbines would function below par. Silt would also be deposited in the river Hooghly and endanger Calcutta port. In the long run, this would entail the construction of a barrage at Farakka to reinvigorate the Hooghly by diverting waterflows. Farmers and workers would suffer water shortages in the canals and the inefficiency of the turbines. These criticisms were made even before the foundation stone was laid, let alone completion of the DVA in 1958.[48]

There was concerted and determined resistance to a large dam in Hirakud, Orissa, as early as 1946. Local Congress leaders even organized workshops to debate its social and economic benefits and costs. A large group of protesters, 4000-strong, greeted the minister for irrigation and power. The key issue was rehabilitation for those displaced by the project. Protest over the dam with wider political issues merged with wider issues. The Communist Party of India also played a role, but police dispersed their agitators. Nehru inaugurated the dam in April 1948. He admonished people, saying they would have to suffer so that the country could move ahead: this is oft quoted.[49] The import of this was clear: despite his Romantic interest in nature, Nehru was a modernizer.

In this he was not as much of a loner as is often made out. Nearly two decades before this incident, Mahatma Gandhi had urged those being displaced by the Mulshi Petha dam being constructed by the Tata Power Company to negotiate for the best deal they could get.[50] Around the same time that the prime minister was at Hirakud, his deputy was speaking elsewhere on similar lines. Sardar Vallabhai Patel asked farmers protesting land acquisition for an aerodrome to get a fair price but not block the project.[51] Yet, none of this can take away from the fact that in a country where over twenty million were to be displaced by mega projects by 1980, the precedents in

48 Bhattacharya, *Bangaldesher Nod*; Roy, 'The Politics of the Environment—I, pp. 354–61.

49 Khagram, *Dams*, pp. 36–7.

50 Rodrigues, *Rural Political Protest*, pp. 108–34.

51 Gandhi, *Patel*.

the Nehru period were far from positive. In Hirakud, for instance, only a tiny fraction of those displaced were rehabilitated.[52]

Desiccation as Past and Future

Nehru found allies for his projects in the most unlikely quarters, specifically in K.M. Munshi, union minister and later governor of Uttar Pradesh. Munshi differed on the cultural content of nationalism, clashing famously with the prime minister on the issue of rebuilding the Somnath temple in Gujarat. Yet Nehru's interest in the Rajasthan Canal, inaugurated in 1956, found an uncanny echo in Munshi's call to fight and push back the advance of the desert. If Nehru saw the waters of the canal as the instrument to reclaim land for the plough, Munshi's programme of Vana Mahotsava (a tree-planting festival) carried the undertones of a nation afflicted by drought and desiccation. It was the duty of Indians to plant and raise 2000 crore (20 billion) trees.[53] Only by planting trees would the people of his native Gujarat stop what he claimed was a millennium-long march of the desert sands from neighbouring Rajasthan.[54] Groves of trees would revive the splendour of Krishna in the Ganga valley.[55] Munshi saw the issue as one of reviving the glorious past of Hindu India. He even spoke at Somnath of Krishna as the presiding deity of the groves.[56] Clearly, the symbolism he drew upon excluded some and included others, a point over which discord with Nehru was to be public. These differences were about Somnath, not tree planting. Munshi did add that every village needed 'a forest of its own from which fuel and timber could be supplied.'[57]

Nehru took aboard the Vana Mahotsava idea, though not with all its trappings. There were differences of approach and emphasis.

[52] Thukral, *Big Dams*, pp. 13–14; Khagram, *Dams*, p. 37.
[53] Munshi, 'The Vanished Glories of Giri Govardhan', p. 184.
[54] K.M. Munshi, 'The Kankaria Lake', p. 184.
[55] Munshi, *Governor's Anvil.*
[56] Munshi, 'The Vanished Glories of Giri Govardhan', pp. 299–301.
[57] Munshi, 'A Forest for Every Village', pp. 297–8.

Speaking a month before Independence, he had compared the killing of a tree to the murder of a human being. Both were 'painful and intolerable' acts.[58] The quest for industrial raw material had depleted forests that had myriad competing uses, as resource catchments and potential arable. Popular movements in the 1940s anticipated several such issues.[59]

Conclusion

Looking back over four decades after his death, it is difficult not to see in Nehru's economic ideas several blindspots of his own time and place. The fascination with technology overrode egalitarian notions in the five-year plans. Despite the regard for Adivasi (Scheduled Tribal) and forest cultures, there was a sense that these were romantic cultural modes to be protected—but in the larger scheme of a modernizing economy. The assumptions of a golden age of post-World War II economic growth as ceaseless process were common to statesmen and women of the time. He was not only no exception but was an exemplar of this approach.

Yet to place him in context also requires careful engagement with his dilemmas and ideas. Nature as embodiment of harmony went well with the idea that human differences were to be settled through peace, not war. The sense and thrill of discovery of the wild made him and his colleagues far more open to ideas about keeping some space aside for nature than one might have imagined in a country with mass poverty and land hunger. The large projects of land clearance for agrarian extension were consequent upon a half-century of near-stagnant agriculture; the dams aimed to generate power for industry. Science provided a corrective, as did a sense of the aesthetic. There is none of the triumph over the natural world that marked post-revolutionary societies in their views of nature, most so in China.[60]

[58] Anon., 'On the Importance of Trees', Speech by Nehru.
[59] Hardiman, *Gandhi*, pp. 144–55.
[60] See Schapiro, *Mao's War*; also Coggins, *The Tiger and the Pangolin.*

There were, of course, clear limits to such brakes as existed in his lifetime. Having been born in the late nineteenth century and with a powerful overlay of Fabian socialism and of fascination with modern technology, it would have been hard for him to grasp the extent to which the planet was getting crowded with people, artifacts, and the ecological consequences of economic growth. A more acute sense of the problems of nature, of its endangerments and the imperative of renewal, was more marked even early on in their correspondence in the consciousness of his daughter Indira.[61] In his own case, industrialization as overriding project though tempered by science was the key to a new India. The consolidation of authority over the forest and hill and the taming of nature were central to a project of the nation-state. It is still notable that there were interstices in the edifice and cracks in the walls and it is no surprise that his legacy, while controversial, should elicit enquiry.

References

Akbar, M.J., *Nehru: The Making of India,* Delhi: Penguin, 1988.

Ali, Sálim, *The Fall of a Sparrow,* Delhi: Oxford University Press, 1987.

Anon., 'On the Importance of Trees', *Hindustan Times,* 2 July 1947.

Bhattacharya, Kapil Dev, *Bangaldesher Nod, Nodi, O Porikalpana,* Calcutta: Bidesoy Library Pvt. Ltd, no date.

Chatterji, Basudev, ed., *Towards Freedom: Documents on the Freedom Movement in India, 1938, Part 1,* Delhi: Indian Council of Historical Research and Oxford University Press, 1997.

Coggins, Chris, *The Tiger and the Pangolin: Nature, Culture and Conservation in China,* Honolulu: University of Hawaii Press, 2003.

Easvara Rao, B., 'Colonial Discourses on Dam Technology and Its Consequences: A Study of the Godavari Anicut', unpublished paper presented at the Conference on the Environmental History of Asia, Jawaharlal Nehru University, New Delhi, December 2002.

Farmer, B.H., *Agricultural Colonization in India since Independence,* Delhi: Manohar, 1974.

[61] See Rangarajan, 'Ideology, the Environment and Policy: Indira Gandhi', pp. 50–64.

Gandhi, Rajmohan, *Patel: A Life*, Delhi, 1990.

———, *Rajaji: A Biography*, Delhi: Viking Penguin, 1995.

Gandhi, Sonia, ed., *Freedom's Daughter, Letters between India Gandhi and Jawaharlal Nehru, 1922–39*, London: Hodder and Stoughton, 1989.

———, ed., *Two Alone, Two Together: Letters between Indira Gandhi and Jawaharlal Nehru, 1940–1954*, London: Hodder and Stoughton, 1992.

Giri, V.V., *Jobs for the Millions*, Madras, 1944.

Gopal, S., ed., *Jawaharlal Nehru: An Anthology*, Delhi: Oxford University Press, 1983.

———, ed., *Selected Works of Jawaharlal Nehru, Second Series (SWJN)*, multi-volume set, Delhi: Nehru Memorial Trust, 1985.

Guha, Ramachandra, *India after Gandhi: The History of the World's Largest Democracy*, Delhi: Picador, 2007.

———, *Mahatma Gandhi and the Environmental Movement: The Parisar Annual Lecture 1993*, Pune, 1993.

Hardiman, D., *Gandhi in His Time and Ours*, Delhi: Permanent Black, 2003.

Khagram, Sanjeev, *Dams and Development: Transnational Struggles for Water and Power,* Delhi: Oxford University Press, 2004.

McNeill, J.R., *Something New under the Sun: An Environmental History of the Twentieth Century*, New York: Allen Lane, The Penguin Press, 2000.

Mitchell, B.R., *International Historical Statistics: Africa, Asia and Oceania, 1750–1988*, New York: Stockton Press, 1995.

Morrison, Kathleen, *Daroji Valley: Landscape, Place and the Making of a Dryland Reservoir System,* Vijayanagara Research Project Monographs, Delhi, 2009.

Munshi, K.M., 'A Forest for Every Village', 28 August 1953, in K.M. Munshi, *Sparks from a Governor's Anvil, Volume I: June 1952–December 1953*, Lucknow: Publications Division, Directorate of Information, 1956.

———, 'The Kankaria Lake, Fifth Centenary Celebrations', Munshi, in K.M. Munshi, *Sparks from a Governor's Anvil, Volume I: June 1952–December 1953*, Lucknow: Publications Division, Directorate of Information, 1956.

———, 'The Vanished Glories of Giri Govardhan', 31 August 1953, in K.M. Munshi, *Sparks from a Governor's Anvil, Volume I: June 1952–December 1953*, Lucknow: Publications Division, Directorate of Information, 1956.

Nehru, Jawaharlal, *An Autobiography*, 1936; London: John Lane, the Bodley Head, rpnt. Delhi: Jawaharlal Nehru Memorial Fund and Oxford University Press, 1986.

———, *Glimpses of World History*, 1934; Allahabad, rpnt. Delhi: Oxford University Press, 1984.

Nehru, Jawaharlal, *Nehru's Speeches, 1949–53*, Delhi: Ministry of Information and Broadcasting, 1953.

Omvedt, Gail, *Ambedkar: Toward an Enlightened India*, Delhi: Penguin, 2004.

Randhawa, M.S., *A History of Agriculture in India, Vol. IV: 1947–81*, Delhi: Indian Council of Agricultural Research, 1987.

Rangarajan, Mahesh, 'From Princely Symbol to Conservation Icon: A Political History of the Lion in India', in Nariaki Nakazato and Mushirul Hasan, ed., *The Unfinished Agenda: Nation-building in South Asia*, Delhi: Manohar, 2001.

———, 'Ideology, the Environment and Policy: Indira Gandhi', Delhi: *India International Centre Quarterly*, 33 (2006).

Rodrigues, L., *Rural Political Protest in Western India*, Delhi, 1998.

Roy, Dunu, 'The Politics of the Environment—I', in Anil Agarwal and Sunita Narain, ed., *The State of India's Environment: The Second Citizens' Report, 1984–85*, New Delhi: Centre for Science and Environment, 1985.

Saha, Meghnad, 'A Scientist's Philosophy of Industrialization', *Modern Review*, 64 (1938).

Schapiro, Judith, *Mao's War against Nature: Politics and the Environment in Revolutionary China*, New York: Cambridge University Press, 2001.

Thukral, Enakshi G. *Big Dams, Displaced People: Rivers of Sorrow, Rivers of Change*, Delhi: Sage, 1992.

7

Five Nature Writers

Jim Corbett, Kenneth Anderson, Sálim Ali, Kailash Sankhala, and M. Krishnan

Jim Corbett (1875–1955) is among India's best-known Indo-Anglian authors after Rudyard Kipling and E.M. Forster. The dramatic encounters between the shikari colonel and his elusive, dangerous adversaries are like jungle versions of Sherlock Holmes, which continue to enthrall new generations of readers long after man-eaters have become a distant memory. *The Man-eaters of Kumaon* (1944), Corbett's first book, remains his most famous.[1] Corbett was a sport-hunter long before he took to the pursuit of marauding leopards and tigers. He remained one even after he gave up the trail of such animals. The pride of a sportsman is often evident in his accounts and it is erroneous to suppose, as many people do, that he only shot man-eaters.

One of his finest narratives in *Man-eaters* that does not involve a man-killer is the shooting of a huge male tiger named the Bachelor of Powalgarh. An easy familiarity with individual tigers in the forests of Kumaon is Corbett's hallmark. The Bachelor was far from

[1] Corbett, *Man-eaters of Kumaon.*

his usual haunts and, wary of people, had long evaded the bullets of stalkers. Corbett eventually got the better of the tiger and admits to a sense of joy at having bagged such a fine specimen. The animal was duly measured and proclaimed one of the largest tigers taken in the province. To be fair to Corbett, his sense of achievement is mingled with remorse.[2]

His sporting ethic, all the same, did not measure up to more recent notions of total preservation. It would be anachronistic to associate such ideas with Corbett. Celebration of life in the outdoors was, in his day, centred around the chase and the hunt, the ability to read pug-marks on a jungle trail, the skill of 'calling up' a tiger in order to be able to shoot it. Fish (especially the great mahseer) were taken with rod and line, deer and peacocks killed for meat, and leopards shot for their skins. This was the world Corbett grew up in and never fully transcended. It was the gun, not the camera, that was his chief, though not sole, instrument.

Corbett's was a keen eye and his vivid descriptions of trees and birds and hills reveal another side to his character. His animal biography of the Pipal Pani tiger, first published in *The Hog Hunters Annual* (1931) and included in *Man-eaters,* is a fine sketch of a young tiger's life.[3] There is an attention to detail that takes us to the forest floor in a manner that many have attempted but in which few have succeeded. The animal lived for a time in the huge log of a tree felled for no apparent reason and hollowed by porcupines. In *The Man-eating Leopard of Rudraprayag* (1948) we take a break from the tale of terror spread by the marauder to glimpse, through Jim's eyes, the beauty of the Vale of Kashmir. Corbett was stalking the Kashmir stag, a much-sought-after quarry when—

> I stepped into a fairyland, for the hail that carpeted the ground gave off a million points of light to which every glistening leaf and blade of grass added its quota. Continuing up for another two or three

[2] Corbett, 'The Bachelor of Powalgarh', in *Man-eaters of Kumaon*, pp. 95–108.

[3] Corbett, 'The Pipal Pani Tiger', in ibid., pp. 159–67.

> thousand feet, I came upon an outcrop of rock, at the foot of which was a bed of blue mountain poppies. The stalks of these, the most beautiful of all wild flowers in the Himalayas, were broken; even so, these sky blue flowers standing in a bed of spotless white were a never to be forgotten sight.[4]

A few lines later we are back to the Alaknanda river where Corbett spends another long night waiting for the man-eater.

The story of the stag is exceptional in terms of the setting. So attuned are we to his little world that it is easy to overlook how far afield Corbett had travelled. Born in Naini Tal to domiciled English parents, he was raised there and at Kaladhungi. He first went shooting junglefowl and deer with his brother Tom, then graduated to leopards and tigers. It was here he learnt how to read tracks on the trail and to tell, from the calls of langurs and peafowl, the movements of big cats along forest paths. He trained soldiers in jungle warfare in Central India, served in Burma, felled trees for railway fuel in Bihar, hunted in the marshlands of the North Indian terai, and finally ran a shikar firm in East Africa.[5] Very few episodes from his business and professional life appear in his books. It is the foothills of the Himalayas that occupy centrestage. One wishes there was more about the lion or cheetah in Africa, or of the dry Central Indian jungle, but this is to miss out on the importance of Kumaon and Garhwal in Corbett's eyes. That was his background, his patch of wild grass. His heart was never far from the mountains and his pen rarely takes us to forests outside them.

A sense of terror remains with the reader long after the Corbett classic is put away. *Rudraprayag* is especially fascinating for it is a full-length story of one hunt. All the other books are collections, including the underrated but gripping *The Temple Tiger and More*

[4] Corbett, *The Man-eating Leopard of Rudraprayag*, p. 145.

[5] Kala, *Jim Corbett of Kumaon*; Booth, *Carpet Sahib*. It is not well known that Corbett was the son and grandson of domiciled Europeans, a class able to mingle with home-born Englishmen (or Britons) but not quite considered their equal. We owe this observation on Corbett in particular to two acute American scholars: Geoffrey C. Ward and Diane R. Ward, *Tiger Wallahs*, pp. 53, 55.

Man-eaters of Kumaon (1954).[6] The leopard of the former book was so feared that it 'imposed a night curfew' over a huge swathe of the Garhwal countryside. Roads that bustled with life fell prey to 'an ominous silence' because of its depredations. Similarly, the Thak man-eating tiger held up forestry work in an entire valley.

In *The Man-eaters of Kumaon* we learn of how contractor and labourer alike looked to Corbett to rid them of the animal. Trees had been marked for felling in the summer of 1938 and, unless the tiger was shot by November, the entire felling cycle would be in jeopardy.[7] This paternal attitude of Corbett as saviour is often evident in his work but should not detract from his uncanny ability to recreate, some might say embellish, the narrative of the chase. Out on foot, sitting up on a machan, stalking a dangerous killer in thick cover—these are the highpoints in a Corbett narrative, the moments that readers want to relive time and again. It is not bloodlust as much as the cunning of the man-eaters, especially of the leopards, that stands out. Caught up in a terrain bustling with human activity and turning to prey on stock or people, they seem to hold sway over an entire population until they run into Corbett. This celebration of victory, so essential to the genre of shikar literature, is evident in all his works. The climax in *The Temple Tiger* provides proof of this sense of achievement: 'Word travelled round the night that the man-eating tiger was dead and when we carried him to the foot of the *ficus* tree next morning to skin him, more than a hundred men and boys crowded round to see him. Among the latter was the ten-year-old brother of the Chuka man-eater's last human victim.'[8]

The killing of man-eaters is always accompanied by a disavowal of any effort to wipe out the tiger as a species. The big cat was a 'large hearted gentleman of boundless courage . . . preying on people due to the force of circumstance.'[9] In *My India* (1952)

[6] Corbett, *The Temple Tiger*.
[7] Corbett, 'The Thak Man-eater', in *Man-eaters of Kumaon*, p.169.
[8] Corbett, 'The Chuka Man-eater', in *The Temple Tiger*, p. 116.
[9] Corbett, 'Author's Note', *Man-eaters of Kumaon*, p. xv.

Corbett blames a large hunting party for wounding an innocent beast. The group used several riding-elephants and tied up over a dozen baits, which Corbett did not like: 'The rifle shot I had heard three days previously had shattered the tiger's lower jaw, the most painful wound that can be inflicted on an animal.' The body of the tiger was found ten days later.[10] In other cases, tigers wounded by gunshot or more natural causes (such as porcupine quills) became a menace. Yet in his books Corbett is mostly silent about the tiger shoots he organized for governors and viceroys, and about his experiences as a member of the pig-sticking club at Meerut. He takes pains to show himself as a hunter, not a wanton killer.

The reason for this silence is significant. By the time he wrote his first book, Corbett was turning to photography. He managed to create a small jungle 'studio' by damming a small stream and setting up a hide in a tree. Here, he became one of the first persons to shoot on cine film a group of seven wild tigers, including a wild white tigress. Appropriately enough, he entitles this section of his first book 'Just Tigers' and reminds us that most of the striped cats fall into this category, troubling neither people nor stock.[11] This episode is matched by other small telltale signs: the admission in *My India* that he felt guilty about shooting peafowl by moonlight but did so only for food. The camera, which would record nature on film, was preferable to the gun. A photo was of interest to all, the trophy only to its owner.[12] But this transition was never complete. It is true that he sounded the alarm call for conservation, but he did not actually lead the struggle to achieve it.

It would be unjust to omit what is perhaps the most distinctive feature of Jim Corbett's India: his picture of village society. He is

[10] Corbett, *My India*, pp. 36–7.

[11] Corbett, 'Just Tigers', in *Man-eaters of Kumaon*, pp. 216–18. It is notable that Linlithgow, viceroy of India, wrote of Corbett as the most knowledgeable of any men he had hunted with in his time in India: 'Foreword', in ibid., p. vii.

[12] Corbett, 'On Shooting Peafowl', *My India*, p. 134; 'Just Tigers', in *Man-eaters of Kumaon*, p. 217.

even sympathetic to the dacoit Sultana, whom he helped track down and capture. Corbett sees the bandit as a local Robin Hood, a victim of social circumstances due to his birth in a so-called Criminal Tribe.[13] Corbett's best tales include an inimitable portrayal of his childhood friend and shooting mentor, Kunwar Singh. 'We had a name', he writes, 'for every outstanding tree, and for every water-hole, game track, and nullah.'[14] These stories in *My India* reveal the desire in Corbett, living in Kenya at the time of writing, to look back to another age in India when he led, and was trusted by, the poor of the country.[15]

His life at the loading yard at Mokameh Ghat includes a chilling account of poverty and death in the time of cholera. This ability to identify with privation in forest or village is what makes Corbett more than a chronicler of the hunt. His narratives carry such a strong emotive charge because their protagonist, usually Corbett himself, sympathizes so fully with the underdog, whether the underdog is a mauled tiger or a hounded bandit. There is also here a strong familiarity with superstition and the spirit world of the Indian peasant, especially in *Jungle Lore* (1953), and a facility with homespun, idiomatic English, which makes Corbett a rather unique writer of Indian-English prose.[16] His sympathies are so quintessentially with the Indian landscape, its flora and fauna, its inhabitants, while his linguistic skills are derived from the best tradition of British folklore and storytelling for pleasure.

Once he left India in 1947, he had to rely on memories of a world he had lost. It is striking that his last work, *Tree Tops* (1955), finds him comparing the night scenes in the Aberdare forest in Kenya to his own Kumaon. The African forest was, to his trained ear, 'disappointingly silent' except for the laugh of the hyena and the grunt of the rhino. The big cats of Africa hardly appear at all. The pamphlet is a short story about Princess Elizabeth's night at

[13] Corbett, 'Sultana: India's Robin Hood', in *My India*, pp. 90–131.

[14] Corbett, 'Kunwar Singh', in ibid., p. 23.

[15] Ibid., pp.16–28.

[16] Corbett, *Jungle Lore.*

a forest lodge. For once, the writer reveals his ability to interact with the powerful and the famous. For the first time in history, he remarks, a princess ascended a tree to spend the night in a tree-top lodge and came down the next day to become a queen: her father, the king of England, had died even as she slept. Corbett had stood guard that night.[17] But the British empire was dying, and with it the old days of man-eaters and their hunter-storytellers—among whom Corbett reigns supreme.

By this time, southern India threw up a new claimant for the slot of the raconteur of the chase. Kenneth Anderson (1910–74) was a planter of Scottish stock. Unlike Corbett, he chose to stay on in newly independent India. It is unfortunate that his work gets small recognition: this is one of the disadvantages of writing in Corbett's powerful narrative shadow. But Anderson deserves attention on many counts. For one, his terrain is so strikingly different: it is the deep South, varied in its ecology and wildlife. The denizens of the forest are often diverse, ranging from elephants to wild dogs, sloth bears to crocodiles. Anderson's books—beginning with *Man-eaters and Jungle Killers* (1957), down to the last one, *Jungles Long Ago* (1976)—provide rare insights into a changing world.[18]

His descriptions of animal behaviour are excellent, the drama of woodland life being of keen interest to him. We read of a herd of gaur, the great jet-black wild cattle of the southern Indian hill forests, warding off a hungry tiger. In *The Black Panther of Sivanipalli* (1959) he writes with warm sympathy of animals. The sloth bear is aptly described in another work:

> The sounds he emits can resemble anything from a bag-pipe being inflated to the droning of an aeroplane, from the buzzing of an angry wasp to the huffing of a blacksmith's bellows, the latter being a sort of background accompaniment to the buzzing and humming sounds. He will twist and contort his body into all shapes provided he can get at the tasty roots . . . He snores so audibly as to be heard at a distance.[19]

[17] Corbett, *Tree Tops*, pp. 26–9.

[18] Anderson, *Man-eaters and Jungle Killers*.

[19] Anderson, *This is the Jungle*, p. 17. Also see Anderson, *The Black Panther*

The sporting ethic is deeply inscribed in his worldview, but he has prejudices common to elite hunters of his day: his delight in one animal's antics is matched by a deep bias against certain other species. He is ashamed to shoot dead a pregnant panther by mistake and he kills elephants only when they are a danger to humans. But the russet-coloured, terrier-sized wild dog, a pack hunter with a wide range in the South Indian forest, is the subject of his ire. Wild dogs are described as 'merciless hunters' and 'implacable killers' and he is happy to shoot them dead and collect a bounty paid by the government.[20] Competing as they did with sportsmen for deer, wild dogs were seen as rivals for big game. Crocodiles are another species out of favour with Anderson. Fisheries department staff encouraged the destruction of crocodiles in the Cauvery, using fish hooks, and he describes their killing with a rather ghoulish delight.[21] On such counts Anderson's views closely mirror those of his time. Animals that were branded cruel or merciless, or that were seen as plain ugly, had no right to live. His books often celebrate their wholesale elimination.

Not so with the panther and tiger. He is keenly aware of their plight even as he shoots them for trophies or to get rid of cattle-lifters and man-killers. There is the tiger of Tumkur, a district which 'did not boast of a regular forest but was covered with ordinary scrub jungle', a small island of thickets in a sea of cultivated fields. This account in *Nine Man-eaters and One Rogue* (1961) is not exceptional. We read of panthers who live much more often in the proximity of villages, in small patches of tree cover and bush. The larger tiger, wandering into such grounds, finds life more difficult. The 'mauler' of Rajnagar, which injured and attacked many humans but rarely deigned to feed on their flesh, made its home in rocky terrain broken by grass jungle and boulders, stream beds and bamboo clumps. The tiger took to killing milch

---

of Sivanipalli, esp. the essay on the gaur, 'The Big Bull Bison of Gedesal', pp. 211–22.

[20] Anderson, *This is the Jungle*, pp. 73, 149.

[21] Ibid., p. 2.

cows and mauling herdsmen. In such cases Anderson displays a keen sense of the complexity of the situation. He lived in a period when the conflicts were more acute than in Corbett's day. There are occasions when he seems ambivalent. He celebrates 'progress' even as he bemoans its impact. An engineer praised for carving out a farm from hill jungles also turns out to be making money felling huge trees for charcoal.[22]

The diverse landscapes we are taken through are a patchwork quilt of dry scrub jungle and riverine thicket, of teak forests and village grazing grounds, plantations and woodlands. There is not one but many a drama in progress. Lambani tribesmen catch crabs in hill streams, travellers walk down mountain paths. Honey attracts not only a bear with a sweet tooth but also honey collectors out to take some to the nearest market.

The jungles Anderson tramps through are not a pristine wilderness but the habitat of a bustling and vigorous human society. There are people chopping wood, grazing cattle, setting traps for birds, gathering flowers and herbs, and foraging for fuel. Such people assist him in his pursuits or ask his help in ridding them of an animal that has lost its ingrained fear of humans. The cast of actors is large and the sportsman's is only one among many faces. Not being a forest officer, he often winks at the subsistence poacher. In turn, Byra of the Chinar jungle promises him an aphrodisiac guaranteed to win over 'the memsahib you love'. But there is anger at the man who uses a rusty matchlock to slay sambar at a waterhole. Anderson's deep ambivalence is partly due to his own immersion in the world of shikar. He is proud of his son's bag of seventy panthers but deeply perturbed by city-based hunters who traverse the forest in jeeps, shooting everything on four feet.[23]

In *Jungles Long Ago* this concern for the future of wildlife takes him to sanctuaries where no shot may be fired. He goes to a different part of the subcontinent, the Gir Forest, the last home of

[22] Anderson, 'The Hermit of Devarayandurga', in *Nine Man-eaters*, pp 154–64; on the habitat of panthers and the tiger, pp. 154-5.

[23] Anderson, 'Byra the Poojaree', in *Nine Man-eaters,* pp. 167, 168.

the Asian lion. The man whose bullets stopped many a tiger in its tracks now marvels at the relationship of deep trust between forest guards and wild lions. The lions do not react even when a khaki-clad guard pulls at their kill to secure it to a tree (and thereby help the tourists get better pictures)! From looking at animals down the gunsights of a rifle, Anderson is here coming round to the view of the photographer and the tourist.[24]

A striking thing about Anderson's jungle pictures is that the sounds and sights are so well described. There are fig trees near a Muslim shrine heavy with fruit, the dining place of hordes of bats. Drought is a time of spiky dry grasses, when a single match can set a jungle ablaze. He sits in the deep, cool shade of a tamarind tree, listening to the cooing of doves and the cries of peafowl. Dusk leads to a change of cast as the distant hoot of the horned owl takes over. A pall of destruction hangs over the forest. But only in his last book does he venture from his hunting grounds into a sanctuary. This itself is an indicator of how much things had changed from the time of his first book to his last.

Sálim Ali was a different sort of figure. Born in Bombay in 1896, he became a world-renowned ornithologist and was lionized widely by the time of his death in 1987. While his many bird books, starting with *The Book of Indian Birds* (1941) down to the ten-volume *Handbook of the Birds of India and Pakistan* (the latter with S. Dillon Ripley, finally completed in 1976), are very much for the specialist or the birdwatching amateur, his autobiography, *The Fall of a Sparrow* (1985), is a classic of fine prose in its own right. It is significant that German-trained Ali in his collaboration with S. Dillon Ripley wrote the notes on taxonomy behaviour and ecology while the American did the manual work of taxidermy. This reversed the usual metropolitan expert *vis-à-vis* colonized person division of labour.[25] It shows us the multifaceted character of a man whose accounts of people are no less interesting than those

[24] Anderson, 'Some Indian Game Sanctuaries', in *Jungles Long Ago*, p. 127.

[25] Ali, *Book of Indian Birds*; Ali and Ripley, *Handbook of the Birds of India*

of birds. His wit and irreverence towards holy cows is among this book's enduring features.

Sálim Ali grew up in Bombay, a city which still had orchards on its outskirts and forested hills near Vihar Lake, where you could meet the occasional panther or boar. In his autobiography he recounts how his romance with birds began. Like his elders in a mercantile Muslim family, he wielded the gun as a small boy, shooting sparrows in the garden. Usually, these birds were cooked in butter and garnished with spices, but one day a strange thing happened: the bird in question turned out to have a yellow throat, and on his elders' urgings he took it across to the Bombay Natural History Society. Sálim walked into a world of trophies, of dead and stuffed animals, to meet the curator of the museum. He was shown drawers full of the carcasses of many different kinds of sparrows. Here he was thunderstruck by the beauty and diversity of India's birdlife. His own life could never be the same again. By the time he went to Burma in 1914 as a young man in search of a future in wolfram mining, he had already made birdwatching a passion. It was to dominate his life.

But the writer in him is careful to give us glimpses of the narrow ledge on which Indians and Europeans met and worked together. There would be sharp differences on political matters in a climate of growing nationalism: Col. R. Meinertzhagen, his mentor, would exclaim: 'Sálim is the personification of the educated Indian and interests me a great deal. He is excellent at his own theoretical subjects but has no practical ability . . . His views are outstanding. He is prepared to turn the British out of India tomorrow and govern the country himself.'[26] Sálim Ali was one of the early Indians not from a princely or aristocratic lineage to venture into the world of nature studies. His surveys of the countryside and its birdlife were

---

and Pakistan; Ali, *Fall of a Sparrow*; on the division of labour, see Lewis, *Inventing Global Ecology*, p. 66 (on the reverse of the North–South divide).

[26] Ali, 'To See Ourselves as Others See Us', quote from diary of Col. Richard Meinertzhagen, 20 May 1937, in *Fall of a Sparrow*, pp. 248–9.

made possible by his contacts with civil officials and princes. There is much that has the touch of adventure: his wife and he drive through jungle only to find their vehicle stuck in a stream, to be pulled out by bullocks. In Hyderabad state's forests there would be 'the thrill of seeing the forest roads covered with fresh pug-marks of tiger, bear and other wildlife every morning.'[27] Chenchu tribal trackers and game guides in the South win his admiration for their expert knowledge of the land. The real twists come not in stalking big game but in the unexpected turns in his personal life. As a jobless youth, he began observing baya weaver birds build their nests in Kihim and ended up making new discoveries about bird behaviour. The autobiography shows us how Sálim Ali viewed his subjects—not in a coldly scientific way but with a keen eye for humour. He reveals how male birds all weave nests which their mates inspect before choosing one. Success in love depends on skill in nest-building.

By the 1930s he was already seen as an authority on India's birds and all doubts were silenced by his continuing stream of books on them. In *Indian Hill Birds* (1949) he talks of how walking on hill tracks was 'particularly delightful' due to the changing ecological milieu as 'one passes from one zone of altitude to another'.[28] At such a time, he admits, it was still not clear to many of his relatives that his work would ever lead to something of lasting value. One of his uncles believed birdwatching was merely an excuse to justify Sálim's tendency to be a 'shirker and a waster'.[29] Though written when he was a venerable and internationally respected scientist, Ali's autobiography is replete with a mildly self-deprecating humour which, like Corbett's, links his prose to one strand of British non-fictional storytelling—in this case to the tradition of pleasant self-mockery and slightly tongue-in-cheek way of saying things, whether about birds or about his family and other animals.

[27] Ibid., p. 71.
[28] Ali, *Indian Hill Birds*, p. ix.
[29] Ali, *Fall of a Sparrow*.

His dogged defence of sport-hunting was, by this time, to lead to strong criticisms from a younger generation of conservationists. But Sálim Ali's views were shaped by his own early life. It was quite normal to shoot antelopes from a car without a licence and sell them to a leading Bombay hotel. On his own camping trips, he often shot animals for food. Ali actually felt the sportsman who adhered to the spirit of fair play was not a danger to wildlife and was also a deterrent to the poacher.[30]

In fact, his dexterity with a shotgun was essential to his work as a student of birdlife. Taxonomic studies were only possible if you shot a type specimen of each species. To shoot the bird, then skin the body, record its size, weight, and plumage, preserve it in formalin, and catalogue details about its habitat required the scientist to know the crafts of hunting and taxidermy. In a sense, his own background helped enormously. Long before he had set his heart on ornithology, he was acquainted with the outdoors and with stalking. His account of a hunt of the elusive houbara bustard—always a gourmet's delight—in the desert of Sind, shows how difficult shooting could actually be. He also carefully reminds the reader that the bird was not chased towards waiting hunters, as this would be unsporting. Sálim Ali was a guest of his uncle in the civil service, and he commandeered a good riding-camel from a willing landlord. On camelback the sport was challenging: 'You suddenly realize that the bird you have been watching slowly walking away . . . has suddenly vanished, in the twinkling of an eye. It has squatted flat on the foot of a diminutive bush, neck stretched out on the ground. The shikari pulls up your camel and nudges you excitedly to shoot but for you the bird is simply not there.'[31]

Sálim Ali's work as a scientist and conservationist was, however, far more central in his writings than the pleasures of the hunt. This distinguishes him from Corbett and Anderson. There was little point cataloguing the wealth of nature unless something could be

[30] Ibid., p. 52. Hotels gladly paid five rupees for a 'dead deer', as venison was on the menu.

[31] Ibid., p. 200.

done to help save it. He recalls how Bharatpur, once a great hunting ground for mass shoots of ducks and geese, was converted into a reserve for wildlife. Through his works, the joy of discovery takes over from the thrill of the hunt. His life is a journey in quest of the mysteries and marvels of the natural world, where every thicket holds a secret, where the bird in the bush is truly worth two in the hand.

Another writer who was never a shikari and very much a preservationist shared Sálim Ali's concern about conservation. Kailash Sankhala (1925–94) was unlike the other nature writers in two major respects: he was an administrator and the architect of what, at the time of its launch, was the single largest wildlife preservation effort undertaken anywhere in the world. It is no surprise, therefore, that the challenge of conservation runs like a thread through his books.

The first and last tiger Sankhala shot with a gun was a male in a dry thorn forest of the Aravalli hills and it is appropriate that the event is described at the very outset of his autobiography, *Tiger! The Story of the Indian Tiger* (1978).[32] This is the tale of not only the man and his life but of the animal that for him symbolized the spirit of the Indian jungle. As a young forest cadet in the 1950s, he too was required, like all aspirants to the Forest Service, to 'bag a tiger'. This rite of passage had the opposite effect and his words are a strange but moving tribute to the victim of his bullet. He saw 'The tiger dead, his legs up and his eyes open. He seemed to look into my eyes and ask the reason for his death. Is this the sport where all rules are in your favour?'[33] The book itself is the story of how his life was now dedicated to another cause: saving the tiger and its forest home.

This was the heyday of commercial shikar and he did not find it easy to make headway. His native Rajasthan was ecologically different from Corbett's hunting grounds in the foothills of the Himalaya or Anderson's terrain in the deep South. Half the land

[32] Sankhala, *Tiger!*
[33] Ibid., p. 20.

was desert, the rest was forest-clad hills dotted with lakes. The latter was where the princes of yore had organized tiger hunts, and which had now become a huge killing field for shikar outfitters. The young Kailash recalled conversations about who had bagged how many tigers and the best way to shoot quarry.

By the 1960s, when he was moving up the ranks of the service, a major shift was taking place in attitudes to wildlife. What Corbett had suggested as a remedy-protecting wildlife was now looking like a dire necessity. Even the idea of the 'man-eater' came under attack. Sankhala became one of the first to take on Corbett in print, refuting the notion that man-eating was ever as rife as had been suggested. The man-eater was more a victim of increasing human intrusions that denied the predator its living space and natural food. Corbett was now blamed for exaggerating the danger that tigers posed to people and indirectly legitimizing the culture of the hunt. The tigers of Corbett Park, Sankhala asserted, would have doubts about the conservationist credentials of the great slayer of man-eaters. In Corbett's place, Sankhala suggested that the less known F.W. Champion be seen as the precursor of the conservation movement.[34] This was a forester who, in the 1920s, had abandoned the gun for the camera. This reworking of history had a dual purpose: it gave Sankhala's own efforts greater legitimacy and undermined an ethos of hunting which was still widely prevalent. This effort was critical for it went against the general ethos of his fellow officers—who saw cash in every tree and a trophy in every tiger or leopard. Sankhala talks of how he has shot 'only 43 tigers' and would love to score a century—only in this case you hardly need reminding that these tigers were 'taken' on film, and not with a gun.[35]

As a student of the tiger's life and ecology, Sankhala's works included the lavishly illustrated *Wild Beauty* (1973) and *Tiger Land* (1974).[36] These are the writings of an ecological nationalist

[34] Ibid., p. 138. See also Champion, *Tripwire for a Tiger*.
[35] Sankhala, *Tiger!*, p. 209.
[36] Sankhala, *Wild Beauty*; idem, *Tiger Land*.

for whom the blackbuck and the bird colonies of Bharatpur, the dry Deccan plateau and its wildlife, as also big-game animals everywhere, make up the splendour and riches of India. In Sankhala's work we notice that the natural world is less a terrain and more a heritage to be cherished. In this respect it sets the stage for the story of his own endeavours as Director of Project Tiger (1973–7), during which he established a network of reserves to save the great cat and the myriad plants and animals that shared its jungle home. The tiger is now transformed from a potential killer into an emblem of life. It stands at the apex of the food chain, the whole of which is to be saved in select stretches of wild land. Reversing the march of cultivation into forest, the core areas of the reserves become a *sanctum sanctorum* for nature. The religious imagery is far from coincidental. Sankhala wrote in 1978 of how 'No axe falls in the forest, no saw moves on dead and fallen wood.' Here, the cycles of renewal and decay, of death and life, continue uninterrupted by the hunter and the logger.[37]

The canvas is broadened to go beyond the destiny of the tiger. Nearly all of Sankhala's works contain an account of the ceaseless activity at a waterhole in the Aravallis in summer. Beasts and birds from the smallest to the largest, from the quail to the tiger, arrive to quench their thirst. Sankhala, perched in a hideout, records their departures and arrivals on film and in his notebook. The very forest tract where he shot a tiger with a gun has become a refuge for wild creatures. From a keeper of captive animals he becomes a protector of the wild. He writes of the men in the field with an enthusiasm that is infectious: 'Panwar is mad about his Minolta camera, capturing the ecological changes in the Kanha meadows, C.B. Singh protests even about angling with a rod and line in the Ramganga river in Corbett park. He is a purist. Deb Roy exchanges fire with poachers even at night in Manas. They know full well that he is a crack shot . . . The commitment is total and the team is perfect.'[38]

[37] Sankhala, *Tiger!*, p. 200.
[38] Ibid., p. 199.

Later works, written after his retirement from service, return to the same theme. *The Gardens of God: The Waterbird Sanctuary at Bharatpur* (1984) is a charming account of the small bird sanctuary where he had served early in his career.[39] In an article he wrote in *Sanctuary* magazine, in 1985, even the Thar desert becomes not a barren stretch of land but a place teeming with life. Gazelles scamper in bush country and sandgrouse fly in their thousands to the few waterholes.[40] The following sample of his prose indicates the tenor of his writings:

> When I close my eyes I see the nests of half a million flamingoes in the Rann of Kutch, the carpet of a million flowers in the Himalayan meadows, the deciduous forests in late February with their extravagant reds, the lushness of the evergreen forests. I see shaded brooks with ferns, with frolicking deer coming down to drink or a tiger sleeping half submerged in a pool unaware of my presence. Inspite of some inevitable moments of sadness and frustration when I look back over the past half century, I feel I have lived one glorious day after another, watching the splash of colour of the setting sun, hearing the alarm calls of chital and sambar, warning of the presence of a predator prowling in the night.[41]

The revised version of his autobiography, entitled *Return of the Tiger* (1993), has a sense of foreboding, and not only in a personal sense. In it he warns of the inroads of new development projects and admits the need to relate to the people who rely on the forest in a more meaningful way. In the Kachida valley of the Ranthambore Wildlife Reserve he climbs to the top of a hill to tell a fellow conservationist how he has redeemed his pledge. Twenty years earlier, he had promised to save the valley, and now he can look back on a job well done.[42] He died the following year. His accounts survive as a record of a magnificent wildlife heritage, ours to cherish or destroy.

[39] Sankhala, *The Gardens of God.*

[40] Sankhala, 'Destination Desert Sanctuary', pp. 40–8.

[41] Sankhala, *Tiger!*, p. 209.

[42] Sankhala, *Return of the Tiger*; Sahgal, *Sankhala's India*, is a fine small collection.

If Sankhala was a man of action, he had a counterpart in a man of ideas. M. Krishnan (1913–96), the most articulate proponent of total preservation, was undoubtedly the most widely read Indian naturalist of the twentieth century. Armed with a degree in Botany, he served briefly as adviser to the ruler of Sandur, a princely state in Mysore. In 1948–9 he began his career as a freelance writer and photographer. Always known as a 'lone wolf', he remains notable for both the outstanding quality of his writings and his black-and-white photographs. His Country Notebook, a fortnightly column in *The Statesman,* Calcutta, was published for nearly half a century. Some of the early pieces are collected in *Jungle and Backyard* (1961).[43]

Krishnan was scrupulous in his attention to changes in the countryside, and a recurrent theme is the cycle of the seasons. March is the time when the Indian roller goes crazy as it begins its courtship rituals; summer is the season of mango blossoms and of the koel song; November, the month for harvesting, is the time to stalk the grey partridge. Krishnan was among the first to sound the warning bell about the wildlife of the dry grasslands and the scrub forests. Of the blackbuck antelope he wrote, 'When every acre is held precious . . . I think the beasts and birds of the open country must look to the blackbuck for their salvation, for it is the one claimant for protection among them whose arresting good looks and swift charm might succeed in attracting notice.'[44] Having witnessed the rapid demise of the great herds of the buck in the Deccan, he was already clinically analysing the causes of their decline. The meat-hunters, often servicing the markets in the towns and bazaars, used both traditional and modern techniques against the animals, but the *coup de grâce* was delivered by the extension of cultivation into the areas it inhabited. Krishnan was way ahead of his times,

[43] Gee, *The Wildlife of India,* for the term 'lone wolf' who did not care for committees and boards, p. 22; Krishnan, *Jungle and Backyard.* Also see Rangarajan, 'Nature's Chronicler', pp. 7–9.

[44] Krishnan, 'The Fastest Thing on Legs', in *Jungle and Backyard,* p. 24. The only anthology of his Tamil writings is Baskaran, *Mazhiakalamum Kuyilosaiyum.*

for until very recently Indian conservation efforts have focussed not on grasslands, mangroves, and wetlands, but on forests.

Modesty was never one of Krishnan's traits. Unlike many urban wildlife lovers he had deep roots in Tamil and Sanskrit literature and an intimate knowledge of the southern Indian countryside in particular, which give all his writings a distinctly Brahmanical air of knowing precisely what is best and necessary. In 1965 he won a Jawaharlal Nehru fellowship to study the ecology and status of the large mammals of peninsular India. The study, published in 1975 under the title *India's Wildlife, 1959–70,* is a masterpiece. It also reflects his other great strength: his long familiarity with the denizens of the monsoon forest, the gaur and the sambar, the chital and the elephant. His view of wildlife never excluded the rich assemblage of India's plants on which its fauna depends. In the book he highlights the destructive forces unleashed in independent India. Hunting menaced not only the survival of species but also radically forced herds of deer to become 'shy and fugitive creatures of the night.'[45] In the past, the forest and sown lands had often been in a tug of war. The boundaries of the jungle had not been fixed; but in his own lifetime the retreat of the woodlands became permanent.

Krishnan's response to these changes was unequivocal. In each of his works, including the superbly illustrated *Nights and Days: My Book of Indian Wildlife* (1985), he argues in favour of a kind of ecological patriotism.[46] India's identity has as much to do with plants and rivers, trees and birds, insects and animals as with the languages and cultures of its people. A sense of national pride required that at least some tracts be preserved in their natural state.

In *Nights and Days,* a photograph accompanies each anecdote of encounters with animals. This was what his Country Notebook looked like: in the anthology he put together a selection of his best pieces. The calls of nesting spoonbills draw his attention. 'I can

[45] Krishnan, *India's Wildlife.*

[46] Krishnan, *Nights and Days*; see also Chandola, *et al.*, *Eye in the Jungle*, a superbly remastered set of M. Krishnan's photographs.

only describe [it] as a strange mixture of a hiss and a growl. It even has an alarm call, a soft sneezing call, very like a man suppressing a sneeze politely in company.'[47] An account of owls large and small reveals how much he likes them, though he reminds us they are 'soft-plumaged, silent-winged, night hunters'.

In the wet grassland of Kaziranga in Assam he sensed the agony of a mother rhino whose calf had been lifted by a tiger. His sympathy for creatures great and small was not matched by any tolerance for error in human beings.[48] Krishnan's sometimes acerbic remarks are often unforgettable. In *Jungle and Backyard,* turning on Sarojini Naidu's poetically pedantic observation that a koel calls 'Lira, Liree', he says devastatingly: 'I have not heard the call. Nor has anyone else.'[49]

Krishnan was very much with Sankhala in his advocacy of a centralized effort to establish inviolate nature reserves. Though familiar with village-based traditions of protecting waterbirds and sacred groves, he felt that only punitive measures could hold back industrialization and population growth from nature reserves. The logger and hunter, the gatherer of fruits and flowers and the tourist, all had to be subordinated in protected areas to the interest of the wild. In the *Sunday* magazine annual in 1977 he warned of the need to be vigilant in protection and to resist the temptation to interfere with nature, 'to gild refined gold and paint the lily.'[50]

Krishnan represents the voice of the unrelenting preservationist. In this role his eloquence has not been matched. There is no dearth of zealous wildlife protectors now, but no one has the same literary flair, that eccentric ability to convey the lived quality of life in the wild and the imperatives of keeping it alive.

[47] Krishnan, 'Spoonbills', *Nights and Days*, pp. 87–90.

[48] Ibid.; Gee, *Wildlife*, p. 22; Krishnan, 'A Day's Span of Life', in *Nights and Days*, p. 77.

[49] M. Krishnan, *Jungle and Backyard,* 'The Voice of Spring', p. 55.

[50] Krishnan, 'The Environment: Disaster Ahead', *Sunday*, Annual, 1977. Especially valuable is Shanti and Ashish Chandola, *Birds and Birdsong*; an invaluable earlier collection is Guha, *Nature's Spokesman.*

The wonderful literary connection between wildlife and rivetting storytelling, established in India by the work of these five nature writers, is a curious and quite uniquely remarkable corner of the Indo-Anglian tradition of prose writing. The other interesting fact to remember, in this context, is that Jim Corbett is almost certainly the highest selling Indian writer of imaginative English prose of all time; and Sálim Ali's collected writings on India's birdlife may well come a very close second. No one who cares for the craft of prose, and its importance in delivering an implicit or explicit conservationist message to large audiences can ever undervalue the achievement of such prose.

References

Ali, Sálim, *The Book of Indian Birds*, Delhi: Oxford University Press, 1941.

———, *Indian Hill Birds,* Bombay: Oxford University Press,1949.

———, *The Fall of a Sparrow,* Delhi: Oxford University Press, 1985.

———, and S. Dillon Ripley, *Handbook of the Birds of India and Pakistan,* 12 vols, Delhi: Oxford University Press,1948–76.

Anderson, Kenneth, *Man-eaters and Jungle Killers*, 1957; rpnt. Delhi: Rupa, 1991.

———, *The Black Panther of Sivanipalli*, 1959; Delhi: HarperCollins, 1991.

———, *This is the Jungle*, London: Allen and Unwin, 1964.

———, *Jungles Long Ago*, 1976; rpnt. Delhi: Rupa, 2012.

———, *Nine Man-eaters and One Rogue*, Delhi: HarperCollins, 1991.

Baskaran, S.T., ed., *Mazhiakalamum Kuyilosaiyum. Ma Krishnanlyarkaiyiyal Katturaikal*, Madras: Kalachuadu Pathigam, 2002.

Booth, Martin, *Carpet Sahib: A Life of Jim Corbett*,1986; rpnt. Delhi: Oxford University Press, 1990.

Champion, James, ed., *Tripwire for a Tiger: Selected Works of F.W. Champion,* Chennai: Rainfed Books, 2012.

Chandola, Ashish, Shanthi Chandola and T.N.A. Perumal, ed., *Eye in the Jungle,* Hyderabad: Universities Press, 2006.

Chandola, Shanthi and Ashish Chandola, ed., *Birds and Birdsong,* Delhi: Aleph, 2012.

Corbett, Jim, *The Man-eaters of Kumaon,* Bombay: Oxford University Press, 1944.

———, *The Man-eating Leopard of Rudraprayag*, 1947; rpnt. Delhi: Oxford University Press, 1973.

———, *Jungle Lore*, Delhi: Oxford University Press, 1953.

———, *The Temple Tiger and More Man-eaters of Kumaon*, 1954; rpnt. Delhi: Oxford University Press, 1994.

Corbett, Jim, *Tree Tops, Bombay*: Oxford University Press, 1955.

Gee, E.P., *The Wildlife of India*, London: Fontana-Collins, 1964.

Guha, Ramachandra, ed., *Nature's Spokesman: M. Krishnan and Indian Wildlife*, Delhi: Oxford University Press, 2000.

Kala, D.C., *Jim Corbett of Kumaon*, 2nd rev. edn, New Delhi: Ravi Dayal, 1999.

Krishnan, M., *Jungle and Backyard*, Delhi: National Book Trust, 1961.

———, *India's Wildlife, 1959–70*, Bombay: Bombay Natural History Society, 1975.

———, *Nights and Days: My Book of Indian Wildlife*, Delhi: Vikas, 1985.

Lewis, Michael, ed., *Inventing Global Ecology: Tracing the Biodiversity Ideal in India 1945–1997*, Hyderabad: Orient Blackswan, 2003.

Rangarajan, M.,'Nature's Chronicler and Defender', *Indian Review of Books*, Chennai, 9 (2000).

———, *India's Wildlife History: An Introduction*, New Delhi: Permanent Black, 2001.

———, ed., *The Oxford Anthology of Indian Wildlife*, 2 vols, New Delhi: Oxford University Press, 1999.

Sahgal, Bittu, ed., *Sankhala's India: Lest We forget*, Mumbai: Sanctuary Asia, 2008.

Sankhala, Kailash, *Wild Beauty*, Delhi: National Book Trust, 1973.

———, *Tiger Land*, London: Fontana-Collins, 1975.

———, *Tiger! The Story of the Indian Tiger*, London: Fontana, Collins, 1978.

———, *The Gardens of God: The Waterbird Sanctuary at Bharatpur*, Delhi: Vikas, 1984.

———, 'Destination Desert Sanctuary', *Sanctuary*, 6 (1991).

———, *Return of the Tiger*, Delhi: Lustre Press, 1993.

Thapar, Valmik, ed., *Saving Wild Tigers 1900–2000*, New Delhi: Permanent Black, 2001.

Ward, Geoffrey C. and Diane R. Ward, *Tiger Wallahs: Saving the Greatest of the Great Cats*, Delhi: Oxford University Press, 2009.

8

The Politics of Ecology

The Debate on Wildlife and People in India 1970–1995

Introduction

In 1979, in a lecture delivered in Delhi, the naturalist M. Krishnan referred to the choice before the conservation movement in India as one between Vedanthangal and Asoka.[1] The metaphors used require some explanation. Vedanthangal (Tamil for hunter's tank, a misnomer if there ever was one) is a bird sanctuary near the city of Madras where, oral tradition has it, nesting waterbirds have been protected for nearly two millennia. When British soldiers shot at the storks in 1798, the residents of the village marched off in protest to the Collector, who issued a proclamation saying no one would be allowed to harm the birds again. Krishnan acknowledged the efficacy of such conservation attempts growing out of religious custom or tradition, but then

I am grateful to Seshagiri Rao, Ram Guha, Vasant Saberwal, K. Jagdish, Seema Bhatt, the late Shambu Prasad, Ashish Kothari, V. Thapar, and M. Vyas. I owe a special word of thanks to the fellows of the Nehru Memorial Museum and Library. The usual disclaimers apply. This essay appeared earlier in the *Economic and Political Weekly*, vol. 31 (1996), pp. 2391–410.

[1] Krishnan, Monthly Lecture. On elephants in early India, see Trautmann, *Elephants and Kings*.

turned to another precedent. The emperor Asoka in the third century BCE had in his Pillar Edicts decreed certain animals and birds as protected. There was also evidence in the *Arthashastra* that reserves known as *abharanyas* (or *hastavanas*) had been set aside especially to safeguard elephants. The historicity of these references need not concern us here as much as the conclusion drawn from history. The past was invoked by Krishnan to suggest a strategy for the future. There was a choice between local efforts from the grass-roots, and state-sponsored schemes from above. One was founded on voluntary participation and the other on the coercive ability of the government. Krishnan warned that there was no time to try the Vedanthangal way. The pressures of demographic and economic expansion left no option but relying on state machinery to save India's wildlife from certain extinction. If there was a tradition to be followed, it was the Asokan one.

Krishnan had served in several, including the advisory body known as the Indian Board for Wildlife set up in 1952 and on the Steering Committee for Project Tiger. Launched in 1973, Project Tiger was at the time the world's largest single wildlife conservation programme. The basic philosophy of the project was identical to the one championed by Krishnan in his lecture and other writings. It was essential to set aside some land, preferably 5 per cent, to be preserved 'free of all human activities' (except for protection).[2] A country could otherwise be lost, not by invasion or conquest but by 'dissipation of the entity from within', and for its own cultural identity it was essential for an India of the future to retain representative patches of fauna and flora in their original state. While the precise quantum of the area to be set aside was specified differently at various times, the nub of the argument was clear.[3] Total environmental preservation in a few selected areas was

[2] Krishnan, 'Preservation in Perpetuity', Annexure II, pp. 89–92. The committee was chaired by N.D. Tiwari (hereafter Tiwari Report).

[3] Krishnan, 'The Environment'; idem, 'A Wildlifer's Apprehensions', pp. 12–14; idem, 'Can it Fail?' In 1989 he argued in favour of 10 per cent of the land being set aside for total preservation.

central to a strategy for conservation. It is also important that the key instrument of change was to be the union government. State governments were seen as hostages to special interests that would prevent any long-term programme from getting off the ground. If necessary, additional areas could, it was suggested, even be leased by the Centre for ninety-nine years and administered for posterity.[4]

Krishnan's observations seem especially striking if we examine the present debate about the fate of the Protected Areas. Wildlife sanctuaries and national parks now cover 5 per cent of the land area of India while their core areas constitute about 1 per cent of the land mass.[5] While their number and area have expanded considerably, there is little disagreement on one basic point: they are in peril. Encroachment by various industrial and commercial interests on their borders and even within their precincts is not new, but it has grown rapidly since 1991. In the new climate of liberalization, sanctuaries have been denotified to facilitate the location of extractive industry (mining), tourist resorts, manufacturing plants, and other 'development' projects.[6] Secondly, the administration of Protected Areas is often under attack from local residents living either within or on the perimeter of parks. They point to the double standards that deny them access for livelihood needs while allowing commercial forestry and other allied activities.[7]

The line taken by Krishnan is still very much the core of official policy. In contrast with the significant, if limited, steps in the direction of Joint Forest Management, the appeals for participatory or joint management of protected areas have made little headway. This is despite the fact that the number of people living in and around the Protected Areas is now provisionally estimated at

[4] Krishnan, 'Preservation in Perpetuity', p. 82.

[5] The best source for the area, status, and conflicts is Kothari, *et al.*, *Management of National Parks*. See also Rodgers and Panwar, *Planning a Wildlife Protected Area*.

[6] Sahgal, 'Denotify and be Damned'.

[7] Dogra, 'Parks and People', pp. 59–61. The workshop was held at the Lal Bahadur Shastri Academy of Administration, Mussoorie, October 1993.

4.5 million and the removal of all such populations or the closure of all access is neither administratively nor politically feasible.[8] The rights of future generations and non-human inhabitants of the planet are seen by wildlifers as being under threat from pressing human demands of the present day.[9] In contrast to the 1970s, some preservationists are willing to invest in ecologically sound development around the sanctuaries in return for further curbs on resource use within the tracts.[10] In common with their predecessors, they see the continued survival of such areas in their natural state as an insurance and an investment in terms of protecting potentially useful species. The moral and ethical aspects are stressed equally forcefully.[11] The implication of all this is to retain intact the present structure of bureaucratic control of Protected Areas under the Forest Department. The congruence of interests, of ideologically charged notions of preservation, and the specific interests of foresters is striking.[12]

At the same time, the once-unified ranks of middle-class groups are now divided. There is discord even on central issues such as the mechanisms and aims of wildlife conservation. Who is to conserve what and for whom? The wildlife movement has been seen as possessing two distinct levels, one with a middle-class constituency and another in rural centres. This is really a reworking of Krishnan's classification, though the sympathies of

[8] Kothari, 'Is Joint Protected Area Management Desirable and Possible?' (hereafter Kothari, JPAM). The papers are available in Kothari, *et al.*, *People and Protected Areas*.

[9] Singh, 'JPAM—Some Policy Issues'. Singh, one of the co-authors of the1989 report, disagreed strongly with Kothari's advocacy of joint management. The notion of rights of nature and of the limits to carrying capacity were carried forward uncritically from the 1989 report: see Kothari, *Management*, p. 13.

[10] Thapar and Manfredi, 'Saving Our Forests', pp. 27–30.

[11] World Wildlife Fund, *World Conservation Strategy*, p. 2.

[12] See Guha, 'Deep Ecology'; Rangarajan 'Wildlife–Human Conflicts', pp. 19–22.

analysts are now in the reverse order.[13] While useful, the two-way split between 'wilderness preservationists and popular conservation' misses the several shades of grey that lie between such extremes. Even in a limited sense, it cannot account for several consequences of the preservationist projects that transcend the specific aims of their proponents. Supporters of statist projects could be active proponents of voluntary village-level efforts, even if in a very limited way.[14] Further, the specific interests of wildlife enthusiasts should not blind us to the wider issues of ecologically sound development or of humankind's ethical responsibility to the kind of nature that they put on the agenda.

I will also try to show how even a narrow and limited social group can, over time, generate fresh initiatives and ideas that break up old alliances. Analysts have often written wildlife enthusiasts off as flamingo-lovers and fans of tiger cubs. Guha is appreciative of how they extend the concept of equity from across classes and nations to other species and generations.[15] Beyond that, he rarely analyses them critically. The question of how to actualize this vision has given rise to new sensibilities that try to take account of the human dimensions of the wildlife question. Key actors in the drama too have changed their views and their constituencies.[16] These ideological debates cannot be divorced from the wider context of both the environmental questions in India today and their linkage not only with the ecological problem but with the political and social order that may be conducive to addressing it. A brief look at the preservation agenda is necessary.

[13] Gadgil and Guha, *Ecology and Equity.*

[14] Lavkumar, 'The Need for a New Conservation Approach', pp. 8–9; Shahi, 'Kokrebellur ke peehar', pp. 22–4; Abraham, 'The Karanjikulam Breeding Bird Sanctuary', pp. 549–72.

[15] Dasgupta, 'The Environment Debate', p. 400. Also in Guha, 'Ideological Trends', pp. 2577–81.

[16] Sahgal, 'If Nature Does Not Survive', describes the Collector as the *maai-baap* or paternal protector for the people. See his 'People and Sanctuaries'; also, Sahgal, *Environment and Wildlife.*

Preservation: From Ascendancy to Crisis

The India of the early 1950s had important continuities in the attitudes and lifestyles of the elite. Hunting continued to be both a privilege and a pastime for officials, princes, and the landed classes—as it had earlier in the century. In the Madras Presidency, S.K. Chettur joined the ruler of Venkatagiri in hunting sloth bears from specially constructed towers.[17] When the civil servant Yezdi Gundevia was posted to Mirzapur in 1939 he suspected that no Indian had held the charge till then on account of the excellent opportunities for shikar in the area! Much of his time was spent following up tigers in jungles and shooting geese in ponds and lakes.[18] Visiting heads of state could travel out from New Delhi into the hills of Rajasthan to try their luck. Prince Philip, for instance, hunted in Ranthambore as a guest of the Maharaja of Jaipur.[19] Until the abolition of privy purses in 1969, many rulers retained shikar rights in their former princely hunting reserves. There were efforts to protect endangered wild animals and birds, but the continuities in the personnel are striking. The Indian Board for Wildlife had its first meeting at Mysore in 1952, with the maharaja as the host. Among the key personalities in policy formulation in the early years were English tea and coffee planters like Randolph Morris and E.P. Gee, foresters such as P.D. Stracey, and the princes of Bhavnagar (in Gujarat) and Sandur (Karnataka).[20] It was no great surprise that even the attempts to control the shooting of tigers in the

[17] Chettur, *The Steel Frame and I*, pp. 97–9.

[18] Gundevia, *Districts of the Raj*, pp. 163–5.

[19] Prince Philip, Foreword to Thapar, *Tigers—The Secret Life*, pp. xvii–xviii. Tigers were not protected at the time in India but the point is to emphasize the cultural continuities with Raj days.

[20] Ghorpade, *Development Ethos*. His father H.Y. Ghorpade and he were both prominent wildlife enthusiasts and were from the former royal family of Sandur. Dharamkumarsinhji was from Bhavnagar, Lavkumar and Shivrajkumar from Jasdan. P.D. Stracey wrote the manual, *Wildlife—Its Conservation and Control*. See Ali, 'R.C. Morris', pp. 192–6, and idem, 'P.D. Stracey', pp. 191–2.

breeding season in Rajasthan were shot down. As the author of the proposal later recounted, virtually all the members of the Advisory Board that considered the issue were keen hunters.[21]

The legal continuities were equally significant. Most of today's wildlife parks have been carved out of either princely hunting grounds or Reserved Forests. The latter were part of the vast network of government forests taken over mainly for revenue and strategic reasons from the late nineteenth century onwards. The appropriation of forest wealth was accomplished by outlawing or severely restricting hunting and other kinds of forest use by Adivasis (Scheduled Tribes) and other forest-dependent peoples. Though these efforts were often resisted by both overt and covert means, the legacy of the game laws was to be very significant for early Indian middle-class wildlife enthusiasts.[22] They often uncritically identified with efforts to penalize quail trappers and deer catchers, even when the trappers were mainly engaged in activities essential for their livelihood.[23] Keen hunters themselves, they felt obliged to control those who were competing for the same resource. This extended beyond the human world to certain categories of wild animals. Thus, Randolph Morris and Sálim Ali called for increased rewards for killing Himalayan black bears to help build up the number of the Kashmir stags.[24] They aimed to save the deer from extinction, not shoot it for trophies, but this was to be achieved by imposing their own rule over nature. Similarly, Stracey praised the killing of jackal cubs to help game birds and urged the eradication of wild dogs 'by every possible means' in order to help herbivores.[25] The notion that predators had a role to play in nature's system and would not wipe out a prey species only acquired full official sanction with the launch of Project Tiger. For many conservationists, the preservation of wildlife was

[21] Sankhala, *Tiger!*, pp. 19 and 184; see also Rangarajan, *Oxford Anthology of Indian Wildlife*.

[22] Abdul Ali, 'Some Notes on the Painted Partridge', pp. 446–8.

[23] Sankhala, *Tiger!*, p. 185.

[24] Morris and Ali, 'Game Preservation in Kashmir', pp. 229–33.

[25] Stracey, *Wildlife*, pp. 47–8 and 58–9.

equated with protecting game birds and animals whose natural enemies were to be wiped out or controlled through intrusive measures.

The development of aesthetic sensibilities in relation to wild animals in general and to the much-despised large carnivores specifically were on the horizon though this may not have been realized at the time. In 1961 a young Indian and her two sons recounted the scene in the Kenyan reserve of Amboseli in a letter home: 'It was fun to drive around and come across that comic, supercilious creature, the giraffe, the prosperous and plump zebra, fleet-footed gazelles of various kinds and the lordly and kindly (looking at least) lion and his family . . . Earlier we had seen a most captivating lion family: two lionesses and cubs.'[26]

Two decades later, now as a keynote speaker at a UN conference in Nairobi, the same Indian travelled to the Maasai Mara reserve on the Tanzanian border.[27] Already, in the 1960s, before her critical role in facilitating and pushing through a preservation project, Indira Gandhi was perhaps symbolic of a new generation of Indians who related to nature not through the barrel of a gun but with binoculars and field guides. As a child she had lost her fear of snakes: her mother's youngest brother Ranjit Pandit was 'passionately interested' in all sorts of animals and, at one time, 'anything you opened in the house' was likely to have a snake in it.[28] In her letters to the imprisoned Jawaharlal she wrote in the winter of 1943 about watching and identifying, and seeing two new species in the garden. In Teen Murti House, where Nehru lived as prime minister, the family kept a variety of pets, including two tiger cubs, a young leopard, and two red pandas.[29] The first red panda was presented to Indira Gandhi on a visit to Assam and was only identified with the aid of a book in a library; and an injury

[26] I. Gandhi to J. Nehru, 25 August 1961, in Gandhi, *Two Alone*, p. 670.

[27] Alexander, *My Years with Indira Gandhi*, p. 69.

[28] Gandhi, *In Conversation with Pupul Jayakar*, p. 9.

[29] I. Gandhi to J. Nehru, 21 September 1943 and 21 October 1943, in Gandhi, *Two Alone*, pp. 272 and 291, respectively.

to one of her tiger cubs was the cause of great anguish even to her busy father, Jawaharlal Nehru.[30]

At a public level Indira Gandhi hosted the first meeting of the Delhi Bird Watchers Society. She was on its executive committee and briefly served as its president.[31] The society itself was a very low-key group, with talks and meetings at Teen Murti House.[32] Though politicians are often given to hyperbole, Mrs Gandhi was perhaps not exaggerating when she later claimed that she was 'one who had been interested in this subject long before I ever heard the word "ecology".'[33] Aesthetic pleasure was always central to her notion of a different relationship with the natural world: there were visits to the Himalayas during which she compared the world to 'Wordsworth's daffodils, an ever-refreshing memory.'[34] These romantic overtones were perhaps also to do with a city dweller's idealization of the world of pastures, forests, and hills. The idea of the oneness of life and a fascination for the powers of modern science also recur in her writings.[35]

While Nehru wrote the foreword to a book on India's wildlife by the naturalist Edward Gee a few weeks before his own death, it was only under Indira Gandhi that the wildlife issue began to receive attention from the head of government.[36] One critical

[30] Gandhi, *Rajiv's World*, pp. 6–7; Jayakar, *Indira Gandhi*, pp. 144–5.

[31] Indira Gandhi, presented by F. Pouchepadass, *My Truth*, pp. 72–3. At the time, she equated protection of monuments (the human heritage) with that of wildlife (the natural heritage): p. 185.

[32] Anon., 'The Delhi Bird Watchers Society', p. 595.

[33] Gandhi, *Collected Speeches*, p. 443.

[34] Norman, *Letters to a Friend*, p. 169, and see also p. 96; Gandhi, *Eternal India*, pp. 249–50.

[35] The classic on urban perceptions of the countryside remains Williams, *The Country and the City.* See Gandhi, *Eternal India*, pp. 105–7, 32–3, and her ecstatic letter on modern sciences to Nehru written on 9 February 1940; Gandhi, *Freedom's Daughter*, p. 16; the philosophical overtones are clear in the letter (13 April 1940), p. 53.

[36] Gee, *Wildlife of India*. Indira Gandhi accompanied him on his visit to Kaziranga sanctuary, Assam, which is described in the book: pp. 158–9. See also Guha, *Gandhi and the Environmental Movement*.

feature of this new development was the close personal equation she developed with a variety of wildlife enthusiasts. These included officials with a keen interest in conservation, most notably Kailash Sankhala, who, as director of the Delhi zoo, once turned up on her birthday with three tiger cubs in a basket.[37] He went on to serve as the first Director of Project Tiger from 1973 to 1977. The hunter-turned-conservationist Arjan Singh, a gentleman farmer from Lakhimpur Kheri in UP, also received support from the PM, who asked the chief minister of UP to assist Arjan Singh who, she said, had been 'ploughing a lonely furrow'.[38] Sálim Ali, the famous ornithologist who appealed to her to save the Silent Valley rain forest, enjoyed a close rapport over decades and later praised her for having 'lent her full support to the movement'.[39] Thus, both among the bureaucracy and middle-class groups who took up the wildlife cause, Indira Gandhi had a core of support. The relationship was a complex one. Being an enabling force for their projects, she cultivated a small constituency that saw her as being above petty politics. The importance of such links in the Western world, where eminent scientists and public figures expressed admiration for her, is not to be underestimated.[40] It was even more crucial during critical periods of the Emergency and after her return to power. Support for conservation could tide her over her human rights record.

Her own role was to be critical at several junctures, though this also points to the extent to which this set of issues both reflected

[37] Sankhala served as Director of the Delhi zoo from 1965 to 1970: Sankhala, *Tiger!*, pp. 140–52; for the tiger cubs, see his *Wild Beauty*.

[38] Singh, *Legend of the Man Eater*, p. 98. Arjan Singh was also encouraged by the chief minister of U.P., Charan Singh.

[39] Ali, 'In Search of the Himalayan Quail', pp. 16–17.

[40] The people of letters included Ivan Illich, Sir Peter Scott, Buckminster Fuller, and S. Dillon Ripley. In addition, Guy Mountfort, Prince Philip, and Prince Bernhard (of the Netherlands) were influential public figures: Norman, *Letters*, pp. 121, 137; Anon., 'The Order of the Golden Ark', pp. 4–5. The award was given to her by Prince Bernhard; Jackson, 'Birth of Sanctuary', pp. 8–9, on how Scott and others lobbied for the protection of Sultanpur Lake in Haryana.

and helped legitimize the centralization and personalization of decision-making power.[41] The run-up to Project Tiger saw her play a crucial role at virtually every step. In 1969, at the meeting of a leading international conservation body in Delhi, she won encomiums for the support she gave to a ban on the trade in tiger and leopard skins. Foreign exchange was important, but 'not at the cost of the life and liberty of some of the most beautiful inhabitants of the country.'[42] The international conservation community, in particular the World Wildlife Fund (WWF) headed by members of European royal families and scientists, had a hand in the process. Its trustee, Guy Mountfort, an expert negotiator, personally lobbied her to constitute a committee that would report to her personally. Such reliance of conservationists on single heads of government also extended to dictatorial regimes. Thus, Sálim Ali regarded it as 'unfortunate' that General Ayub Khan fell from power in Pakistan just when he was becoming pro-conservation.[43] Inside India, diverse groups would also directly approach the prime minister for action at a local level. In 1982 the coastguard was deployed to protect nesting sea turtles on the Orissa coast following a study by the Madras Snake Park biologist J. Vijaya.[44] Such rapport did not exclude the Gandhian environmentalist Sunderlal Bahuguna, who got an ancient oak tree in Nainital saved from the army by writing to the prime minister.[45]

Even this brief list shows the variety of conservationists who had close personal links with Indira Gandhi. They included a

[41] Ali, 'Review of G. Mountfort', pp. 307–8; see Zafar Futehally's letter to Mountfort asking the latter to take up protection of lions with the prime minister as it 'might do the trick', quoted in Mountfort, *Back from the Brink*, p. 123.

[42] Gandhi, *The Years of Endeavour*, pp. 265–6.

[43] Mountfort, *Saving the Tiger*, p. 91.

[44] Whitaker, *Snakeman*, p. 98.

[45] Bahuguna, 'My Work Will Go On'. Nostalgia for Indira Gandhi was also expressed by the Malayali poetess Sugatha Kumari, who felt that 'If Indira and Rajiv had been alive, not an inch of forest would have been touched.' Surendran, 'Government's Volte Face'.

forester (Sankhala), a dedicated wildlife lover (Arjan Singh), and a grassroots leader on forest issues (Bahuguna). At an organizational level, both old and new groups were represented: Sálim Ali headed the Bombay Natural History Society (BNHS) founded in 1883, and the reptile specialists were from the Madras Snake Park founded in 1971. The centralization of powers was at both an executive and later at the juridical level. Her letters to the Bihar chief minister in July 1972 did not mince words. She referred him to a complaint on the release of forest lands and said: 'Please look into it and stop it.'[46] In the 42nd Amendment to the Constitution in 1976, forests and wildlife were annexed to the Concurrent List instead of the States List. This gave the Union the formal right to overrule state decisions and laws on these subjects. What is important is the fact that the small but influential wildlife lobby had won significant gains in a short span of time due to support from the PM.[47]

Her powers, even when in office, were not unlimited, especially in the face of pressures for fresh development projects. This became clear in the case of Silent Valley in Kerala, where the state government wished to build a dam in one of the last areas of wet evergreen forest. The green light had been given by Morarji Desai in 1979. Though his successor, Charan Singh, leaned in favour of cancellation, it was Indira Gandhi who defused the issue by appointing two Central Review committees and eventually scrapping the project in 1983. In doing so she also proposed alternative ways of generating power and irrigation water: as she told a senior UN official, 'Each province or region gets emotionally attached to some schemes.'[48]

[46] Letter to Kedar Pande, CM of Bihar, 5 July 1972, in Shahi, *Backs to the Wall*, pp. 142–3. This letter was written from Shimla, where Indira Gandhi was holding talks with Pakistan after the Indo–Pak war of 1971.

[47] Shahi, 'Mrs. Gandhi and Wildlife'. Shahi was a senior forester who led a delegation to meet Indira Gandhi on her visit to Patna in 1978, when she was out of power.

[48] Indira Gandhi to M. Tolba, *Selected Speeches and Writings, Vol. IV*, pp. 306–12. See D'Monte, *Temples or Tombs?*

New initiatives included the end of all tiger hunting, the creation of core zones in tiger reserves—where commercial forestry was halted—and the expansion of the Protected Area system in 1980–4. The number of National Parks increased from nineteen to fifty-two.[49] In the process, however, the wider human dimensions of wildlife conservation, especially the vexed issue of local rights, received little attention. The eloquence of Indira Gandhi in her speech to the Stockholm Conference on the need for measures sensitive to people was often not matched by her decisions on the ground.[50] She admitted that people who lived in and around forests could hardly be urged to preserve wildlife unless their own conditions of living were improved.[51] Pressure on the lifestyle of tribals was 'causing her great distress'. But power has its own logic and in the same speech she pressed for more stern measures to ban tree-cutting in ecologically sensitive areas. But her ire was targeted at contractors rather than at the process of commercialization itself.[52] The attempt to enact a new forest law which would be much more stringent was given up because of Adivasi protest against a measure which seemed to reduce their own rights while not reining in industry.[53]

In Indira Gandhi's case the key point is that her personal awareness of the need for conservation has to be set against the structure through which she sought to achieve these aims. While she did refer to popular religious traditions like those of the Kashmiri saint Nand Rishi on the protection of trees, she was cast in an Asokan mould.[54]

[49] Singh, 'Indira Gandhi', *Cheetal*, pp. 1–4. The major expansion of the PA network was in the late Indira and the Rajiv Gandhi years. Over a third of the acreage of PAs as of 1995 consisted of land taken over in and after 1983.

[50] For a lucid analysis of the ideological roots of slum demolition in Delhi during 1975–7, see Viswanathan, 'Ancestors and Epigones', pp.14–24. There is a parallel with the eviction of villagers from wildlife reserves.

[51] Gandhi, 'Man and His World', pp. 60–7.

[52] Gandhi, Speech to State Forest Ministers, pp. 91–7.

[53] People's Union for Democratic Rights, *Undeclared Civil War*.

[54] 'Food lasts only as long as forests do' was a saying of Nur-ud-din Wali which she quoted in the McDougall lecture, *Peoples*, p. 183.

There was in her a major transition in terms of aesthetic sensibilities and often more so in her realization that the ecological question had relevance and peculiar complexities for developing countries in an unequal world. But the emphasis on equity was absent in the world of *realpolitik*. It is also clear that wildlife conservation issues helped Indira Gandhi cultivate a small but influential lobby in the Western world, even as her Stockholm speech affirmed her role as leader of the developing countries.

The salient features of the preservation model evolved during her first spell in power were clear. Recovery centred on the extension of conservation areas, and on intensified protection wherever possible. The latter was attempted in the 'core areas' of Project Tiger and in any other national parks where the political circumstances permitted. All bounties for 'vermin' were scrapped, and even the removal of dead trees was halted in the core zones. The maxim of 'do nothing and don't let anybody do anything' did not stop with forestry, but included local resident people. The continuity lay not in ecological terms but in a wider social sense. The environmental heritage was to be saved through bureaucratic intervention in selected tracts. Wider environmental deterioration was a concern for preservationists but it was not prominent on their agenda. This uniform model of preservation was applied to lands with diverse ecologies. But biological conservation was founded on the premise of the exclusion of resident peoples. Even when the latter were tolerated in the 'buffer' zones of Project Tiger, they were seen as a necessary evil.

But by now there were other voices in the debate. The new currents questioned not only the glaring inequities that often accompanied the statist model but went beyond by advocating alternatives. What follows is an attempt to sketch out the evolution and basic features of the alternatives. The first group are the 'pragmatic conservationists' who hope to retain the existing system while making it sensitive to specific grievances. Next come the 'constructive workers', also close to the government apparatus, but much more geared to generating employment through a more efficient use of natural resources. The third are members of the 'urban intelligentsia', often more forceful in their criticism of the existing administrative system as well as of market-driven strategies. The last but the most politically crucial are 'rural activists', who often see local control as the starting point for change. While each of these strands has its roots in the past, my attempt here is to focus on the last two decades.

The critics of the problem are by contrast drawn from a variety of backgrounds and, in turn, approach the issue of people and wildlife from very different standpoints. They all agree that the dominant wildlife preservation methods are in a crisis. Where they differ from the preservationists is in their perception of what constitutes the problem. In particular, they draw distinctions between different groups of human beings and different kinds of ecologies. Many of the issues they raise are of wider importance. In particular, the kind of role they envisage for market forces and the bureaucracy on the one hand, and rural producers on the other, is of much interest for students of social change.

The categories are used here not as 'ideal types' but as classifications that will help tease out the rich and complex processes at work. They have been grouped together in terms of their responses to four critical aspects of the wildlife–people debate: their view of state control, their view of commercialization, the importance attached to livelihood, and their interests in maintaining biological diversity. As will become evident, their attitudes to these issues vary widely but still fall into a pattern.

Two caveats are in order. None of the groups of critics subscribes to the prevalent model of growth. Most would agree with the preservationists that the reworking of the people–nature relationship is integral to a vision of a different society. The overlap goes even further: often, as in the case of opposing the denotifications of sanctuaries to make way for industrial exploitation, they may all find themselves on the same side of the fence. In fact, many critical voices today are those of people who were hardline preservationists until quite recently. But that is to jump ahead of the story.

The second caveat is simple but crucial. These are not watertight categories and are not meant to be mutually exclusive. It is possible that the activities of a person or activist group have undergone considerable shifts over time. The interaction between different groups, like the urban and rural activists, has often gone so far as to make a division between them difficult. But distinctions are indispensable in identifying patterns and processes of change.

Pragmatic Conservationists

Pragmatic conservationists share many of the premises of the preservation lobby but seek to attain their objectives very differently. Their main disagreement is not with the creation of Protected Areas or with totally protected core zones, but with the way in which officials exercise their powers. Their view is shaped by their own experience as field biologists, which often leads them to advocate a more proactive policy to control marauding animals or to intervene in natural processes. Livelihood issues concerning the rural poor are important to pragmatic conservationists, who see no future for wildlife without informed and sensitive steps to reassure cultivators or stock-keepers of their own security and prosperity.

In March 1977 Indira Gandhi lost the elections and Morarji Desai headed the first non-Congress government in India since Independence. A worried Sálim Ali was impolitic enough to remind Desai that 'whatever little success' they had achieved had been because Indira Gandhi was a dedicated nature lover. But Morarji set the wheels turning when he urged the ornithologist to consider afresh that he was only 'preaching to the converted' in the cities. It would be so much more difficult to persuade a villager 'to preserve the tiger or leopard that has deprived him of his sole worldly possession.' The veteran scientist promptly wrote an editorial in the popular magazine *Hornbill*, urging, 'an earnest all-out effort to tackle the problem at the grassroot level.'[55] There was no longer any point in looking at issues in isolation; the 'wider polity which utilizes resources' had to be understood more clearly to achieve

[55] Ali, 'Wildlife Conservation and the Cultivator', pp. 3–4.

success.[56] Sálim Ali's brief article sums up the potential and limits of the pragmatic conservationist approach, but its worth was only realized in the years ahead.

A year later, one of his associates in the Bombay Natural History Society (BNHS) helped approve a grant to a young doctoral student at Bangalore who wanted to study the dynamics of elephant–human conflict in South India.[57] Raman Sukumar's findings gave teeth to a new perspective on wildlife management. Saving the Asian elephant was the major objective underlying the research project, but, besides detailed field surveys of the species, Sukumar set out to look at the question of crop-raiding by this huge animal. His main finding was that a disproportionate amount of crop destruction was by a relatively small number of male elephants. Herds led by females, dubbed 'matriarchs', also did some damage, but it paled in comparison. In order to alleviate the sufferings of *ragi* cultivators, he favoured capturing male elephants that were certified crop raiders. The study weighed up various other factors, such as the fragmentation of the natural habitat by plantations, fields, and dams, but the pattern of rogues and raiders stood out.

Interestingly, when these findings were first sent to a biology journal they were not published as it was anathema to recommend the capture, let alone the killing, of a threatened species. This 'ivory tower attitude' to conservation missed seeing the dual significance of the study,[58] which sought to ensure the protection of biological diversity and address pressing human concerns. This dual emphasis was not entirely unique. Others had also urged decision-makers to pay attention to the fears of people on the periphery of wildlife parks.[59] Harjot Singh, a resident of Sampurna Nagar on the outskirts of a national park in Uttar Pradesh, was quoted saying,

[56] Ali, 'Conservation in Evolution', p. 22.

[57] Sukumar, *Elephant Days and Nights*, p. 5; see also his monograph, *The Asian Elephant*.

[58] Sukumar, 'Management of Large Mammals', pp. 93–102.

[59] Saharia, 'Human Dimensions', pp. 183–90; contrast this with the triumphalist tone in Panwar, 'What to Do'.

'The law is a cruel joke. If a man kills a tiger he has to pay a fine of Rs 50,000 and undergo ten years' imprisonment. If a tiger kills a man, the compensation paid is Rs 5000. If the government wants to protect tigers, why should it be done over our heads?'[60] In West Bengal, some forest officers came up with innovative solutions to ward off tigers from attacking fishermen and woodcutters in the mangroves of the Sundarbans.[61] But Sukumar's work was presented in a scientific study in a verifiable format. It may not have been evident at the time, but it was the first in the line.

The wider problem his work pointed to was the need to craft a solution to issues that continued to bedevil many areas in India with large populations of mega-herbivores or carnivores. The general picture of the retreat of wildlife under human pressure at the subcontinental level had to be squared with realities at the local level. It was possible for a species to be rare at the macro level but to be present in large numbers in certain regions. The problem was to weigh which kind of human land-use was exacerbating conflict, and to identify particular aspects of the behaviour or ecology of a particular species that made it, or people, prone to conflict.

While elephants are creatures of the relatively wetter forests in South Asia, another large mammal living in more open, dry areas in northern and Central India had been reduced to one relict population in Gujarat. The Asiatic lion, protected by the Nawab of Juangadh from around 1900, went through two population bottlenecks, but by the 1970s was recovering under protection. The relocation of pastoralist settlements had enabled a part of the reserve to be free of livestock.[62] Though some graziers remained in the rest of the 1500 sq km sanctuary, the objective was still 'the restoration'

[60] Shahi, 'Dudwake Baghon'. See also the report of a student team from Delhi on the Betla tiger reserve in Palamau: Sharma, 'Tigers versus People', pp. 11–12; idem, 'Project Tiger', pp. 19–22.

[61] Rishi, 'Man, Mask and Man-eater', p. 915; for later work, see Mallon and Nurbu, 'Conservation Programme', pp. 89–97.

[62] Joslin, 'The Environmental Limitations', pp. 648–64; Berwick, 'The Gir Forest', pp. 28–40.

of the rest of the reserve by the progressive withdrawal of the remaining cattle.'[63] As wildlife staged a recovery, the Gir saw a spate of attacks by lions on human beings.

In the late 1980s a new study by Ravi Chellam from Saurashtra University overturned much of the earlier logic.[64] Chellam pointed out that the lion population in the reserve had built up and the territorial nature of the prides forced a spillover into adjoining areas. Here, the lions came into conflict with people and cattle. Other researchers found that the Scheduled Caste labourers who worked on pumpsets at night were the most vulnerable to lion attacks. The policy suggestion was similar to Sukumar's: remove excess lions by capture or shooting. The new researchers argued that there was no need to remove Maldharis from the rest of Gir. The policy of relocation was held to be sound but its implementation tardy and insensitive.[65]

Pragmatic solutions also appeal to another genre of researchers who worked with wildlife *outside* forested areas. The birds and animals of scrub and grassland often live in the proximity of villages where setting up large Protected Areas is simply out of the question. The extension of cultivation over the plains regions and river valleys has advanced so far as to make it impossible to locate large stretches of land that are uncultivated. The Aligarh biologist Asad Rafi Rahmani, an associate of Sálim Ali, advocated a flexible strategy to protect the Great Indian Bustard. This ground-loving bird, the second heaviest on earth, returns to certain patches for courtship displays and nesting. The key was to ensure the protection of tracts often only a few dozen hectares in size. As these areas often fell within revenue lands and on village grazing grounds, Rahmani favoured a mix of preventive and participatory measures.[66]

[63] Mountfort, *Back from the Brink*, p. 123.

[64] Chellam, 'Ecology of the Asian Lion'.

[65] Saberwal, *et al.*, 'Lion–Human Conflict', pp. 501–7; contrast this with the uncritical acceptance of official claims in Berwick, 'The Ecology of the Maldhari Grazier', pp. 81–94.

[66] Ali and Rahmani, *Study of Certain Endangered Species of Wildlife.*

A similar but more conflictual situation emerged in studies on the wolf, unlike the tiger an inhabitant of the countryside in tracts with dryland farming and sheep- or goat-rearing. The wolf has not only been known to lift children in areas like Palamau in Bihar but more often stock animals.[67] The picture put together is complex. Wolves in western India actually gain from dryland farming as they can take cover in the fields before the harvest with their young cubs. The extension of perennial irrigation, as in the case of the Rajasthan Canal, will transform the situation by changing cropping cycles.[68] At another level, in areas like Nanaj near Pune, while shepherds disliked the animal because of raids on their stock, cultivators saw it as the key to controlling antelope numbers.[69] Clearly, ensuring survival for the wolf required an approach that took account of basic facts about its biology and behaviour. As a wide-ranging animal living in low densities, it perforce comes into contact with human settlements. Many shepherd communities regularly kill wolf cubs to protect their herds: the only answer would be to provide the wolf with a system of 'perpetual care'. The continued existence of vanishing species requires sustained attention to the problems of people who share habitats with such species.[70]

Certain basic features about the pragmatic conservationists are worth further attention. The conflicts between people and animals were broken up and viewed in a disaggregated way. Neither lions nor elephants were inherently dangerous, but certain individual specimens were prone to come into conflict with people. An understanding of their life cycles and the vulnerabilities of different groups of human land-users was crucial. In one case, grain cultivators and in the other labourers and cattle-keepers were the most vulnerable group. Here, we see a widening of sensibilities towards different groups of humans. The preservation of an organism is critical

[67] Shahi, 'Status of the Gray Wolf', pp. 493–502.

[68] Jhala, 'Status and Conservation of the Wolf', pp. 476–83.

[69] Kumar, 'Wolf in Bustard Country', pp. 26–33.

[70] See Zimen and Boitani, 'Wolf, Italy', pp. 99–102; Boitani, 'Wolf Management', pp. 125–32.

but they feel they do not have a duty to conserve 'each and every individual of the species'.[71] The efficient management of a resource rather than an ethically driven campaign to make all human–animal relations equal marks the attitude of the pragmatic conservationists. The emphasis is less on the inalienable right of all living things to life and there is a candid openness about the possibilities of earning more revenue or generating better incomes. The element of pragmatism is crucial. In the absence of strict measures against aberrant carnivores, the result would be a 'backlash'. None of these scientists sees an alternative to a role for enforcement agencies of the state, but they advocate exercising power in a very different way. For one, knowledge would not be gathered only through the official machinery, which is often incapable of flexible responses because of a lack of information or research capabilities.

Constructive Work

Sukumar's own initiation into wildlife biology had begun as a birdwatcher in a small forest then at the edge of the southern Indian metropolis of Madras. By this time the forest, the Guindy Park, was already the site of innovative approaches to reptile conservation that were harbingers of change. It was here, in the Madras Snake Park, that Rom Whitaker and his team first perceived that the organization of wildlife-economy-based Adivasis could be a step towards controlling the trade in Indian wildlife. Whitaker's biographer is correct in observing that this idea was ahead of its time, but in retrospect it was a step in a new direction.[72] Constructive work may be the best category in which to fit the activities aimed at creative solutions around existing skills and within the exchange economy. In the process, such groups have often widened the terms of debate from being about preservation or total protection to being about possible sustainable long-term use. Whitaker's group

[71] Rodgers, 'Policy Issues in Wildlife Conservation', pp. 461–8; the need to control man-eaters and cattle-lifters was accepted in the Indian Board for Wildlife, *Report of the Task Force for Eliciting Public Support*.

[72] Whitaker, *Snakeman*, pp. 149–51.

worked in close conjunction with the Irulas, Adivasis who once trapped small-game animals, rodents, and snakes for a living, but who were being marginalized by urbanization and the clearance of scrub forests on the south-western coastline. The effort was to draw upon Irula skills, to which the exchange economy was not alien, and to provide means by which they could get better terms of trade without depleting reptiles. These two broad features of pushing for change by improving the bargaining position of 'losers' in development, and of augmenting the resource base, remain the hallmark of constructive work groups.

In the case of the Madras Snake Park, the origins lay in a protection venture centred on the captive breeding of reptiles. The small captive breeding plot adjacent to Guindy Park was a hive of activity, but the dilemma facing the Irulas soon became evident. The snakeskin trade was of the order of thousands of skins a year, and the tribals found it profitable to catch the reptiles. Zai Whitaker summed up the attitude in the Snake Park: 'Russel's viper, burning bright/ Do not hiss and do not bite/ We are trying to save your skin/ From hand bags, wallets and their kin.' But the flipside was that snake venom was extremely valuable, the poison from a krait being worth as much as Rs 3000 a gram. By the late 1960s the Irulas were not only the 'backbone of the snakeskin trade' but were also catching snakes to extract venom with which to make antivenin. The bid to form a snake-catchers co-operative made only slow progress but the organization was registered in 1978. Every Friday Irulas from the areas surrounding Madras would make their way to the park with the deadly quarry, which would be 'milked for venom' and released a few weeks later in the wild. The ban on snakeskin exports and the curbing of the trade had worsened the plight of the Irulas but the venom trade provided fresh opportunities. Amendments in the Wildlife Protection Act, 1972, also allowed the capture and 'milking' of snakes, in contrast to the normally strict ban on killing or trapping species that were endangered and under Schedule I of the Act.[73]

[73] Ibid., pp. 149–51, poem on p. 179.

But it was not with snakes, though, that the break with preservation lobbies came. It happened via crocodiles. The three species of crocodiles in India were rescued from almost certain extinction through a programme of captive hatching and breeding in which the Snake Park and the Food and Agriculture Organization played a critical role. Nationwide surveys showed a decline in numbers from a variety of factors, including dams on rivers, killing for skins, and for bounties. Crocodile eggs were gathered and hatched for captive rearing, especially in the newly created Crocodile Bank near Madras. The notion of a 'bank' was a deliberate one: this would be a bank where crocodiles and not money would multiply.[74]

By 1994 there were over 20,000 animals in captive collections, both in the Bank and in Forest Department collections. However, the original purpose of the project was to supply skins to the market using captive-bred specimens. The idea was to harvest a resource in captivity while the wild population was augmented through protection and the release of captive-bred specimens. The part of the programme relating to marketing skins has never been realized as the necessary legal changes have not been brought about. There is virtually no public record of criticisms of marketing crocodile leather, but two points are often raised by preservationists. One is the problem of enforcement, for poachers could start a parallel trade. The other is the belief that such a trade would mark the triumph of an instrumentalist and exploitative attitude while undermining the ethical notion that all organisms have a right to life. In 1990 such views impelled the Ministry of Environment and Forests to order the confiscation of a dancing bear from its owner.[75]

The upshot of this is clear: the preservationist lobby has defended its stance. The problem is that such a view of nature, however moral it may be, does not often provide much by way of alternatives. The Irula Co-operative itself is only a small pilot venture.

[74] Whitaker and Andrews, 'The Madras Crocodile Bank', pp. 77–83; Whitaker and Whitaker, *Status and Conservation of the Asian Crocodilians*.

[75] Goyle, 'Proposal for Sloth Bear Rehabilitation'.

But the principle of combining traditional skills with modern management techniques is a significant one. A recent proposal is to permit the controlled harvesting of turtle eggs in the great nesting grounds of Gahirmatha on the Orissa coast, not for trade but for local consumption. As several hundreds of thousands of eggs are destroyed by the tides, this would not affect reproduction rates. Until the sanctuary was created in 1975, the local zamindar collected an *anda kara* (egg tax) from fisherfolk and the foresters took the rest of the eggs for sale! The proposal is not to revive the old hierarchies or the trade but to give people 'a vested interest' that will create a socio-economic base for conservation.

Similar sustained use systems have been proposed for as many as six reptile species: these include captive-bred populations as well as wild ones.[76] The point about cruelty is acknowledged but, as Indraneil Das asks: if domestic animals can be used, why not wild ones?[77] The observation is of wider significance: nature does not exist untouched by human presence and the practices of capture or consumption by tribals or other direct resource-users seem cruel to middle-class people.

The 'constructive work' programmes concerned with forest revival are both better developed and more widely known. There are important parallels as well as contrasts with the debate on faunal resources. The struggle for control over forest lands in the colonial period had echoes in independent India, where the broad parameters of legislation and executive practice have if anything become even more stringent. Foresters have often seen trees in terms of their worth as timber, while across much of the peninsula peasants and other villagers have drawn a wider variety of usufruct-based products from the forests. These include nuts, fruits, leaf manure, and twigs. The commercialization of non-wood products, such as tendu leaves and harra fruits, sal seeds and mahua flowers, has not been matched by better terms of trade

[76] Das and Reptile Group, *South Asian Herpeto Fauna*, pp. 5–12.

[77] I. Das, Research Officer, Interview, Crocodile Bank, Mahabalipuram Road, 3 February 1994.

for those who gather them. This exploitation of produce-gatherers by mercantile capital and governmental agencies is paralleled by an exclusive focus on the regeneration of tree species critical for timber, such as sal, teak, pines, and eucalyptus. Constructive work initiatives in the forestry sector have moved beyond the agenda of employment towards regeneration through entitlement rights for direct resource-users.[78]

The orientation of such projects, towards multi-species forests rather than monoculture stands, is conducive to a wider variety of bird and animal life. The reafforestation programmes of the Dasholi Gram Swarajya Mandal over the last quarter-century have not only seen a very high rate of success in terms of survival rates but also focussed on broadleaf tree species that are central to livelihood. This is in contrast to official programmes in Uttarakhand that have historically been oriented to plantation of conifers that are of limited use in the agrarian economy. The forest protection initiatives in three districts of West Bengal—Midnapur, Purulia, and Bankura—are perhaps the best known, but they have their counterparts in Orissa and Bihar. A share of forest products for villages in return for protection of the forests on a voluntary basis has enabled extensive regeneration of the sal forests. This itself marks a major shift in terms of technologies of forest management away from production of wood (from the tree trunk) to a host of products (taken from the crown) like twigs, seeds and leaves. The relative success of Joint Forest Management (JFM) in comparison to government forestry has to be seen in perspective: over 60 million hectares are under the Forest Department, and only a small fraction of the land is under JFM.[79] There is no evidence that these practices may not be extended to the Reserved Forests.[80] But the broad

[78] Chambers, Saxena, and Shah, *To the Hands of the Poor*, pp. 155–9. The employment generation potential of oilseeds from trees such as the mahua alone is of the order of 4.4 million labour days a year. For a gendered view of the issue of land and forest rights, see Agarwal, *A Field of One's Own*.

[79] Poffenberger, *Joint Management for Forest Lands*.

[80] Guha, 'Forestry Debate and Draft Forest Act', pp. 2192–6.

principle of joint control has been given due place in rhetoric. Such efforts are significant because they expand the ability of people, whether peasant women in Chamoli or Adivasis in West Bengal, to control their own lives. They should not be dismissed as 'reformist' as they are often a highly creative response to difficult conditions and have positive consequences at a wider level.[81]

More recently, there have been efforts to extend such an approach of Joint Management to the Protected Areas (JMPA). This effort seeks to build on existing arrangements while lobbying for legal and administrative changes. The central premise is that the long-term future of sanctuaries and national parks rests on the co-operation of local people with any open-minded forest officer willing to be more accommodating about their needs.[82] The arguments used are out of the book of the pragmatists as the claim is that this will help meet the long-term objectives of conservation. As Ashish Kothari writes, 'I do not believe the Forest Department can exercise control even if it wanted to . . . It is not a question of whether we should try such alternatives or not; we have no choice but to.'[83] While he refers to several cases where popular action has stalled development projects, Kothari points to constructive efforts at conservation around the sanctuaries. Forest Protection Committees formed with the help of a voluntary organization are helping check timber poaching in the Ranthambhore Tiger Reserve.[84] In Nagaland, the Naga Mothers' Association has campaigned against indiscriminate hunting. Unlike government agencies, such groups can motivate people through educational efforts and mobilize their energies. In official eyes they play an auxiliary role and not a central one. The provision of basic services via voluntary efforts is also seen by

[81] Agarwal and Narain, *Towards Green Villages.*

[82] For early critiques that anticipate many of the present initiatives, see Bhatt, 'Project Tiger'; Sarabhai, Bhatt, and Raju, *People's Involvement in Wildlife Management.*

[83] A. Kothari, IIPA, to S. Deb Roy, Ministry of Environment and Forests, 29 March 1995.

[84] Desai, *et al.*, 'Human Resource Development'.

some preservation groups as integral to their own objectives: by relieving pressure on the forests, they create alternatives for people living near parks.[85]

Yet it is not on issues of voluntary support for protection but on increased or secure access to forest products from Protected Areas that the constructive work groups have run into barriers. Even a sympathetic forester observed that conservation was not compatible with continued use of an area. People's support for conservation was 'essential', but Deb Roy felt that if people are partners in management they 'would certainly bring forward human interest before ecology.'[86] While the debate continues, the broad orientation of the constructive work efforts is clear: it is to push for incremental change by highlighting success at the grassroots. There is clear ground for co-operation with preservation groups in joint operations against commercial interests and for participatory management outside Protected Areas. Such efforts may even achieve a measure of success within low-intensity conflicts between government authorities and people, but a lot depends on the 'officer on the spot'. The space that exists within the system often hinges on his or her attitude to such efforts.[87] Conversely, without legislative reform, such efforts will remain few and far between.

Constructive workers, unlike some urban intellectuals, do not valorize tradition over modernity. The very nature of their work impels them to combine practices with very different origins. An Irula bringing in a venomous snake for poison extraction may be deploying a traditional set of skills but is doing so for a new

[85] Manfredi, 'Art for Conservation's Sake', pp. 24–30.

[86] S. Deb Roy to A. Kothari, 1 May 1995. There are dissenters within the Forest Department. For instance, M.L. Ramprakash, Conservator of Forests in Karnataka, favours collection of non-wood produce from the buffer zone of the Bandipur tiger reserve: *Joint Protected Area Management Update*, no. 3 (March 1995), p. 1.

[87] In Guindy, access to a sacred spring increased illegal trespass but taps were provided to devotees outside the park perimeter in 1993. S. Datt, Wildlife Institute of India, personal communication.

purpose. Venom extraction is part of modern medicinal practice and the co-operative is a modern form of organization. Similarly, women's groups taking up tree planting may be extending their own productive role in gathering fodder or firewood to regeneration through protection or planting. But the institutional mechanisms of *mahila mandals* (women's committees) or of co-operatives with recognized forest rights may be new innovations. Both in terms of technology and social practice such efforts cannot simply be labelled 'traditional'; nor are they uncritical exponents of modernization.

Actually, existing practices are much richer than such labels can suggest. This gives them their strength. The problem is that in order to succeed these efforts may need legal recognition, but that may be denied. Voluntarist constructive work cannot thus escape the legal and administrative hurdles placed in its way.

The emphasis is on incremental change, more so with the market and even more with statist control regimes. Of course, such activities may also be integral to the programmes of organizations with a more agitational mode of work. While livelihood is central to their agenda, the actual importance of biodiversity may vary widely, depending on the priorities of the group in question. In general, biological diversity may gain as an offshoot of other programmes, such as the planting of indigenous tree species.[88] In specific cases, the protection of groves of trees of a wetland, a patch of grassland, or of scrub jungle may have worked only because of conscious local efforts.

The Urban Intelligentsia

One set of critics whose platform calls for a more drastic overhaul of the conservation regime may be classified as members of the urban intelligentsia. Though their social background is often similar to that of other middle-class groups, their own research and informal interaction with rural protest groups has led to a reappraisal of the development process itself. In their daily lives they are often

[88] Daniels, 'A Conservation Strategy'.

shielded from the direct impact of degradation of ecosystems to a greater degree than are rural activists and constructive workers. In particular, they have been willing to take up specific cases of the denial of local rights by the government and the destruction of resources by industry. In general, they are not uncritical supporters of tradition, but they question the style and kind of modernization that has taken place. Livelihood is important to these critics, but increasingly they favour more far-reaching steps for the empowerment of disadvantaged social groups. Biological diversity was often the starting point for many such researchers and activists, but they hope to protect it through innovative and participatory measures, not coercive government machinery.

Perhaps the first attempt to systematically study 'conservation from below' was a report on the sacred groves of the hills around Pune in Maharashtra.[89] The conservation efforts of groups like the Bishnois, a tribe mainly living in Rajasthan, are a *cause célèbre* among environmentalists.[90] The historian D.D. Kosambi had investigated the changing cultural and religious significance of sacred sites around Pune. But no one had tried to assess the conservation value of such sites.[91] The findings of the botanist V.D. Vartak and the ecologist Madhav Gadgil were revealing. The former was a senior botanist with extensive field knowledge of the region and the latter a young ecologist. The choice of the topic was also influenced in an indirect way by Gadgil's personal acquaintance with Kosambi and with the sociologist Iravati Karve, both of whom were based in Pune.[92] The groves, varying in size from a clump of trees to several acres in size, often remained the last stands of vegetation in large areas of countryside. Several rare plant species have since

[89] Gadgil and Vartak, 'Sacred Groves', pp. 313–20. A brief paper had already been read out in the Indian National Sciences Academy, but it did not attract much notice. Gadgil had also written a popular article in *The Illustrated Weekly of India*, 2 September 1973.

[90] Vyas, 'And the Blackbuck Lives'; Sankhala, 'People, Trees and Antelopes', pp. 205–10.

[91] Kosambi, 'At the Cross-road', pp. 87–107.

[92] M. Gadgil, Interview, Bangalore, 14 June 1995.

been located in the precincts of such groves elsewhere in India, some of which have survived intact for over 500 years.[93] The two authors argued that self-restraint had been the key to survival of these tracts: extraction of wood was either banned or very limited. Yet the picture was far from idyllic, and a coal trader from the town of Mangaon was eying the groves to make charcoal. The perspective of the preservationists was reversed in two ways. Conservation was located in the everyday practices of rural people and this tradition was seen as qualitatively better than state-inspired attempts.

K.C. Malhotra, a student of Iravati Karve's, joined forces with Madhav Gadgil in a study of different styles of resource-use. Already in the mid-1970s their work, a combination of that of an ecologist and an anthropologist, suggested fresh insights into the relationship of different types of land-use and levels of biological diversity. In their study of pastoralism and hunting in western Maharashtra they argued that the older systems of trapping game animals were not depleting wild animals in any significant way. Peasants as well as the largely pastoral Nandivalas caught the occasional deer, while the Phasepardhi tribals mainly captured blackbucks. What had completely transformed the region and made such practices unsustainable was the Panchet hydel project and attendant pressures on the land from a mix of market forces and new forms of agriculture.[94]

This model could and did often lead to simplistic conclusions but it represented a major breakthrough at the time.[95] First, the roles of villains and heroes were reversed.[96] The picture of the

[93] Chandran, 'Vegetational Changes', Figs 8.11 and 8.13. Some of the Dipterocarps in the groves are over five centuries old and will only grow on patches where there has been no cultivation or use of fire.

[94] Gadgil and Malhotra, *A People's View of Eco-development*, pp. 7–25; Malhotra, Khomne, and Gadgil, 'Hunting Strategies', pp. 1–39.

[95] Gadgil and Guha, *This Fissured Land*; but see Guha, *Environment and Ethnicity*.

[96] Gadgil and Berkes, 'Traditional Resource Management Systems', pp. 127–41.

ecologically profligate tribal was not the only casualty. After all, the question raised by this was of much wider import. While it shared with previous anthropological writings on Adivasis a tendency to romanticize rural society, it went much further than them. The development process itself was directly questioned; it was essential to promote growth but, given the way dams were being built, failures were inevitable. Urban decision-makers were several stages removed from direct dependence on natural resources and were therefore immune from the immediate consequences of unbalanced development processes. Peasants and tribals depending much more directly on natural resources bear the brunt of the development process.[97] The dominant mode of wildlife protection was not spared as it aimed at preservation in the amusement parks of the privileged classes. Gadgil pointed out how 'the very same people' who favoured the toleration of the occasional killings of people by tigers in the Sundarbans believed that 'monkeys must be shot out because they damage ornamental gardens in cities.'[98]

A significant shift was taking place here, away from reliance on governmental control and towards a more locally rooted system. But it was far from complete. Uncultivated lands were important for rural subsistence, while unchecked commercialization was undermining the basis of survival of wildlife and poor people alike. Gadgil and Malhotra still advocated the creation of nature reserves in 3 per cent of the land area which would be 'totally free' of human interference and devoted to the preservation of biological diversity.[99] But the seeds of change were contained in fieldwork which pointed to a long history of human use of even supposedly 'pristine' lands. Critical interventions in public debates on dams and on forest policies by scientists also prepared the ground for more sustained critiques not only of forestry itself but of the wider

[97] Gadgil, 'Hills, Dams and Forests', p. 300.

[98] Gadgil, 'Wildlife Resources of India', pp. 1–28.

[99] Gadgil and Malhotra, *Eco-Development*, pp. 23–4; see Gadgil and Malhotra in Tiwari Report, pp. 69–70, where they are critical of the Zuari fertilizer factory in Goa for denuding a forest.

systems of resource access that were weighted in terms of resource-extensive use by elites.[100]

Events on the ground moved ahead at a faster pace. Unlike the government which attempted to enact a more stringent law on forests in 1982, a section of urban researchers and activists veered towards the view taken by tribal groups. There were signs of this even earlier, as in the support extended to the Chipko movement in 1974 by botanists from Delhi and in the integration of ecological issues in local-level studies of development.[101] But these did not have the wider resonances of the great debate over the 1982 Bill. Deforestation and the decimation of wildlife were seen as the outcome of commercialization and of the degree to which forest-dependent people had no direct role in the control of natural wealth. The survival of diverse multi-species forests was seen as linked with the struggle against commercially oriented monoculture plantations. Mixed forests were seen as crucial in both ecological terms (as they harboured several plant and animal species) and for social reasons (as the Scheduled Tribes and non-tribal peasants and artisans used a multitude of species).[102] The battle lines were drawn much more clearly when a student group from Delhi took up the issue of firing on cattle grazers in the Keoladeo Ghana national park near Bharatpur in November 1982.[103] The former hunting reserve of the local ruler, the park had become a bone of contention between cattle owners and the wildlife authorities. The Indian Board for Wildlife meeting in October 1982 (with Prime

[100] Gadgil and Malhotra, 'Questioning the Bedthi Hydel Project', pp. 25–30.

[101] Veerendra Kumar of Zakir Husain College, Delhi University, prepared a critique of the forestry practices in Chamoli at the request of the village committees spearheading protest: see Roy, 'Proposal for People's Science Institute'; Roy, *et al.*, *Planning the Environment.*

[102] People's Union for Democratic Rights, *Undeclared Civil War*; Kulkarni and Fernandes, *Towards a New Forest Policy.*

[103] Dhawan, Prasad, and Singh, *Report of the Kalpavriksh Team*; Anon., 'Project Tiger and the People', pp. 1380–3.

Minister Indira Gandhi in the chair) decided to close the area to all cattle. The decision was implemented overnight and in the ensuing tension the police shot and killed nine people.

The report on it by the Kalpavriksh team had much in common with civil liberties team reports; it blamed the government for not giving adequate warning to the crowds. Patients were interviewed and the issue of compensating deaths was raised. But equally significant was the stance of the group, which was an environmental action group, not a civil liberties forum. The closure of the sanctuary was held to be unjust as no alternative had been provided by the authorities. The report had a dual agenda of local rights and wildlife conservation. It also quoted a BNHS researcher who felt that cattle access was not harmful to the waterbirds as it controlled the aquatic grasses.[104] Such findings did not receive much attention at the time but subsequently became important.

The next question was inevitable. Was it possible that conservation did not require areas totally free of human presence? Even where these were necessary, local-level decisions might suffice. In any case, the core areas of wildlife parks were being reserved for scientific or aesthetic use, but this was a political point. The issue still remained of whether it was at all valid to search for a natural space that would be freed of biomass extraction in toto. The legitimacy of schemes like Project Tiger were from the very outset based on terms wider than aesthetic sensibilities. The creation of inviolate natural areas free of human presence, other than the protective umbrella of the authorities, was justified in terms of its contribution to protecting the spectrum of living things. By safeguarding these core areas from human beings, preservationists had argued they were ensuring that biological diversity was kept intact at least in these few oases. They could be baseline areas for research into the working of natural ecological systems. In addition to potentially useful plant species in the wild, researchers could document the complex interrelations between water, soil, and

[104] These points were later recorded in Vijayan, 'Keoladeo Ghana'.

fauna/flora. The view of these tracts as relict natural areas and their value in terms of biological diversity were central to the case.

It was on both these counts that fresh perspectives soon began to emerge. Even in the Amazon basin, this notion of nature freed of human presence has increasingly come under critical scrutiny. The great basin supported large populations before the Spanish conquest and even now is critical to the livelihood of not less than 2 million people.[105] Similarly, in eastern and southern Africa, the notion of a primeval Eden was itself central to a notion of the continent as an uncivilized domain awaiting conquest. The same idea was adopted by many modern conservationists.[106] The notion of a 'wilderness' had even less validity in a subcontinent like South Asia with a much larger human population and many millennia of agrarian civilization. The problem would not be one of discovering nature in its pristine state but of working out which kinds of human activity significantly reduced or enhanced biological diversity. But to do this it became necessary to see the forests, scrublands, and marshes as existing within human history. In the struggle for control of these areas, the notion of creating a wilderness was a means of ensuring control by preservationists at the cost of competing land-users. The issue was not one of nature versus people, it was one of certain groups versus others. The notion of an inclusive idea of conservation meshed very well with innovative research in other parts of the world, particularly in Latin America, and even in some of the American-Indian-controlled areas in the southern US.[107] The keynote was not a romantic idealism about such communities but hard-headed scientific work about what kinds of biodiversity could coexist in and around areas subject to continuing but regulated human use.

The survival of rare plants in the sacred groves of the Western Ghats no more seemed like an isolated or unique case, but part of

[105] Gomez-Pompa and Kaus, 'Taming the Wilderness Myth', pp. 271–9; Hecht and Cockburn, *The Fate of the Forest.*

[106] Anderson and Grove, *Conservation in Africa.*

[107] Oldfield and Alcorn, *Biodiversity.*

a wider pattern. Unlike state systems which had till recently focussed mainly on large mammals, these practices encompassed a wider spectrum of diversity.[108] This struck deep at the older stereotype. In recent work in the alpine regions of the Western Himalayas, other writers have also suggested a much more nuanced view of rural relations with the natural world.[109] Not only do they eschew a romantic 'harmony', they show how specific patterns of use may not be as damaging as was once believed. For instance, it has been argued that decades of Gaddi pastoralism in Himachal have not degraded the forests, unless the degradation is seen merely in terms of the density of timber trees. Similarly, mountain ungulates seem to be able to coexist with the Gaddis provided there is a degree of tolerance by the armed men who accompany the flocks on the trails. Such views are not uncontested but at least there is a serious informed debate grounded in fresh research. It is notable that the debate about levels of diversity has been posed by scholars in terms of extensive forms of land-use, such as pastoral production and swidden cultivation.[110] The levels of plant diversity in various systems of traditional agriculture, or of local breeds of livestock, can only be maintained if stock-keepers and cultivators have a central role to play in the process of conservation.[111] Scientific work parallels and complements efforts of social scientists to study the dynamics of collective action systems, of how they work and why they break up.[112]

The major break then is on the casualty of the erosion of genetic diversity and the best way to conserve and enhance it. Gadgil

[108] Toledo, 'Patzcuaro's Lesson', pp. 147–71; ibid., pp. 119–26.

[109] Saberwal, 'Rethinking Biodiversity Conservation in India'; Fox, *et al.*, 'Wildlife Conservation and Land-use Changes', pp. 39–60.

[110] Ramakrishnan, *Shifting Agriculture and Sustainable Development*; Kothari, *Conserving Life*.

[111] For another view of science and the ecological dilemmas, see Shiva, *Staying Alive*; on East Africa, Homewood and Rodgers, 'Pastoralism and Conservation', pp. 431–8.

[112] Jodha, 'Common Property Resources', pp. 1169–86.

and Rao argue the case in a recent draft Bill on Nature, Health, and Education.[113] The bureaucracy is ill equipped to meet the emerging problems of the ground, be it in terms of shifts in species abundance or diversity, or fresh threats due to pollution or other degrading factors. Conversely, the diversity of resource-use systems is so enormous even over small stretches of the Indian countryside that they are simply not amenable to efficient or just bureaucratic land control. The rich regenerative potential of local systems of resource-use may not always be evident to a distant mandarin. More seriously, the information-gathering system at the disposal of land managers as well as their skills may not register major changes fast enough. In contrast, local users have several practices that could be the core of a new strategy for conservation. They would be backed up with technical assistance and co-ordination but would have a central role in the process. The present Protected Areas as well as sacred groves and ponds, patches of grassland and deserts scrub outside the PA system would be managed as 'safety sites'. Unlike the 'supply sites', which would include the 23 per cent of the land area now under the Forest Department and the 6 per cent now under the Revenue Departments, the criterion of control would be 'safety' rather than 'supply'. The foresters and other technical personnel would remain in the picture but their role would be akin to that of the Agriculture Department in terms of providing support, services, and incentives, not direct management. The PA system would not be managed in isolation but be treated as part of a wider regime of control.

There are many possible problems in this alternative model, but it is ideologically significant as it makes a break with a statist system of control. The early work on sacred groves or on rural lifestyles in the Deccan was much more limited in scope and suggestions but carried the seeds of these proposals. Incentives to

[113] Gadgil and Rao, *People's Health*; idem, 'A System of Positive Incentives', pp. 2108–17; the bill is reproduced in *The Hindu Survey of the Environment*, pp. 217–23.

protect diversity of cultivators were suggested in the case of the Nilgiri Biosphere Reserve. The Second Citizens' Report on India's Environment also took a step in this direction.[114] This represents a politically significant development because a section of the skilled and educated literati is making common cause with disadvantaged groups. Such work brings together specialist knowledge with the emerging ground-level situation and offers a critique. At an international level, both biologists and social scientists are presently engaged in a debate over such issues and the Indian experience is not an isolated one.

The Bill draws together these findings and seeks to articulate elements of an alternative structure. The actual problem in such models is their treatment of market forces. The community is to serve as a line of defence against corrosive impact, such as species extermination, to meet market demand or to mediate in case of conflicts over resource-use. But it is not at all clear what is to stop a hamlet from cutting down a forest or draining a wetland for immediate economic returns. Many collective-action systems in montane and semi-arid areas, where they are probably still the most resilient, are in a transitory phase. They were never static in the past but the levels of internal differentiation and the external pressures today are of an unprecedented nature. The question is not whether such devolution must take place. There is little doubt that many of the points made by urban intellectuals are valid: these systems are more flexible than a bureaucracy and involve people with more direct stakes in the viability of forests of wetlands with distant administrators.

But the issue is a more complex one, of designing a structure of incentives that will enable such initiatives an existence on the ground to endure the impact of pressures. This, in turn, will only be possible in the context of wider changes in the system of land-use. The challenge is to try and work out a system of control that combines local control with tangible benefits that enable a

[114] Gadgil, *et al.*, *Report on the Nilgiri Biosphere Reserve.*

better livelihood yet also enhance the resource base. This is easier said than done. But it is a vast improvement on a tunnel vision that concentrates solely on a few protected zones under guns and guards. Over two decades, urban intellectuals have gone from studying alternative systems to favouring a radical shift in the power structure to meet the dual demands of conservation and human livelihood. They have taken a step towards a notion of empowerment of disadvantaged groups, a programme which has often been integral to many movements of political assertion, but which is now being supported on new grounds: its ability to conserve biological diversity.

Rural Activists

Of the groups mentioned above, only constructive workers have any direct material stakes in the outcome of human–wildlife conflicts. Rural activists are engaged in efforts to secure a direct participatory role for resource users in the control of open-access or common-property lands, government forests, ponds, pastures, and wildlife sanctuaries. The improvement of rural livelihood and living conditions is central to their perspective and recent attempts to defend natural areas from developers have to be seen in this light. The creation of wildlife sanctuaries seems to such groups to be simply one in a long line of events that have deprived them of their land rights. In the past, this loss of entitlement often entailed a deeper sense of cultural loss. Rural activists, obviously, do not work or exist in isolation from wider networks of protest groups that include those in towns and cities. Being based largely in villages, they share the consequences of ecological deterioration and social dislocation with those affected by wildlife conservation, big dams, and commercial forestry. What matters less are the social origins of particular activist groups, and much more the kind of issues they focus on. They take up mobilization against dominant groups to a greater extent than do constructive workers. In fact, Koya Adivasis petitioned a government committee in 1960 against the creation of a wildlife reserve in Andhra Pradesh. Their complaints were explicit and clear: the creation of a game sanctuary in the Narasampet meant that 'They cannot hunt. They cannot even get wood from contractors; they cannot extract kopi grass which they have always used for making ropes. The once proud Koyas, hunters and lords of the forest . . . are today forbidden even to enter the forest and are deprived of all rights and privileges they formerly had. They cannot even remove a few stones from the area to pave the paths of their villages.'[115] Yet such concerns remained at the margins until they were again taken up in the 1980s.

The new wave of social movements did not often directly take up the wildlife question but the implications were clear, as in the case of Chipko. The Valley of Flowers sanctuary was not far from the hamlet of Reni where village women stopped a sports firm from felling trees in 1974. This movement, 'Chipko Andolan', soon won wide acclaim, and by 1980 some of its leaders were vocal in their criticism on restrictions on usufruct rights in the Valley of Flowers. The area had long been important to nearby villagers who harvested wild tubers but this limited use was seen as destructive by the Forest Department.

This marked a wider agenda inclusive of plant diversity than existed in official strategy.[116] It forms a parallel to the drive by the preservation lobby to halt commercial forestry in the core areas of tiger reserves. The difference is crucial: the activists saw the survival of the mixed forests as essential for the sustenance of rural people. Meanwhile, the displacement of villages to make way for wildlife, though not without precedent, had been taken up under Project Tiger areas and in the Gir Forest. Since then the terms of resettlement and the question of how far displacement is essential have been a major bone of contention. At the time there was little sustained protest.

[115] Elwin, *Report of the Committee*, pp. 318–19; for the dissonances around game laws in the colonial period, see Rangarajan, *Fencing the Forest*, esp. chapter 5; Guha and Gadgil, 'Forestry and Social Conflict', pp. 141–77.

[116] Gadgil and Meher-Homji, 'Role of Protected Areas', pp. 143–59; Guha, *The Unquiet Woods*.

But such strategies of creating 'people-free' zones at the core of wildlife sanctuaries were attempted in many other areas. They were linked with the much wider problem of the restriction of usufruct rights. Under the Wildlife (Protection) Act of 1972, there were no rights of access in national parks. In many areas, this led to protests. The Bharatpur firing in 1982 has already been discussed. In this case, the investigators were drawn from a metropolis and could not make much headway as the villagers were intimidated by the local authorities. Since then the degree of mobilization in and around the PAs and new sorts of links, this time with the small-town intelligentsia, have caused a sea change. The expansion of the network of Protected Areas and the intensification of protection measures have provoked a strong response from resident people in many areas.

This pattern emerges clearly in the case of the Rajaji Park near Hardwar. Carved out of the governor general's old shooting blocks, the park is home not only to diverse wildlife, including UP's largest population of wild elephants, but also to several people. In 1979 the government decided to move out the Gujjars and resettle them in a housing colony. The local Gujjars, who are allied to the group Vikalp, rebut the Forest Department's charges that they are overgrazing the area. Their case has wider significance. Firstly, they point to the shrinking of lands along their old travel routes on account of the extension of cultivation and forest; confined to a smaller area, they see themselves as the victims of the process of development. Secondly, they refer to the extensive encroachment on the forests of the area by an irrigation channel, an army ammunitions depot, and several public and private sector industrial units. In addition to mass protests in 1991–4, they also challenged the administration to hand over the park to them for direct management.[117]

More recently, in conjunction with the Bombay-based Indian People's Tribunal for Human Rights, they organized public hearings

[117] Vikalp, 'Rajaji National Park'; Relinks is another group working in the area.

by a retired Chief Justice of a high court. Among other issues, Justice Potti also enquired into possible alternatives to defuse tensions while protecting forests. The report itself is complex: it offers a critique of the existing arrangements for rehabilitation and a more acceptable package that addresses the needs of the Gujjars. Justice Potti raised the issue of compensation for victims of animal attack and suggested they be made equal to those given to aircrash victims. In the longer term, Vikalp argues that the survival of Rajaji and nearby forests is not possible simply through sacrifices by the resident population. The diverse groups in the area—the Gujjars, the inhabitants of the Forest Villages who are tenants of the Forest Department, *taungya* cutters who were brought in to raise tree crops, artisans who collect *baan* grasses from the forest for rope-making—all took part in the consultations.

This itself was significant as the diversity of interest groups is often held as a reason against local control. No easy panacea emerged but the very existence of the process was significant.[118] The destruction of the forest is the consequence of wider processes of social and economic change that need to be taken up. This can be illustrated with reference to the firewood demands of the nearby town of Hardwar, which powers the denudation of substantial areas. In fact, travelling to Hardwar from Delhi, it is impossible to miss the multistoreyed flats that are creeping towards the river. Such changes are cutting off the route for the few bull elephants still courageous enough to make the journey.[119] The Gujjar and the elephant are both hanging in the balance but the former is fighting back.

Nor is this an exception. The general impact of industrialization and the double standards adopted by the administration to forest-dependent people led to the organization of the *Jungle Jeevan Bachao Yatra* ('Save the Forests, Save our Lives' march) in 1995. In the more recent past this technique of processions crisscrossing the

[118] Singh and Kothari, 'Balancing Act', pp. 96–9.

[119] Trip by the author, September 1994.

countryside to bring together affected and concerned citizens has been a favourite of the environmental movement. There have been many yatras, like the Askot–Arakot march by Chipko students in 1974. There was Sunderlal Bahuguna's Kashmir–Kohima trek in 1982, the fisherfolks' march along the sea coast in 1989, and the long march of the anti-dam protestors in the case of the Narmada project in 1992.[120] But this was the first time that the wildlife–people issue was taken up this way. At the end of the 15,000 km march the organizers issued a statement denouncing the creation of *'sarkari sher aur sarkari ped'* (governmental tigers and trees).[121]

In most places on the route, at the Gir Forest in Gujarat or at Rajaji, the tale was a similar one. Disallowing access to forests and natural areas had deprived people of sustenance while opening the area to contractors and other rapacious developers. It is noteworthy that groups like the Tarun Bharat Sangh in Sariska have done more than protest against closure of access. They have planted indigenous trees on common lands, and fought mining interests to a standstill until the state government stepped in on the other side. This consciousness is also evident in the revival of protected forests known as *rhoonds*, and *deobanis* that are protected by villagers.[122] As in Rajaji, the 'petty oppressions' by the Forest Department have been a major grievance. They only illustrate the wider dilemma of a department with rights over residents and usufruct right-holders.[123]

The upshot of the yatra of 1995 was itself mixed and attracted criticism from some quarters for not being strident or radical enough.[124] The debate continues but the significance of the event is easy to miss. The yatra was designed to act as a stimulus for further contact and dialogue and, even in the six months that followed it,

[120] See Gadgil and Guha, *Ecology and Equity.*

[121] Anon., 'Sarkari Tigers Neglected'.

[122] Anon., 'Good as Gold', p. 23.

[123] Mitra, ' No More Bribes', pp. 22–5; Deshpande, 'Vile Report', p. 2.

[124] Iyer, 'Journey to Nowhere', pp. 22–5; Deshpande, 'Vile Report', p. 2.

grassroots groups in three states organized their own networks to continue contact and exchange of information.

What are the main contributions of the rural activists involved in the yatra and elsewhere in the country? Firstly, it will now be difficult to use coercive powers to relocate or displace people in and around Protected Areas. Unlike urban intellectuals or pragmatic conservationists, most rural activists live and work among the communities whose cause they espouse. Their strength is also linked to a significant change: the willingness of politicians to be more sensitive than previously to rural protests.[125] Such changes come from executive action and rural activists' demand for legal rights. At present, the Collector may grant concessions under an amendment in the Wildlife Act made in 1991.[126] Livelihood issues are paramount for rural activists, who see the bureaucracy as failing to improve the living conditions in these areas. Commercial interests, in particular of non-tribal traders and large industry, are regarded as exploiters of both people and nature.

If these terms seem ambiguous it is necessary to reiterate that, unlike the other groups studied here, rural workers are not attached to institutions of higher learning and are often engaged in mobilization against heavy odds. Their view of nature and the question of biodiversity requires more elaboration and attention. One approach has been to see them as standard bearers of traditions that are more in harmony with nature than the industrial mode of development, socialist or capitalist. Since wildlife is not always central to the agenda, as in the case of preservationists, rural activists are often pilloried for not being sensitive to long-term issues. In fact, the point can be turned around. In several cases certain projects which would be deeply damaging not only to wild animals or plants but also to the ecology of vast areas have been stalled

[125] Dakshina Murthy, 'Karnataka Tribals to be Allowed to Stay Put in Park', *Hindustan Times*, 25 February 1995.

[126] Kothari, JPMA. For a pragmatic conservationist's view, critical of the foresters but firm on relocation of Gujjars, see Johnsingh, 'Rajaji National Park'; a more conventional view is by the Park Director: Khati, 'Problems in Paradise', pp. 15–21.

only because of rural protests by disadvantaged social groups. What is valid is the fear that a successful movement for assertion may not be able to control deeper market forces that may corrode the resource base. But bureaucratic regimes have hardly done very well on this count and have facilitated and assisted such corrosive forces.

The preservationists are strident against claims of rural activists who advocate continued use of the protected areas. Surely something is seriously wrong with a system that cannot provide for the disadvantaged from what is left over after reserving of 5 per cent of the country's land area. Rural activists reply that they were not involved in demarcating the 5 per cent and, in any case, this struggle for control is by no means restricted to these areas. The other problem, of providing safe havens for plant and animal life freed of people, does not appeal to rural activists in the way that it does to preservationists. Activists feel that tribals and pastoralists have a better record of living with natural systems than do urban and rural elites. Sacred groves and religious taboos on harvesting wildlife are cited to buttress such claims. If at all core areas are to be set aside, activists would claim that residents have to play a part in delineating the zone. Such areas can possibly be created elsewhere, but the nub of the problem will lie in participation and control which cannot be left solely with the authorities.

The emergence of networks among action groups working on the periphery of protected tracts is a major landmark. As with the forest question, local experiences are now being discussed at a wider level, not only in terms of solidarity and joint action, but also to evolve a common platform. The actual evolution of institutions and mechanisms for rural control has a long way to go, but the process has begun. Local control cannot, in itself, resolve issues: the wider institutions of governance can often be more than willing to bend over to industrial interests.

A Process of Interaction

Critics are largely united in their disaffection with the prevalent mode of preservation. They do not believe in a policy of total environmental protection. Their grounds for criticism and levels of alienation from the dominant model vary and there is also room for mutually contradictory views among them. In their own ways each is questioning the Forest Department's monopoly of power and knowledge in parks and sanctuaries. Though their concerns and prescriptions vary, the critics stand for changes of strategy and policy in the conservation of biological diversity.

This is most clearly evident in the case of rural activists and pragmatic conservationists. The former have a constituency that primarily consists of the rural poor in hilly and mountainous regions, areas with dryland agriculture and animal husbandry. These are populations partially or wholly reliant on gathering forest products, whether for subsistence or sale. The relocation of such villagers, whether Adivasis or caste Hindus, to make way for wildlife, is strongly opposed by rural activists. Pragmatic conservationists, while often critical of the administration's insensitive methods, broadly agree that people must be removed from prime wildlife habitats if this is essential for rare species.

The question goes beyond one of rehabilitation and relocation to usufruct rights. Pragmatic conservationists are mainly wildlife biologists whose prime aim is to evolve management programmes for specific species or ecosystems. They approach the issue from the standpoint of enhancing the survival prospects of their target species or ecosystems. Their findings often pit them against the older 'hands-off' approach of the preservationists, but their methodology is still geared to wildlife much more than to people. Rural activists, at least those who are sensitive to ecological matters, see the issue in terms of the livelihood and survival of social groups marginal to the power structure. It would make little tactical sense for them to admit that the sustenance of disadvantaged groups may at times be in irreconcilable conflict with wild plants or animals. Their prime focus is not only on redressing grievances—which pragmatic conservationists are willing to acknowledge. Some voluntary groups have gone so far as to ask that they and other local residents in and outside the park be given control of the area.

Such a prospect would not be welcome to even the most open-minded of pragmatic researchers. Where there is room for joint action, it is with regard to specific grievances, such as wild animal depredations on crops or attacks on people. The biologists who have documented these problems in detail are in a position to lobby governments to be much more responsive, both in preventive terms and to provide effective compensation. Ironically, the very structure of consultation that incorporates such experts also slows down remedial action.

Professional foresters are apt to look upon researchers as upstarts and drag their feet on implementing programmes for culling male elephants and lions. Research scholars who have logged several hundred hours tracking wild animals or assessing crop damage are still marginal to the community of forestry. They may have the expertise but they lack directorial power. As members of the middle class or literati they do not experience the problems of deprivation so clear to the rural activists. But there is little doubt that pragmatic conservationists are the most ambivalent of all the groups of dissenters and critics. Their findings point in one direction and their professional life makes it essential for them to remain in close contact with the very branch of government whose choices they often disagree with. The growth of autonomous research institutions has increased their leeway and given them a separate institutional base outside the Forest Department, but they can go a certain distance and not beyond.

Rural activists have a much wider agenda and programme. They seek to question not only wildlife conservation policies but the wider gamut of issues related to development. These include the terms of trade with mercantile groups and administrators who purchase timber or non-wood forest products, the denial of land rights and credit to the poor, and the more mundane but critical problems of the lack of even basic social services such as health and education. The strategy is one of struggle, all the more so because they are often at loggerheads with the Forest Department, their overlord controlling access to grazing grounds. Increasingly, human rights violations have come to be prominent in the issues raised by such groups. These efforts are now backed up by their allies in urban areas who also call for an alternative mode of conservation and development.

The urban intelligentsia has come to identify with the rural activists' agendas much more closely than in the past. Alternative systems of protection such as sacred groves were initially seen as an adjunct to the existing PAs but the debate has now moved ahead. The emergence of cross-regional and state-level co-ordination has had a lot to do with the joint efforts of the urban intelligentsia and rural activists. What is equally important is the strong advocacy of decentralized systems of resource control. The Gadgil–Rao Bill of 1995 calls for an extensive restructuring of control of the existing Protected Areas as 'safety sites', giving village-level committees a central role in delimiting boundaries, assessing crop damage, and ensuring protection from rapacious commercial interests. It is true that links on the wildlife front are still nascent compared with the networks on large dams or commercial forestry. But this has to do with both the new wave of protest against sanctuaries and the awareness among both urban and rural concerned citizens that the destruction of natural areas was not their objective. The issue being contested is not only one of equity but also of sustainability: this may have been implicit in many Adivasi or peasant movements in the past but it is being made explicit now.

There are still differences in emphasis between the urban and rural advocates of local control. The former attach considerable importance to biological diversity and often favour service charges to groups who protect rare plants. They who would once have scoffed at the notion of rights of nature having an intrinsic worth have come to champion such notions. They ground their case in the continued existence of tribal or peasant traditions that view nature not as separate from the human world but as part of a unified whole. Urban intellectuals, often a part of the middle class, acknowledge the role of such ideas but they are more sceptical of their viability in the face of market forces.

Perhaps, this is the strongest and weakest part of their case. They are on good grounds in favouring positive incentives for conservation. This at least makes an ideological point, namely, that it is the Maldharis of the Gir who should be rewarded for coexisting with lions. They can and should be turned from antagonists or victims into protectors and it is the duty of society at large to assist them in every way possible. But it is still not clear how such incentives are to be worked out in economic terms. Local protection is often a success because it is rooted in cultural or religious notions and practices. It may not be possible to affix a monetary value on the protection of pipal trees in a village grove or of sacred crocodiles in a lake. In trying to defeat the market system, urban intellectuals have to beware of siding with the very forces that may undermine their wider airms.

At another level, some among the urban literati have probably gone too far down the road in romanticizing traditional systems. This is significant in that at least it displaces the old stereotype of rapacious and destructive tribals or peasants who will destroy the fauna and flora unless checked by government. It is also important that the ways of relating to nature that were earlier considered the preserve of the ethnographer are now studied by biologists or historians. The division between 'science' and 'local knowledge' may have been necessary two decades ago to prevent uncritical glorification of the former and outright dismissal of the latter. But it may be useful to simply have a critical perusal of 'actually existing practice' rather than romanticize traditional systems. This is especially necessary considering the degree of market integration and the rates of demographic expansion that we are often dealing with. Self-reliant agrarian communities linked in a loose federal arrangement may or may not be ideal, but they are hardly practicable in today's world. In any case, dialogue about actually existing practice will enable much more creative and relevant interventions both at a conceptual and practical level.

Rural and urban critics need to be much more specific about what is meant by local control. Many Protected Areas contain people living within their confines, on the perimeter, and groups that may reside further away but use the tract at certain times of the year for limited purposes.[127] Further, there are those who draw on fodder reserves in sanctuaries during pinch periods, as when the rains fail. It is often not clear on what basis local control will work, whether the criterion is to be the length, or place of residence. Even more complicated is the conflict between locally resident cultivators who may use a forest and nomadic groups with herds who are themselves the victims of land acquisition by government but add to the pressure on the resource base in or around a sanctuary. The usual answer is to allow such issues to be decided by consensus and open negotiation. This still does not explain what the minimal points of agreement will be and how they are to be ascertained. Even more crucially, who is to play the mediating role if not the government in a democratic system? And if the mediator is to be the administration, there is the vexed question of which element in the bureaucracy is to be given weightage and how it is to be made accountable and transparent. Local control can only work within a wider framework conducive to conservation and less prone to encouraging short-term growth of the kind that corrodes the resource base. There has to be a role for the state but it will have to be very different from what it is today.

There is also some sign that, as in several strong agitations against de-notification to facilitate industrial interests, local people will have a prior say before such denotification is permitted. Similarly, the existing arrangements under which the Wildlife Wing assists in protection of sacred groves and waterbird sanctuaries maintained by villagers could be given a new legal status as 'people's protected areas'. Yet these measures may not go far enough. There is an urgent need to go much further in evolving alternative systems of control that build on existing efforts and strengthen them. If the rural or urban critics of preservation are to succeed, they have to evolve alternative structures of power.

[127] For a perceptive assessment of the problems of local control, see Pelusso, 'The Political Ecology of Extraction', pp. 49–74.

Constructive work groups have a very critical role to play. Their strength lies in their ability to evolve creative solutions to existing problems that not only improve livelihood but also increase elbow room for disadvantaged groups in their struggles. In the process, such groups have come up with workable alternatives that expand the scope for reform within the existing system. The question which still remains is how far these efforts can supplement the work of rural activists or urban reformers in evolving an alternative framework. The problem of tapping market forces for conservation is all the more problematic. If it is a question of organizing co-operatives for venom extraction or for tendu leaf trade, there is no question that such organization is essential to bargain with middlemen or government agencies. The danger here is that constructive work may often stop at just that, and the massive funds now being given may simply give a fresh lease of life to the old way of operation, in which government departments increase their own clout.

Conclusion

If the older preservationist agenda looks like it is in deep trouble, it still has a lot of life left in it. The crisis of an old order need not necessarily be a prelude to its collapse. None of the critics named here has much sympathy for the agenda of unreconstructed developmentalism that the preservationists did so much to critique. Their shortcoming was their reliance on the state machinery, in particular on the legislative and executive power of the union government. The power of the union (or federal) government in development policy is now much more limited than in the early 1970s, for both political and economic reasons, but the pressure to generate revenue and attract industrial investment is all too real at the state-government level. Critics today often equate preservationists with the forces of short-sighted development. This is perhaps correct insofar as both support the existing power structure and only disagree with the way power is to be exercised. One wants to cut down a forest to make way for a dam, the other to save it for scientific research and leisure. There is still a deep antagonism between the constituencies of the middle-class preservation lobby and rural activists. Wildlife enthusiasts feel that animals have primacy over villagers, at least within wildlife reserves. There is 'no other way to successfully run a reserve, *and there can be no compromise on the issue.*'[128] This is the nub of the issue: in their own ways, all the other groups studied here are convinced of the viability of alternatives. Nowhere will the struggle for control be as sharp as between rural activists and the preservation lobby. The protection of wildlife 'for its own sake' was both a utilitarian and a romantic endeavour. It was preserved for certain kinds of uses (scientific research or wildlife watching) in preference to other uses (livelihood and survival).[129] In the Indian case, neither a technocracy or bureaucracy—acting as the arbiter of conflicts—nor a free market system which tilted towards the privatization of open-access resources would address ecological issues adequately. The assertion of people's rights has the potential for a different kind of conservation-oriented control of their lives and lands. The very idea of a forest separate from people is seen as 'an illusion' that only denies 'the unalienable relation of nature to man'. The question becomes one of working out a new set of relations with the forest which will be enduring for both people and the natural world.[130]

At a time of demographic growth and agrarian intensification, this will be a major challenge and site-specific approaches will probably play a vital role. These issues cannot be divorced from the wider ecological dilemma. Local institutions may be open to corrosion by market forces, due to a combination of external pressures and social change among what may seem like homogeneous rural communities. The risks inherent in political reform must not be allowed to postpone change but the wider economic context of incentives for destructive behaviour has to be changed if there is

[128] Dalal, 'A Wild Way to Go', *The Times of India*, 9 October 1983, emphasis added.

[129] Worster, *Nature's Economy.*

[130] Savyasachi, 'Tiger and the Honey-Bee', pp. 30–4.

to be any hope. This issue calls for more thought and action. Some arch-preservationists may look back on the 'golden era' of the Indira years and yearn for them.[131] But the clock cannot and should not be turned back. The maturing of democracy and political assertion by disadvantaged sections is now far more advanced than in the Indira era. The traditions represented by Vedanthangal are now locked in contest against those symbolized by Asoka.

References

Abdul Ali, Humayun, 'Some Notes on the Painted Partridge around Bombay', *Journal of the Bombay Natural History Society* (*JBNHS*), vol. 61 (1964).

Abraham, S., 'The Karanjikulam Breeding Bird Sanctuary in Ramnad District of Tamil Nadu', *JBNHS*, vol. 70 (1973).

Agarwal, A., and S. Narain, *Towards Green Villages*, New Delhi: Centre for Science and Environment, 1989.

Agarwal, B., *A Field of One's Own: Gender and Land Rights in South Asia*, Cambridge: Cambridge University Press, 1995.

Alexander, P.C., *My Years with Indira Gandhi*, New Delhi: Vision Books, 1991.

Ali, S., 'Review of G. Mountfort's *The Vanishing Jungle*', *JBNHS*, vol. 67 (1970).

———, 'P.D. Stracey', *JBNHS*, vol. 87 (1977).

———, 'R.C. Morris', *JBNHS*, vol. 87 (1977).

———, 'Wildlife Conservation and the Cultivator', *Hornbill*, June 1977 (unnumbered).

———, 'Conservation in Evolution—The Silent Valley Project', *Hornbill*, no. 4 (1979).

———, 'In Search of the Himalayan Quail', *The Illustrated Weekly of India*, 14 July 1985.

———, and A. Rahmani, *Study of Certain Endangered Species of Wildlife and Their Habitats, 1982–84: The Great India Bustard*, Bombay: BNHS, 1984.

[131] Sankhala, 'After the Carnage', p. 81, where he says of tiger poaching in Rajasthan: 'Had She [Indira] been there, many heads will have rolled.' For a more self-critical appraisal, see Sankhala, 'Future of National Parks in India', pp. 791–8.

Anderson, D.M., and R.H. Grove, ed., *Conservation in Africa: People, Problems, Practice*, Cambridge: Cambridge University Press, 1988.

Anon., 'Good as Gold', *Down to Earth* (*DTE*), 31 March 1994.

———, 'Project Tiger and the People: A Report on Simlipal', *EPW*, vol. 20 (1985).

———, 'Sarkari Tigers Neglected', *Hindustan Times*, 2 March 1995.

———, 'The Delhi Bird Watchers' Society', *JBNHS*, vol. 49 (1950).

———, 'The Order of the Golden Ark', *Cheetal*, vol. 23 (1982).

Berwick, M., 'The Ecology of the Maldhari Grazier in the Gir Forest, India', in J.C. Daniel and J.S. Serrao, ed., *Conservation in Developing Countries: Problems and Prospects*, Bombay: Oxford University Press, 1990.

Berwick, S., 'The Gir Forest: An Endangered Ecosystem', *American Scientist*, vol. 64 (1976).

Bhatt, S., 'Project Tiger: A Success Story?', Yale School of Forestry and Environmental Sciences, unpublished paper, April 1989.

Boitani, L., 'Wolf Management and Conservation in Italy', *Biological Conservation*, vol. 61 (1992).

Chambers, R., N.C. Saxena, and T. Shah, *To the Hands of the Poor: Land, Water and Trees*, Delhi: India Book House, 1989.

Chandran, Subash, 'Vegetational Changes in the Evergreen Forest Belt of Uttara Kanada district of Karnataka State', PhD thesis, University of Dharwad, Karnataka, 1993.

Chellam, Ravi, 'Ecology of the Asian Lion', PhD thesis, University of Saurashtra, Gujarat, 1994.

Chettur, S.K., *The Steel Frame and I: Life in the ICS*, Bombay: Asia Publishing House, Bombay, 1962.

D'Monte, D., *Temples or Tombs? Industry vs Environment, Three Case Studies*, Delhi: CSE, 1985.

Dakshina Murthy, K.S., 'Karnataka Tribals to be Allowed to Stay Put in Park', *Hindustan Times*, 25 February 1995.

Dalal, N., 'A Wild Way to Go', *The Times of India*, 9 October 1983.

Daniels, R.J., 'A Conservation Strategy for the Birds of Uttara Kanara District', PhD thesis, Centre for Ecological Sciences, Indian Institute of Science, Bangalore, 1989.

Das, I., and Reptile and Amphibian Specialist Group, *South Asian Herpeto Fauna Conservation Action Plan*, Bangkok: IUCN, 1994.

Dasgupta, B., 'The Environment Debate: Issues and Trends', *EPW*, vol. 13 (1978).

Desai, K., S. Sachdeva, J. Lall, A. Jindal, A. Shreyasa, and M. Joshi, 'Human Resource Development for JPMA', Delhi: IIPA Workshop, September 1994.

Deshpande, A., 'Vile Report', *DTE*, 30 June 1995.

Dhawan, H., A. Prasad, and D. Singh, *Report of the Kalpavriksh Team Sent to Investigate the Firing in the Bharatpur Sanctuary on November 7, 1982*, Delhi: Kalpavriksh, 1982.

Dogra, B., 'Parks and People—Report from a Workshop', *Sanctuary*, vol. 13 (1993).

Elwin, V., *Report of the Committee on Special Mutipurpose Blocks*, Delhi: Ministry of Home Affairs, Government of India, 1960.

Fox, J.L., C Nurbu, S. Bhatt, and A. Chandola, 'Wildlife Conservation and Land-use Changes in the Trans-Himalayan Region of Ladakh, India', *Mountain Research and Development*, vol. 14 (1994).

Gadgil, M., 'Hills, Dams and Forests', *Proceedings of Indian Academy Science*, vol. 2, pt 3 (1979).

———, 'Wildlife Resources of India', National Academy of Sciences, *Golden Jubilee Volume*, Delhi, 1980.

———, and F. Berkes, 'Traditional Resource Management Systems', *Resource Management and Optimisation*, vol. 18 (1991).

Gadgil, M., and R. Guha, *This Fissured Land: An Ecological History of India*, Delhi: Oxford University Press, 1992.

———, *Ecology and Equity: The Use and Abuse of Nature in Contemporary India*, Delhi: Viking Penguin, 1996.

Gadgil, M., and K.C. Malhotra, *A People's View of Eco-development*, Delhi: WWF-India, Environment Services Group, 1980.

———, 'Questioning the Bedthi Hydel Project: An Experiment in People's Participation', in K. Mathur and H. Sethi, ed., *Action Research for Development*, Delhi: IIPA, 1983.

Gadgil, M., and V.M. Meher-Homji, 'Role of Protected Areas in Conservation', in V.L. Chopra and T.N. Khooshoo, ed., *Conservation of Productive Agriculture*, New Delhi: Indian Council for Agricultural Research, 1986.

Gadgil, M., and P.S.R. Rao, 'A System of Positive Incentives to Conserve Biodiversity', *EPW* (6 August 1994).

———, *People's Health, Nature and Education Bill*, Bangalore: Centre for Ecological Sciences, Indian Institute of Science, Technical Report, February 1995.

Gadgil, M., S.R. Bhagwat, G. Mukundan, and J. Joseph, *Report on the Nilgiri Biosphere Reserve*, Department of Environment, 1985.

Gadgil, M., and V.D. Vartak, 'Sacred Groves of India—A Plea for Continued Conservation', *JBNHS*, vol. 72 (1975).

Gandhi, Indira, *Collected Speeches: The Years of Endeavour*, Delhi: Publications Divisions, 1975.

———, *Eternal India*, Delhi: BI Publications, 1980.

———, *My Truth*, Delhi: Vision Books, 1981.

———, 'Man and His World', Speech at the Stockholm Conference on the Human Environment, in idem, *On Peoples and Problems*, London: Hodder and Stoughton, 1982, 2nd edn, 1983.

———, 'Speech to the Conference of State Forest Ministers', 18 October 1982, *Indira Gandhi on Environment*, New Delhi, Department of Environment, 1984.

———, *Selected Speeches and Writings, Vol IV: 1980–81*, New Delhi: Publications Division, 1985.

———, *In Conversation with Pupul Jayakar*, New Delhi: Indira Gandhi Memorial Trust, 1986.

Gandhi, S., ed., *Freedom's Daughter: Letters between Indira Gandhi and Jawaharlal Nehru, 1940–64*, London: Hodder and Stoughton, 1992.

———, ed., *Two Alone, Two Together: Letters between Indira Gandhi and Jawaharlal Nehru, 1940–64*, London: Hodder and Stoughton, 1992.

———, ed., *Rajiv's World*, New Delhi: Viking Penguin, 1994.

Gee, E.P., *The Wildlife of India*, London: Collins, 1964.

Ghorpade, M.Y., *Development Ethos and Experience*, Bangalore: Southern Economist, 1991.

Gomez-Pompa, A., and A. Kaus, 'Taming the Wilderness Myth', *Bioscience*, vol. 42 (1992).

Goyle, R., 'Proposal for a Sloth Bear Rehabilitation Centre-cum-Safari', World Wide Fund for Nature, India, April 1960.

Guha, R., *The Unquiet Woods: Ecological Change and Peasant Resistance in the Himalaya*, 1989; 2nd rev. edn, Delhi: Oxford University Press, 1999.

———, 'Deep Ecology or Deep Wilderness', typescript, Yale University, 1988; rpnt. in *Environmental Ethics*, vol. II.I (1989).

———, 'Ideological Trends in Indian Environmentalism', *EPW*, vol. 23 (1988).

———, *Gandhi and the Environmental Movement—The Parisar Annual Lecture*, Pune, 1993.

———, 'Forestry Debate and Draft Forest Act: Who Wins and Who Loses?', *EPW*, vol. 29 (1994).

———, and M. Gadgil, 'Forestry and Social Conflict in British India', *Past and Present*, no. 123 (1989).

Guha, S., *Environment and Ethnicity in India, 1200–1991*, Cambridge: Cambridge University Press, 1999.

Gundevia, Y.D., *In the Districts of the Raj*, Bombay: Orient Longman, 1992.

Hecht, S., and A. Cockburn, *The Fate of the Forest: Developers, Destroyers and Defenders of the Amazon*, London: Penguin, 1989.

Homewood, K.M., and W. Rodgers, 'Pastoralism and Conservation', *Human Ecology*, vol. 12 (1984).

Indian Board for Wildlife, *Report of the Task Force for Eliciting Public Support for Wildlife Conservation*, Delhi: Department of Environment, 1984.

Iyer, M., 'Journey to Nowhere', *DTE*, 31 March 1995.

Jackson, P., 'Birth of Sanctuary', *Newsletter for Bird Watcher*, vol. 14 (1974).

Jayakar, P., *Indira Gandhi*, Delhi: Viking Penguin, 1988.

Jhala, Y.V., 'The Status and Conservation of the Wolf in Gujarat and Rajasthan, India', *Conservation Biology*, vol. 5 (1991).

Jodha, N.S., 'Common Property Resources and the Rural Poor', *EPW*, vol. 27 (1986).

Johnsingh, A.J.T., 'Rajaji National Park', *National Mail*, Bhopal, 3 April 1995.

Joslin, P., 'The Environmental Limitations and Future of the Asiatic Lion', *JBNHS*, vol. 81 (1984).

Khati, D.S., ' Problems in Paradise', *Sanctuary*, vol. 13 (1991).

Kosambi, D.D., 'At the Cross-road: A Study of Mother-goddess Cult Shrines', in idem, *Myth and Reality: Studies in the Formation of Indian Culture*, Bombay: Popular Prakashan, 1962.

Kothari, A., *Conserving Life: Implications of the Biodiversity Convention for India*, Delhi: Kalpavriksh, 1994.

———, 'Is Joint Protected Area Management Desirable and Possible', paper at a workshop on JMPA, Indian Institute of Public Administration (IIPA), New Delhi, 1–3 September 1994.

———, N. Singh, and S. Suri, ed., *People and Protected Areas: Towards Participatory Conservation In India*, Delhi: Sage, 1996.

Kothari, A., P. Pande, S. Singh and D. Variava, ed., *Management of National Parks and Sanctuaries in India—A Status Report*, New Delhi: Indian Institute of Public Administration, 1989.

Krishnan, M., 'The Environment—Disaster Ahead', *Sunday*, Annual Number (1977).

———, 'Can it Fail?', *Project Tiger Newsletter*, no. 1 (1978).
———, Monthly Lecture, National Museum of Natural History, New Delhi, 10 November 1979 (unpublished).
———, 'Preservation in Perpetuity of 5 per cent of India's Heritage', *Report of the Committee for Recommending Legislative Measures and Administrative Machinery for Environmental Protection*, New Delhi: Department of Science and Technology, 1981.
———, 'A Wildlifer's Apprehensions', *Hornbill*, vol. 2 (1989).
Kulkarni, S., and W. Fernandes, ed., *Towards a New Forest Policy: People's Rights and Environmental Needs*, Delhi: Indian Social Institute, 1982.
Kumar, S., 'Wolf in Bustard Country', *Sanctuary*, vol. 14 (1994).
Lavkumar, K.S., 'The Need for a New Conservation Approach in India', *Newsletter for Bird Watchers*, vol. 14 (1974).
Malhotra, K.C., S.B. Khomne, and M. Gadgil, 'Hunting Strategies among Three Non-pastoral Nomadic Groups in Maharashtra', *Man in India*, vol. 63 (1983).
Mallon, D., and C. Nurbu, 'A Conservation Programme for the Snow Leopard in Kashmir', *Proceedings, of the Fifth International Snow Leopard Symposium*, Dehra Dun: International Snow Leopard Trust, 1988.
Manfredi, P., 'Art for Conservation's Sake', *Sanctuary*, vol. 14 (1994).
Mitra, A., 'No More Bribes, Gujjars tell Foresters', *DTE*, 31 March 1995.
Morris, R.C., and S. Ali, 'Game Preservation in Kashmir', *JBNHS*, vol. 53 (1955).
Mountfort, G., *Back from the Brink: Successes in Wildlife Conservation*, London: Hutchinson, 1978.
———, *Saving the Tiger*, London: Michael Joseph, 1981.
Norman, D., ed., *Letters to a Friend, 1950–84*, London: Weidenfeld and Nicholson, 1986.
Oldfield, M., and J.B. Alcorn, ed., *Biodiversity—Culture, Conservation and Development*, Boulder, Colorado: Westview Press, 1989.
Panwar, S., 'What to Do When You've Succeeded: Project Tiger Ten Years Later', in J. McNeely and K. Miller, ed., *Conservation and Development: The Role of Parks in Sustaining Society*, New York: Smithsonian, 1984.
Pelusso, Nancy Lee, 'The Political Ecology of Extraction and Extractive Reserves in East Kalimantan', Indonesia', *Development and Change*, vol. 23 (1992).
People's Union for Democratic Rights, *Undeclared Civil War*, Delhi, 1982.
Philip (Prince), Foreword, in V. Thapar, *Tigers—The Secret Life*, Delhi: Elm Tree Books, 1989.

Poffenberger, M., *Joint Management for Forest Lands: Experiences from South Asia*, Delhi: Ford Foundation, 1990.

Ramakrishnan, P.S., *Shifting Agriculture and Sustainable Development in North East India: An Interdisciplinary Study*, Delhi: Oxford University Press, 1993.

———, 'Wildlife–Human Conflicts', *Seminar*, 426 (1994).

———, *Fencing the Forest*, Delhi: Oxford University Press, 1995.

———, ed., *The Oxford Anthology of Indian Wildlife, Vols. I and II*, Delhi: Oxford University Press, 1999.

Rishi, V., 'Man, Mask and Man-eater', *Tiger Paper*, vol. 15 (1988).

Rodgers, W., 'Policy Issues in Wildlife Conservation', *Indian Journal of Public Administration*, vol. 35 (1989).

———, and H. Panwar, *Planning a Wildlife Protected Area Network in India*, 2 vols, Dehra Dun: FAO, 1988.

Roy, Dunu, 'Proposal for People's Science Institute', typescript, Shahdol, Madhya Pradesh, June 1984.

———, A. Gupta, S. Gotge, and A. Deshpande, *Planning the Environment: Based on Research Conducted in Shahdol District, Madhya Pradesh*, Madras: Gandhigram Press, 1980.

Saberwal, V., 'Rethinking Biodiversity Conservation in India', Yale University, typescript, 1995.

———, Ravi Chellam, and A.J.T. Johnsingh, 'Lion–Human Conflict in the Gir Forest, India', *Conservation Biology*, vol. 8 (1994).

Saharia, V.B., 'Human Dimensions of Wildlife Management—The Indian Experience', in J. McNeely and K. Miller, ed., *Conservation and Development: The Role of Parks in Sustaining Society*, New York: Smithsonian, 1984.

Sahgal, B., 'If Nature Does Not Survive Neither Will Man', *Sunday Express*, 13 October 1985.

———, 'Denotify and be Damned', *Sanctuary*, vol. 13 (1993).

———, *Environment and Wildlife: The Parisar Annual Lecture*, Pune, 1992.

———, 'People and Sanctuaries', in A. Agarwal and S. Narain, *State of India's Environment: The Second Citizens' Report, 1984–85*, Centre for Science and Environment, in *Sanctuary*, 1993.

Samar Singh, 'Indira Gandhi, The Environmentalist', *Cheetal*, vol. 26 (1988).

Sankhala, K.S., *Wild Beauty*, New Delhi: National Book Trust, 1973.

———, *Tiger! The Story of the Indian Tiger*, London: Collins, 1978.

———, 'People, Trees and Antelopes in the Indian Desert', in F. McNeely and D. Pitt, ed., *Culture and Conservation: The Human Dimension in Environmental Planning,* Dublin: Croom Helm, 1984.

———, 'Future of National Parks in India', *Indian Forester,* vol. 117 (1991).

———, 'After the Carnage', *Frontline,* 5 November 1993.

Sarabhai, K.V., S. Bhatt, and G. Raju, *People's Involvement in Wildlife Management: An Approach to Joint Sanctuary Management of the Shoolpaneshwar Wildlife Sanctuary,* Ahmedabad: Viksat, 1991.

Savyasaachi, 'The Tiger and the Honey-bee', *Seminar,* no. 423 (1994).

Shahi, J.P. 'Dudwake baghon ko narbhakshi kaon bana raha hai', *Ravivar,* Delhi (April 1982, in Hindi).

Shahi, S.P., *Backs to the Wall: The Saga of Wildlife in Bihar,* Delhi: East-West Affiliated Press, 1977.

———, 'Kokrebellur ke peehar mein pakshi parivar ka basera', *Cheetal,* vol. 27 (1981; in Hindi).

———, 'Status of the Gray Wolf (*Canis lupus pallipes*) in India: A Preliminary Survey', *JBNHS,* vol. 79 (1982).

———, 'Mrs. Gandhi and Wildlife', *Hindustan Times,* 4 November 1984.

Sharma, Mukul, 'Project Tiger: Jahan janvar aadmi ka shikar karte hain', *Samkaleen Janmat,* Patna (February 1982; in Hindi).

———, 'Tigers versus People', *Nature: The Environmental Action Newsletter,* Delhi (October 1983).

Shiva, V., *Staying Alive: Women, Ecology and the Politics of Survival,* Delhi: Kali for Women, 1988.

Singh, A., *Legend of the Man Eater,* Delhi: Ravi Dayal Publisher, 1993.

Singh, N., and A. Kothari, 'Balancing Act: Report on Rajaji', *Frontline,* 30 June 1995.

Singh, Shekhar, 'JPAM—Some Policy Issues', IIPA Workshop, 1994.

Stracey, P.D., *Wildlife—Its Conservation and Control,* Delhi: Manager of Publications, 1963.

Sukumar, R., *The Asian Elephant: Ecology and Management,* Cambridge: Cambridge University Press, 1989.

———, 'The Management of Large Mammals in Relation to Male Strategies and Conflict with People', *Biological Conservation,* vol. 55 (1991).

———, *Elephant Days and Nights: Ten Years with the Asian Elephant,* Delhi: Oxford University Press, 1994.

Thapar, V., and P. Manfredi, 'Saving Our Forests', *Seminar,* vol. 426 (1994).

Toledo, V., 'Patzcuaro's Lesson: Nature, Production and Culture in Indigenous Regions of Mexico', in M. Oldfield and J.B. Alcorn, ed., *Biodiversity—Culture, Conservation and Development*, Boulder, Colorado: Westview Press, 1989.

Trautmann, Thomas R., *Elephants and Kings: An Environmental History*, Ranikhet: Permanent Black, 2015.

Vijayan, V.S., 'Keoladeo Ghana National Park Ecology Study', *Annual Report*, Bombay: BNHS, 1987.

Vikalp, 'Rajaji National Park: Conservation, Conflict and People's Struggle', Delhi: IIPA workshop paper, September 1994.

Viswanathan, S., 'Ancestors and Epigones', *Seminar*, 330 (1987).

Vyas, M., 'And the Blackbuck Lives', *Echoes from the Wild*, Delhi, October 1979.

Whitaker, R., and H.V. Andrews, 'The Madras Crocodile Bank', *Contributions in Herpetology* (1992).

Whitaker, R., and Z. Whitaker, *Status and Conservation of the Asian Crocodilians*, Crocodile Specialist Group, Species Survival Commission, Morges: IUCN, 1989.

Whitaker, Z., *Snakeman: Story of a Naturalist*, Delhi: India Magazine Books, 1989.

Williams, R., *The Country and the City*, London: Oxford University Press, 1973.

World Wildlife Fund, UN Environment Programme, International Union for the Conservation of Nature, *World Conservation Strategy*, Morges, 1980.

Worster, D., *Nature's Economy: A History of Ecological Ideas*, New York: Sierra Club Books, 1977.

Zimen, E., and L. Boitani, 'Wolf, Italy', *WWF Yearbook, 1972–73*, Morges, 1973.

9

Parks, Politics, and History

Conservation Dilemmas in Africa

The conservation dilemmas of Africa are of pressing concern to people everywhere. In recent years, works of history as well as of science have questioned the older stereotypes. The Victorian idea was of a continent fit for conquest, carved up by various European powers whose rule (or misrule) left a mark in more ways than one, not only on people but also on the landscape and wildlife. In recent years the Southern and Central African region has come to be better known for new and innovative experiments that try to place conservation on a co-operative basis. But such an enterprise requires an engagement with history as well as with science.[1] The past matters as it can illustrate how the present came about. By knowing better what choices were made in

This was first published as a review essay on four books: J. Carruthers, *The Kruger National Park: A Social and Political History*, Pietermaritzburg: University of Natal Press, 1995; R.P. Neumann, *Imposing Wilderness: Struggles over Livelihood and Nature Preservation in Africa*, Berkeley: University of California Press, 1998; David Western, *In the Dust of Kilimanjaro*, 1997; Washington: Island Press, rev. edn, 2002; Bill Weber and Amy Vedder, *In the Kingdom of the Gorillas: Fragile Species in a Dangerous Land*, New York: Simon and Schuster, 2001.

[1] See Beinart, 'The Politics of Colonial Conservation', pp. 143–62; and Anderson and Grove, 'The Scramble for Eden', pp. 1–12.

the past, when and why, the dilemmas of the present can be seen in a more holistic way. Equally important is a critical appraisal not of the biological sciences in a narrow sense but of the role played by scientists and the knowledge they generate. Since conservation is as much about relating to people as it is about plants, animals, landscapes, and soils, there is no escaping the wider question: What has been the experience of scientists who try to intervene in real-life situations and devise models or approaches of conservation that can work?

Southern Africa looks especially interesting to a student of the politics of conservation in South Asia. Both regions had a history of colonial rule, but in ecological terms there were significant contrasts as well as similarities. Both were major trophy-hunting grounds by the late nineteenth century. But in South Asia it was the creation of large forest reserves for timber and the expansion of canal networks that were at the heart of the colonial remaking of the landscape. In Anglophone and Belgian-ruled Africa the emphasis was more on soil conservation, stock control, game protection, and hunting. All were pursued using a range of means, some of them draconian. No wonder that nationalist movements in eastern Africa often entailed resistance to the forced labour that was recruited for public works. But the cutting edge of statist conservation lay in South Africa. It is in the fitness of things that a look at recent works should begin with the politics of preservation in the continent's first National Park, Kruger.

The Kruger Park: From Myth to History

Jane Carruthers is a pioneering historian of South African conservation. Not surprisingly, her monograph on the political and social history of Kruger Park begins by explicitly acknowledging how famous the place is. She presciently observes how for several people South Africa is epitomized both by the former system of apartheid and by the Kruger National Park. However, unlike apartheid, the park is a compelling emblem; nature conservation is seen as intrinsically benign. But the story is not quite so simple. For tourists the vast 19,000 sq km park simply showcases wilderness. Watching wildlife from a gasoline-powered automobile is an innovation that dates back to the 1920s, but until recently the experience reinforced an alliance of English- and Afrikaans-speaking white settlers. The railroad had been an ally of the creation of America's first national park: the internal combustion engine played a similar role fifty years later in Africa. Such an act of creating a park was a gesture not merely to 'save' nature, but to redefine who owned it. The exclusion of black Africans culminated in the birth of apartheid in 1948, a political system founded on racial distinctions and unequal rights. Kruger, a symbol of the triumph of the camera over the culture of sport, was simultaneously a central emblem of apartheid for decades.

The idea was that the park for white tourists from all parts of South Africa would showcase the land 'as the Voertrekkers saw it'. Paul Kruger was first reinvented as a pioneer of preservation; later Henrik Verwoerd, who presided over South Africa as State President in the 1960s, was credited with the creation of the Augrabies National Park. Kruger was not just a national park: it was part of a much larger political drama.

The history was easy to elide over, for the wilderness has often seemed to exist outside of and beyond the political realm. But the Kruger was already a magnet for wildlife enthusiasts by the mid-twentieth century. Writing in the *Journal of the Bombay Natural History Society* in 1954, St J. MacDonald was struck by how even the lions seemed like domestic animals. He compared watching animals favourably to the thrill of the chase and the hunt. 'The watchful experience I have from a car compares with any thrill I experience awaiting a driven tiger, a rogue elephant, or closing in with a tracked bison or tsine . . . Man in his car [is] but as a spectator and regarded as no more than some other form of life in the Reserve by its denizens.'[2] Interestingly, even though he visited the

[2] MacDonald, 'Wildlife Preservation', pp. 1–4.

country within the first decade of India's Independence in 1947 and the victory of the National Party in the South African whites only election of 1948, the author was blind to the politics of the park. Even early writers of conservation history tended to marginalize the black majority.[3]

In a later era, as the apartheid regime came under increasing pressure from within and without, the park and other wildlife reserves were used as symbols to try to defuse criticisms. By preserving the wild in a large park, the white racist regime killed two birds with one stone. It staked a claim to being a responsible benefactor of immense natural wealth for the world at large. It also won legitimacy in Western eyes. By the 1970s the parks enabled white South Africa to woo support overseas amidst wider anti-apartheid boycotts in the international community. For instance, the 1001 Club of the World Wildlife Fund, launched as a fund-raising campaign by Prince Bernhard of the Netherlands, required a contribution of 10,000 dollars as entry fee. The number of white South Africans who signed up were three hundred times the number of Americans who did—in proportion to their total numbers.

Few other international fora were willing any more to admit white South Africans. Many appear to have been from the secret white supremacist brotherhood, Broederbund.[4] By this time, the recovery of numbers of rare herbivores enabled a form of 'zoological diplomacy'. White rhinos from Natal's parks were sent to white-settler-ruled Rhodesia (now Zimbabwe) and two independent African states, Kenya and Swaziland.[5]

The idea of setting aside game reserves and national parks arose at a very specific point in time. It was forerun by a mass slaughter that was integral to the process of conquest and subjugation of the land and the people. There was no perfect harmony before the conquest by the Dutch and the subsequent entry of the British. The

[3] Khan, 'Soil Wars', pp. 439–59.

[4] Bonner, *At the Hand of Man*, pp. 68–9.

[5] Sparks, *Animals in Danger*, pp. 49–50.

Zulu ruler Shaka, for instance, had hunting reserves demarcated in Umfolozi, Natal, to ensure there was enough game. Yet the first major mammal extinctions took place as a consequence of the coming of modern technologies of warfare and hunting and the inability of two large herbivores (the bluebok and the quagga) in the Cape Colony to adapt to the major changes in the land.[6] Early conservation concerns were centred on the mid-nineteenth-century fears of desiccation, the idea that deforestation would lead to a shortage of water supplies and agricultural destabilization.[7]

The attitude to wildlife itself underwent considerable shifts over time. Wild animals were a source of revenue in the initial stages, with no limits on bags or a thought to the morrow. Hunters like William Cornwallis Harris, who had also fought and hunted in India, made their hunting exploits the stuff of early bestsellers. Hides, horns, and ivory continued to be a major source of revenue in the late nineteenth century, but the agrarian frontier moved north, pushing back 'native' pastoralists and large herds of wild ungulates in its wake. The first reserves were created in the 1890s, when there were fears of the all-out and final extinction of game. Earlier regulations via Game Rules were largely a failure.

It was in this context that the Sabi Game Reserve came to be of prominence. It was not the first such area but it was the one that lasted. Carruthers shows how the creation of Reserves was also a device to assert competing land claims. Land-grab was easier to justify when cloaked in the garb of conservation: the Pongola area was protected to forestall British land claims. But there was more to it all than mere annexation ambitions. A section of white settlers became advocates of protection. In their view the real threat to wildlife arose from another group. In 1903, writing to the Colonial Secretary, the local Game Protection Association warned that 'The destruction of game by the natives . . . enables a large number to live by this means who would otherwise have

[6] Silverberg, *The Dodo*, pp. 97–106.
[7] Grove, 'Early Themes in African Conservation', pp. 21–37.

to maintain themselves by honest labour.'[8] The absence of direct interests of settlement in the area by white landowners and the lobbying by Abel Chapman eventually led to the appointment of a warden and curbs on hunting. James Stevenson Hamilton was to serve as the warden from 1902 till 1946: a man in command on the spot who was often able to do as he liked. One era had given way to another.

While there is little doubt the curbs hit non-whites more seriously, a section of settlers was also affected by the new rules. There were protests, for instance that the area was now a 'lion-breeding centre', the big cats being seen as marauders of domestic livestock. Despite many competing pressures and claims, the reserve survived, unlike many others in South Africa.[9] In 1924 politicians like J.M. Hertzog explicitly championed the renaming of the Sabi Game Reserve on the Mozambique border after Paul Kruger. The creation of a national park was not a simple victory of 'good versus evil', nor was the idea just an implant from the USA.

The other voices were all too easily ignored. These included the story of people evicted from the tract or subject to labour levies and curbs on use of the land for livelihood. Game wardens were part of the South African police force, and they did not hesitate to seize or deny firearms to blacks, or fine them for trespass and for keeping domestic dogs. An earlier generation of white hunters had compared peoples like the San to baboons and the Khoikhoi to bush pigs. Such attitudes were often reinforced, not discarded as conservation gave them a sharper edge.

Carruthers deftly demonstrates the evolution of the Afrikaner notion of conservation from the 1940s onwards. Black Africans were depicted as cruel and destructive; the Parks Board claimed to be nature's voice. Initially, African settlements were allowed to stay, but in 1905 over 3000 were evicted from a now much larger Sabi Game Reserve. Later there was a decades-long struggle

[8] Carruthers, *The Kruger National Park*, p. 32.

[9] Beinart and Coates, *Environment and History*.

by the Makuleke community against expansion of the park. The community lost out in 1969 and was relocated. Such dislocations were part and parcel of highly intrusive and racially skewed land-use allocations in the apartheid era. Those living off the land were not the only ones who felt the brunt of exclusion. There were even segregated camps for white and black tourists, the latter with much worse facilities and services.

White managers were not homogeneous, there being major rifts over how to manage the park. The evolution of wildlife biology in the 1950s in the white universities of South Africa led to significant differences of opinion on how best to deal with carnivores in the Kruger. In much of southern Africa the first generation of park officials comprised former military officers. This was the case of East Africa's game wardens too: George Adamson, Bruce Kinloch, David Sheldrick, and J.P. Ionides in British East Africa.[10] Ironically, scientists revived the old policy of killing off carnivores. Lion hunting, halted since 1926, was renewed in order to safeguard the rare sable antelope. The idea of 'management by intervention', a hallmark of the South African model of conservation, crystallized in this period. It was no coincidence that to save species like the mountain zebra and bontebok from extinction white settlers had founded several smaller reserves. A Kruger warden told a visiting British biologist in the 1970s that the park itself was not a natural unit but the result of human ingenuity. To save it meant to actively intervene. To the visitor it looked more like a 'gigantic game ranch', complete with man-made watering points, inoculations for rare ungulates, tranquillizer guns, animal relocations, and border fences. Far from being wilderness free of human intervention, the area, its plants and animals, have been re-natured in myriad ways. The question has often been: Who does the reshaping and why?[11]

The park was an artefact of politics as much as of wildlife managers. No wonder that the end of apartheid in the 1990s led to strident calls for its abolition in the new democratic South Africa.

[10] Adamson, *Bwana Game*; Kinloch, *The Shamba Raiders*.

[11] Hamilton, *Battle for the Elephants*, p. 68.

It is a measure of the statesmanship of Nelson Mandela and his successors that these calls have not won response. But even as they strive to make the park the heritage of all South Africans irrespective of colour, status, and income, there is no escaping its troubled history. Older concepts have resurfaced in new forms. The notion that game can be cropped as a resource is now advocated for the region and various parts of the world. The recovery of the rhino and elephant under managed conditions is seen not as a leftover of the apartheid era but as a positive contribution for conservation everywhere. Some advocates have even favoured it as an ideal model for other species and continents.

But interestingly, the idea of commercialized hunts and game culls can be seen as a product of the unique mix of large blocs of landed estates and exclusive landownership in South Africa's recent past.[12] A bloc of southern African states has advocated highly intrusive forms of management, with culling as standard practice as a model in the 1980s. The same nation-states continue to champion such an approach after the end of the apartheid era too.[13] More important is the notion of Peace Parks along the border, and Kruger is the centrepiece of a major initiative with South Africa's adjacent countries.[14] The legacy of the apartheid past has not vanished but the new socio-political order based on universal franchise and a multi-party polity faces a difficult task. It has to remodel conservation while breaking out of its draconian past.

Contesting the Wilderness

Carruthers' book is a highly skilled work of history. She lucidly pieces together key moments in South Africa's history and the conflicts that need to be understood in the search for a just future.

[12] Rolfes, *Who will Save the Wild Tiger?* See Beinart and Coates, *Environment and History*, p. 88, for a rate list for hunts on a private game reserve.

[13] Ellis, 'Of Elephants and Men', pp. 53–69. For a critical view of co-operative conservation in Zimbabwe, see Alexander and MacGregor, 'Wildlife and Politics', pp. 605–27.

[14] Duffy, 'The Environmental Challenge', pp. 441–51.

A different study by the geographer Roderick P. Neumann takes up the 137 sq km Arusha National Park in Tanzania but focusses much more on local displacements and perceptions. Arusha's past intersected with Kruger's in the 1920s, a decisive decade in Africa's wildlife. Eastern Africa remained a largely peasant-based society, with a much thinner overlay of white settlers. Even the politics of hunting, parks, and game was much more closely tied with the changing fashions at a pan-imperial level than was ever the case in South Africa.[15] When Tanzania gained independence in 1961, there were significant continuities in government policy with the late colonial era, especially in the field of conservation. What was earlier the white man's game became a potential source of foreign exchange—so much so that the country has National Parks and equivalent reserves extending over a fourth of its land mass. This was far more than the 3 per cent set aside for parks in South Africa.

The British took control of the region after 1918 and were keenly aware of the new conservationist initiatives in South Africa. While German concerns had centred more on forestry, the Mt Meru state forests were re-gazetted as a Complete Game Reserve in 1928. The presence of the Merus in the region dated back over three centuries. There had been conflicts earlier, as between Merus and the Arusha peoples, but European incursions in the 1890s marked the start of a new era. The initial military encampments by the Germans gave way to land annexation for plantations, as well as for forest reservation. Early British Game Rules were softened by fears of disorder that enforcement might provoke. Agriculture officials found a 'hardening of African opinion' undermining conservation efforts. A London-based lobby, the Society for Preservation of Fauna in the Empire (the SPFE) became a focal point for those lobbying for tougher enforcement. Though formed around 1900, its influence in the empire increased in later decades.

[15] Mackenzie, *The Empire of Nature*; Anderson and Grove, *Conservation in Africa.*

Its clarion call for natural resource-use conservation anticipated post-World War II international conservation organizations. The US and South Africa, that were upheld as models for East Africa's parks, allowed no human settlers in their confines.

The ground realities of eastern Africa were more prosaic. Licences for hunting were rarely given to villagers: one analysis shows only one in twenty given to black Africans between 1922 and 1939.[16] It took three years to finalize the borders of what became the world-famous Serengeti Park. Even this agreement between the Parks Board and the Maasai pastoralists was explicitly on the basis that the latter's rights would be unaffected. It is a different matter that these assurances were later violated. As in South Africa, there were often double standards. The Ngorongoro Crater, a focus of contests between officials and herders, had earlier been opened to a German rancher who kept cattle and shot wildebeest. Eventually, the Maasai found their access curtailed: rights became conditional, were reduced to privileges, and access was only retained after protracted conflicts. The Serengeti and Ngorongoro were only a few hours' drive from the Kenyan border and, with the outbreak of the Mau Mau rebellion in 1951, officials trod warily. There were some brakes on the pace of exclusion. A Maasai memorandum from the Serengeti plains quoted by Neumann put it very simply: 'From time to time, we see white hunters posing with the trophies of the animals they have shot . . . It is the very same people and their friends who wish to evict us from the National Park, yet we think it is they who are the enemies of the game rather than us.'[17]

A thinly disguised distrust of the Africans' ability to rule themselves meshed well with concerns that they would devastate their wild birds, animals, and landscapes. Such concerns were common as decolonization loomed, but only rarely were they expressed as candidly as with reference to Africa. Bernhard Grzimek,

[16] Parker and Amin, *Ivory Crisis*, p. 128.

[17] Maasai of the National Park, Memorandum, 1957, quoted in Neumann, *Imposing Wilderness*, p. 122.

the legendary German zoologist who co-authored *Serengeti Shall Not Die*, was a typical case. Though claiming that 'A Negro is an equal and a brother', he still warned against 'the over-hasty conversion of coloured colonies into independent democratic states.' The Green agendas of colonizers were contrasted with the more immediate day to day preoccupations of their subjects. Conservation was a pretext for the continuance of colonialism. The book by Dr Grzimek was first published in 1959 and translated into eighteen languages.[18] Such fears were misplaced.

Two years later his platform was taken over by erstwhile nationalist agitators who now replaced the British. The 'idea of wilderness' had found fresh adherents. In his Arusha Manifesto, President Julius Nyerere (r. 1961–85) struck a note that warmed the hearts of Western wildlife lobbies. Tanzania's natural treasures were held 'in trusteeship' for the whole world. Recent scholarship has shown that members of the very conservation groups who lauded its contents prepared the actual draft! That still hardly makes it clear who was using whom. Nyerere wanted developed countries to pay for the protection. He had other reasons too. As he had famously remarked, he did not 'want to spend his holidays watching crocodiles. Nevertheless I am fully in favour of their survival.' Many foreign visitors made tourism the largest source of revenue for Tanzania, after diamonds and sisal.[19] But this did not resolve the conflicts on the ground: it often only deepened them. The issue of what Africa *really* ought to look like is contentious.

There were differences not only between but also within nations. Lines of continuity with the colonial era could sometimes be striking. In the Serengeti case the notion of a natural space devoid of the presence of pastoralists meshed well with independent Tanzania's dominant ideology of self-reliant socialism. As of 2003 the Selous Game Reserve, a 44,000 sq km tract, was the scene of

[18] Grzimek and Grzimek, *Serengeti Shall Not Die*, pp. 178–9.
[19] Bonner, *At the Hand of Man*, p. 65; Nash, *Wilderness and the American Mind*.

the Maji Maji rebellion against the Germans in the early 1900s. Two decades later it saw forcible evictions by the British during tsetse fly control drives. The rulers of the new nation took up further resettlement. Nyerere eventually had eight of ten villages in the country regrouped under the Villagization scheme as this was seen as key to socio-economic development. The eviction of the Maasai from Serengeti was not an exception: such relocations and displacements were a major feature of conservation policy until very recently. In most parks, displacement was seen as a prerequisite for successful preservation.[20]

The great insight of the work is the author's grasp of what the changes meant and still mean for local peoples. The issue as he suggests goes beyond their immediate grievances—like denial of access to ancestral lands, curbs on resource use, and conflicts with wildlife on cultivated lands. The steady erosion of rights continued through the 1960s and the 1970s. But it has recently given way to more emphasis on community involvement in conservation. Several sites of conflict in the past are now scenes of an array of approaches that include sharing revenues from tourism, co-operative protection, and expenditure on welfare. Serengeti, Arusha, and Selous: all familiar as scenes of conservation mired in conflict are now sites for new approaches.[21] Yet, the past is never so far away. Difficult issues refuse to go away. Even benefit-sharing is no panacea. For instance, the construction of classrooms may not directly be linked to the reduction of grazing trespass. Conversely, only very rarely has the restitution of customary claims been a matter for renegotiation. Still, redress has not come merely due to changes in conservation ideology and shifting donor preferences. It is also the result of a growing assertion of rights on the ground that rarely takes the form of open rebellion but endures in myriad other forms. Costs often still outweigh benefits: this is the picture that emerges in Arusha.

[20] Shao, 'The Villagization Programme', pp. 219–39.

[21] Rodgers, Hartley, and Bashir, 'Reflections on Community Involvement', pp. 324–82.

In Kilimanjaro's Shadow

The great advantage of the historical insights of studies like those of Kruger and Arusha is the way they illumine processes by which specific decisions and conflicts in the past shaped the present. But the evolution of alternatives on the ground is far more difficult. For Carruthers the historian and Neumann the geographer, the past is a guide to what the present should *not* be about. Crafting alternatives on the ground is perhaps equally if not more challenging. A sense of disquiet with conservation via coercion is a starting point. It still opens up dilemmas on how to ensure participation without damaging core conservation goals such as protecting ecological integrity and maintaining species diversity.

One person who was central to the search for other, more inclusive, models of conservation was David Western. The son of a former British Indian Army officer who became a professional hunter in Kenya, his own life bridged many transitions. There was the shift to the Kenya of *uhuru* (freedom) in a polity dominated by the Kikuyu tribe. Equally, there was a shift from the world of old white hunter naturalists and wardens to a new Africa where independence went together with a growing role for professional scientists. Western's own life is fascinating: he has played a key role at critical junctures in conservation debates. These include the great debates of the 1980s on whether and why elephant numbers were declining, culminating in the CITES ban on ivory in 1989.

But much of his life and the story told here centres on his work in Kenya's Amboseli. Like neighbouring Tanzania, Kenya was a former British colony: Jomo Kenyatta ruled as its president till 1977 and was succeeded by Daniel Arap Moi. The stable one-party state was more open to the West through the Cold War years than Tanzania. More importantly, it was an early leader in developing sport-hunting and wildlife-based tourism. By the late 1960s, when Western was a young researcher, Amboseli already attracted 60,000 tourists a year. By this time the first generation of African park and wildlife administrators was also making its presence felt. Kenya was also different in other ways. Nairobi University and the Institute of Development Studies became the focus of African-born researchers. The seeds of alternatives may have lain in the past. There had been centuries of coexistence (though not absolute harmony) of Maasai pastoralists and wildlife. Some ground had been broken by middle-of-the-road ideas of some colonial administrators.

The dominant ideology of preservation still held sway where it mattered most. Western strongly argues that the late colonization of eastern Africa was a blessing in disguise. The region was spared the kind of wipe-out of wildlife that took place in parts of southern Africa. Late Victorian sensibilities braked slaughter even if there was often indifference to the hardship of cultivators, local hunters, and cattle keepers. At the same time, the coming of freedom opened up the chance to try out new ways of protection. The key was in giving value to wildlife. He quotes a Maasai friend who felt wild animals could be a 'second cattle' for the Maasai. The key lay in reversing a century of marginalization of the Maasai. They had lost their best lands to European settlers and were now in danger of losing out to parks. The idea was to move beyond the idea that wildlife was a white man's first right and a black man's burden. This meant both hard bargaining and ecological insight. Both rested on political spadework at the local, county, and national level. The New York Zoological Society's support proved the most vital ingredient. The local equation was a simple one. If the Maasai were not given stakes in Amboseli, they could destroy it. 'Retaliatory spearing' of rhinos was an index of a breakdown of relations. But in times when there has been co-operation, as in the late 1970s, the numbers of rare species have increased, poachers have been apprehended, and the Maasai have acted as guardians of nature.

Neither Maasai nor wildlife are frozen in time. But the changes do not fit any preconceived neo-Malthusian pattern. There is one central narrative from the late 1960s onwards: a deep realization of the complex links between nature and people: 25,000 wild ungulates could not subsist on Amboseli's 400 sq km area alone. The herds required access to forage and water in a larger expanse of land ten times the size of the park. The Maasai needed the water supplies within Amboseli in times of drought and in the annual dry season.[22]

Mount Kilimanjaro, which looms in the background, had a role to play. The alluvial soil run-off and groundwater made the tract more productive than the surrounding red-soil region. Much of greater Amboseli is not cultivable and pastoralists rely on a hardy local breed of cattle. Denudation of the reserve due to overgrazing was a well-worn trope in conservation literature. Western and his colleagues challenged it, presenting evidence to the contrary. They traced the phenomena to more complex patterns of ecological change, including increasing water salinity, and the longer time cycles of ecological transitions.

In fact, there was no 'steady state equilibrium'. Fire, elephants, and cattle opened up the thorn scrub. Cattle-grazing on the savannah opened up spaces for the regeneration of thickets of trees. But there were often variations: elephants created grasslands by knocking down trees. The latter grew back over time: a cycle longer than one person's lifetime, but clear enough if one consulted older records. Places like the Mara-Serengeti ecosystem attracted international attention as huge herds of zebra and wildebeest gathered in open savannah. But the grasslands were part of a continuum with thickets and mature tree forest. Taking one place at a time out of context tended to give a misleading impression of timeless harmony in nature.

The Maasai were also agents of change. Human and cattle numbers grew and aspirations changed. Western maps the contrasts of Oloitiptip, the senior Maasai leader in national politics, and a new generation of educated leaders. The older ways of life, never static, were now changing at a faster pace. In the 1973 drought even those Maasai who liked the pastoral way of life tried their hand at owning land, which was let out for cultivation. Here there lay the seeds of a second critical danger. Private farms could wreak havoc in

[22] Western, 'Amboseli National Park', pp. 302–8.

an insidious way. The privatization of land into plots and the spread of fences could cut off migratory routes for wild animals. These would undermine the ecological integrity of the whole region. The segregation of park and herder would damage the interests of both. Western's is only one view of a complex, multifaceted process. What is significant is that a scientist should take on board social concerns at the heart of his own work. This marks a major change from an exclusive focus on biotic systems to the exclusion of human impact. It is also significant that he distinguishes different groups and classes of human resource users.

There were several distinct phases in the evolution of a co-operative model, with many difficult moments.[23] In the first phase, the idea of a role for the Maasai in Amboseli did not gather enough support among key decision-makers. President Kenyatta himself decreed the creation of a National Park, with only its size reduced to defuse disaffection. It had been a game reserve for over a quarter-century: the local Maasai now opposed the creation of a park. Alternative ideas slowly gathered support.

In 1973 an attempt was made to quantify the opportunity costs of creating a National Park in Amboseli. The estimate was beguiling. It was possible to earn far more by combining stock-keeping with wildlife. There would have to be give and take on both sides, but the key lay in coexistence, not separation. In the mid 1970s a World Bank-funded scheme was launched; Maasai leaders even met the president of Kenya. The project effected a series of careful compromises: resources and responsibilities were to be shared. The Maasai agreed to leave the park zone. In return they were promised a share of tourism revenues, adequate water supplies for cattle, and fees for commercial hunts on their own lands. The project worked well for about five years and then came unstuck. Government halted payments, cut off the water supply, and reneged on agreements. Changes of personnel and a merger

[23] A concise version can be found in Western, 'Ecosystem Conservation', pp. 15–52.

of the Game and Parks departments did not improve matters. Parashino, the Maasai, did not appear incorrect in his cynicism: 'A park means the Maasai lose.'[24]

Western was not always directly engaged with Amboseli, being drawn to research. He was also a key player in major conservation policy debates, mainly on the issue of the African elephant. But even these, such as the factors behind the sharp decline in elephant numbers, brought him back to Amboseli later. In a sense the place never left his life. It drew him back not merely as a scientist but an active negotiator for change. The chance to influence policy came amidst a major crisis and propelled him centrestage. Fresh waves of poaching decimated the rhino and elephant across much, though not all, of sub-Saharan Africa. Kenya alone lost as many as 140,000 elephants in a matter of two decades: many heads started to roll. By the late 1980s African nation-states were ready for draconian measures to save their wildlife from poaching rings.[25]

The creation of the Kenya Wildlife Service (KWS) and the appointment of Richard Leakey heralded major changes. Western was Leakey's successor as head of the Service and is cautious in criticisms of the former's tenure (1987–94 and 1998–2000). There were, however, major differences in emphasis. Leakey trusted the old 'fortress-like' methods more; Western leaned as always in favour of reform. Amboseli was the litmus test. Leakey promised a change in attitudes towards people but tough policing remained the core of his approach. Leakey's ouster was a result of his wresting of the famous Maasai Mara Reserve from the powerful Narok District Council.

Western's own policies sought to reverse the trend. Only 5 per cent of all visitors to parks were Kenyan. Fees for them were halved in a 'Parks for Kenyans' drive. A review team brought scientists, politicians, and community representatives together. Landowners' associations were encouraged to take up wildlife conservation.

[24] Western, *Kilimanjaro*, p. 105.

[25] Ibid., p. 245. For a different view stressing Western popular and institutional pressures, see Bonner, *At the Hand of Man*, pp. 281–5.

Public hearings were held to enable people to air their grievances. Kenya resisted donor (especially World Bank) pressure to cut back on fifty of the fifty-six reserves and parks. Despite changes in personnel, Western's core philosophy has won more adherents. There has been progress on more participatory conservation, if in a piecemeal manner. Many early initiatives have now borne fruit. In 1997–2002 alone over 2500 sq km of land was set aside for wildlife protection by communities and landowners in Kenya. The preservationist model continues in the national parks but it is no more the only approach to protection. The book ends on a positive note, with an account of a meeting of the Laikapia Wildlife Forum in June 2001. The Speaker of Kenya's National Assembly even claimed: 'We do not need the Kenya Wildlife Service any more but we do want to work with them.'[26] The broader constituency for conservation is now a reality, even though many challenges lie ahead.

Year of the Gorilla

Kenya and Tanzania are more politically stable than adjacent Rwanda, a country recently at the centre of international attention on account of the civil war and genocide. In conservation terms it has long been a focus of attention because of the occurrence there of a rare and charismatic primate: the mountain gorilla. Few large vertebrates can match its popular appeal. The largest of primates occurs in eleven countries, but the mountain gorilla is a rare sub-specie. Only 600 survive. Save for a handful in Uganda, *Gorilla gorilla berengei* inhabits only former Belgian possessions in East and Central Africa.[27] The Congo and to a greater extent Rwanda have a long but troubled history of gorilla conservation. *In the Kingdom of the Gorilla* chronicles an innovative attempt to ensure a secure future for the species. But the region's history has been very different from that of eastern and southern Africa. As in

[26] Western, *Kilimanjaro*, p. 294.
[27] Butynski, 'Africa's Great Apes', p. 13.

Western's case, here too is an instance of scientists grappling with field-level choices of how best to promote conservation with a human dimension. This has been compounded in no small way by the existence for a while of much harsher, even racially informed, approaches in the same site.

The sub-specie has remained fascinating to scientists ever since it was first described for modern science by Captain Oscar von Beringe in 1902. At the time, Rwanda and Burundi were German colonies. The Congo became the 'personal property' of the ruler of Belgium in 1885, followed by direct Belgian rule. Prince Albert's visit to Yellowstone National Park in the USA won him over to the idea of a refuge for the gorilla. Carl Akeley's lobbying marked the start of an active role for American biologists in the region. By the time of his death in 1926 Akeley had travelled widely across Africa for three decades: to Somaliland, to East Africa, and into the Virunga volcanoes on expeditions towards filming, hunting, and collecting specimens for the American Museum of Natural History. A year before this the Parc d'Albert came into being: the continent's first park outside South Africa. Five years later his spouse and associate Mary Jobe Akeley described it as the first park ever to be established for 'purely scientific purposes'.

But the genesis of conflict was already evident. To avoid conflicts between 'native rights' and nature there would be curbs on cultivation and hunting. A new research centre would include 'buildings designed for use of white men unaccustomed to the tropics.' Gorillas would be secure as long as the rulers and their co-equals could study them: those who lived in the Virunga had a secondary role.[28] Not that all apes were safe. Akeley shot a gorilla family for a New York museum. Domination had begun but conservation proved a harder act to follow. The scientific centre never took off; the Belgians began to lose their hold by the end of World War II.[29] Imperial powers had started engaging with

[28] Akeley, 'Belgian Congo Sanctuaries', pp. 289–300. Haraway, *Primate Visions*, pp. 31–45 for an insightful perspective on Akeley's legacy.

[29] Haraway, 'Universal Donors', esp. pp. 340–2.

species conservation precisely when their grip on colonies was slackening.

There were many changes and new challenges in the post-1945 era. George Schaller made a significant observation: newly independent Rwanda's park was far better protected than the one in Belgian Congo. The latter had been 'abandoned long before independence to graziers, poachers and woodcutters.' Warden Amicet Mburanumne stringently protected the Rwandan park. In November 1960 he spoke of the keys to success: conservation, scientific co-operation, and the expansion of tourism.[30] But Rwanda's wildlife would not continue to be so fortunate. Much depended on the agendas of the rulers. A pioneer of primate behaviour in Tanzania noted how the cultivators adjacent to reserves hoped to reclaim land for growing crops. The authorities resisted such demands both during and after British rule.[31] However, the Belgians in Rwanda did not create a clear administrative system for conservation. In 1958 they opened up a fifth of the reserve to grow pyrethrum, a source for bio-pesticides in Europe. After Independence, the Ministry of Agriculture oversaw the park till as late as the mid-1970s. Axe and plough got to work in the forest. In 1969 40 per cent of the park was opened up for cultivation in a project funded by the European Common Market.

This was the backdrop against which Dian Fossey entered the region. First attempting research in the Kivu region of Congo, she soon shifted to Rwanda, growing into a defender of the species against poachers and encroachers. Entering a scene where the park administration was in a rundown state, she organized anti-poaching patrols, conducted censuses, lobbied international funding agencies, and founded a research centre at Karisoke. Fossey's model of 'active' as opposed to 'theoretical conservation' enabled her to free a small tract from rival human intrusions. This found her often usurping

[30] Schaller, *Year of the Gorilla*, p. 161.

[31] Goodall, *In the Shadow of Man*, p. 30. Goodall was writing of Gombe Stream Reserve for chimpanzees, Tanzania, in the late 1950s, just before the end of the colonial era.

the role of the park authorities. Such strategies attracted fierce controversy long before her murder in December 1985. Fossey's books and articles placed the issue of the mountain gorilla before a global audience. Her dedication was undeniable, but the means adopted were self-defeating.

Bill Weber and Amy Vedder arrived in the country to work with Fossey in 1978. They were unable to identify with her philosophy of conservation. The authors' criticisms of her condescending attitude to local people are not to be dismissed lightly. Fossey tortured and beat up intruders, used black magic, and even killed off cattle found in the park. Her own account includes several unsavoury episodes. Even admirers had qualms over her scorched-earth tactics. On one occasion an American colleague tried to dissuade her when in a poachers' camp but failed. Fossey later recalled how, 'As I stood there breaking bamboo snares one by one, she stood apart and in a very firm way asked what right I had, an American, here in Africa for only a few months, to invade the rights of Africans whose country it was. I went on breaking traps, though I couldn't help but agree with her—Africa belongs to Africans.'[32]

Rifts with park authorities worsened this attitude. Fossey's style deeply offended the sovereignty of a newly free country and won few allies for the cause she represented. Only white researchers were recruited: apes, it was said, had 'only known Africans as poachers in the past.' Not a single Rwandan researcher was trained or inducted in the entire Fossey period, in contrast to Jane Goodall in the Gombe, Tanzania, where Tanzanian nationals took over virtually all research from around 1975.[33] Even the Rwandan director of the park felt that the Virungas were set aside for 'white people only'. Fossey went so far as to assert that 'Africans are not allowed to approach my gorillas *on account of their skin colour.*'[34] The Karisoke Centre bypassed park officials. In a fascinating anecdote,

[32] Mowat, *Virunga*, pp. 68, 104, 123–4; Goodall, *The Wandering Gorillas*, p. 60.

[33] Fossey, *Gorillas in the Mist*, p. 57; Haraway, *Primate Visions*, pp. 167–70.

[34] Fossey, quoted in Mowat, *Virunga*, pp. 235–6.

the director of the park accosted Weber and Vedder and asked them if two Rwandans could walk into Yellowstone and commence research without any permission whatsoever.

The defence of gorillas against poachers' forays was not enough to save them when officials and local inhabitants were treated with disdain. The authors tried a different approach, lobbying the authorities and assessing local opinions through surveys. The park lacked clear local support; 80 per cent of Rwandan farmers favoured the survival of the great apes. But one out of two hoped the park would be converted to arable land; 40 per cent collected firewood from the park. Over 100,000 people lived within a five-mile radius of its borders.

The merely scientific value of the species and its global popularity meant little to farmers and herders. Nor was it enough for park officials to convince the political leadership of the country. Yet, there was some ground for hope. The recently founded park authority, ORTPN, shared the positive assessment of gorilla-centred tourism. Unlike in British East Africa, the conservation body was given an institutional basis more than a decade after Independence. The park authorities became allies against agrarian extension. The mountain gorilla emerged as the symbol of Rwandan nationalism.

The species would win a lease of life because of its unique importance to a small developing country. Even 'crazy white people' who would pay $ 1000 for a four-member party to trek into a forest within touching distance of the apes became allies for a cause. They gave the decision-makers of a poor country strapped for foreign exchange a convincing reason to keep the park intact. When a Belgian-funded cattle-raising project threatened to further reduce the habitat, tourism seemed a better bet. Three thousand tourists paying twenty-five dollars each would generate more revenue than the cattle-raising scheme.

The promise of foreign exchange helped forestall denudation. The scheme also combined job generation with eco-tourism. The pied wagtail, a traditional Rwandan symbol of goodwill, was the emblem of an education programme in schools. A younger generation of Rwandans saw wildlife films on their country for the first time and debated whether and how to conserve their natural heritage.

The Mountain Gorilla Project began in 1979 in response to a crisis; it soon became a viable alternative to an approach that relied solely on exclusion and policing on a vigilante basis. By now gorillas totalled 260, with only 30 silver back males. Recovery was quicker than anybody expected. By 1989 losses of animals to poachers dropped from ten a year to only three in ten years. Enforcement improved once local people became allies. The first joint census by Uganda, Rwanda, and the Congo showed an overall increase of nearly 25 per cent in the gorilla population. Income from park fees reached a million dollars the same year. Tourists in the country spent five times as much.

The Nyungwe Reserve in southern Rwanda with its colobus monkeys and wealth of birdlife became a second tourist destination. In landscape terms both reserves offered a very different option from the savannah of the Akagera Park, which was more akin to East African parks. Primate-based tourism gave Rwandan decision-makers the kind of rationale for conservation previously known only in larger East African countries. There were still many limitations, notable being the absence of revenue-sharing with local communities and low progress on wider environmentally sound schemes to arrest soil erosion and improve firewood supplies. The profits from tourism and wildlife films too rarely went into the pockets of Rwandans on the rim of the gorilla habitat. But the breakthroughs were still significant in a situation that had seemed almost devoid of hope.

Much of the success hinged on political factors that later came undone in the genocide and civil war of the mid-1990s. Rwanda's people were divided into the majority Hutu and the minority Tutsi, with the former being the dominant group in national politics. From 1973 till 1994 the army general Juvenal Habariyama held power. His patronage was critical for Dian Fossey as much as for Bill Weber and Amy Vedder. The latter scheme ensured a flow of revenues to his power centres in the north while the Nyungwe project added to patronage. By the late 1970s population growth was at the rate of 3.7 per cent and the density of people per sq km was as high as 500 in some tracts.[35] But the breakdown was a political rather than a demographic one. Political turmoil in neighbouring Uganda led to a more assertive mood among the Tutsi. Some formed an armed insurgent group to try seizing power in Rwanda, while a section of Hutus too grouped into an extremist force. Clashes till 1993 and an abortive accord could not forestall the genocide of 1994, in which more than a million people were killed and hundreds of thousands rendered homeless.

Yet Rwanda witnessed 'conservation nationalism' of a sort the world has rarely seen in the past. It is tempting to compare the saga of the mountain gorilla to another rare species that barely made it through wars in its only home in the wild, the European bison. Also a creature on shifting borderlands (between Poland, Germany, and Russia), a huge number were slaughtered in the First World War (1914–18) by German troops. The population was augmented with captive-born specimens in the post-war period.[36] In the closing years of the twentieth century Rwanda presents the contrasting case of a very different approach to a rare species. Its experience shows how ideas of protection can even find unlikely but valuable adherents. In the initial years of the Rwandan civil war only *one* gorilla was killed, with all insurgent groups agreeing they were too valuable to be killed. This did not prevent another sixteen losing their lives between 1995 and 1998. Still, things could have been worse. Even the Hutu rebel armies freed the park guards in the Virungas and asked them to get back to work. The gorilla as a national icon had a power that transcended its appeal as a symbol of conservation. Only once the two images merged could its survival be assured.

[35] Rwanda's population growth rate has since declined sharply from 3.5 per cent in 1970–95 to just over 2 per cent by the year 2000: UNDP, *Human Development Report 2002*, pp. 163–5.

[36] Schama, *Landscape and Memory*, pp. 37–74.

The wider tragedy affected many Rwandans who had worked hard to save the endangered species. Those who did not fall in line with armed groups often paid with their lives. These included ranger Jonas Guitonda, who refused to share profits with cattle traffickers in the park, and two former Karisoke workers, Nshogoza and Kanyarogano. The travails are far from over but the foundations laid in the country in the late 1970s have held firm. Many former staff freed from gaol drifted back to rejoin work. Eugene Ratagumara, jailed by insurgents, was released and assumed duties again in the Nyungwe Park. By 2001 a fresh census found another increase in gorilla numbers in the Virungas. A new generation of wild gorillas now with African not Anglophone nicknames wins acquaintance with 2000 tourists a year, only a third of the peak level of the pre-war years but a renewal nevertheless.[37] The atmosphere of co-operative conservation among the three gorilla range states has given way to deep animosity and suspicion fuelled by conflicting interests in the continuing civil war in the Congo. Doubts over the consequences of ape-centred tourism have never quite died away, especially due to the threat of diseases from human visitors. As many as seventy tourists with guides visit the gorillas on an average day at peak season: the dangers are ever present.[38]

There is still a wider insight into the processes by which the efforts symbolized by the Mountain Gorilla Project won fresh ground, despite problems remaining. Rwandans in responsible positions were central to saving the species. Its forest home won a lease of life only when they saw tangible benefits from conservation. Even genocide, civil war, interstate strife in the region, and Great Power manoeuvres did not override such enlightened self-interest. It was active on-site conservation that succeeded, not pure research and internationally funded policing alone. The Virungas were unlike Kibale in neighbouring Uganda, where there were sharp conflicts

[37] Anonymous (2002), Interview with Bill Weber, pp. 52–3; also see Schaller, 'Gentle Gorillas, Turbulent Times', pp. 65–8.

[38] Butynski, 'Africa's Great Apes', pp. 29–36.

with human settlers within and around the park. There were fewer people–park conflicts on the perimeter of the gorilla reserve. No settlers lived within.[39] The volcanoes' refuge did not suffer the fate of Akagera, the Rwandan park on the Tanzanian border, which was cleared and cultivated by destitute refugees. Though the park covers only 0.5 per cent of Rwanda, the international appeal of the gorilla made it a prize worth guarding.

Africa and South Asia: Contrasting Legacies in Conservation

Amidst the tragedies, hope springs anew. This perhaps is the message of the history of Africa's parks. Innovative conservation approaches in Amboseli and Parc d'Volcans are part of a growing tableaux of new initiatives in the continent. In a variety of ways, it is better placed than Southern Asia, a region with which I am much more familiar. It is commonplace to assert that the absence of innovation and the more pronounced reliance on exclusion and hard-line preservation in South Asia is due to the higher level of human pressures and the smaller expanse of Protected Areas. There is a grain of truth in such observations. A quick comparison between India and Tanzania shows that the latter has a population density of 33 to a sq km while India's is well over 300. Similarly, the average size of a Tanzanian park or reserve is over 2000 sq km, more than eight times that of the average acreage of an Indian sanctuary or park. As of 2003, the Selous Game Reserve would easily have dwarfed *all* the tiger reserves in India combined. At a macro level, India is three times the size of South Africa but has over a billion people to the former's 43 million.[40]

But there is more to the picture, as is evident in the insights provided by the works on four African countries, each with its

[39] Struhsaker, 'Strategies for Conserving Forest National Parks', pp. 97–112.

[40] Rodgers, Hartley, and Bashir, 'Reflections on Community Involvement', p. 344; Rangarajan, *India's Wildlife History*, p. 103.

distinctive history and political profile. Innovation in part also stems from the institutional logic of the park system: in Kenya, the Wildlife Service, and prior to that the National Parks Department, was able and willing to negotiate the sharing of power. The Virungas case was different, given that ORTPN was only four years into its existence when the Mountain Gorilla Project was launched.

South Asia saw the creation as early as 1864 of a Forest Department, before this happened in the rest of the British empire. The first park was created in the United Provinces nearly a decade after Kruger and the Parc d'Volcans was. Protection of the prince's or the king's game in India had a longer lineage and firmer history than the more half-hearted attempts of the British. These included the Gir Forest in western India, with the last population of lions in Asia, subject to very few royal hunts from 1900.[41] British India was very different from the princely states and accounted for two-thirds of South Asia. Though the Game Rules dated back over half a century, production rather than protection was the watchword till well after Independence. The clarion call for action by popular writers in Africa and South Asia grew after the Second World War but the institutional form of the responses was very different.[42] To this day the Wildlife Wing of the Indian Forest Department administers the parks and sanctuaries. There is no autonomous Parks Board (as in South Africa) or a Department (like in Rwanda) or an equivalent of the Kenyan Wildlife Service. Much of this can be traced back to the institutional legacy of the empire: the foresters who control a fifth of India's land mass are reluctant to part with any of it to a separate wildlife conservation authority.

It is perhaps no coincidence that revenue-sharing with people on the park perimeter has actually taken off in the one region of South Asia never under direct British rule, Nepal. But this experiment in

[41] Rangarajan, 'From Princely Symbol', pp. 399–443. Interestingly, a Game Warden from East Africa surveyed the Forest: see Caldwell, 'Gir Forest Lions', pp. 62–5.

[42] Compare the titles of Seshadri, *The Twilight of India's Wildlife*, and Moorehead, *No Room in the Ark*.

Chitwan has yet to be replicated in any of the other countries of the region. Yet the tract was more comparable to the princely reserves in India.[43] The idea of safeguarding the entire flora and fauna as opposed to populations of key vertebrates became official policy only as late as 1970.[44] Already a late starter in preservation, South Asia has also lagged in taking the initiative in assigning communities a role in conservation. There have been major policy changes in relation to managing forests, for example the introduction of joint forest management. These do not, however, have any clear counterpart in national parks and wildlife sanctuaries. Community-run reserves are a relatively new concept in the policy-makers' lexicon. They have no legal standing or recognition in policy.[45] Conversely, the acreage of Forest Department land in India—23 per cent of the land area—is comparable to the area under parks and wildlife reserves in Tanzania. Even after a tenfold accretion in area over 1969–89, the total percentage of the land mass under parks and sanctuaries is only 5 per cent, far less than even Kenya's 8 per cent.[46]

Other contrasts between and within the two regions are worth reflecting on. Arusha or the Virungas' parks are certainly comparable to reserves in Nepal, Bangladesh, or India in acreage and the intensity of human pressures on the rim. It is true that the great apes of Central Africa, the huge migratory herds of the Serengeti plains or even the South African *veld* have no counterpart in Asia. The spectacle of the last Eden, ahistorical as it may be, has an appeal for tourists from North America, Europe, and Japan that would be hard to match.[47] The landownership system in South Africa and the

[43] Dinerstein, *et al.*, 'Tigers as Neighbours', pp. 316–33.

[44] Indian Board for Wildlife, *Report of the Expert Committee*. Compare this to the Game Reserves Commission Report in South Africa, 1918, in Beinart and Coates, *Environment and History*, p. 75.

[45] Kothari, *et al.*, *Communities and Conservation*.

[46] Rodgers, Panwar, and Mathur, *Protected Area Network*; Bonner, *At the Hand of Man*, p. 195.

[47] Turnbull, 'East African Safari', pp. 26–35.

arrangements for licensed hunts on community lands as in Kenya or Zimbabwe too do not have counterparts in Asia. Interestingly, the latter was actually mooted in Pakistan by the one biologist, George Schaller, who worked in both Africa and South Asia for two decades. But nothing came of his proposal to 'crop' herds of wild goats and sheep in parts of the Pakistan highlands. Again, the region he was dealing with was exceptional. Unlike much of British East Africa, uncultivable due to the absence of adequate rainfall or the tsetse fly, over half of South Asia is cultivable. The forest has been pushed back in much of the river basin and lowlands by the plough and axe. This still leaves several regions with extensive forest cover, but their total acreage is much smaller than in most African countries.[48]

The level of human development and the economic profile of a country or the region in which a park is located are critical in the kind of human pressures it has to handle. Southern Africa in general has higher human development levels than any neo-Malthusian scenario would allow for. Western is prescient in pointing to the decline in Kenya's population growth rate. Once at 3.5 per cent, it is now down to 1.8. Literacy in the entire southern African region is far higher than in South Asia, save for Sri Lanka. Even Rwanda's adult literacy in 2000 was 10 per cent higher than India's, though life expectancy is less than forty years. The levels of spending on health and education are reflected in the levels of human development, but these cannot mask internal inequities. South Africa's 43 million citizens live in cities and towns, compared to 40 per cent in developing nations as a whole. The ability of the apartheid regime to survive economic isolation and boycotts was partly on account of the level of industrial development. The fact that fewer people subsist on the land also makes leeway for more accommodation in the rural hinterland.[49]

Other striking contrasts demonstrate the enormity of the challenge that conservation faces in Africa. It is well known that

[48] Schaller, 'Status of Wildlife', pp. 133–43.

[49] UNDP, *Human Development Report 2002*, pp. 158–9, 163–5, 196–7.

South Africa's level of internal inequality has few parallels. One estimate is that 10 per cent of the population corners 46 per cent of the national income. Equally seriously, the denial of access to modern higher education has left the sciences in general, and ecology- and conservation-related disciplines in particular, dominated by whites. In Central Africa, Belgian colonialism was rapacious and hardly allowed for upward mobility, the army being a partial exception. South Africa developed wildlife biology in the 1950s, with Pretoria University emerging as a centre of excellence, but the doors were explicitly closed to most non-whites.[50] The Serengeti had a world-class centre in Seronera by the late 1960s, but the only black Africans were 'bottle washers or mechanics'. Through 1967 to 1975 sixty graduates and other researchers worked in Gombe: all were foreign and none were of the Tanzanian majority community.

It was only in the mid-1970s that the picture began to change in Tanzania: as Haraway puts it, Third World nationals were beginning to shed the cloak of anonymity.[51] Only a decade earlier, a major conclave on the future of East Africa's wildlife found fifty-one of the fifty-five participants of the former ruling race.[52] There is no doubt there have been major changes since then. The process of engagement is chronicled by authors like David Western, himself a Kenya-born white. Similarly, it was only the Rwandan parks officials and authorities that saved the gorillas of the Virungas through and after the war. But the gap remains an all too real one. Political power may have passed from colonizers to independent nation states in East and Central Africa. Apartheid may be a part of history. But the absence of more black voices in the debates as experts in the sciences remains a big cause for concern.

Here, the picture in South Asia is markedly different, though it has to do with a very different history of British imperialism in the region. By the early nineteenth century eastern India already had a

[50] Carruthers, *Kruger*, p. 115.

[51] Haraway, *Primate Visions*, p. 170.

[52] Western, *Kilimanjaro*, pp. 54, 90.

bilingual intelligentsia, even before Japan did. More central to our theme, the emerging middle classes threw up early scientific figures, often funded by the princes. Of these Sálim Ali, who died in 1987, was only the best known. Ali, who had been exposed to cutting-edge ecological theory in Germany in 1929–30, drew support from the Bombay Natural History Society, which had included Indian literati from the time of its birth. Ali went on to collaborate with the American scientist S. Dillon Ripley from the 1940s.[53]

Over 1947–57 the Indian government began imposing restrictions on primate experts and encouraging collaborations in publishing. The emergence of a small nucleus of Indian scientists, however, soon ceased to directly reflect in debates on conservation policy. Partly due to the breakdown of relations with the US in the early 1970s and also the intransigence of the Forest Department, wildlife biology as a discipline flowered much later in India than in East Africa. George Schaller's work *The Deer and the Tiger* did make a mark, but it took over a decade for it to bear fruit. Nepal was ahead of India in this respect due to the spin-offs from the Smithsonian Institution's research work in the Chitwan National Park.[54] So the picture is very mixed. The social base of science was broader in South Asia but there was greater openness to wildlife biology in much of Africa.

But it is in this respect that the works reviewed here point the way ahead. The Kruger story is salutary. All too often, there is a tendency to see parks as an American import (or export) into other societies, ignoring the ways in which the content could differ from the form. Local political cultures and ground realities make national histories of conservation all too vital, and Carruthers sets a standard that will be hard to equal. *Imposing Wilderness* and Western's work sit well together. One provides searing intellectual critique. The message in a work like *In the Kingdom of the Gorillas* is crystal clear.

[53] Ali, *Fall of a Sparrow*, pp. 96, 180–1.

[54] Lewis, 'Tracking the Biodiversity Ideal', pp. 75, 81–6; Schaller, *Deer and Tiger*.

For too long, popular conservation literature has centred on the lives of researchers and their subjects: Goodall and the chimpanzees, and Fossey and the gorilla being prime examples. The picture of Africa was one without its people, their cultures, their dilemmas. It was almost as if the scientist worked in a void, with only her animals for company. The new genre takes the spotlight to the life stories of women and men of science who grapple with conservation. These are accounts sensitive to ecological constraints but also to the human dimension. The Kenyan case is a fascinating one that stretches back across the decades; the one from Rwanda is truly a tale of hope. Such initiatives show how conservation can begin to move away from a troubled past to a more just future.

References

Adamson, G., *Bwana Game: The Life Story of George Adamson*, London: Collins, 1968.

Akeley, Mary Jobe, 'Belgian Congo Sanctuaries', *Atlantic Monthly* (1931).

Alexander, J., and J. MacGregor, 'Wildlife and Politics: Campfire in Zimbabwe', *Development and Change*, 31 (2000).

Ali, S., *The Fall of a Sparrow*, Delhi: Oxford University Press, 1985.

Anderson, D.M. and R.H. Grove, 'The Scramble for Eden', in idem, eds, *Conservation in Africa: People, Problems, Practice*, Cambridge: Cambridge University Press, 1987.

Anonymous, Interview with Bill Weber and Amy Veder, 'Fragile Species in a Dangerous Land', *Wildlife Conservation*, 52–3 (2002).

Beinart, W., 'The Politics of Colonial Conservation', *Journal of Southern African Studies*, 15 (1989).

———, and Peter Coates, *Environment and History: The Taming of Nature in the USA and South Africa*, London: Routledge, 1995.

Bonner, R., *At the Hand of Man: Hope and Peril for Africa's Wildlife*, New York: Vintage, 1993.

Butynski, T.M., 'Africa's Great Apes', in B.B. Beck, *et al.*, ed., *Great Apes and Humans: The Ethics of Coexistence*, Washington: Smithsonian Institution Press, 2001.

Caldwell, K., 'Gir Forest Lions', *Journal of the Society for Preservation of Fauna of the Empire*, 34 (1938).

Carruthers, J., *The Kruger National Park: A Social and Political History*, Pietermaritzburg: University of Natal Press, 1995.

Dinerstein, E. Rijal, *et al.*, 'Tigers as Neighbours', in J. Seidensticker, *et al.*, ed., *Riding the Tiger: Tiger Conservation in Human-dominated Landscapes*, Cambridge: Cambridge University Press, 1999.

Duffy, Rosaleen, 'The Environmental Challenge to the Nation-State: Super Parks and the National Parks Policy in Zimbabwe', *Journal of Southern African Studies*, 23 (1997).

Ellis, S., 'Of Elephants and Men: The Politics of Nature Conservation in South Africa', *Journal of Southern African Studies*, 20 (1994).

Fossey, D., *Gorillas in the Mist*, 1983; rpnt. New York: Houghton Mifflin, 1987.

Goodall, A., *The Wandering Gorillas*, London: Collins, 1979.

Goodall, Jane van Lawick, *In the Shadow of Man*, 1971; rpnt. 2nd edition, Glasgow: Fontana, 1974.

Grove, R.H., 'Early Themes in African Conservation: The Cape in the Early Nineteenth Century', in D.M. Anderson and R.H. Grove, ed., *Conservation in Africa: People, Problems, Practice*, Cambridge: Cambridge University Press, 1987.

Grzimek, B., and M. Grzimek, *Serengeti Shall Not Die*, 1959; rpnt. London: Collins, 1964.

Hamilton, Douglas, *Battle for the Elephants*, London: Doubleday, 1990.

Haraway, D., 'Universal Donors in a Vampire Culture: Biological Kinship Categories in the Twentieth Century United States', in W. Cronon, ed., *Uncommon Ground*, New York: W.W. Norton, 1995.

———, *Primate Visions: Gender, Race and Nature in the World of Modern Science*, 1989; 2nd edn, London: Verso, 1992.

Indian Board for Wildlife, *Report of the Expert Committee*, Delhi: Ministry of Agriculture, 1970.

Khan, Fareida, 'Soil Wars: The Role of the African National Soil Conservation Association in South Africa, 1953–59', *Environmental History*, 2 (1997).

Kinloch, B., *The Shamba Raiders: Memoirs of a Game Warden*, London: Collins–Harvill, 1972.

Kothari, A., R.V. Anuradha, N. Pathak, and B. Taneja, ed., *Communities and Conservation: Natural Resource Management in South and Central Asia*, Delhi: Sage, 1990.

Lewis, M.L., 'Tracking the Biodiversity Ideal: Transfer and Reception of

Ecological Theories and Practices between the US and India, 1947–1997', Unpublished PhD thesis, Univ. of Iowa, 2002.

MacDonald, St J., 'Wildlife Preservation: The Kruger National Park, An Example', *Journal of the Bombay Natural History Society*, 52 (1954).

Mackenzie, J., *The Empire of Nature: Hunting, Parks and British Imperialism*, Manchester: Manchester University Press.

Moorehead, A., *No Room in the Ark*, London: Collins, 1959.

Mowat, F., *Virunga: The Passion of Dian Fossey*, Paperback edn, 1987; rpnt. Toronto: Seal Books, 1988.

Nash, R., *Wilderness and the American Mind.* New Haven: Yale University Press, 1982.

Neumann, R.P., *Imposing Wilderness Struggles over Livelihood and Nature Preservation in Africa*, Berkeley: University of California Press, 1998.

Parker, I., and M. Amin, *Ivory Crisis*, London: Chatto and Windus, 1983.

Rangarajan, M., *India's Wildlife History*, Delhi: Permanent Black, 2000.

———, 'From Princely Symbol to Conservation Icon: A Political History of the Lion in India', in N. Nakazato and M. Hasan, ed., *The Unfinished Agenda: Nation-building in South Asia*, Delhi: Manohar, 2002.

Rodgers, A., D. Hartley, and S. Bashir, 'Reflections on Community Involvement in Conservation', in V.K. Saberwal and M. Rangarajan, ed., *Battles over Nature, Science and the Politics of Conservation*, Delhi: Permanent Black, 2003.

Rodgers, W.A., H.S. Panwar, and V.B. Mathur, *Protected Area Network in India: A Review*, Dehra Dun: Wildlife Institute of India, 2000.

Rolfes, Michael T., *Who Will Save the Wild Tiger?*, Montana: PERC, 1998.

Schaller, G.B., *The Year of the Gorilla*, London: Penguin, 1964.

———, *The Deer and the Tiger: A Study of Wildlife in India*, Chicago: University of Chicago Press, 1968.

———, 'Status of Wildlife and Research Needs', in IUCN, *Ecological Guidelines for National Parks in the Middle East and South West Asia*, Morges: IUCN, 1976.

———, 'Gentle Gorillas, Turbulent Times', *National Geographic,* 185 (1995).

Schama, S., *Landscape and Memory*, New York: Vintage Books, 1995.

Seshadri, B., *The Twilight of India's Wildlife*, London: John Baker, 1969.

Shao, J., 'The Villagization Programme and the Disruption of Ecological Balance in Tanzania', *Canadian Journal of African Studies*, 20 (1986).

Silverberg, Thomas, *The Dodo, the Auk and the Oryx*, 1967; London: Puffin, 2nd edn, 1973.

Sparks, J., *Animals in Danger*, London: Hamlyn, 1973.

Struhsaker, T.T., 'Strategies for Conserving Forest National Parks in Africa with a Case Study from Uganda', in J. Terborgh, *et al.*, ed., *Making Parks Work, Strategies for Preserving Tropical Nature*, Washington: Island Press, 2002.

Turnbull, C., 'East African Safari', *Natural History*, 90 (1981).

UNDP, *Human Development Report 2002, and Developing Democracy in a Fragmented World*, New York: Oxford University Press, 2002.

Western, D., 'Amboseli National Park: Enlisting Landowners to Conserve Migratory Animals, *Ambio*, 11 (1982).

———, 'Ecosystem Conservation and Rural Development: The Case of Amboseli', in D.M. Western, R.M. Wright, and S. Strum, ed., *Natural Connections: Perspectives in Community-based Conservation*, Washington: Island Press, 2013.

———, *In the Dust of Kilimanjaro*, 1998; rpnt. Washington: Island Press, 2002.

10

Contesting Conservation

Nature, Politics, and History in Contemporary India

Making space for nature in India today is no easy task. But opportunities in a liberal democracy with nearly six decades of adult franchise open up possibilities for new kinds of engagement among citizens with ecology and justice. Writing at the onset of the era of neo-liberal reform, two leading scholars of ecology and equity had argued there were two kinds of development choices before the country.[1] One was highly centralized and extensive resource use and abuse, and the other was founded on devolution, intensive resource use and regeneration.

It is now possible to take a more nuanced view wherein the choices are not so stark. This is not because the deeper contradictions have become less pronounced; it is more due to the emergence, though in a very incipient form, of a middle ground. This is still an emerging and often ambiguous space, and its contours and shape differ in various regions. But it is possible to argue that many of the alternative currents that were visible two decades ago are now more mature, complex, and diverse. This does not mean the challenges are any easier.

The task of reconciling regeneration of the life cycles of rivers and forests, ponds and mountains is still not easy given the geo-physical

[1] Gadgil and Ramachandra Guha, *Ecology and Equity*.

and historical constraints in the country. For a start, it has twice as many people today as it did four decades ago: population density has risen more than fivefold since the 1880s to 400 to a sq km now.[2] Such a country cannot be an easy place to retain landscapes with mostly natural vegetation. It is commonplace to assume the landscape was like this across the centuries, but the reverse is also true. Only over the last two centuries has the cultivated arable land grown to occupy nearly half the land mass. For centuries, it was the ebb and flow of the line of forest and arable land that was a decisive and continuing trend.[3] The growth of modern industry, of railway lines and mines, highways and new townships has also been a major ecological factor. Economic growth, even as it creates wealth, exacerbates conflicts between rival uses for the land and waterscapes. Since 1980 the Indian economy has been the second-fastest-growing in the world. The gap has grown from 275 billion dollars in 1991 to 2 billion by 2014–15. The expansion of industry and conflicts within and between urban and rural society over access to and control of resources are not new but have grown sharper in recent times.

The socio-cultural milieu and political landscape are also in a state of flux, more so because of increasing awareness of rights among the underprivileged as well as the complex relationship of this process to unequal access to natural resources and to economic and social opportunities. The scale and extent of controversy over forest clearances, and the issue of land rights of those whose livelihoods or habitations are displaced are now issues of prime political importance. How far the accumulation of wealth will be reconciled with the clash of rights of those directly reliant on resources is a major issue of political import in forest and coast, dam site and riverfront. This simple question resonates in myriad forms across the country.

Traditionally, discussions about the conservation of nature, and particularly of wildlife, have gravitated towards creating and

[2] Guha, *Health and Population*, pp. 58–60.

[3] Deloche, *Trade and Transportation Routes*, pp. 1–10.

maintaining nature reserves. Several national parks and tiger reserves, elephant reserves and wildlife sanctuaries, have been established or expanded since the early 1970s. Many such sites had their origins in the princely or imperial past, when they were hunting grounds for the landed aristocracy, princes, and British imperial officials. Around four decades ago a new 'ecological patriotism' combined with deep concern over the extinction of rare fauna impelled a major emphasis on saving nature. The acreage of Protected Areas went up tenfold from 1969 to 1989. Indian parks are still small, an average size of about 200 sq km, and there is nothing to compare with Kruger in South Africa.[4] But at a larger level, and anticipating developments in eastern and western Africa, the imperial state had by a century ago annexed over 600,000 sq km of forest. Even more land, a vast estate is to this day owned by state forest departments, a pattern with roots in the colonial past. It is such administrative mechanisms that India's new rulers turned to in the 1970s as they gave preservation a place in the sun.[5]

The strategy of preservation was simple. Spaces on land and water of intrinsic ecological worth were delineated and protection was made the explicit management priority. Preservation was the way to safeguard ecological integrity. Competing social, economic, and cultural claims were shut out by law and executive fiat. Much conservation then has been about the vigorous defence of these reserves and their protection from any activity that compromised wildlife and nature. It is crucial to stress that the vast majority of the forest estate was open to economic exploitation. The forester to this day is less a planter of trees and more a complex land manager: mobilizing labour, laying roads and bridges, cutting fire lines and supervising contracts, regulating the clearance of forest and organizing its regrowth. It may escape memory but nobody should forget what the famous wolf boy Mowgli did at the end of Kipling's *Jungle Book*: he became a forest guard!

Protecting nature has primarily meant locking human influences

[4] Saberwal and Rangarajan, *Battles over Nature.*

[5] Beinart and Hughes, *Environment and Empire.*

out in a small but significant area of land. The limitations of the preservationist approach are self-evident. Vital as they are for heritage and science, such reserves cover a mere 5 per cent of the country's landscape. They do not exist in ecological or economic isolation from a wider matrix. In turn, parks and sanctuaries are part of a larger network of government forests which are also increasingly sites of contest. Crises of survival of rare fauna such as the tiger have resurfaced, leading to debate, controversy, and to some extent introspection among decision-makers. They are increasingly embattled and under pressure, with task forces having been set up on key flagship species such as the tiger and the elephant.[6] Significantly, both these task forces had two features in common: they called for more integration of science in policy-making and for greater transparency, dialogue with, and participation of those living in and around the Protected Areas.[7]

Critics have rightly pointed to the limitations of such piecemeal reform, even as they acknowledge it has some elements of a long overdue paradigm shift in the interrelationship of nature, knowledge, and power. The conflicts such initiatives aim to defuse are acute: two of every three kills of elephants by people in India are by cultivators defending crops. In turn, 400 people a year, mostly farm labourers and farmers, are killed by elephants. But at a wider level this will only work if protection (for both animals and people) and compensations are made accountable at the local level, preferably via elected representatives. This will call for an overhaul not merely of the forest departmental machinery but the revenue administration in general.

Yet this points to a larger scenario where fluidity is a fact and interventions rigid. Lines on the land rarely mean as much as they seem. Animals and birds, water and wind do not obey the boundaries people draw. In any case only 25 of the 650 Protected Areas in India are more than 1000 sq km, a far cry from Selous

[6] Ministry of Environment and Forests, *Joining the Dots*; Rangarajan, *et al.*, *Gajah*.

[7] Madhusudan and Sankaran, 'Seeing the Elephant'.

Game Reserve in Tanzania, which is over 40,000 sq km. Often, a park's wildlife populations can be imperilled by what happens beyond its borders. The catastrophic population crash of the three most common vulture species, first documented in Bharatpur's wetlands, had its origins in the changing practice of veterinary medicine across India. Tigers or elephants can be marooned in small reserves as mega-development projects cut off corridors that animals can now walk across. Reserves with sharp boundaries hold even less meaning in arid and montane landscapes where species share their ranges with human communities. Wolves and snow leopards, for instance, can hardly be contained within park boundaries. Big cats, especially leopards, survive in stable populations in sugarcane fields, calling for strategies that go beyond simple seclusion.[8] Even in urban spaces, remnant nature can persist both in form and substance.

As for rivers and the sea, the vitality of the larger waterscape hinges on much more than policing the extraction of biomass. Large dams have often significantly altered the ecology of rivers, while the coastline is being rapidly transformed by new ports, increased pollution, and urban expansion. The earlier notion of secluded reserves has little meaning given the fluidity of natural systems. It is not without value but it does need careful rethinking, especially given the ways in which the viability of reserves is under threat from actions well beyond their boundaries.

If nature's processes cross borders, so too do the webs of human actions. The recent wiping out of the tiger population of a well-known Indian tiger reserve, Sariska, owed as much to pressures on the habitat from mining and commercial firewood trade from outside the tract as to poachers.[9] Similarly, river pollution is an ever-present threat to unique reptiles and mammals, the gharial in the Chambal river and the Gangetic dolphin in the Ganga.[10]

[8] Athreya, *et al.*, 'Translocation as a Tool', *Conservation Biology*, pp. 1133–41.

[9] Shahabuddin, *Conservation at the Crossroads.*

[10] Lenin, 'Song of the Ganges Gharial', pp. 34–8; Kelkar and Krishnaswamy, 'Restoring the Ganga', pp. 58–80.

The creation of wealth and waste, the movement of goods and people, all combine to limit if not totally undermine the value of enclave-centred conservation. This is no new phenomenon: captive elephants were a major item of trade for over two and a half millennia, while horses, another vital auxiliary of war, were bred or maintained in grasslands. India, for centuries, imported ivory from Africa and shatoosh wool from the Tibetan plateau. The pace and scale of such exchange and extraction have radically changed in the recent past.

So, make no mistake: reserves are not *passé* and still need priority. Preservation remains a valid and worthwhile ideal to strive for. The larger projects of cleaner air and water, sustainable farming and eco-friendly urban spaces, will gain immeasurably from safety sites where we can learn about the workings of nature. The idea of *in situ* preservation has special significance in a country with a population density of well over 300 to a sq km. It is equally vital because India, with just 2 per cent of the earth's land surface, has a fifth, no less, of its domestic ungulates. Unless some areas are kept free of biomass extraction, it will be difficult to get a sense of how nature's system of renewal and repair works. But the matrix requires active intervention, care, and thought. The reserves and the larger landscape milieu are different parts of a spectrum that complement each other.

But there is little doubt that nature reserves are in crisis for reasons well beyond the circumstances responsible for their insular character. Often, the reserves are contested spaces and though the present model that tries to render them inviolate works, it only does so fitfully. Powerful economic factors were checkmated a quarter of a century ago when a hydel power plant in Silent Valley was scrapped to save a rainforest.[11] More recently a major nuclear research facility was disallowed in a critical forest adjacent to the Mudumalai Tiger Reserve, and a bauxite mine disallowed in the Niyamgiri hills in Orissa. The former were mostly about ecological integrity and the latter also about the rights of the Scheduled Tribes

[11] D'Monte, *Temples or Tombs?*

under a key piece of recent legislation, the Forest Rights Act 2006.[12] The latter has been crucial in halting the grant of a bauxite mining lease in the Niyamgiri hills for a major international aluminium company. The ability of the Gram Sabha (village council) to draw on provisions of the Act were central to this denouement, though it is too early to see how far this will be a precedent in other, less publicized conflicts. The Niyamgiri case had important implications for nature protection as the hills are part of a key elephant landscape.

Tiger reserves, national parks, and wildlife sanctuaries still slow down if not hamper major changes in the land in parts of India. But the larger web of the economy cannot but intrude on the world of nature. The market economy has long done so but in recent decades such pressures have grown manifold even in frontier states and interior hill regions.[13] The complex of parks in the Nilgiri Biosphere Reserve is a case in point. About 150,000 people have relied on the Bandipur Tiger Reserve alone for firewood. Over 100,000 cattle graze in it every day. For those eking out modest livelihoods, energy and cash are vital for sustenance, and the forest is a source of both. If the parks sustain the people, the harvest of fuelwood and fodder also undermines its fragile ecology. Conversely, animals like elephants and wild boar raid crops in the adjoining farmlands, while cattle vie with wild grazers and browsers for fodder in the reserved forests. Most conservation efforts here as elsewhere are directly in conflict with the survival needs of such farming communities. Increasingly able to assert their rights, and as active voters, they cannot be stopped from regular ingress to the park. It's a fragile balancing act. The park as entity survives and the livelihoods do too, but the idea of a strict nature reserve is realized only in part. This remains the case even though—unusually for an Indian park—it has no residents within its perimeter. To add to pressures, large infrastructure projects in the greater Nilgiris threaten to slice up this contiguous forest tract.

[12] Padel and Brody, *Sacrificing People*.

[13] Saikia, *Forests and the Ecological History of Assam*.

Conversely, the displacement of resident peoples, whether through physical relocation to create 'inviolate spaces for wildlife recovery' or in a more indirect sense via the denial of usufruct rights to access forest produce, has been a major locus of tensions. The displacement on more than one occasion of fishers, cultivators, and woodcutters in the Sundarban mangroves in 1978 even entailed direct confrontations, with loss of life in police firings. Elsewhere, as in the Central Indian forest of Kuno (Madhya Pradesh) where the Sahariya Scheduled Tribes were relocated, their economic condition has deteriorated rather than improved. In the recent past a far better economic package has been made available by the union government to the tune of one million rupees per family. Prior to this in Bhadra, Karnataka, independent studies indicate higher incomes for most people relocated from a tiger reserve. There is a caveat: unlike in the other two cases cited here, most of the displaced in Bhadra were not Scheduled Tribals or Scheduled Castes, but mainly people from a dominant peasant community. Whether such a practice can be replicated elsewhere is, therefore, an open question.[14] The issue is of central importance as over 50,000 families are possibly to be relocated from Tiger Reserve core areas in the next few years.

There are ways to intervene that alleviate distress. Efforts to facilitate alternative energy and to evolve better farmer-maintained fencing address some of the issues in an innovative way and take the sharp edge off conflict. Perhaps if extended more widely they can do more than just buy time. They can create or secure conservation spaces via co-operation, widening the constituency for conservation beyond those who make gains (or limit losses) arising from protection. And such efforts outside the parks are as integral to making space for nature as creating parks in the first place.

Such efforts are admittedly on a small scale but they may well be harbingers of change. This will of course only be so if they are

[14] Jalais, *Forest of Tigers*; Kabra, 'Conservation Induced Displacement', pp. 249–67.

scaled up and become the nucleus of new and livelihood-friendly conservation practice. Insurance for herders to protect sheep from wolves and snow leopards have worked in the western Himalaya and are being expanded under Project Snow Leopard.[15] Farmers' co-operative fences to keep out elephants have worked well near Bandipur in Karnataka and hold promise elsewhere. Co-operation to save adjacent wetlands and continuing age-old tolerance may be the key to saving the largest crane in India, the sarus. Similarly, the Bodoland Autonomous Council in Assam has enabled the recovery of a major biodiversity site, Manas, as it is seen as an integral heritage of the Bodo Scheduled Tribe which has gained autonomy over the region that contains the reserve. These are but small initiatives, often led and worked on by exceptionally motivated individuals or groups. Elsewhere, there has been an efflorescence of small community-run 'no-go' sites and areas where limited extraction is permissible. Can they be scaled up fast enough? This hinges on legal and administrative changes that enable these to have the stable basis they now lack. And even if they are, will it simply gain some space and win some time but not much more?

As argued above, the larger ecological and economic fabric is under strain and can do with more than just tending fences at the forest edge. It may defy commonly held premises, but recent ecological and social research has shown that significant spaces continue to remain for nature *outside* reserve boundaries. This is true for charismatic vertebrates such as Asian elephants, and even more so for biomes like wetlands, dry savannah, and scrub jungles. An obsession with reserves alone may do these species and habitats grave injustice. For many smaller taxa, habitats outside reserves may often be far more crucial than what may be found inside them.

Policy and practice *vis-à-vis* the lands and waters outside reserves still have crucial implications for conservation. Yet we cannot overlook the fact that outside reserve boundaries, economic, social,

[15] Bhatnagar, 'Project Snow Leopard', pp. 44–8.

and cultural demands will take priority. Thus, on the ground, it is often difficult to view the reserve boundary as a line that clearly separates conservation opportunity from conservation threat. Making space for nature seemed easier in the imperial or princely case, but then the hierarchies of men were reproduced when it came to access to nature.

Should these continue in a democratic society? That they do is undoubtedly true, but democracy is on trial here as much as on other issues of justice. A just society or a state by just means has today to grapple with how to achieve peace with nature. But the burdens of the peace cannot be uneven and the fruits unequally shared. To be egalitarian conservation has to separate itself from its more conservative roots, and perhaps the constructive efforts mentioned here and the more active grassroots movements of protest must both have critical roles to play.[16]

For these hopes to be made reality, change is necessary. Just as conservation must grapple with the serious challenges within reserve boundaries, it must equally embrace the opportunities outside them. To accomplish such a metaphorical blurring of the reserve boundary, we must first transcend the more entrenched ideological boundaries as well. If nature spills beyond borders, thought, policy, and action must follow suit. This is not a prescription to let go of nature reserves. I would argue against a 'let's forget nature reserves' stance with all the emphasis possible. But conservation, whether protection or ecological restoration, cannot stop at reserve boundaries. Nor can it treat the wider matrix as orphaned ecological space.

Such a wider platform for ecology is easy to speak about but hard to create or sustain. Like any other school of thought, the conservation community too is riven across many ideological lines. Biocentric ideologies of *preserving* nature are locked in contest with anthropocentric ideas of *using* nature.[17] Landscape-level approaches

[16] Jacoby, *Crimes Against Nature*.

[17] Gadgil, *Ecological Journeys*; Karanth, *View from the Machan*.

conflict with those that want a hard, sharp edge for reserves to be the prime field of focus.[18] Others focus on small species or reserves as worthwhile and yet others remain focussed on big animals and landscapes playing an umbrella or flagship role. Captive breeding and *ex situ* means of conservation vie with the needs of protecting species *in situ*. Some leverage emerging markets for conservation, others favour a systematic delinking of nature from markets. Some see inclusive, democratic processes that involve a cross-section of society as anchor; others yearn for an earlier age when power and wealth were concentrated with a few and conservation rolled out quickly.

Conservation practitioners have defied all manner of typecasting and continue to adopt a melange of shifting positions. They have cut the cloth to the occasion. Like any crisis-driven response, conservation has often involved on-the-spot responses with the theory later playing catch-up. Many sharp edges in conservation arise from the novelty of the conservation enterprise itself. Managing runaway growth to minimize long-term negative impacts on ecology in a disparate society is hard enough. With so many voices, many strident and each more vocal with time, the task becomes even more complex.

To rethink conservation is to reorder our ideas about nature as much as society. To use Deng Xiao Peng's phrase, it is about crossing the river while feeling the stones. The journey must not be broken but has to negotiate the hidden real-life obstacles. For conservation, the crossing has to be in the mind and heart as much as by how the feet walk the riverbed. Ethics and economics, political and social concerns, all have to blend with ecology. The structures and functions of nature do matter but so too do the ways in which institutions work and cultures change.

These newer engagements can complement older approaches. This may not be easy, especially when the proponents of the older guns-and-guards approach see any change as the start of the deluge.

[18] Karanth and DeFries, 'Conservation and Managemeng', pp. 2865–9.

The deep attachment to the strict enforcement model has been reinforced by recent crises, especially so with threats in the wild to the national animal, the tiger.[19] In a routine all too familiar in South Africa, the emphasis on enforcement can all too easily become a means to simply reinvigorate the bureaucratic stranglehold on rural economies and ecologies without addressing threats to ecological integrity. Further, recent campaigns to save imperilled species, ecologies, and habitats have derived substantial support from the corporate sector, the audio-visual media, and the film fraternity. What is significant is the counterpositioning of threats to nature (in the most recent case represented by a young tiger cub) with its converse, the strong enforcers: hence the call for more contributions for purchase of equipment for enforcers.

There is a significant critique of such centralization of power and the many abuses that accompany it. But what is more crucial is that stringent anti-poaching campaigns in a country such as India hardly begin to address critical threats to the larger flora and fauna complex. Conservation is about the wider ecological integrity of the landscape and even scientists who are proponents of strict preservation do not see poaching as *the* major issue at hand.[20] Proponents of hard-edged reserves are themselves divided on whether the core response is better policing versus poachers or a more integrated habitat preservation model.

But there is also a pragmatic view that is a critique of the preservation via firm-borders position. As the Bandipur case shows, the best-armed guards cannot keep out village cattle. As anthropologists have argued, the forest guard is not merely an agent of government: he is likely to be also a villager with deep social roots.[21] Even were the enforcement of authoritarian agendas possible, as they often are, it raises a critical question of who is to save what and from whom? The idea of nature is after all deeply contested and how

[19] Thapar, *The Last Tiger*; Chundawat, *Panna's Last Tiger*.

[20] Watson, *et al.*, 'Bringing the Tiger Back', pp. 8–9.

[21] Vasan, *Living with Diversity*.

one responds to the issue of where repair and renewal is to begin is a deeply and implicitly political question.

It is more difficult in forests and other such landscapes beyond the urban spaces and intensely cultivated areas. Whereas agrarian rights have been devolved downward—though in an uneven way and save for certain regions not equitably—it is true that the government as property owner and regulator looms larger in the life of basic producers who are in hill, forest, and dry regions. In addition to the Forest Department there are a host of government agencies that impinge on the lives and livelihoods of those who herd, fish, hunt, gather, or cultivate a crop once a year. It is no surprise that the intensity of conflicts in forests is equalled by those on the coast or in dry rangelands and hill pastures.[22]

How can one advance nature-friendly agendas on a wider social and ecological canvas? This requires engagement not only with protection but production, not only 'inviolate spaces' but also with human settlements. Often, groups try going beyond small nuclei of middle class, bureaucracy, and science to reach out to larger political constituencies. There are intimations of change not only in citizen groups and academia, but also in government. This calls for a paradigm shift in which there is a challenge for the larger political system.[23]

Whether this will be a counteracting force to the more destructive trends unleashed by larger economic forces is an open question. The deepening of democracy, as in the case of the Forest Rights Act, is a positive trend. But it sits uneasily with the greater centralization of power and the reinforcing of market-led growth both within and without the country. Similarly, the greater transparency and accountability due to recent changes in policies in the displacement of people from parks are a vast improvement; but whether they change forester–citizen interaction on the forest floor is yet to be seen. The promise of a law-governed democratic state runs counter

[22] Agarwal, Chopra, and Sharma, *State of the Environment*; Gooch, 'Victims of Conservation', pp. 239–48.

[23] Shahabuddin and Rangarajan, *Making Conservation Work*.

to so much in the daily, more crude and brutal realities of grids of power.[24] Iconic animals have indeed made a transition to becoming symbols of ecological awareness, but there is a troubling past of repressive measures to protect hunting grounds which is in danger of being played out in a new setting.[25]

Conservation in practice has to combine ecological sanity with justice, a space for nature with one for livelihoods. There are working approaches with different and often more effective ways of drawing on knowledge and institutions, processes, and practices to create more not less space for nature. Many of these initiatives lie at points in the spectrum that are neither fully statist and centralized nor completely community centred and locally rooted. There is a space that combines elements of both but mixes and matches them in new ways.

It is possible here to draw on Ajantha Subramanian's insightful work on the fishers of the Coromandel coast of Tamil Nadu. She concludes that the state system does more than merely create docile subjects or insurrectionary 'others'. In the case of the fishers, decades of political activity have opened up new spaces for a kind of collective that is deeply engaged within state spaces. These dynamic, contested processes which are the subject of her study are deeply relevant to the debate on the future of nature in India. In fact, the Forest Rights Act has led to consideration of a similar legislative measure providing a legal basis for fisher rights on coasts and in the sea. Of course, as she observes, resource renewal will involve a different set of priorities for production.[26] It is also important to acknowledge that the south-west coast, with its long history of radical social reform and upheaval over the last century, may not in every way be typical of other regions in the country. But there is reason to argue that the level and extent of attempts to redefine

[24] Gopalakrishnan, 'Blame the Forest Management'; Chhatre and Saberwal, *Democratizing Nature*.

[25] Gold and Gujjar, *In the Time of Trees*.

[26] Subramanian, *Shore Lines*, pp. 253–4.

democracy in a way inclusive of rights to forest and coast do have the potential for new engagements with nature as much as among people.

It is important to note that such a cautiously positive view of the present scenario is not shared by many seasoned observers. The frictions around Maosim and related radical currents are sometimes seen as fundamentally challenging the present socio-political order. Bastar, the Central Indian region in Chhattisgarh, which is an epicentre of the often violent encounter between the government and armed rebels, is a well-known forest tract. It has had a long history of upheaval and a century ago witnessed a major rebellion which contested imperial control of the forest and curbs on swidden cultivation. It was here and elsewhere in the Central Indian forest tracts that writers and journalists wrote extensively of social and political contests. What is crucial is that there is a sharp contest not only for the wealth of the forest but for the minerals that lie beneath the soil: bauxite, iron ore, and coal.

Yet it would be misleading to ignore the struggles to protect the forest cover from encroaching mines and industry that are waged on a peaceable basis. It is such protests that played a key role in the denial of the mining lease for bauxite in the Niyamgiri hills. Peaceful protest and law-governed means of struggle have taken up such issues. It is such efforts, not armed Maoist groups, that raise issues of how to rethink development in less destructive ways. Such struggles are replete with potential for they often engage those whose work and livelihood depends centrally on the continued existence of the forest.[27]

But for that, the need to think afresh and create anew has never been more urgently felt. There is no doubt that conservation or ecology, as with any social entity, is a house divided. Which current will prevail and for how long will have much to do with the new denouement. To strive for nature without borders is not just about more of the same. It is about some of the new. This is part of the

[27] Roma, 'Forest Justice Movements', pp. 75–7.

larger challenge of crafting a more just society but in a manner that respects and builds on livelihoods as much as allows nature's systems space and time for repair and renewal. Making space for the cycles of earth and water, forest and mountain hinges on how people combine peace among themselves with the search for justice with nature.

References

Agarwal, Anil, Ravi Chopra, and Kalpana Sharma, ed., *State of the Environment: A Citizen's Report*: Delhi: CSE, 1982.

Athreya, Vidya, Morten Oden, John D.C. Linell, and K. Ullas Karanth, 'Translocation as a Tool for Mitigating Conflict with Leopards in Human Dominated Landscapes in India', *Conservation Biology,* 25 (2010).

Beinart, William and Lotte Hughes, *Environment and Empire,* Oxford: Oxford University Press, 2007.

Bhatnagar, Yashveer,'Project Snow Leopard', *Seminar,* 603 (2010).

Chhatre, Ashwini, and Vasant K. Saberwal, *Democratizing Nature,* New Delhi: Oxford University Press, 2006.

Chundawat, S. Raghuram, *Panna's Last Tiger: How the Management Fails to Protect Our Wildlife,* Delhi: Baavan, 2009.

D'Monte, Darryl, *Temples or Tombs? Industry or Environment—Three Case Studies,* Delhi: Centre for Science and Environment, 1985.

Deloche, Jean. *Trade and Transportation Routes in India Before Steam Locomotion: Volume I: The Land Routes,* New Delhi: Oxford University Press, 1993.

Gadgil, Madhav, *Ecological Journeys: Science and the Politics of Conservation,* Ranikhet: Permanent Black, 2001.

———, and Ramachandra Guha, *Ecology and Equity: The Use and Abuse of Nature in India*, New Delhi: Oxford University Press, 2000.

Gold, Ann Grodzins, and Bhoju Ram Gujjar, *In the Time of Trees and Sorrows,* New Delhi: Oxford University Press, 2003.

Gooch, Pernille,'Victims of Conservation or Rights as Forest Dwellers: Van Gujjar Pastoralists between Contesting Codes of Law', *Conservation and Society,* vol. 7, no. 4 (2009).

Gopalakrishnan, Shankar, 'Blame the Forest Management System', *Economic and Political Weekly,* 46, December 2010.

Guha, Sumit, *Health and Population in South Asia from Earliest Times to the Present,* Ranikhet: Permanent Black, 2001.

Jacoby, Karl, *Crimes Against Nature: Poachers, Squatters, Thieves and the Hidden History of American Conservation,* Berkeley: University of California Press, 2001.

Jalais, Annu, *Forest of Tigers: People, Politics and Environment in the Sundarbans,* New Delhi: Routledge, 2009.

Kabra, Asmita, 'Conservation Induced Displacement: A Comparative Study of Two Indian Protected Areas', *Conservation and Society*, vol. 7, no. 4 (2009)

Karanth, K. Ullas, *A View from the Machan: How Science Can Save the Fragile Predator,* New Delhi: Permanent Black, 2006.

Karanth, Krithi, and Ruth DeFries, 'Conservation and Management in Human-dominated Landscapes: Case Studies from India', *Biological Conservation,* 143 (2010).

Kelkar, Nachiket, and Jagdish Krishnaswamy, 'Restoring the Ganga for its Fauna and Fisheries', in M. Rangarajan, M.D. Madhusudan, and Ghazala Shahabuddin, ed., *Nature without Borders*, Hyderabad: Orient BlackSwan, 2014.

Lenin, Janaki, 'Song of the Ganges Gharial', *Seminar,* 577 (2007).

Madhusudan, M.D., and Pavithra Sankaran, 'Seeing the Elephant in the Room: Human–Elephant Conflict and the ETF Report', *Economic and Political Weekly,* 49 (2010).

Ministry of Environment and Forests, *Joining the Dots: Report of the Tiger Task Force,* Delhi, 2005.

Padel, Felix and Hugh Brody, *Sacrificing People: Invasions of a Tribal Landscape,* Delhi: Orient BlackSwan, 2010.

Rangarajan, M., *et al., Gajah—Securing the Future for Elephants in India: The Report of the Elephant Task Force*, New Delhi: Government of India, Ministry of Environment and Forests, 2010.

Roma, 'Forest Justice Movements', *Seminar,* 613 (2010).

Saberwal, Vasant K., and Mahesh Rangarajan, ed., *Battles over Nature: Science and the Politics of Conservation,* New Delhi: Permanent Black, 2007.

Saikia, Arupjyoti, *Forests and the Ecological History of Assam,* New Delhi: Oxford University Press, 2011.

Shahabuddin, Ghazala, *Conservation at the Crossroads: Science, Society and the Future of India's Wildlife,* New Delhi: Permanent Black, 2010.

———, and Mahesh Rangarajan, ed., *Making Conservation Work: Securing Conservation in the New Century,* New Delhi: Permanent Black, 2007.

Subramanian, Ajantha, *Shore Lines: Space and Rights in South India,* Stanford: Stanford University Press, 2009.

Thapar, Valmik, *The Last Tiger,* New Delhi: Oxford University Press, 2006.

Vasan, Sudha, *Living with Diversity: Forestry Institutions in the Western Himalaya*, Shimla: Indian Institute of Advanced Study, 2006.

Watson, Joe, *et al.*, 'Bringing the Tiger Back from the Brink—The Six Percent Solution', *PBLOS Biology* (2010).